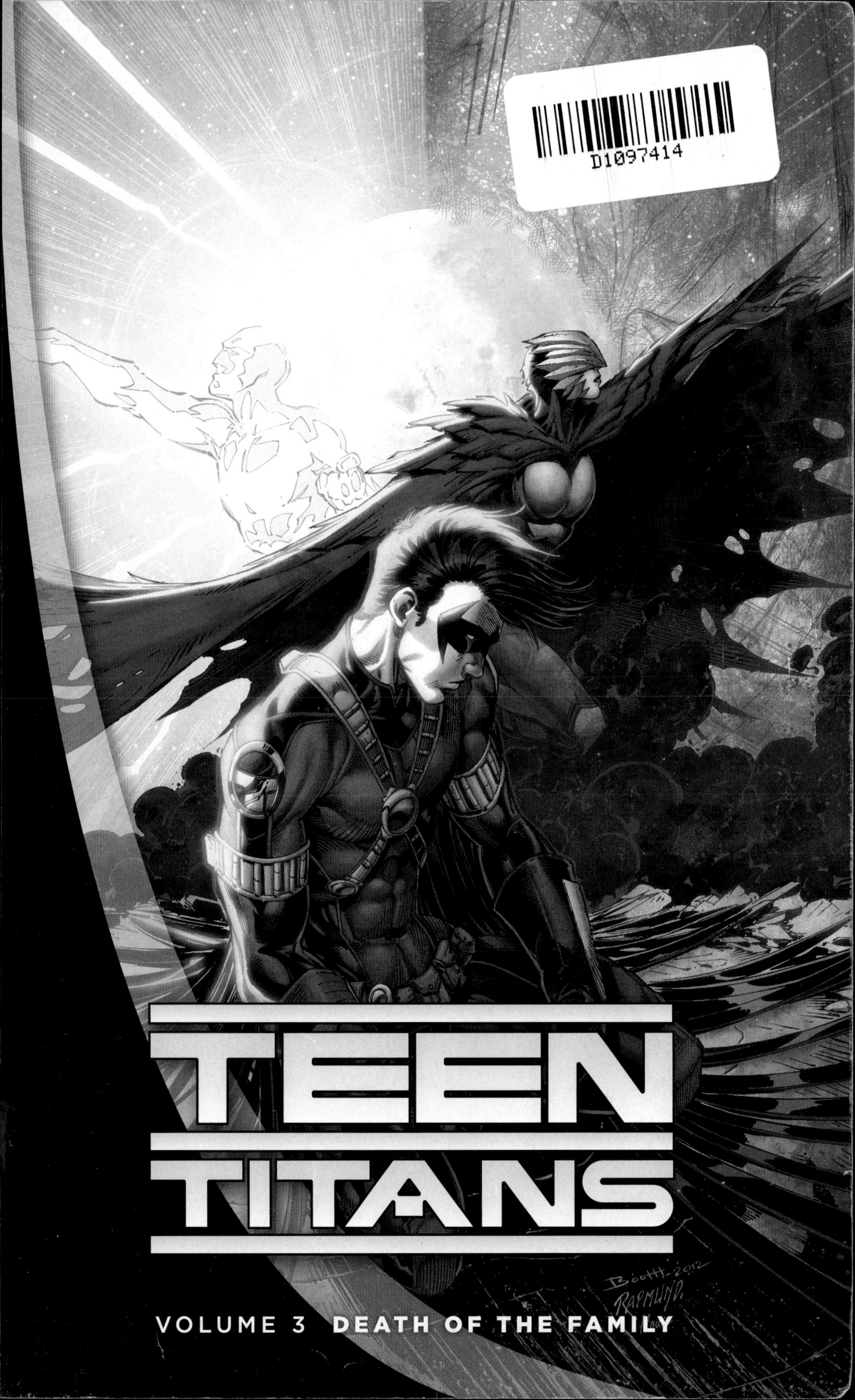
Booth 2012
Rapmund

TEEN TITANS

VOLUME 3 **DEATH OF THE FAMILY**

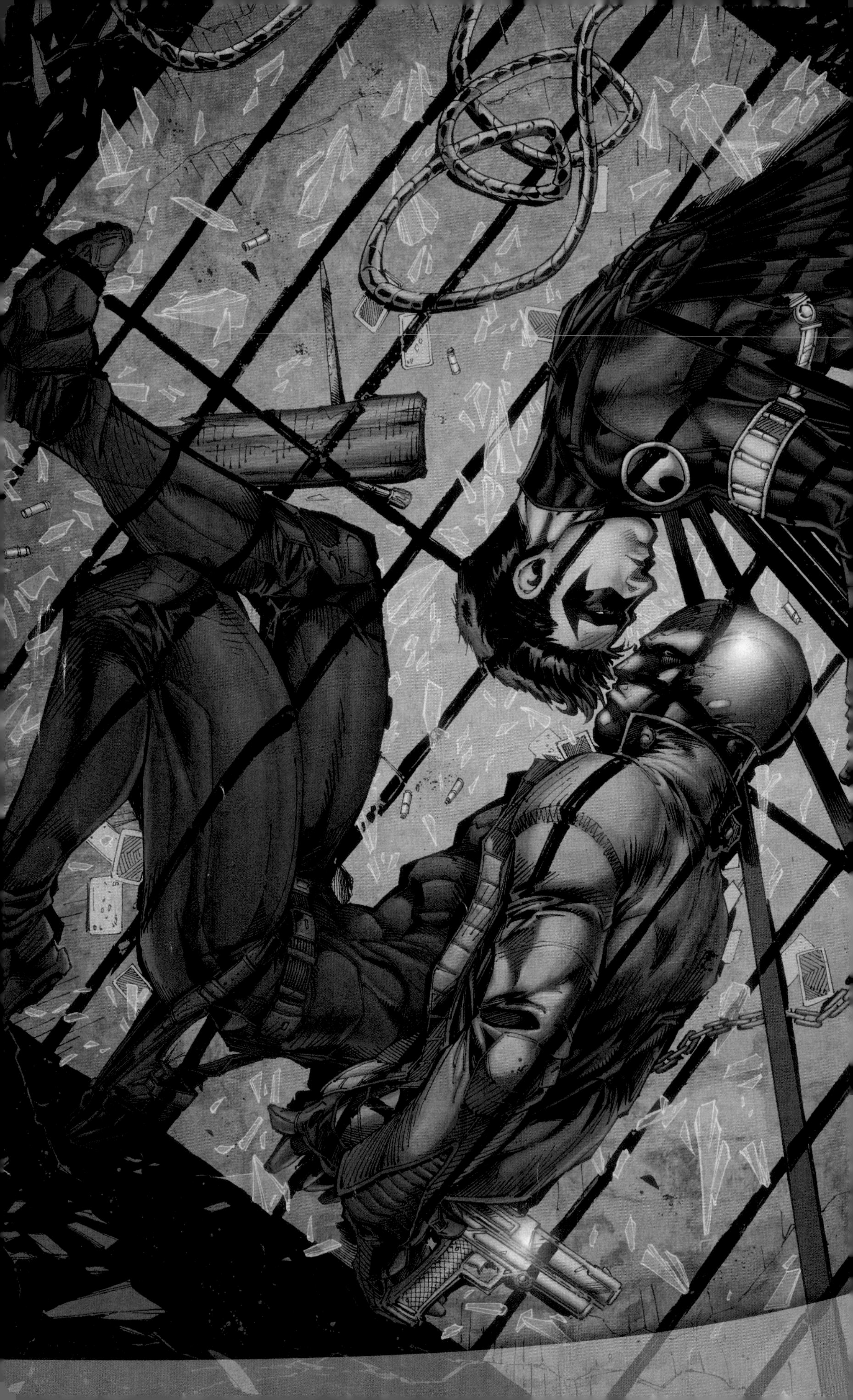

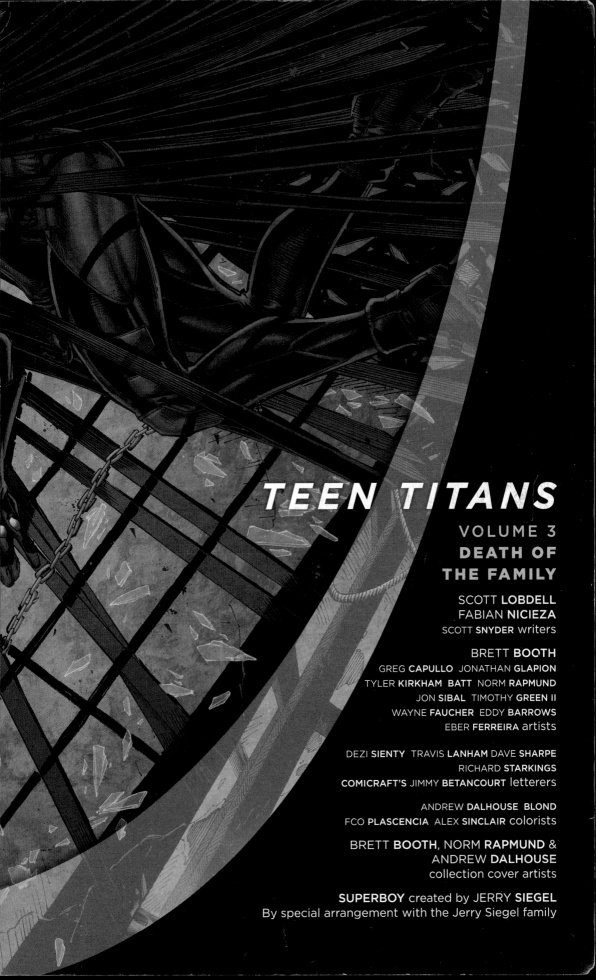

TEEN TITANS

VOLUME 3
DEATH OF
THE FAMILY

SCOTT **LOBDELL**
FABIAN **NICIEZA**
SCOTT **SNYDER** writers

BRETT **BOOTH**
GREG **CAPULLO** JONATHAN **GLAPION**
TYLER **KIRKHAM** BATT NORM **RAPMUND**
JON **SIBAL** TIMOTHY **GREEN II**
WAYNE **FAUCHER** EDDY **BARROWS**
EBER **FERREIRA** artists

DEZI **SIENTY** TRAVIS **LANHAM** DAVE **SHARPE**
RICHARD **STARKINGS**
COMICRAFT'S JIMMY **BETANCOURT** letterers

ANDREW **DALHOUSE** BLOND
FCO **PLASCENCIA** ALEX **SINCLAIR** colorists

BRETT **BOOTH**, NORM **RAPMUND** &
ANDREW **DALHOUSE**
collection cover artists

SUPERBOY created by JERRY **SIEGEL**
By special arrangement with the Jerry Siegel family

EDDIE BERGANZA MIKE COTTON MIKE MARTS Editors – Original Series KATIE KUBERT Associate Editor – Original Series
DARREN SHAN ANTHONY MARQUES Assistant Editors – Original Series ROWENA YOW Editor
ROBBIN BROSTERMAN Design Director – Books ROBBIE BIEDERMAN Publication Design

BOB HARRAS Senior VP – Editor-in-Chief, DC Comics

DIANE NELSON President DAN DIDIO and JIM LEE Co-Publishers
GEOFF JOHNS Chief Creative Officer
JOHN ROOD Executive VP – Sales, Marketing and Business Development
AMY GENKINS Senior VP – Business and Legal Affairs NAIRI GARDINER Senior VP – Finance
JEFF BOISON VP – Publishing Planning   MARK CHIARELLO VP – Art Direction and Design
JOHN CUNNINGHAM VP – Marketing TERRI CUNNINGHAM VP – Editorial Administration
ALISON GILL Senior VP – Manufacturing and Operations HANK KANALZ Senior VP – Vertigo and Integrated Publishing
JAY KOGAN VP – Business and Legal Affairs, Publishing JACK MAHAN VP – Business Affairs, Talent
NICK NAPOLITANO VP – Manufacturing Administration SUE POHJA VP – Book Sales
COURTNEY SIMMONS Senior VP – Publicity BOB WAYNE Senior VP – Sales

TEEN TITANS VOLUME 3: DEATH OF THE FAMILY

DC Comics, 1700 Broadway, New York, NY 10019
A Warner Bros. Entertainment Company.
Printed by RR Donnelley, Salem, VA, USA 11/15/13. First Printing.

ISBN: 978-1-4012-4321-0

Library of Congress Cataloging-in-Publication Data

Lobdell, Scott, author.
Teen Titans. Volume 3, Death of the family / Scott Lobdell, Brett Booth.
pages cm. -- (The New 52!)
ISBN 978-1-4012-4321-0 (pbk.)
1. Graphic novels. I. Booth, Brett, illustrator. II. Title. III. Title. Death of the Family.
PN6728.T34L65 2013
741.5'973—dc23

2013030642

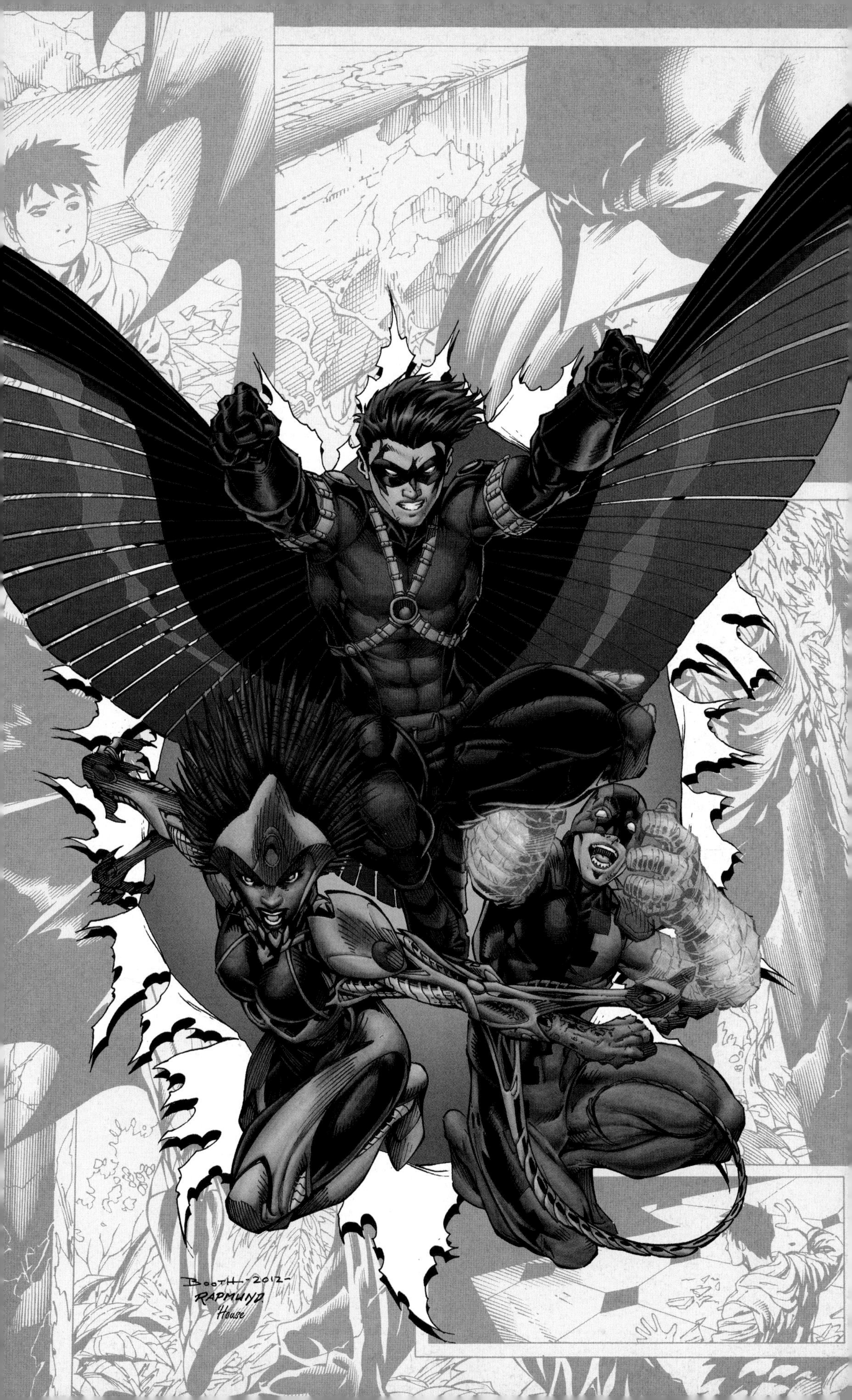
BOOTH -2012-
RAPMUND
House

RED ROBIN

SCOTT LOBDELL writer **TYLER KIRKHAM** penciller **BATT, NORM RAPMUND & JON SIBAL** inkers
cover art by **BRETT BOOTH, NORM RAPMUND & ANDREW DALHOUSE**

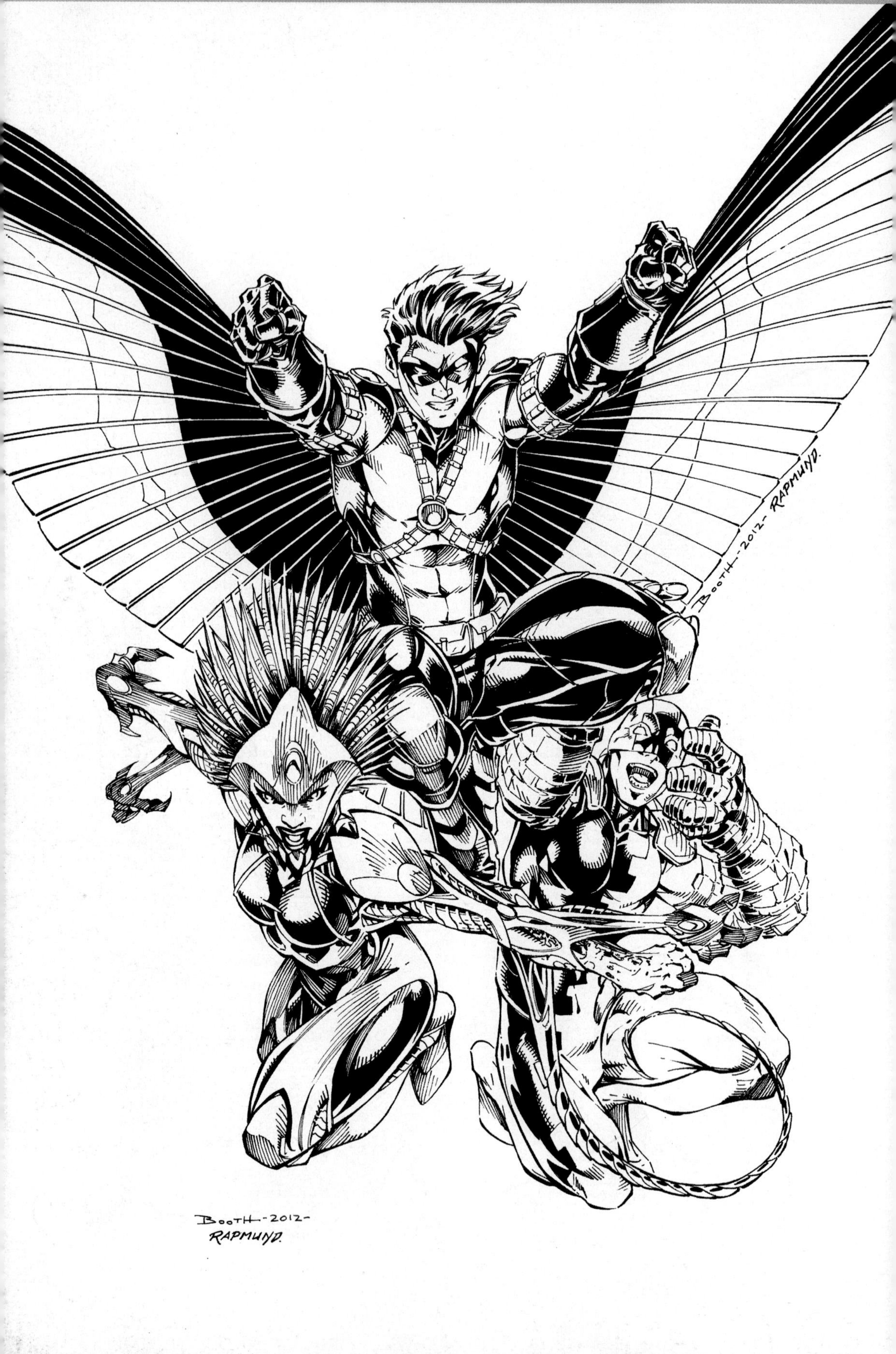
BOOTH -2012- RAPMUND.
BOOTH -2012-
RAPMUND.

DC COMICS™ PROUDLY PRESENTS:

BEFORE THE NEW 52!

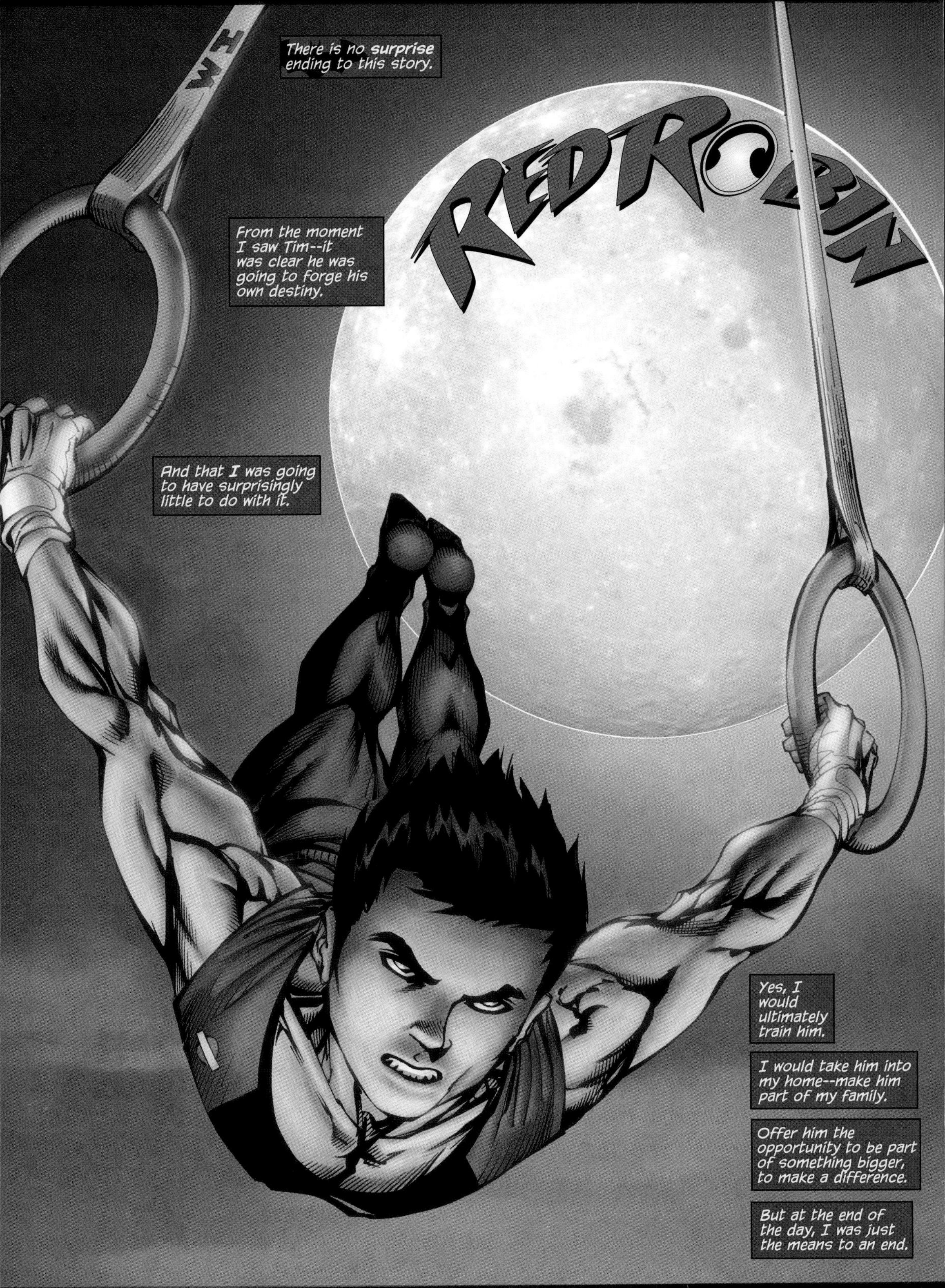
There is no surprise ending to this story.
RED ROBIN
From the moment I saw Tim--it was clear he was going to forge his own destiny.
And that I was going to have surprisingly little to do with it.
Yes, I would ultimately train him.
I would take him into my home--make him part of my family.
Offer him the opportunity to be part of something bigger, to make a difference.
But at the end of the day, I was just the means to an end.

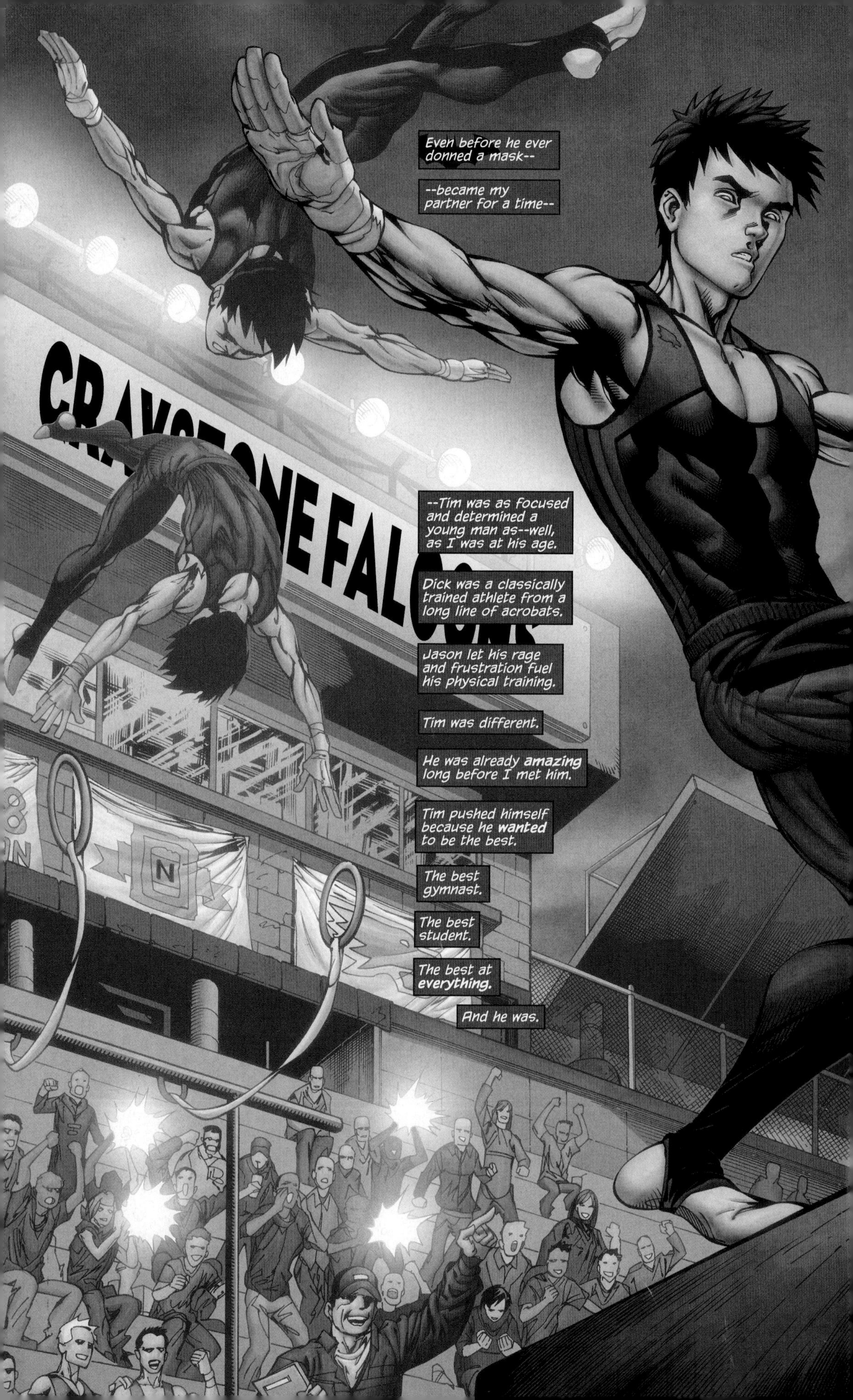
Even before he ever donned a mask--
--became my partner for a time--
--Tim was as focused and determined a young man as--well, as I was at his age.
Dick was a classically trained athlete from a long line of acrobats.
Jason let his rage and frustration fuel his physical training.
Tim was different.
He was already **amazing** long before I met him.
Tim pushed himself because he **wanted** to be the best.
The best gymnast.
The best student.
The best at **everything.**
And he was.

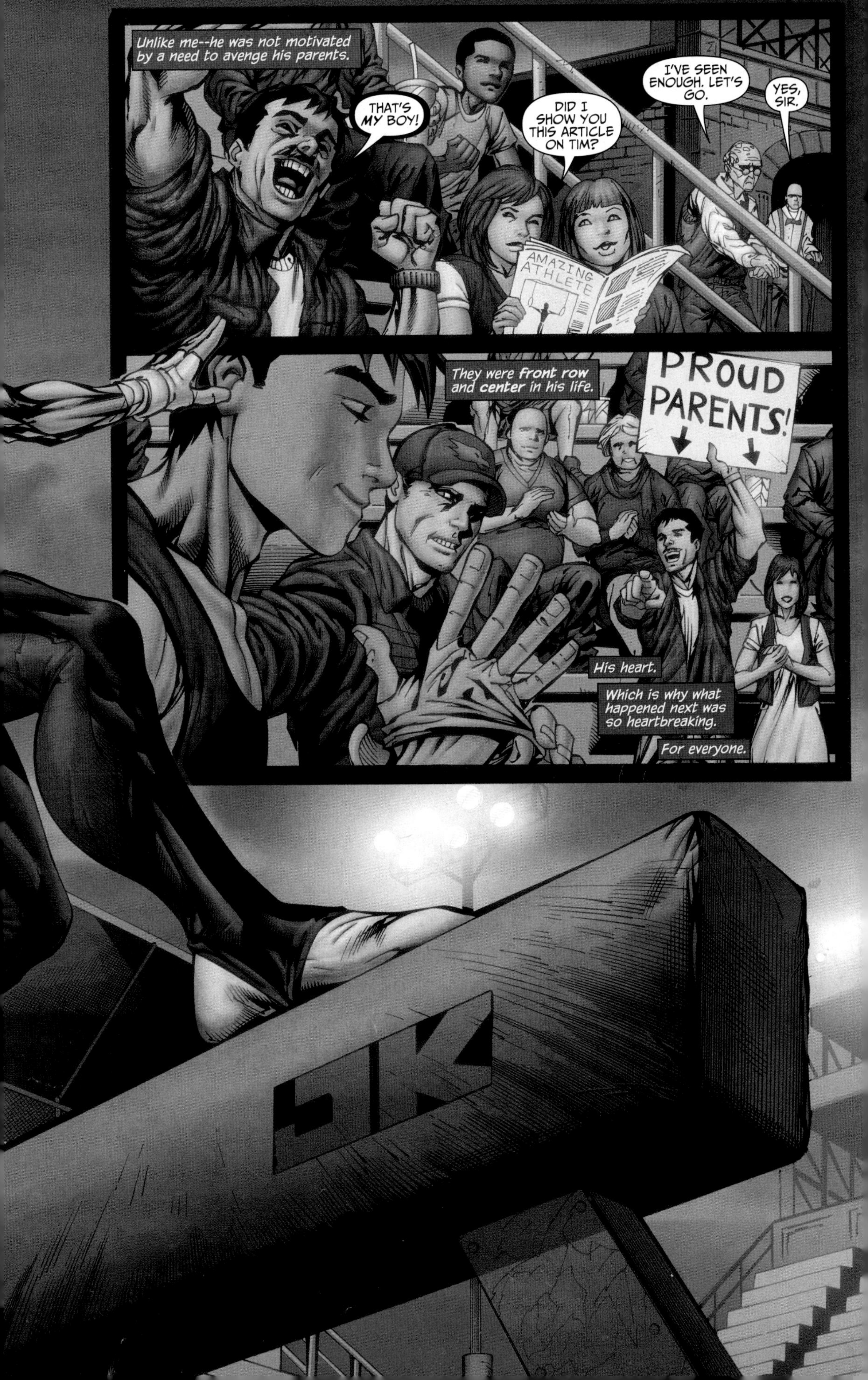
Unlike me--he was not motivated by a need to avenge his parents.
THAT'S MY BOY!
DID I SHOW YOU THIS ARTICLE ON TIM?
AMAZING ATHLETE
I'VE SEEN ENOUGH. LET'S GO.
YES, SIR.
They were front row and center in his life.
PROUD PARENTS!
His heart.
Which is why what happened next was so heartbreaking.
For everyone.

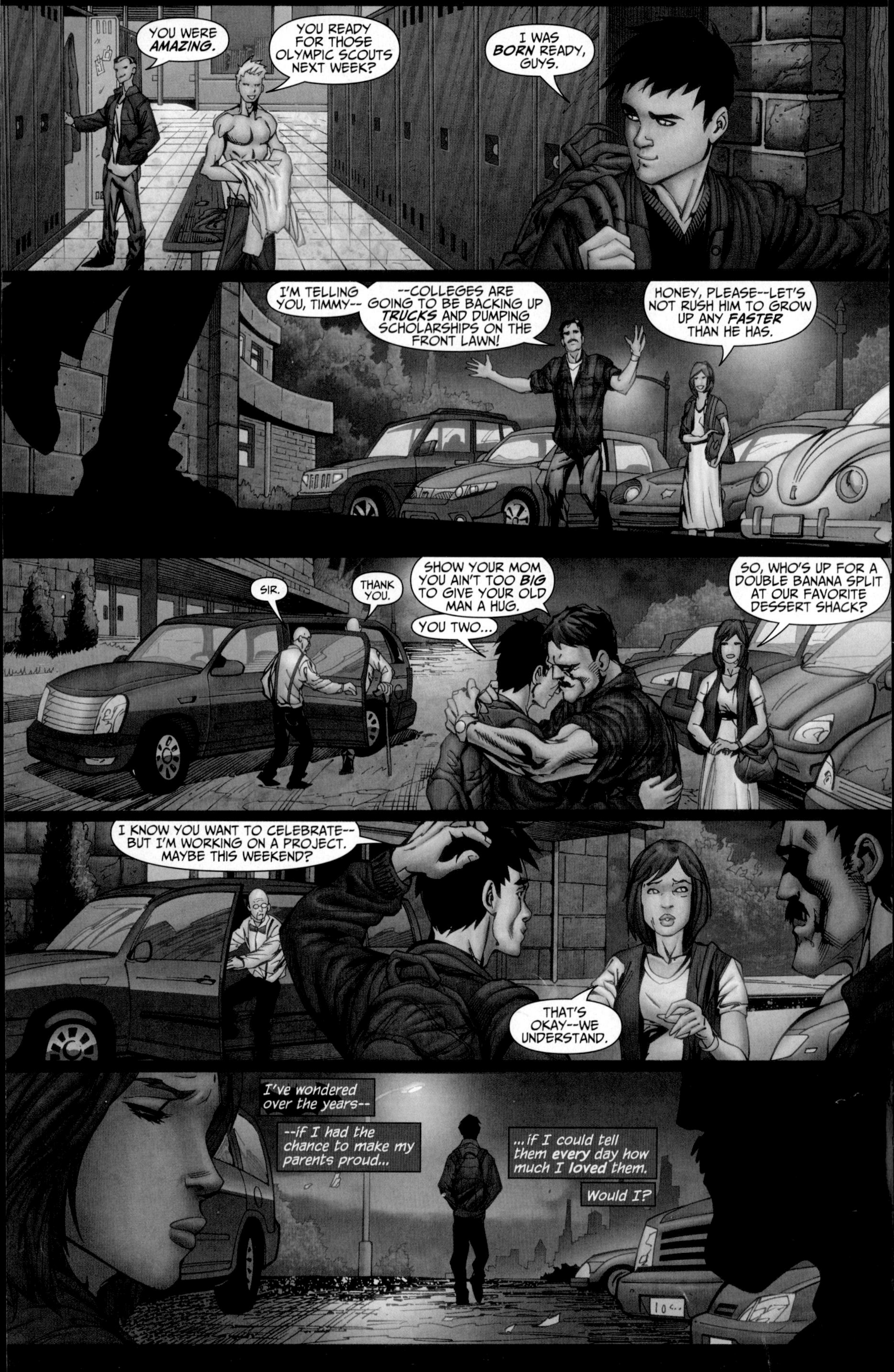
YOU WERE AMAZING.
YOU READY FOR THOSE OLYMPIC SCOUTS NEXT WEEK?
I WAS BORN READY, GUYS.
I'M TELLING YOU, TIMMY--
--COLLEGES ARE GOING TO BE BACKING UP TRUCKS AND DUMPING SCHOLARSHIPS ON THE FRONT LAWN!
HONEY, PLEASE--LET'S NOT RUSH HIM TO GROW UP ANY FASTER THAN HE HAS.
SIR.
THANK YOU.
SHOW YOUR MOM YOU AIN'T TOO BIG TO GIVE YOUR OLD MAN A HUG.
YOU TWO...
SO, WHO'S UP FOR A DOUBLE BANANA SPLIT AT OUR FAVORITE DESSERT SHACK?
I KNOW YOU WANT TO CELEBRATE-- BUT I'M WORKING ON A PROJECT. MAYBE THIS WEEKEND?
THAT'S OKAY--WE UNDERSTAND.
I've wondered over the years--
--if I had the chance to make my parents proud...
...if I could tell them every day how much I loved them.
Would I?

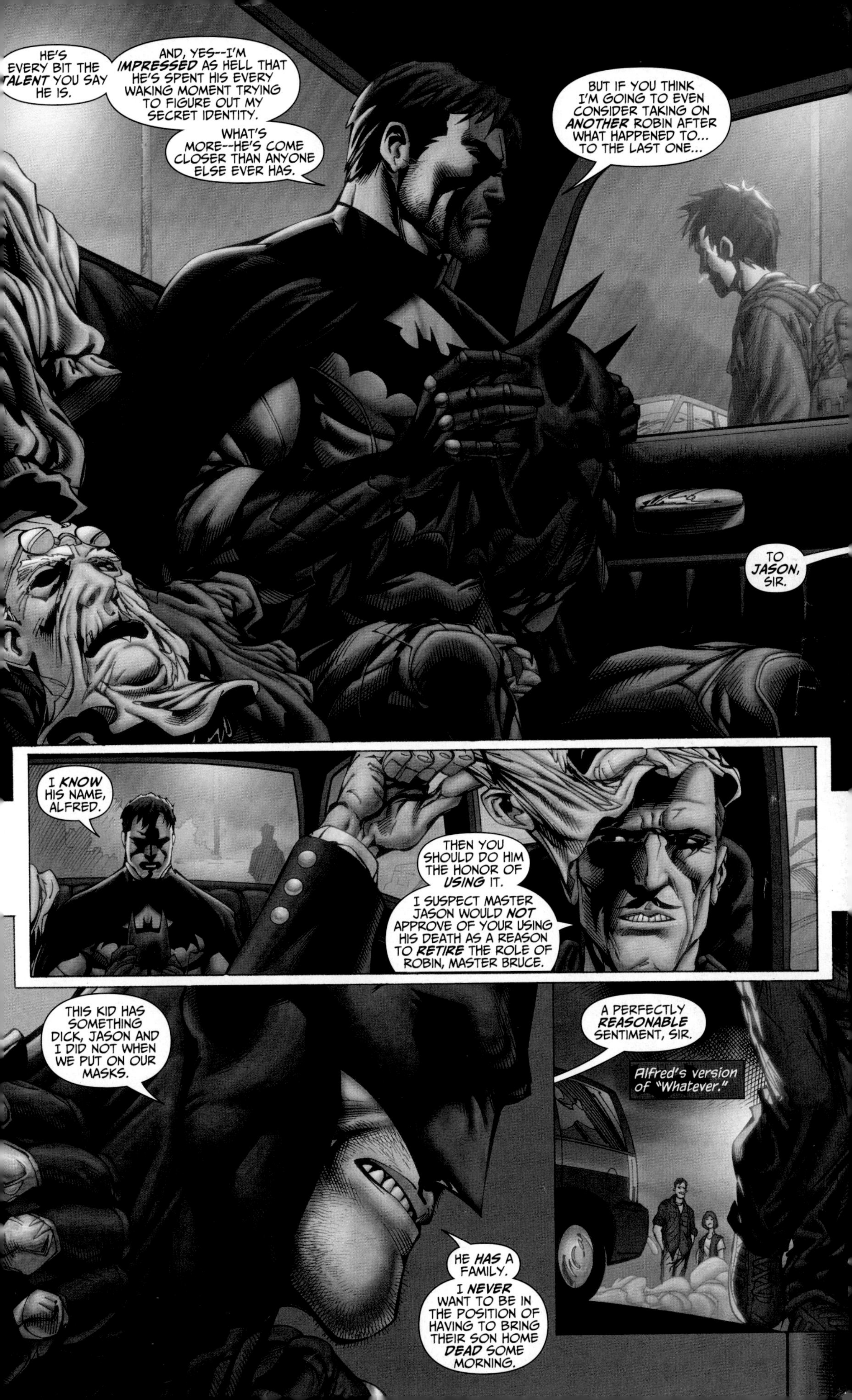

HE'S EVERY BIT THE TALENT YOU SAY HE IS.
AND, YES--I'M IMPRESSED AS HELL THAT HE'S SPENT HIS EVERY WAKING MOMENT TRYING TO FIGURE OUT MY SECRET IDENTITY.
WHAT'S MORE--HE'S COME CLOSER THAN ANYONE ELSE EVER HAS.
BUT IF YOU THINK I'M GOING TO EVEN CONSIDER TAKING ON ANOTHER ROBIN AFTER WHAT HAPPENED TO... TO THE LAST ONE...
TO JASON, SIR.
I KNOW HIS NAME, ALFRED.
THEN YOU SHOULD DO HIM THE HONOR OF USING IT.
I SUSPECT MASTER JASON WOULD NOT APPROVE OF YOUR USING HIS DEATH AS A REASON TO RETIRE THE ROLE OF ROBIN, MASTER BRUCE.
THIS KID HAS SOMETHING DICK, JASON AND I DID NOT WHEN WE PUT ON OUR MASKS.
HE HAS A FAMILY.
I NEVER WANT TO BE IN THE POSITION OF HAVING TO BRING THEIR SON HOME DEAD SOME MORNING.
A PERFECTLY REASONABLE SENTIMENT, SIR.
Alfred's version of "Whatever."

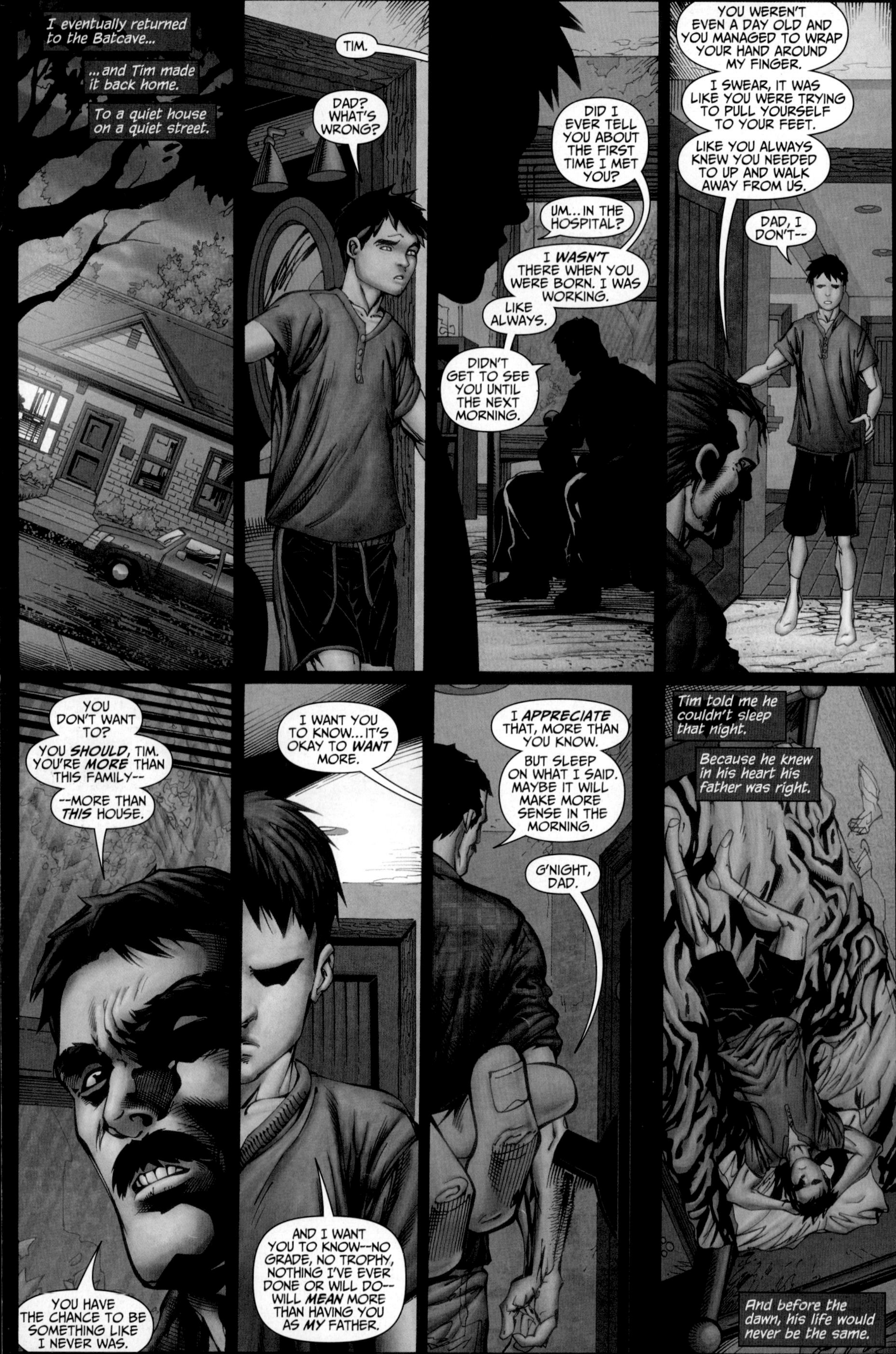
I eventually returned to the Batcave...
...and Tim made it back home.
To a quiet house on a quiet street.
TIM.
DAD? WHAT'S WRONG?
DID I EVER TELL YOU ABOUT THE FIRST TIME I MET YOU?
UM...IN THE HOSPITAL?
I WASN'T THERE WHEN YOU WERE BORN. I WAS WORKING.
LIKE ALWAYS.
DIDN'T GET TO SEE YOU UNTIL THE NEXT MORNING.
YOU WEREN'T EVEN A DAY OLD AND YOU MANAGED TO WRAP YOUR HAND AROUND MY FINGER.
I SWEAR, IT WAS LIKE YOU WERE TRYING TO PULL YOURSELF TO YOUR FEET.
LIKE YOU ALWAYS KNEW YOU NEEDED TO UP AND WALK AWAY FROM US.
DAD, I DON'T--
YOU DON'T WANT TO?
YOU SHOULD, TIM. YOU'RE MORE THAN THIS FAMILY--
--MORE THAN THIS HOUSE.
YOU HAVE THE CHANCE TO BE SOMETHING LIKE I NEVER WAS.
I WANT YOU TO KNOW...IT'S OKAY TO WANT MORE.
AND I WANT YOU TO KNOW--NO GRADE, NO TROPHY, NOTHING I'VE EVER DONE OR WILL DO--WILL MEAN MORE THAN HAVING YOU AS MY FATHER.
I APPRECIATE THAT, MORE THAN YOU KNOW.
BUT SLEEP ON WHAT I SAID. MAYBE IT WILL MAKE MORE SENSE IN THE MORNING.
G'NIGHT, DAD.
Tim told me he couldn't sleep that night.
Because he knew in his heart his father was right.
And before the dawn, his life would never be the same.

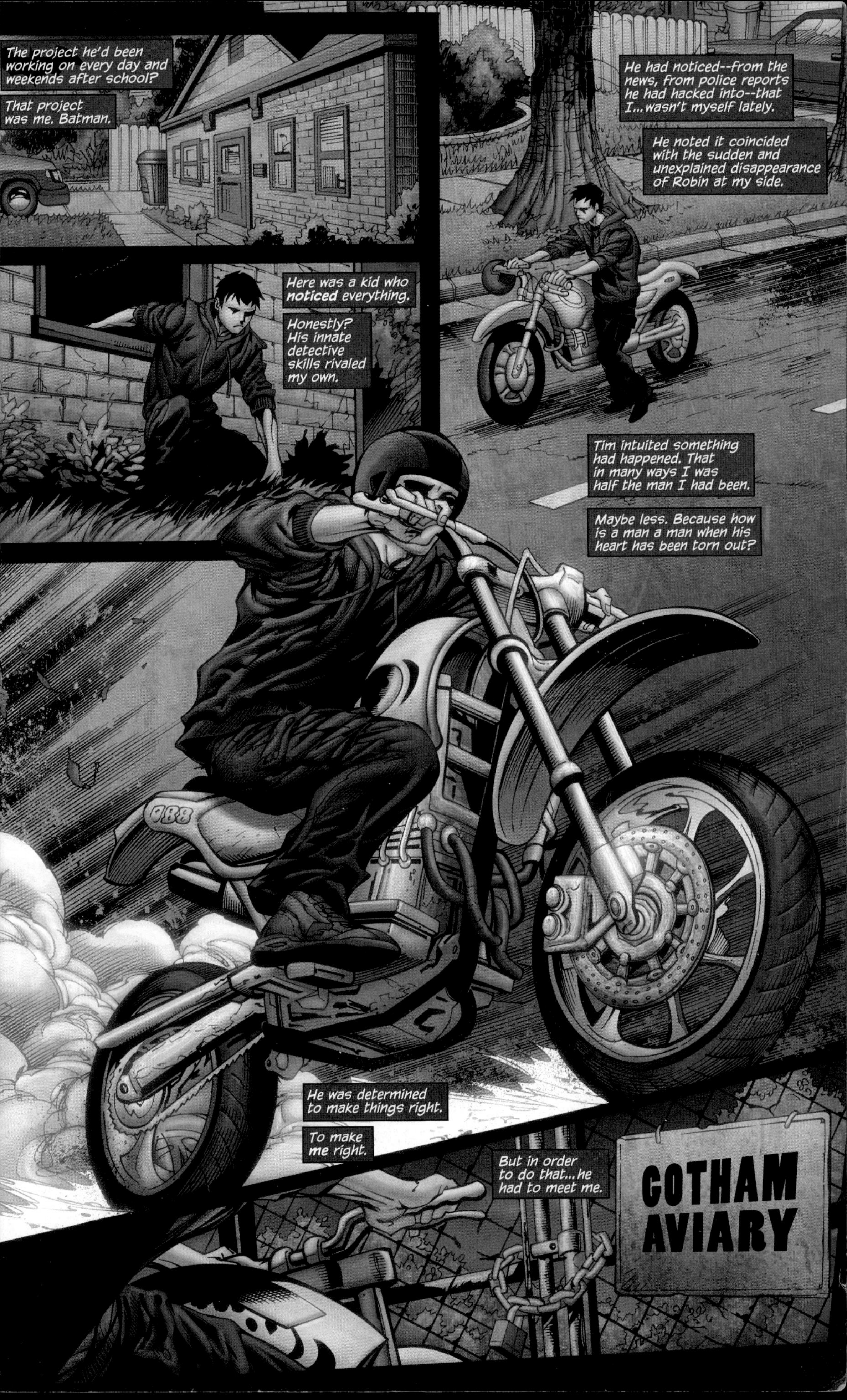
The project he'd been working on every day and weekends after school?
That project was me. Batman.
He had noticed--from the news, from police reports he had hacked into--that I...wasn't myself lately.
He noted it coincided with the sudden and unexplained disappearance of Robin at my side.
Here was a kid who noticed everything.
Honestly? His innate detective skills rivaled my own.
Tim intuited something had happened. That in many ways I was half the man I had been.
Maybe less. Because how is a man a man when his heart has been torn out?
He was determined to make things right.
To make me right.
But in order to do that...he had to meet me.
GOTHAM AVIARY

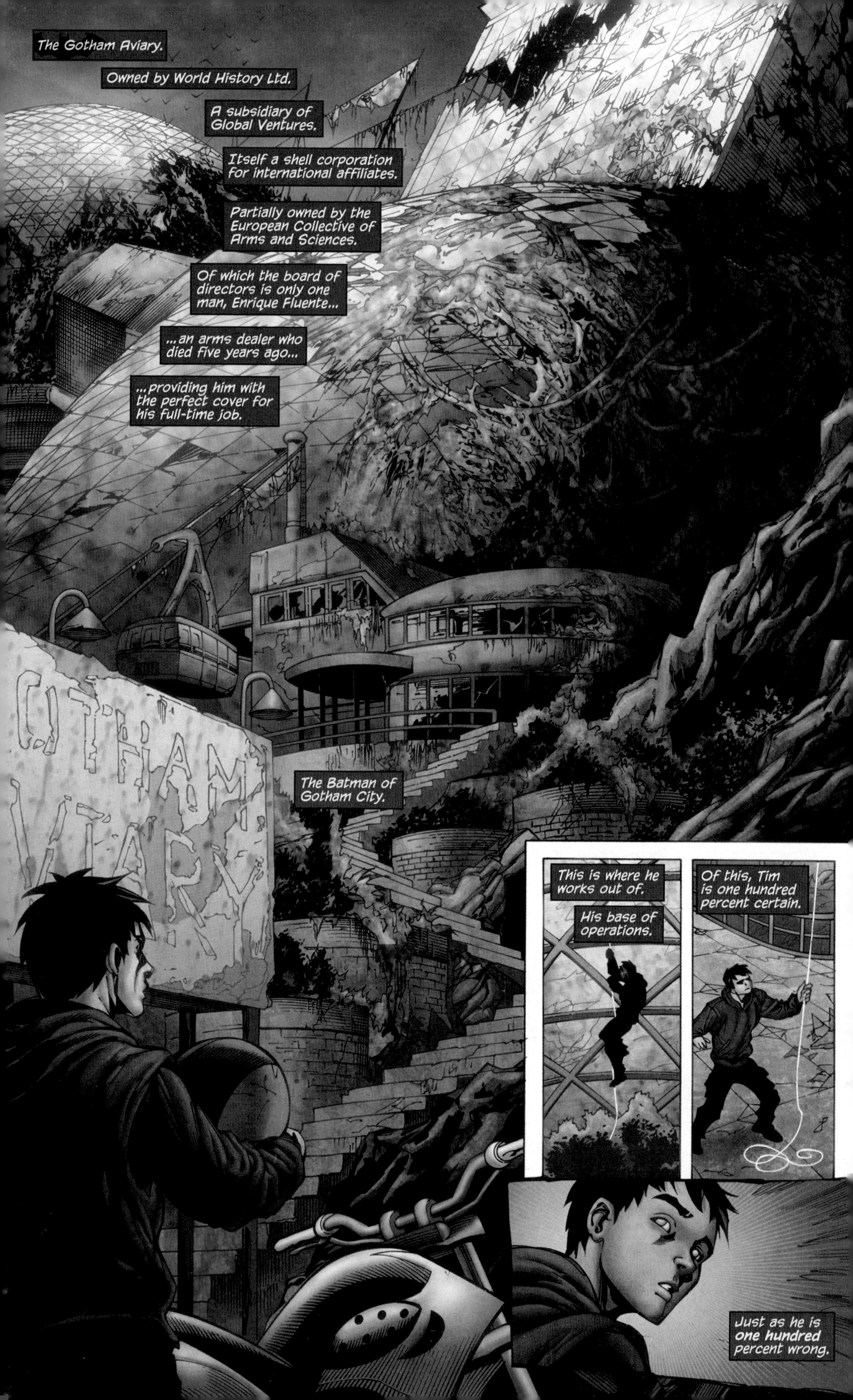

The Gotham Aviary.
Owned by World History Ltd.
A subsidiary of Global Ventures.
Itself a shell corporation for international affiliates.
Partially owned by the European Collective of Arms and Sciences.
Of which the board of directors is only one man, Enrique Fluente...
...an arms dealer who died five years ago...
...providing him with the perfect cover for his full-time job.
The Batman of Gotham City.
This is where he works out of.
His base of operations.
Of this, Tim is one hundred percent certain.
Just as he is one hundred percent wrong.

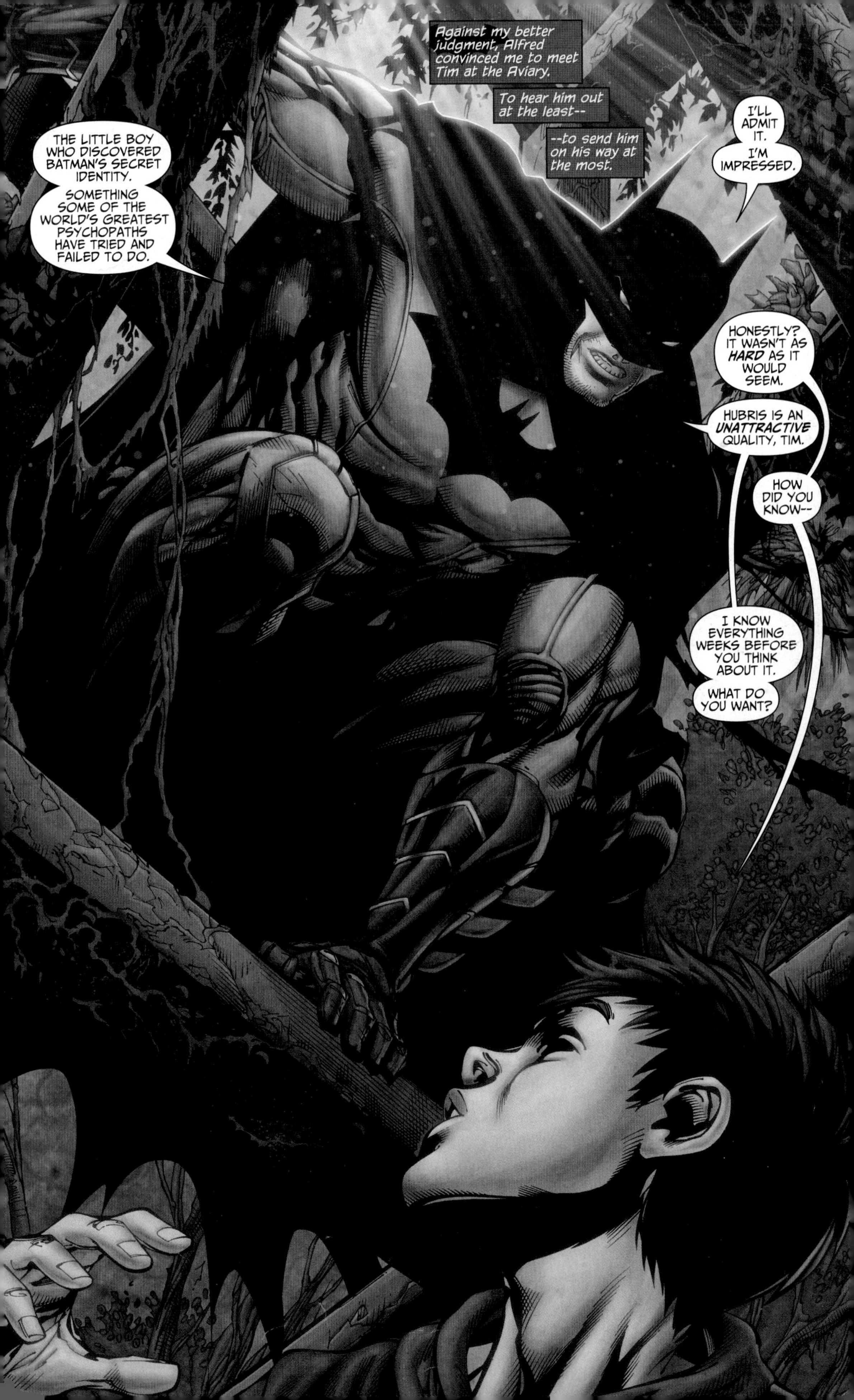

Against my better judgment, Alfred convinced me to meet Tim at the Aviary.
To hear him out at the least--
--to send him on his way at the most.
THE LITTLE BOY WHO DISCOVERED BATMAN'S SECRET IDENTITY.
SOMETHING SOME OF THE WORLD'S GREATEST PSYCHOPATHS HAVE TRIED AND FAILED TO DO.
I'LL ADMIT IT.
I'M IMPRESSED.
HONESTLY? IT WASN'T AS HARD AS IT WOULD SEEM.
HUBRIS IS AN UNATTRACTIVE QUALITY, TIM.
HOW DID YOU KNOW--
I KNOW EVERYTHING WEEKS BEFORE YOU THINK ABOUT IT.
WHAT DO YOU WANT?

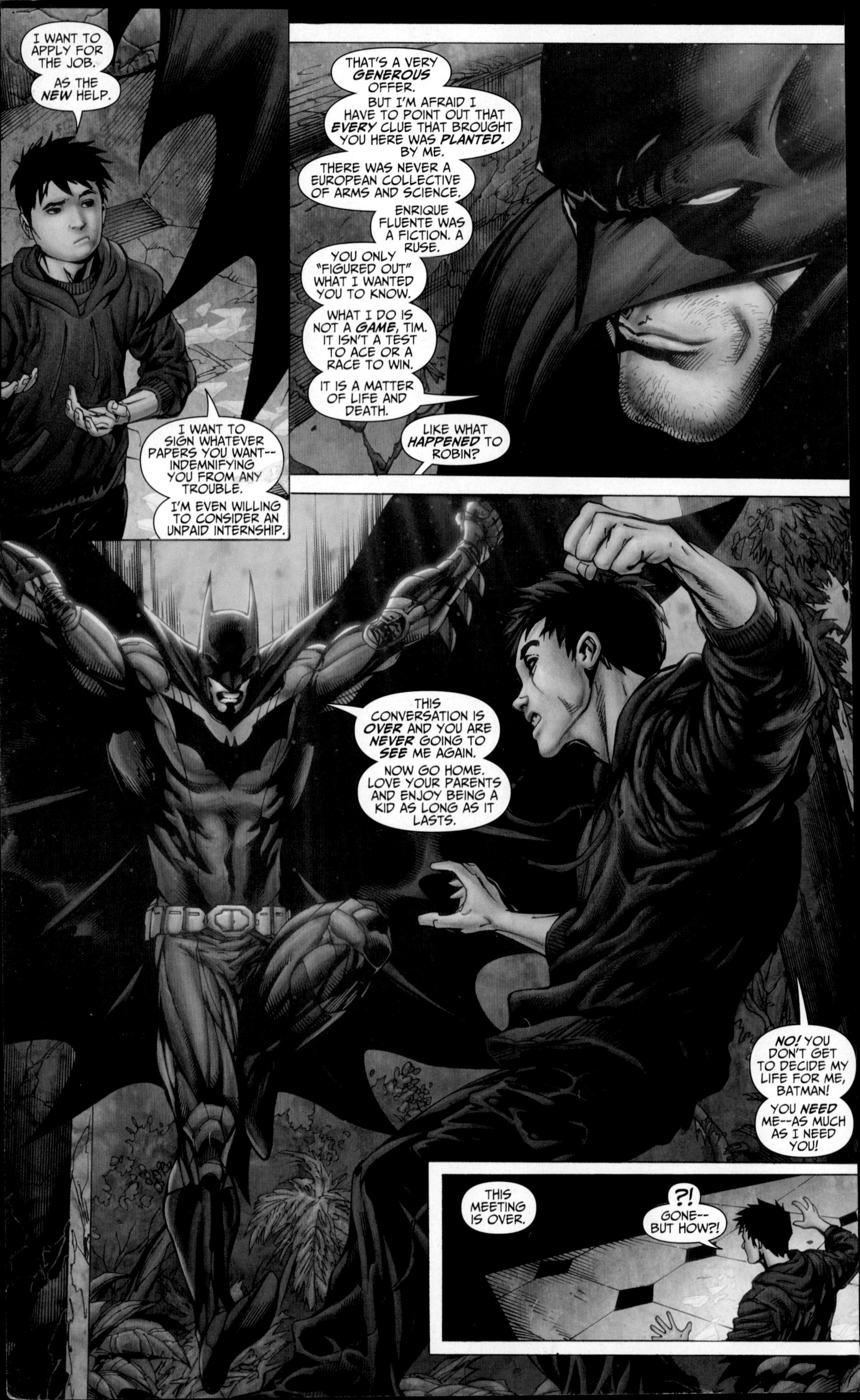
I WANT TO APPLY FOR THE JOB.
AS THE NEW HELP.
THAT'S A VERY GENEROUS OFFER.
BUT I'M AFRAID I HAVE TO POINT OUT THAT EVERY CLUE THAT BROUGHT YOU HERE WAS PLANTED. BY ME.
THERE WAS NEVER A EUROPEAN COLLECTIVE OF ARMS AND SCIENCE.
ENRIQUE FLUENTE WAS A FICTION. A RUSE.
YOU ONLY "FIGURED OUT" WHAT I WANTED YOU TO KNOW.
WHAT I DO IS NOT A GAME, TIM. IT ISN'T A TEST TO ACE OR A RACE TO WIN.
IT IS A MATTER OF LIFE AND DEATH.
LIKE WHAT HAPPENED TO ROBIN?
I WANT TO SIGN WHATEVER PAPERS YOU WANT--INDEMNIFYING YOU FROM ANY TROUBLE.
I'M EVEN WILLING TO CONSIDER AN UNPAID INTERNSHIP.
THIS CONVERSATION IS OVER AND YOU ARE NEVER GOING TO SEE ME AGAIN.
NOW GO HOME. LOVE YOUR PARENTS AND ENJOY BEING A KID AS LONG AS IT LASTS.
NO! YOU DON'T GET TO DECIDE MY LIFE FOR ME, BATMAN!
YOU NEED ME--AS MUCH AS I NEED YOU!
THIS MEETING IS OVER.
?!
GONE--BUT HOW?!

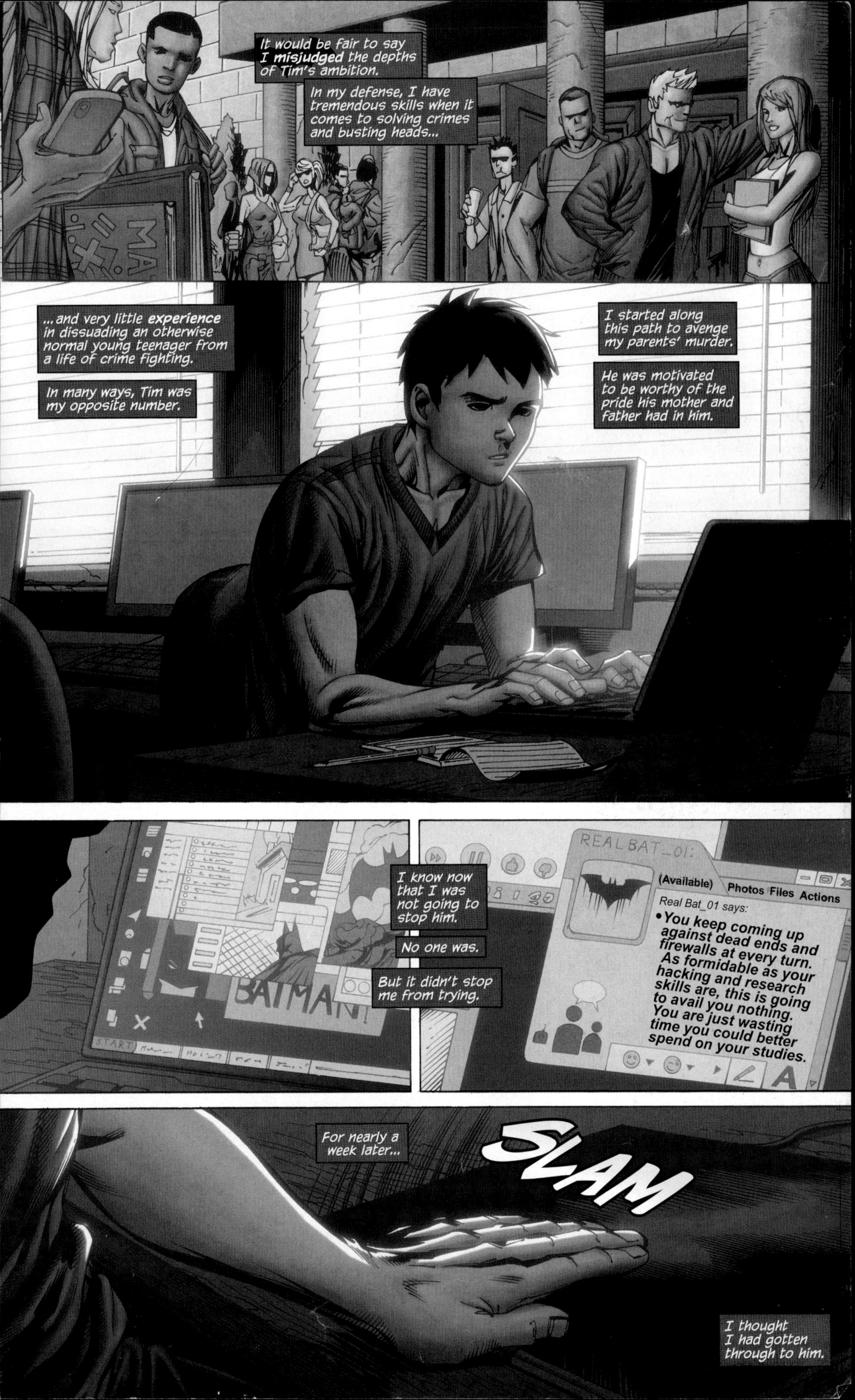
It would be fair to say I misjudged the depths of Tim's ambition.
In my defense, I have tremendous skills when it comes to solving crimes and busting heads...
...and very little experience in dissuading an otherwise normal young teenager from a life of crime fighting.
In many ways, Tim was my opposite number.
I started along this path to avenge my parents' murder.
He was motivated to be worthy of the pride his mother and father had in him.
BATMAN!
I know now that I was not going to stop him.
No one was.
But it didn't stop me from trying.
REAL BAT_01:
(Available) Photos Files Actions
Real Bat_01 says:
• You keep coming up against dead ends and firewalls at every turn. As formidable as your hacking and research skills are, this is going to avail you nothing. You are just wasting time you could better spend on your studies.
For nearly a week later...
SLAM
I thought I had gotten through to him.

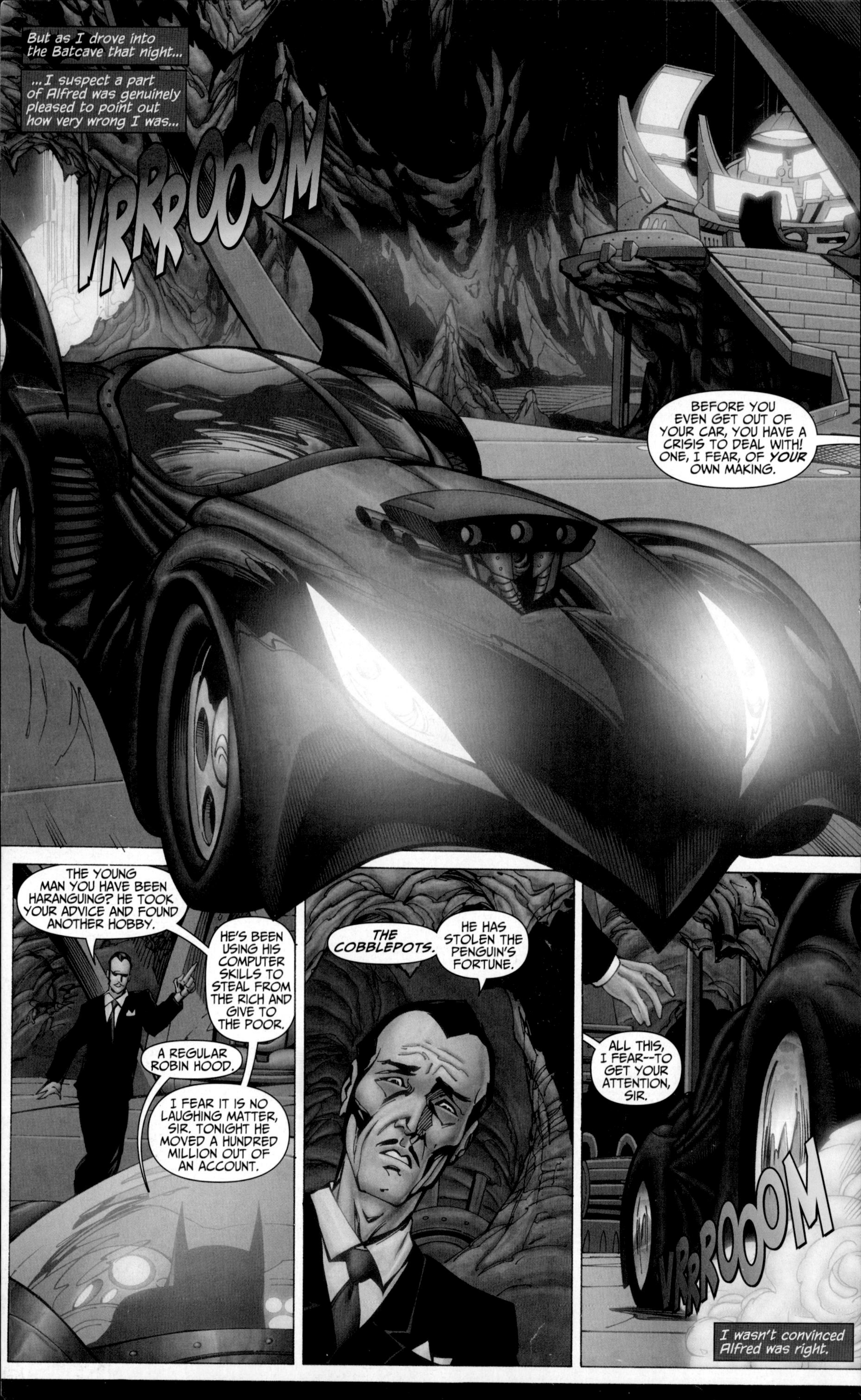

But as I drove into the Batcave that night...
...I suspect a part of Alfred was genuinely pleased to point out how very wrong I was...
VRRROOOM
BEFORE YOU EVEN GET OUT OF YOUR CAR, YOU HAVE A CRISIS TO DEAL WITH! ONE, I FEAR, OF YOUR OWN MAKING.
THE YOUNG MAN YOU HAVE BEEN HARANGUING? HE TOOK YOUR ADVICE AND FOUND ANOTHER HOBBY.
HE'S BEEN USING HIS COMPUTER SKILLS TO STEAL FROM THE RICH AND GIVE TO THE POOR.
A REGULAR ROBIN HOOD.
I FEAR IT IS NO LAUGHING MATTER, SIR. TONIGHT HE MOVED A HUNDRED MILLION OUT OF AN ACCOUNT.
THE COBBLEPOTS.
HE HAS STOLEN THE PENGUIN'S FORTUNE.
ALL THIS, I FEAR--TO GET YOUR ATTENTION, SIR.
VRRROOOM
I wasn't convinced Alfred was right.

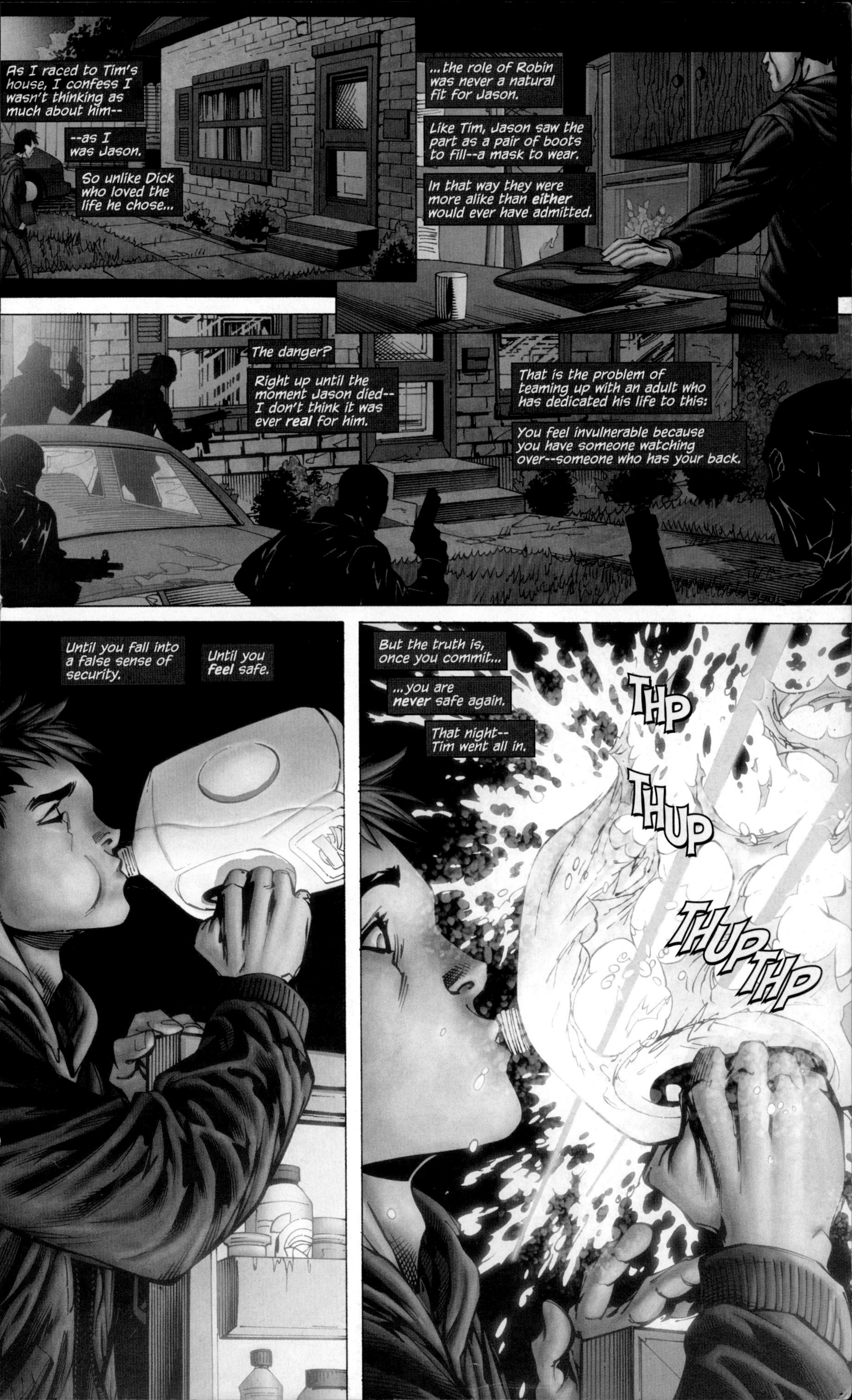
As I raced to Tim's house, I confess I wasn't thinking as much about him--
--as I was Jason.
So unlike Dick who loved the life he chose...
...the role of Robin was never a natural fit for Jason.
Like Tim, Jason saw the part as a pair of boots to fill--a mask to wear.
In that way they were more alike than either would ever have admitted.
The danger?
Right up until the moment Jason died-- I don't think it was ever real for him.
That is the problem of teaming up with an adult who has dedicated his life to this:
You feel invulnerable because you have someone watching over--someone who has your back.
Until you fall into a false sense of security.
Until you feel safe.
But the truth is, once you commit...
...you are never safe again.
That night-- Tim went all in.
THP
THUP
THUP THP

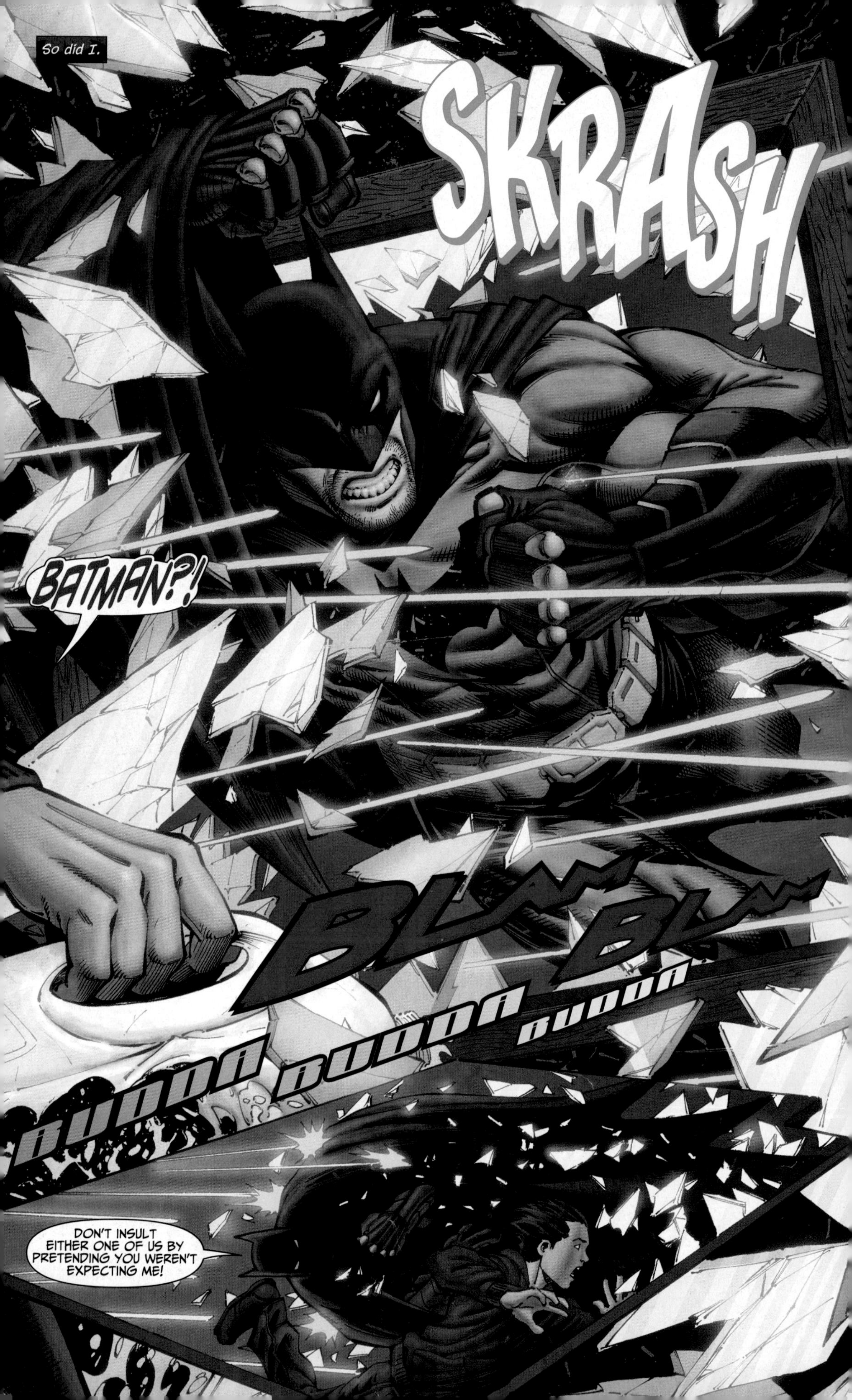
So did I.
SKRASH
BATMAN?!
BLAM BLAM
BUDDA BUDDA BUDDA
DON'T INSULT EITHER ONE OF US BY PRETENDING YOU WEREN'T EXPECTING ME!

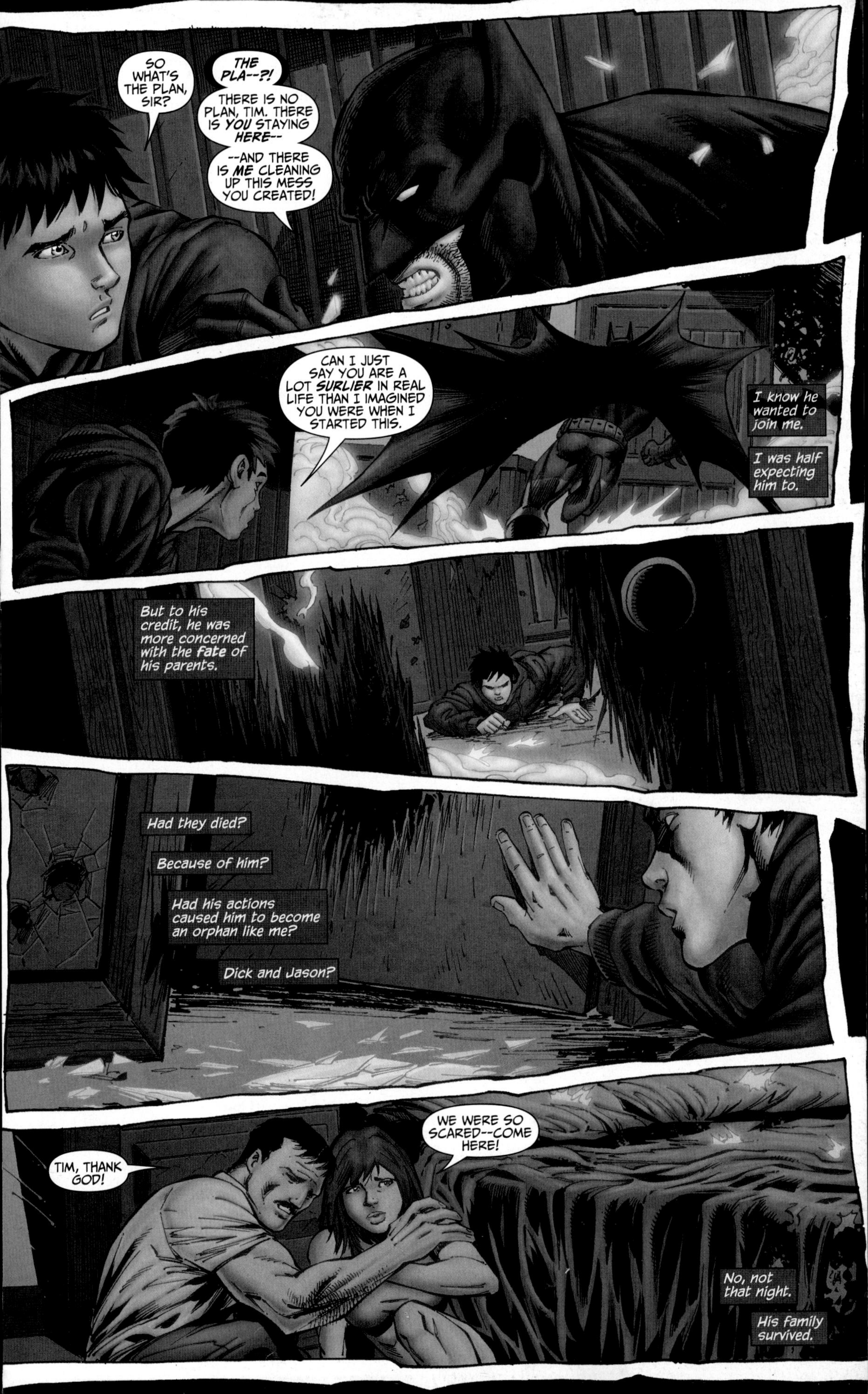
SO WHAT'S THE PLAN, SIR?
THE PLA--?!
THERE IS NO PLAN, TIM. THERE IS YOU STAYING HERE--
--AND THERE IS ME CLEANING UP THIS MESS YOU CREATED!
CAN I JUST SAY YOU ARE A LOT SURLIER IN REAL LIFE THAN I IMAGINED YOU WERE WHEN I STARTED THIS.
I know he wanted to join me.
I was half expecting him to.
But to his credit, he was more concerned with the fate of his parents.
Had they died?
Because of him?
Had his actions caused him to become an orphan like me?
Dick and Jason?
TIM, THANK GOD!
WE WERE SO SCARED--COME HERE!
No, not that night.
His family survived.

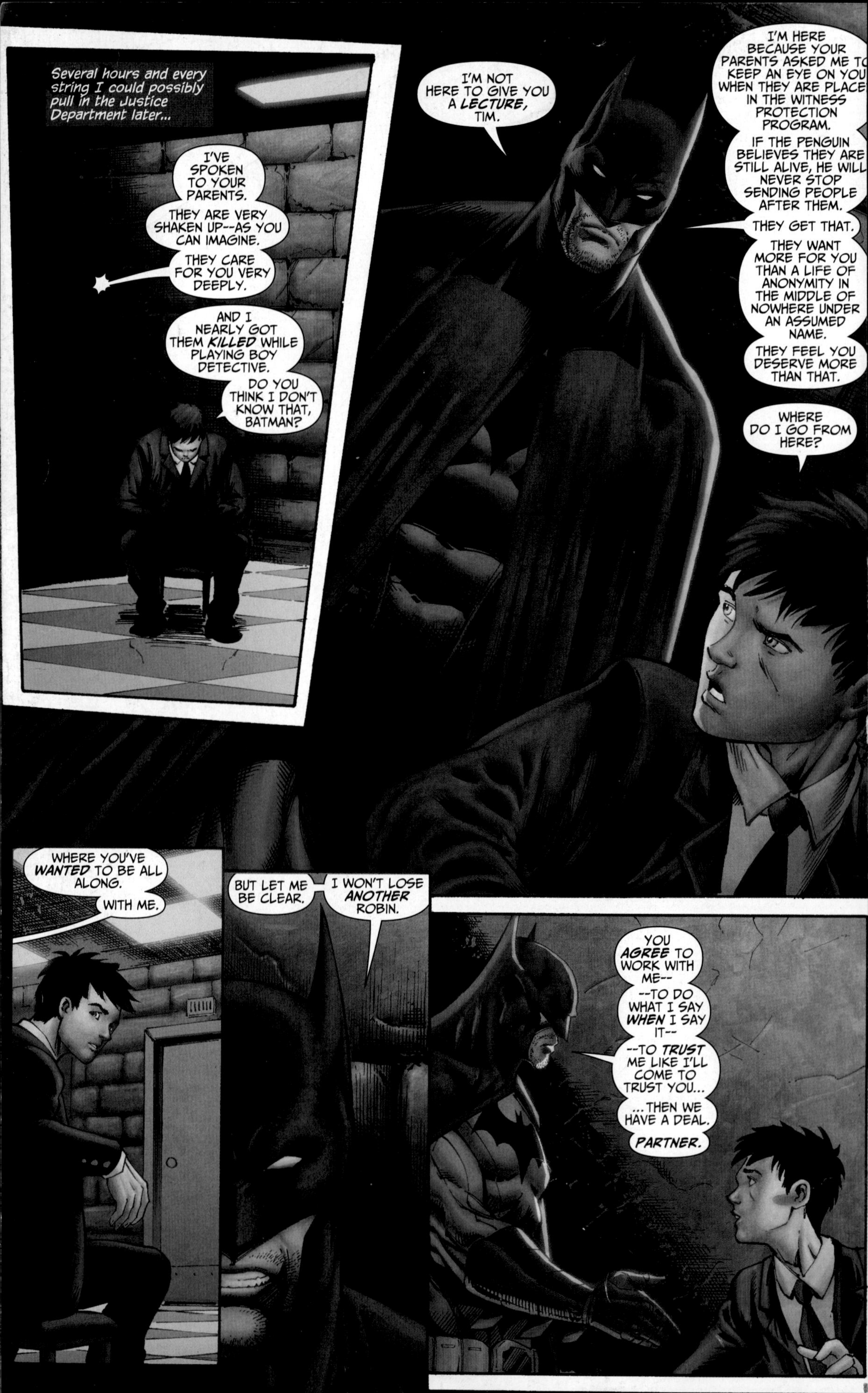
Several hours and every string I could possibly pull in the Justice Department later...
I'VE SPOKEN TO YOUR PARENTS.
THEY ARE VERY SHAKEN UP--AS YOU CAN IMAGINE.
THEY CARE FOR YOU VERY DEEPLY.
AND I NEARLY GOT THEM *KILLED* WHILE PLAYING BOY DETECTIVE.
DO YOU THINK I DON'T KNOW THAT, BATMAN?
I'M NOT HERE TO GIVE YOU A *LECTURE,* TIM.
I'M HERE BECAUSE YOUR PARENTS ASKED ME TO KEEP AN EYE ON YOU WHEN THEY ARE PLACED IN THE WITNESS PROTECTION PROGRAM.
IF THE PENGUIN BELIEVES THEY ARE STILL ALIVE, HE WILL NEVER STOP SENDING PEOPLE AFTER THEM.
THEY GET THAT.
THEY WANT MORE FOR YOU THAN A LIFE OF ANONYMITY IN THE MIDDLE OF NOWHERE UNDER AN ASSUMED NAME.
THEY FEEL YOU DESERVE MORE THAN THAT.
WHERE DO I GO FROM HERE?
WHERE YOU'VE *WANTED* TO BE ALL ALONG.
WITH ME.
BUT LET ME BE CLEAR.
I WON'T LOSE *ANOTHER* ROBIN.
YOU *AGREE* TO WORK WITH ME--
--TO DO WHAT I SAY *WHEN* I SAY IT--
--TO *TRUST* ME LIKE I'LL COME TO TRUST YOU...
...THEN WE HAVE A DEAL.
PARTNER.

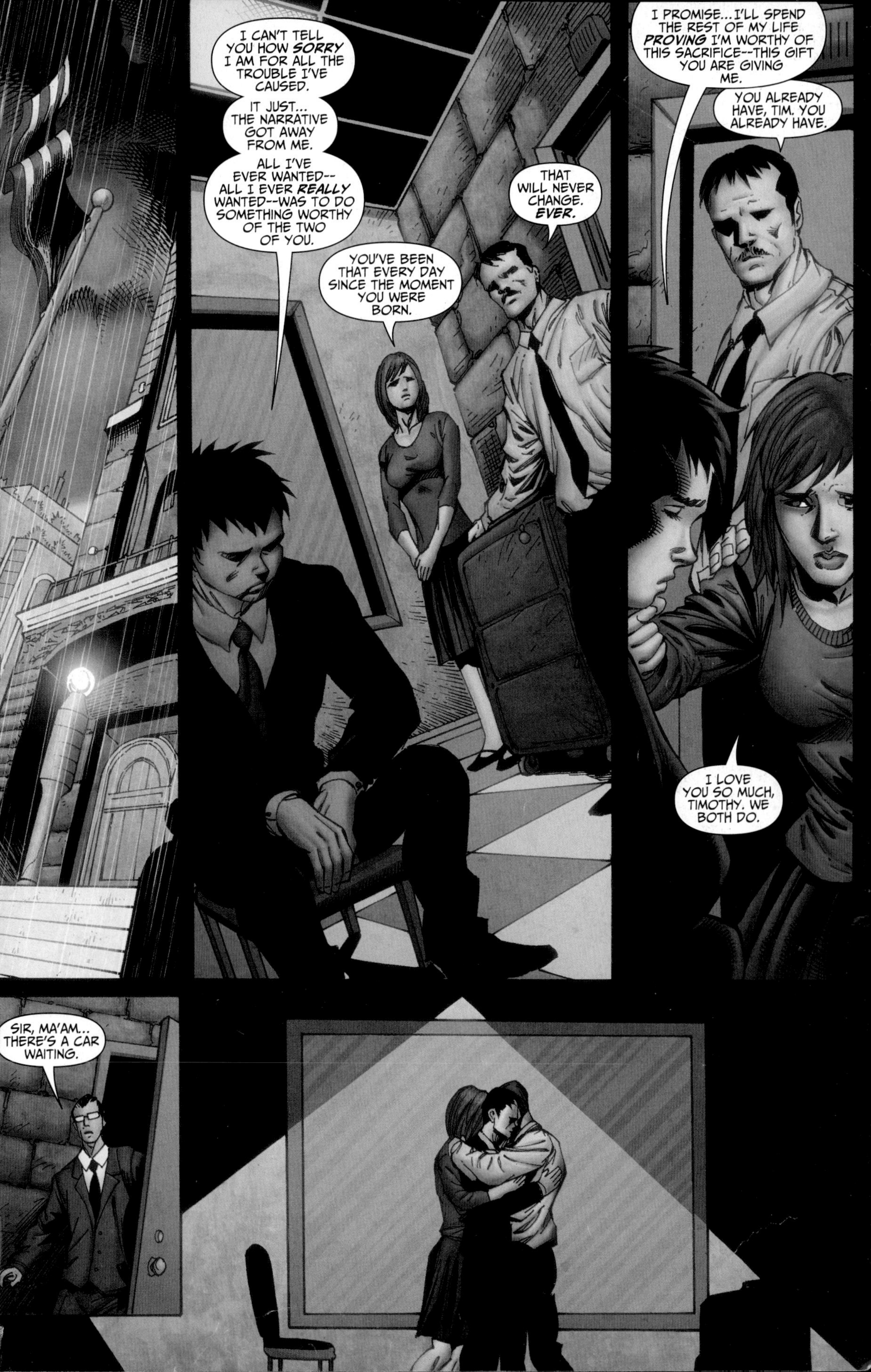
I CAN'T TELL YOU HOW SORRY I AM FOR ALL THE TROUBLE I'VE CAUSED.
IT JUST... THE NARRATIVE GOT AWAY FROM ME.
ALL I'VE EVER WANTED-- ALL I EVER REALLY WANTED--WAS TO DO SOMETHING WORTHY OF THE TWO OF YOU.
YOU'VE BEEN THAT EVERY DAY SINCE THE MOMENT YOU WERE BORN.
THAT WILL NEVER CHANGE. EVER.
I PROMISE...I'LL SPEND THE REST OF MY LIFE PROVING I'M WORTHY OF THIS SACRIFICE--THIS GIFT YOU ARE GIVING ME.
YOU ALREADY HAVE, TIM. YOU ALREADY HAVE.
I LOVE YOU SO MUCH, TIMOTHY. WE BOTH DO.
SIR, MA'AM... THERE'S A CAR WAITING.

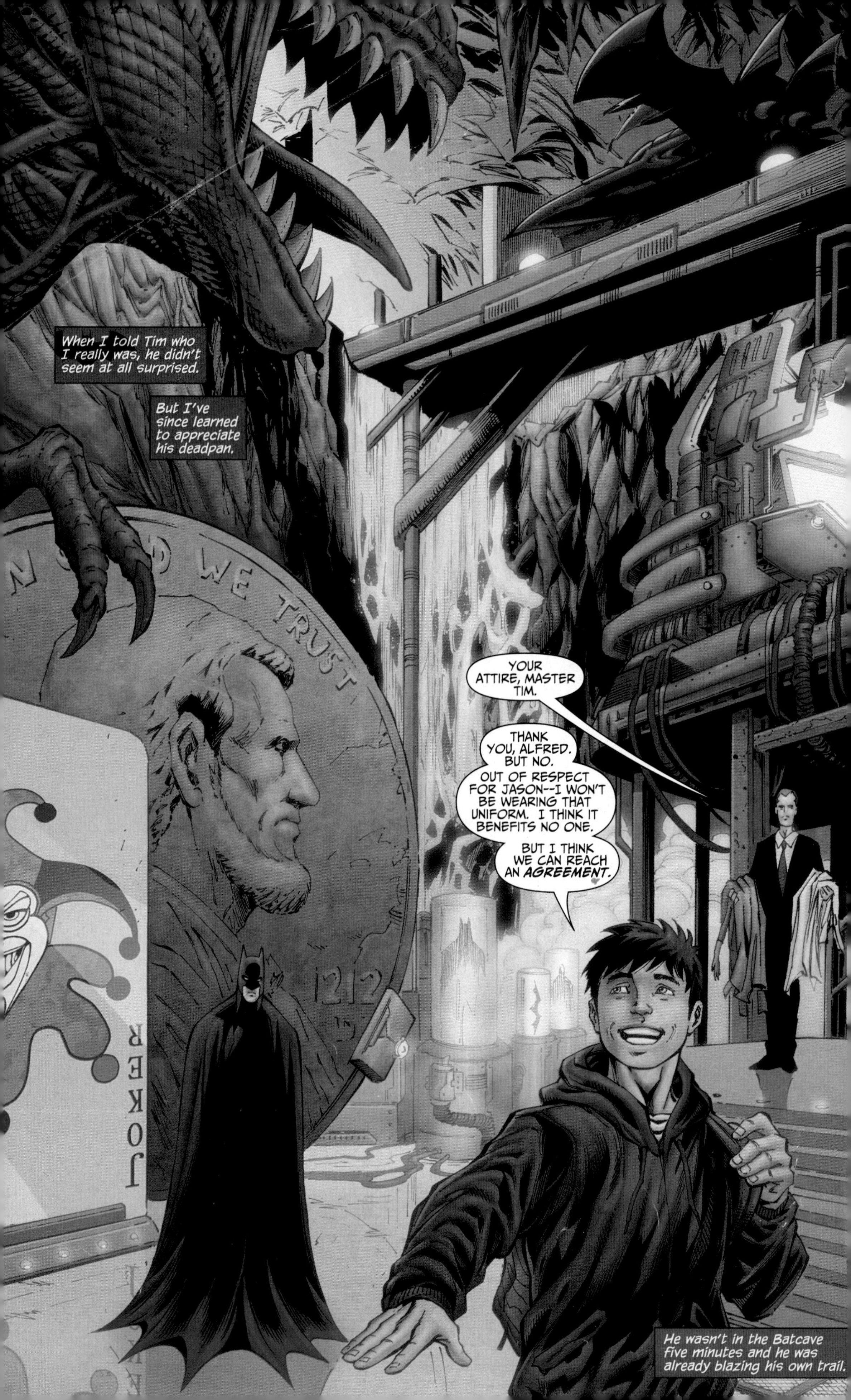

When I told Tim who I really was, he didn't seem at all surprised.
But I've since learned to appreciate his deadpan.
IN GOD WE TRUST
YOUR ATTIRE, MASTER TIM.
THANK YOU, ALFRED. BUT NO.
OUT OF RESPECT FOR JASON--I WON'T BE WEARING THAT UNIFORM. I THINK IT BENEFITS NO ONE.
BUT I THINK WE CAN REACH AN *AGREEMENT.*
JOKER
He wasn't in the Batcave five minutes and he was already blazing his own trail.

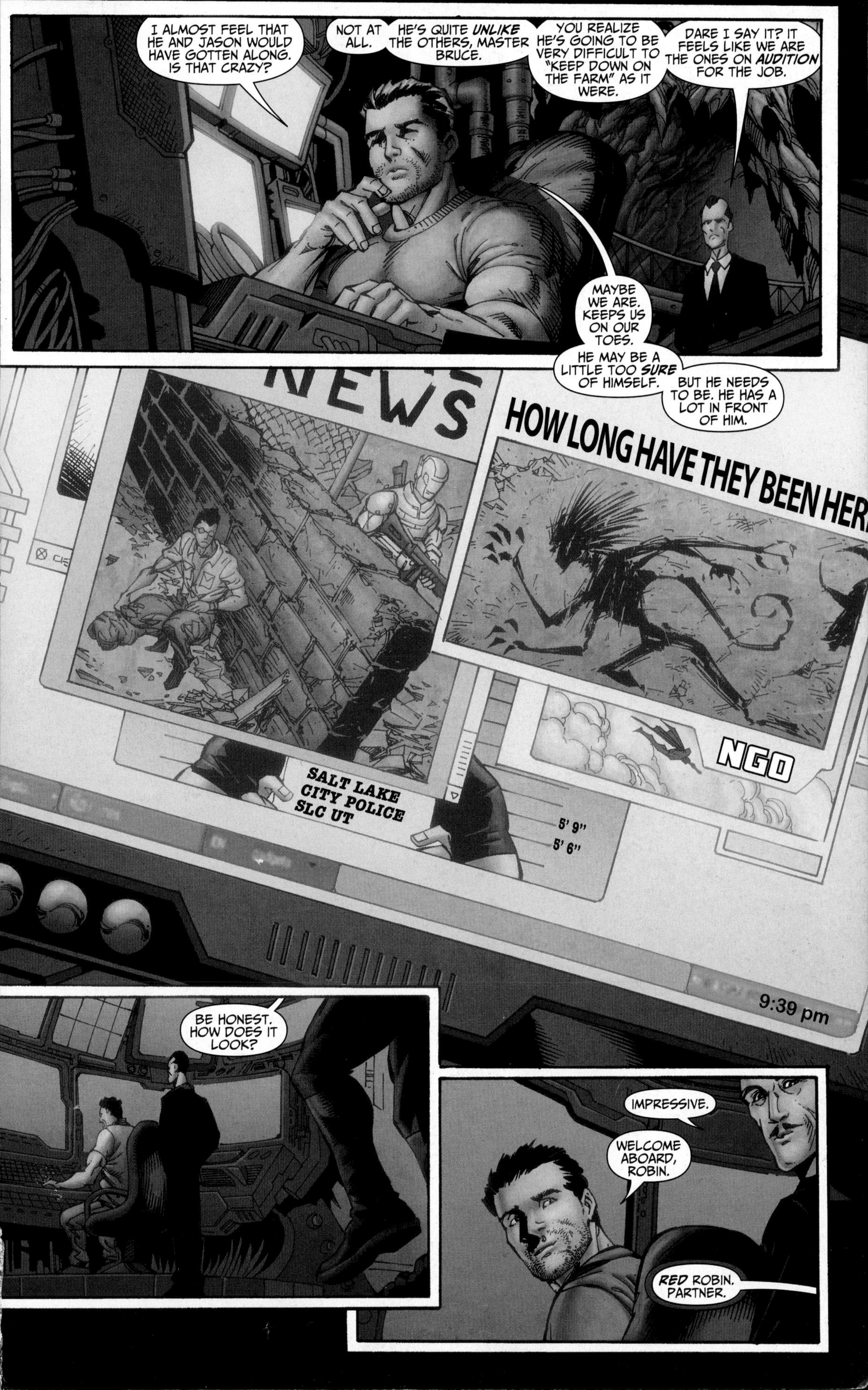

I ALMOST FEEL THAT HE AND JASON WOULD HAVE GOTTEN ALONG. IS THAT CRAZY?
NOT AT ALL.
HE'S QUITE UNLIKE THE OTHERS, MASTER BRUCE.
YOU REALIZE HE'S GOING TO BE VERY DIFFICULT TO "KEEP DOWN ON THE FARM" AS IT WERE.
DARE I SAY IT? IT FEELS LIKE WE ARE THE ONES ON AUDITION FOR THE JOB.
MAYBE WE ARE. KEEPS US ON OUR TOES.
HE MAY BE A LITTLE TOO SURE OF HIMSELF.
BUT HE NEEDS TO BE. HE HAS A LOT IN FRONT OF HIM.
NEWS
HOW LONG HAVE THEY BEEN HER
NGO
SALT LAKE CITY POLICE SLC UT
5' 9"
5' 6"
9:39 pm
BE HONEST. HOW DOES IT LOOK?
IMPRESSIVE.
WELCOME ABOARD, ROBIN.
RED ROBIN. PARTNER.

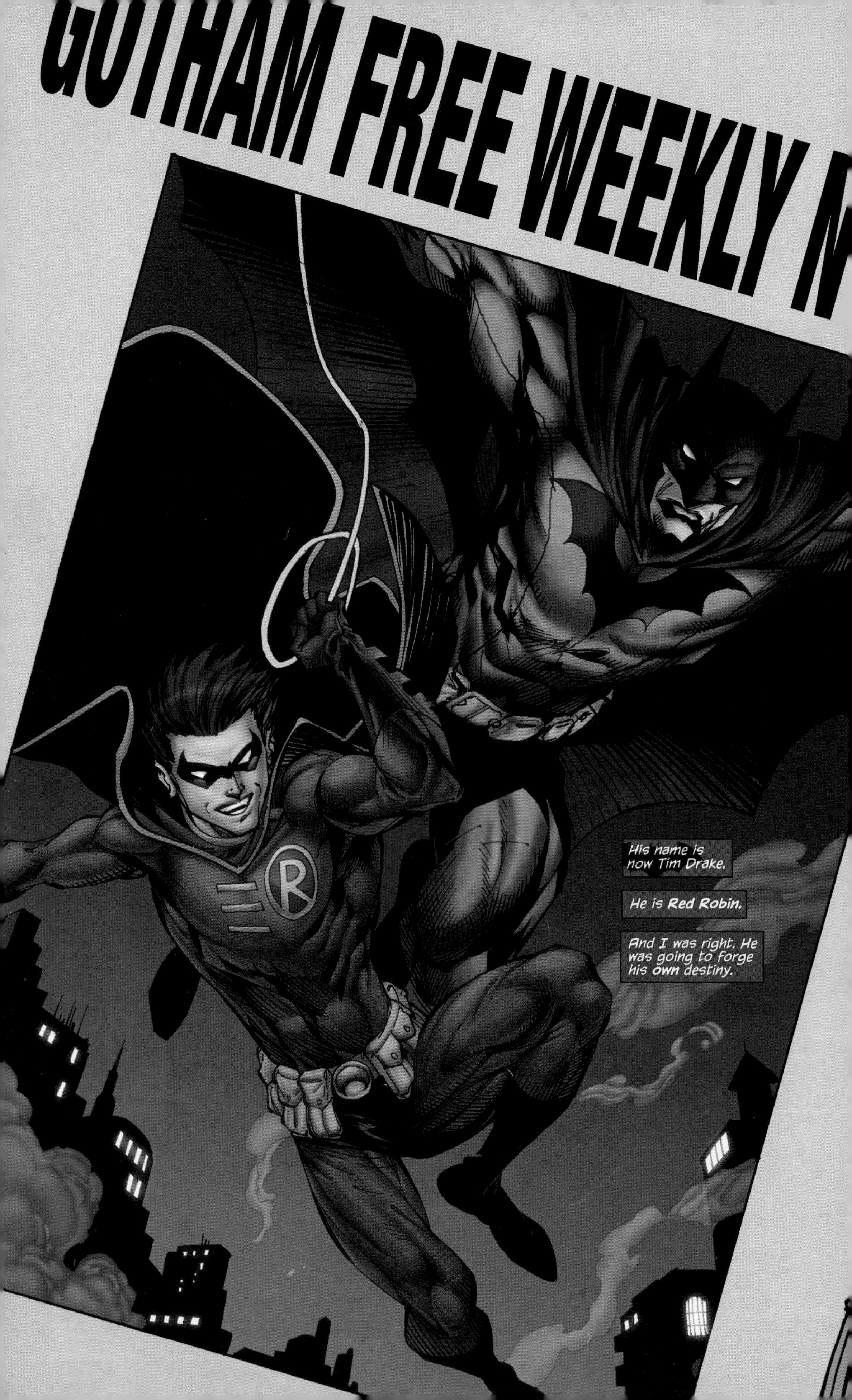
GOTHAM FREE WEEKLY N
His name is now Tim Drake.
He is Red Robin.
And I was right. He was going to forge his own destiny.

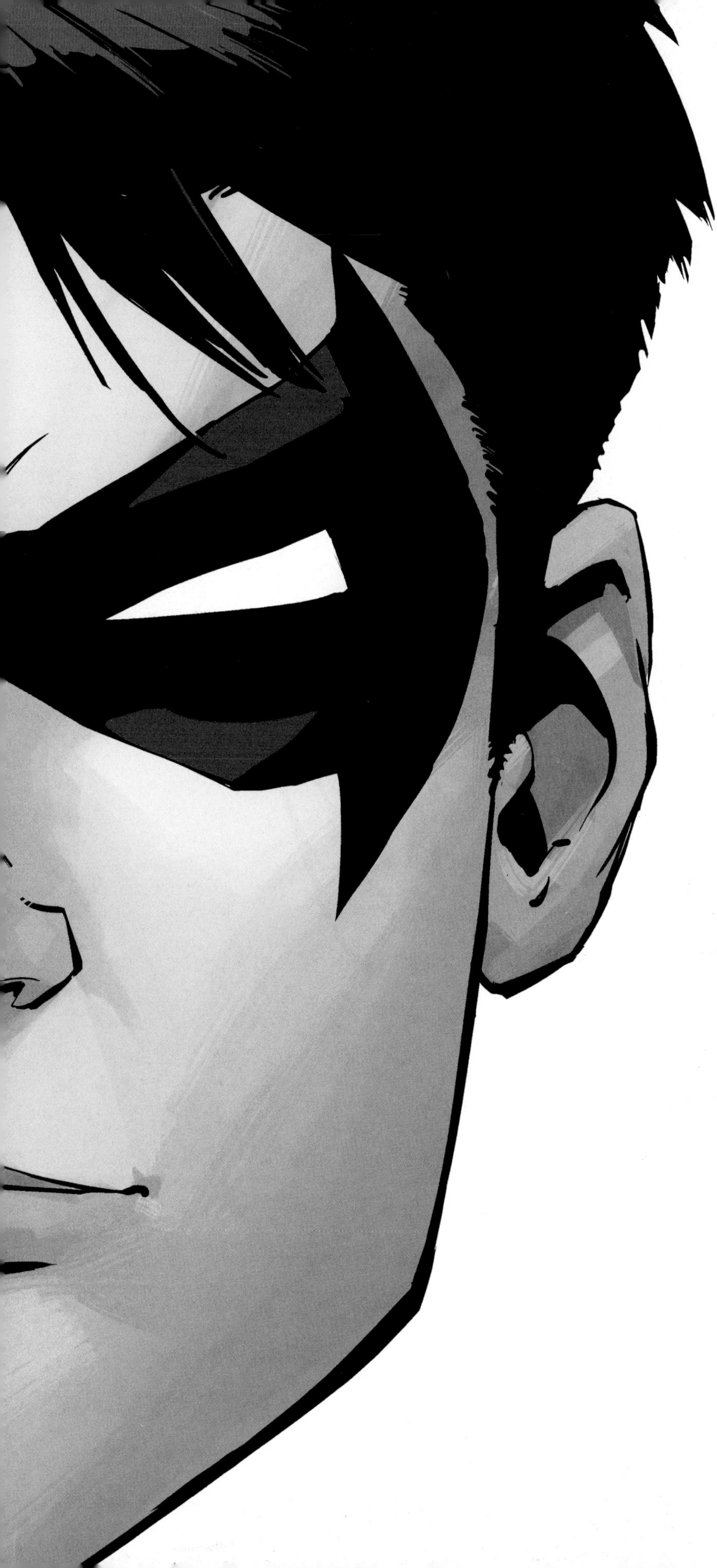

TEEN SCREAM

SCOTT LOBDELL & FABIAN NICIEZA writers BRETT BOOTH penciller NORM RAPMUND inker
cover art by GREG CAPULLO & FCO PLASCENCIA

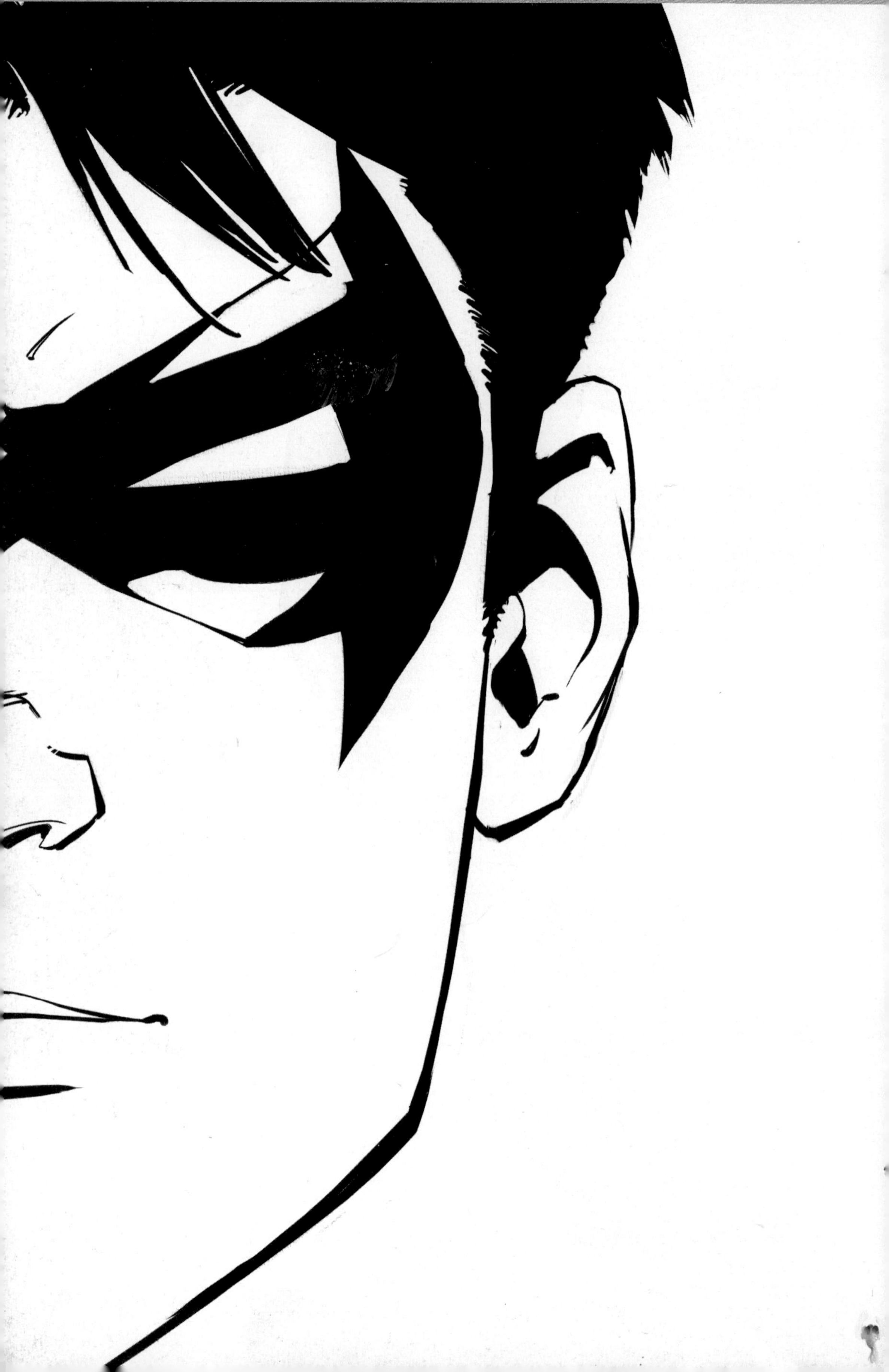

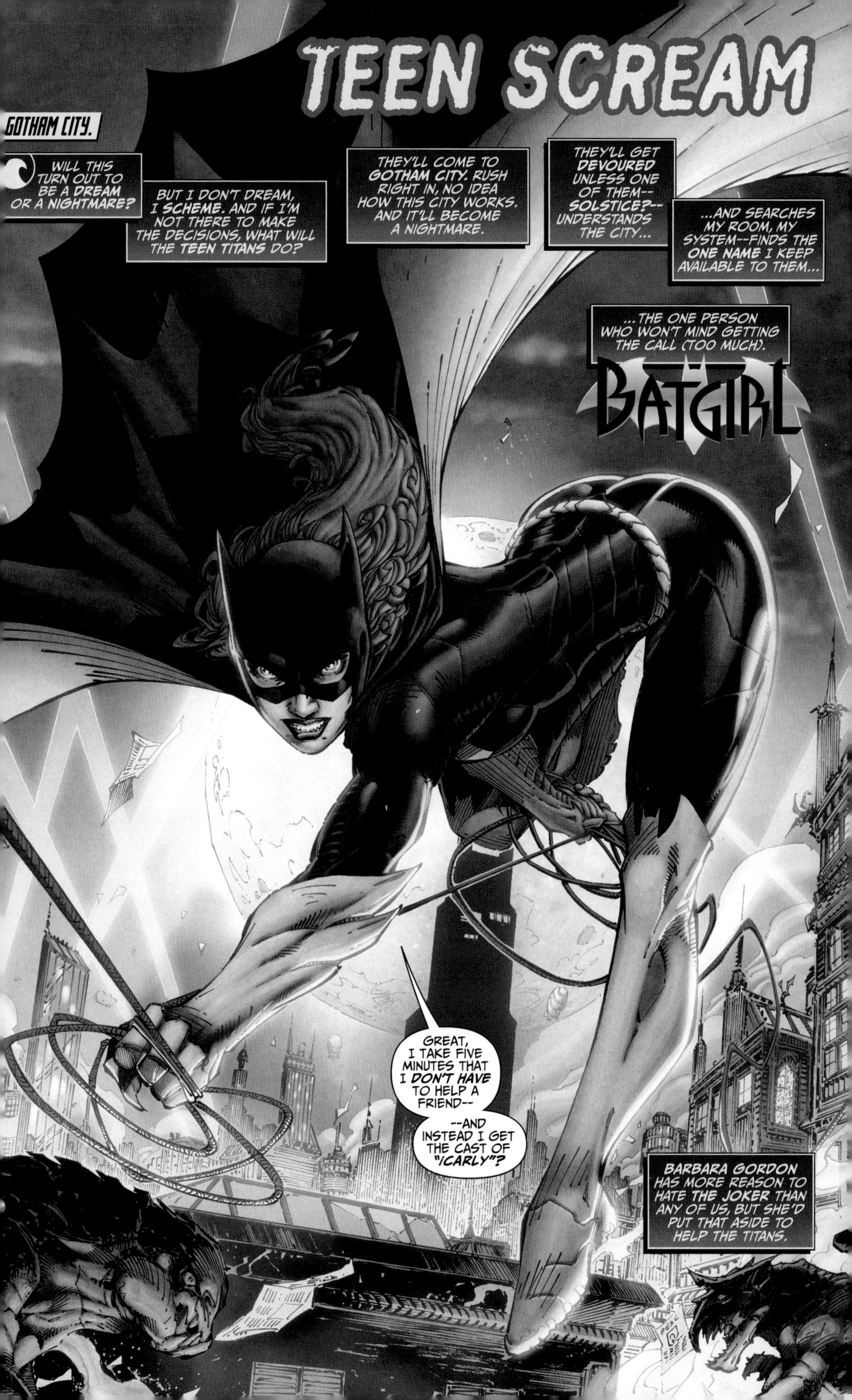
TEEN SCREAM
GOTHAM CITY.
WILL THIS TURN OUT TO BE A DREAM OR A NIGHTMARE?
BUT I DON'T DREAM, I SCHEME. AND IF I'M NOT THERE TO MAKE THE DECISIONS, WHAT WILL THE TEEN TITANS DO?
THEY'LL COME TO GOTHAM CITY. RUSH RIGHT IN, NO IDEA HOW THIS CITY WORKS. AND IT'LL BECOME A NIGHTMARE.
THEY'LL GET DEVOURED UNLESS ONE OF THEM--SOLSTICE?--UNDERSTANDS THE CITY...
...AND SEARCHES MY ROOM, MY SYSTEM--FINDS THE ONE NAME I KEEP AVAILABLE TO THEM...
...THE ONE PERSON WHO WON'T MIND GETTING THE CALL (TOO MUCH).
BATGIRL
GREAT, I TAKE FIVE MINUTES THAT I DON'T HAVE TO HELP A FRIEND--
--AND INSTEAD I GET THE CAST OF "iCARLY"?
BARBARA GORDON HAS MORE REASON TO HATE THE JOKER THAN ANY OF US, BUT SHE'D PUT THAT ASIDE TO HELP THE TITANS.

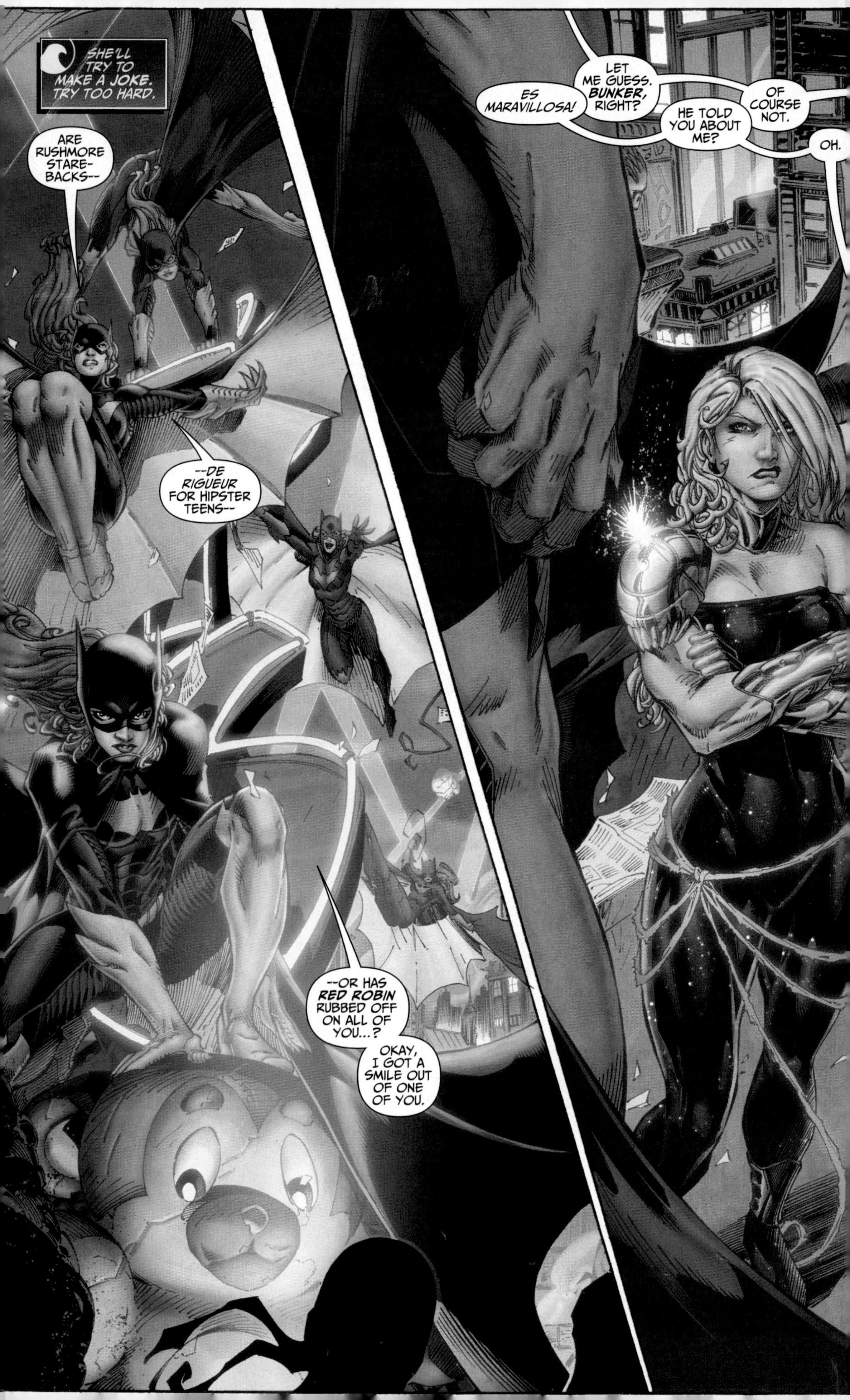
SHE'LL TRY TO MAKE A JOKE. TRY TOO HARD.
ARE RUSHMORE STARE-BACKS--
--DE RIGUEUR FOR HIPSTER TEENS--
--OR HAS RED ROBIN RUBBED OFF ON ALL OF YOU...?
OKAY, I GOT A SMILE OUT OF ONE OF YOU.
ES MARAVILLOSA!
LET ME GUESS. BUNKER, RIGHT?
HE TOLD YOU ABOUT ME?
OF COURSE NOT.
OH.

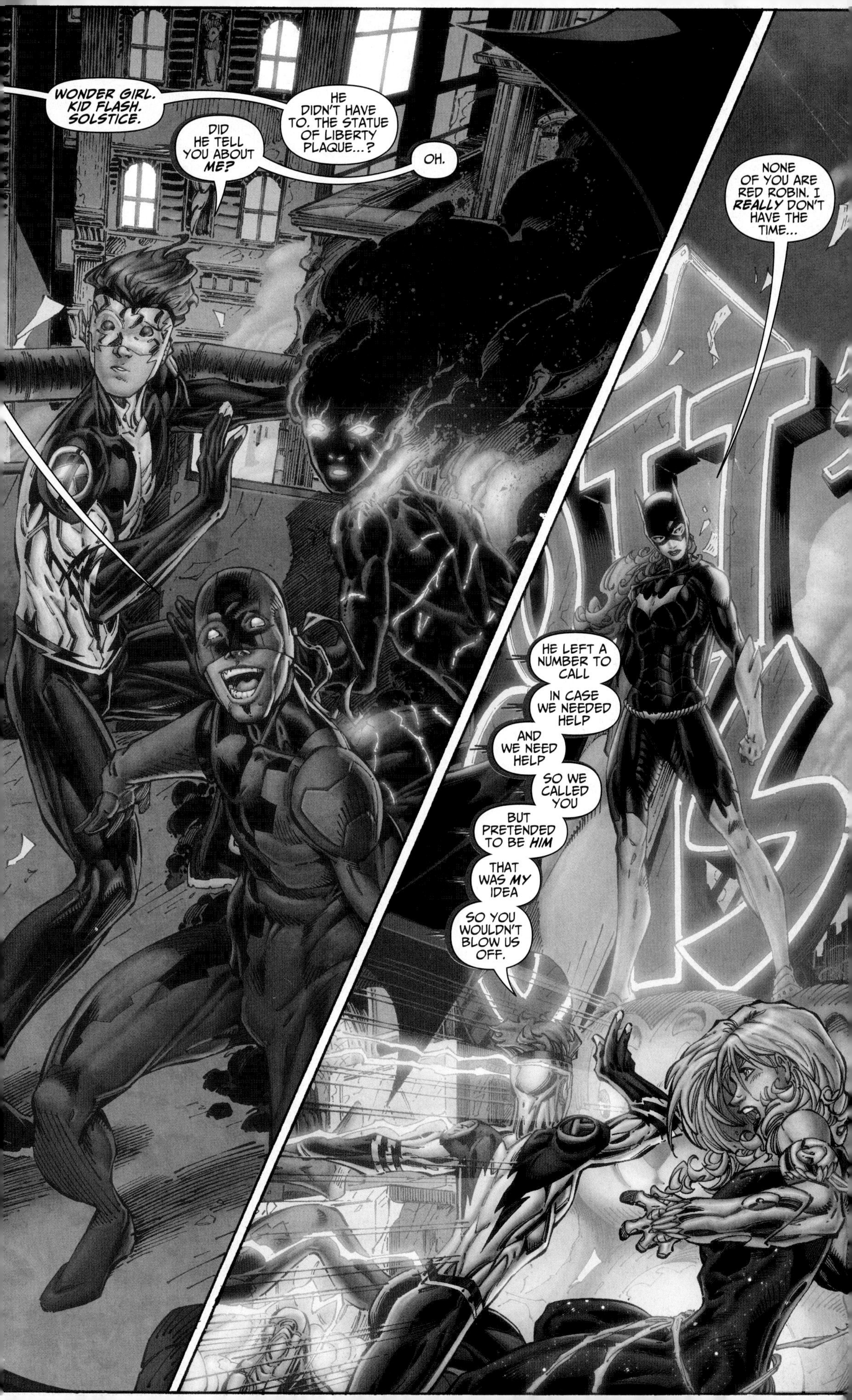
WONDER GIRL. KID FLASH. SOLSTICE.
HE DIDN'T HAVE TO. THE STATUE OF LIBERTY PLAQUE...?
DID HE TELL YOU ABOUT ME?
OH.
NONE OF YOU ARE RED ROBIN. I REALLY DON'T HAVE THE TIME...
HE LEFT A NUMBER TO CALL
IN CASE WE NEEDED HELP
AND WE NEED HELP
SO WE CALLED YOU
BUT PRETENDED TO BE HIM
THAT WAS MY IDEA
SO YOU WOULDN'T BLOW US OFF.

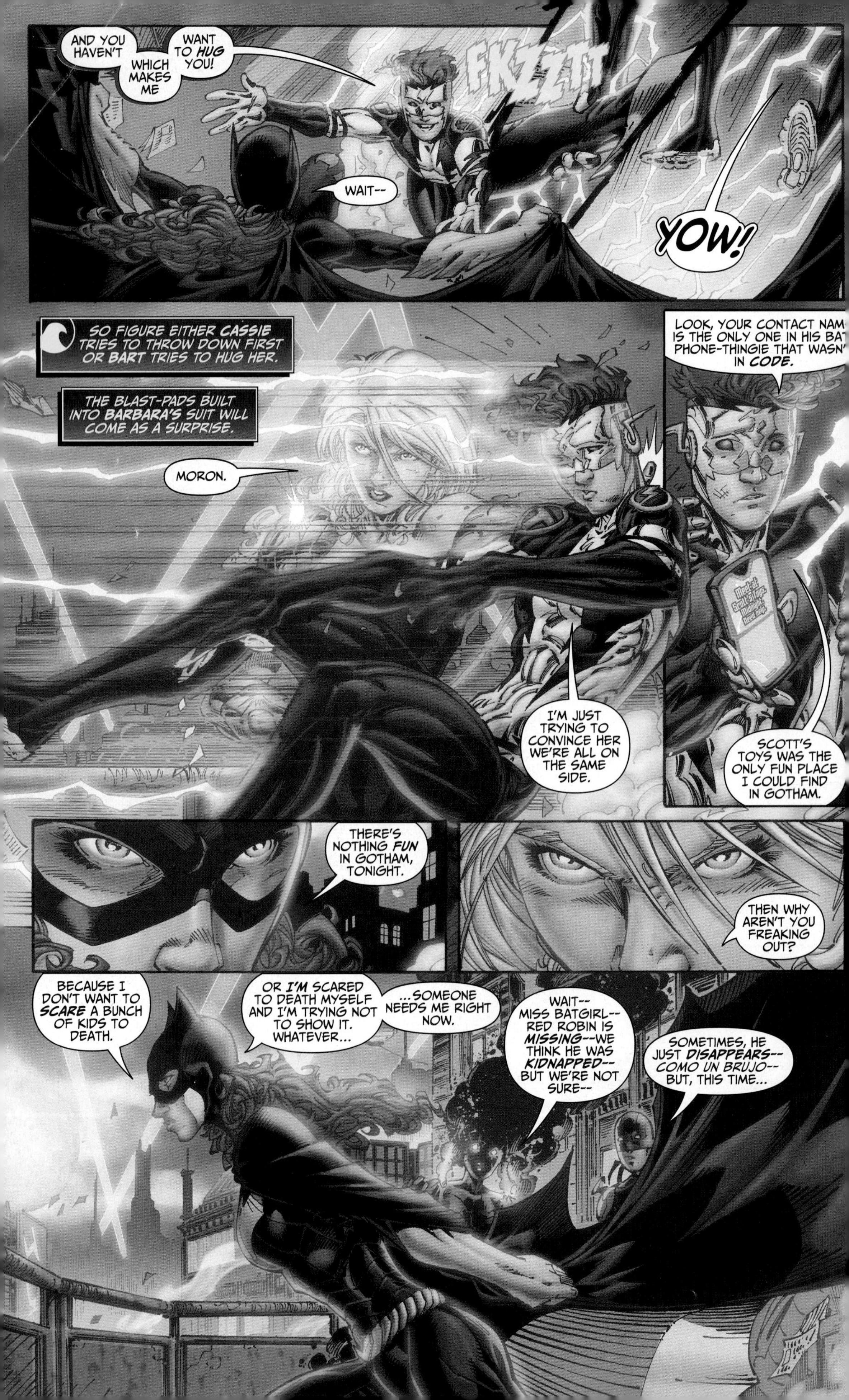
AND YOU HAVEN'T
WHICH MAKES ME
WANT TO HUG YOU!
FKZZTT
WAIT--
YOW!
SO FIGURE EITHER CASSIE TRIES TO THROW DOWN FIRST OR BART TRIES TO HUG HER.
THE BLAST-PADS BUILT INTO BARBARA'S SUIT WILL COME AS A SURPRISE.
MORON.
LOOK, YOUR CONTACT NAM IS THE ONLY ONE IN HIS BAT PHONE-THINGIE THAT WASN' IN CODE.
I'M JUST TRYING TO CONVINCE HER WE'RE ALL ON THE SAME SIDE.
SCOTT'S TOYS WAS THE ONLY FUN PLACE I COULD FIND IN GOTHAM.
THERE'S NOTHING FUN IN GOTHAM, TONIGHT.
THEN WHY AREN'T YOU FREAKING OUT?
BECAUSE I DON'T WANT TO SCARE A BUNCH OF KIDS TO DEATH.
OR I'M SCARED TO DEATH MYSELF AND I'M TRYING NOT TO SHOW IT. WHATEVER...
...SOMEONE NEEDS ME RIGHT NOW.
WAIT-- MISS BATGIRL-- RED ROBIN IS MISSING--WE THINK HE WAS KIDNAPPED-- BUT WE'RE NOT SURE--
SOMETIMES, HE JUST DISAPPEARS-- COMO UN BRUJO-- BUT, THIS TIME...

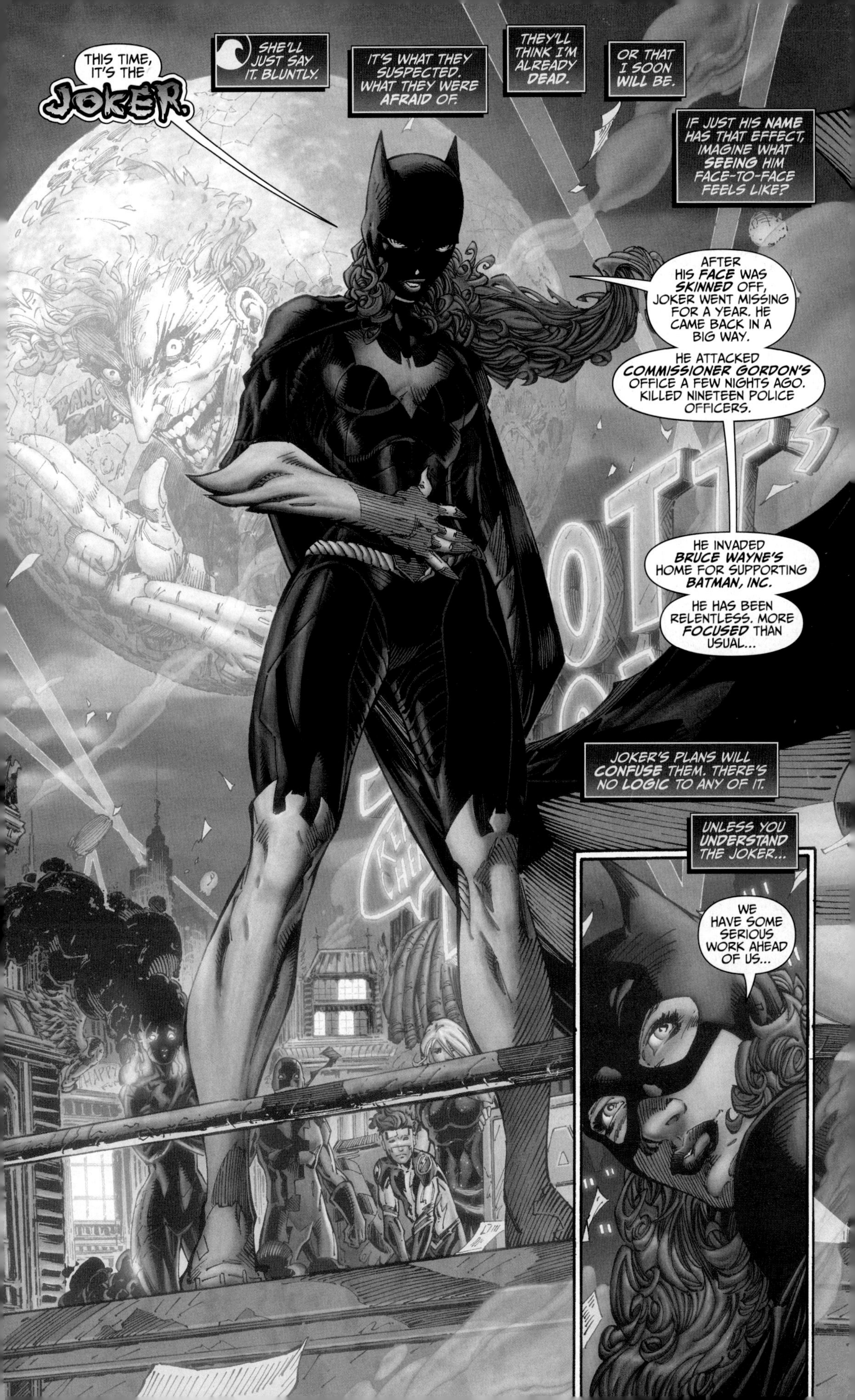
THIS TIME, IT'S THE JOKER.
SHE'LL JUST SAY IT. BLUNTLY.
IT'S WHAT THEY SUSPECTED. WHAT THEY WERE AFRAID OF.
THEY'LL THINK I'M ALREADY DEAD.
OR THAT I SOON WILL BE.
IF JUST HIS NAME HAS THAT EFFECT, IMAGINE WHAT SEEING HIM FACE-TO-FACE FEELS LIKE?
AFTER HIS FACE WAS SKINNED OFF, JOKER WENT MISSING FOR A YEAR. HE CAME BACK IN A BIG WAY.
HE ATTACKED COMMISSIONER GORDON'S OFFICE A FEW NIGHTS AGO. KILLED NINETEEN POLICE OFFICERS.
HE INVADED BRUCE WAYNE'S HOME FOR SUPPORTING BATMAN, INC.
HE HAS BEEN RELENTLESS. MORE FOCUSED THAN USUAL...
JOKER'S PLANS WILL CONFUSE THEM. THERE'S NO LOGIC TO ANY OF IT.
UNLESS YOU UNDERSTAND THE JOKER...
WE HAVE SOME SERIOUS WORK AHEAD OF US...

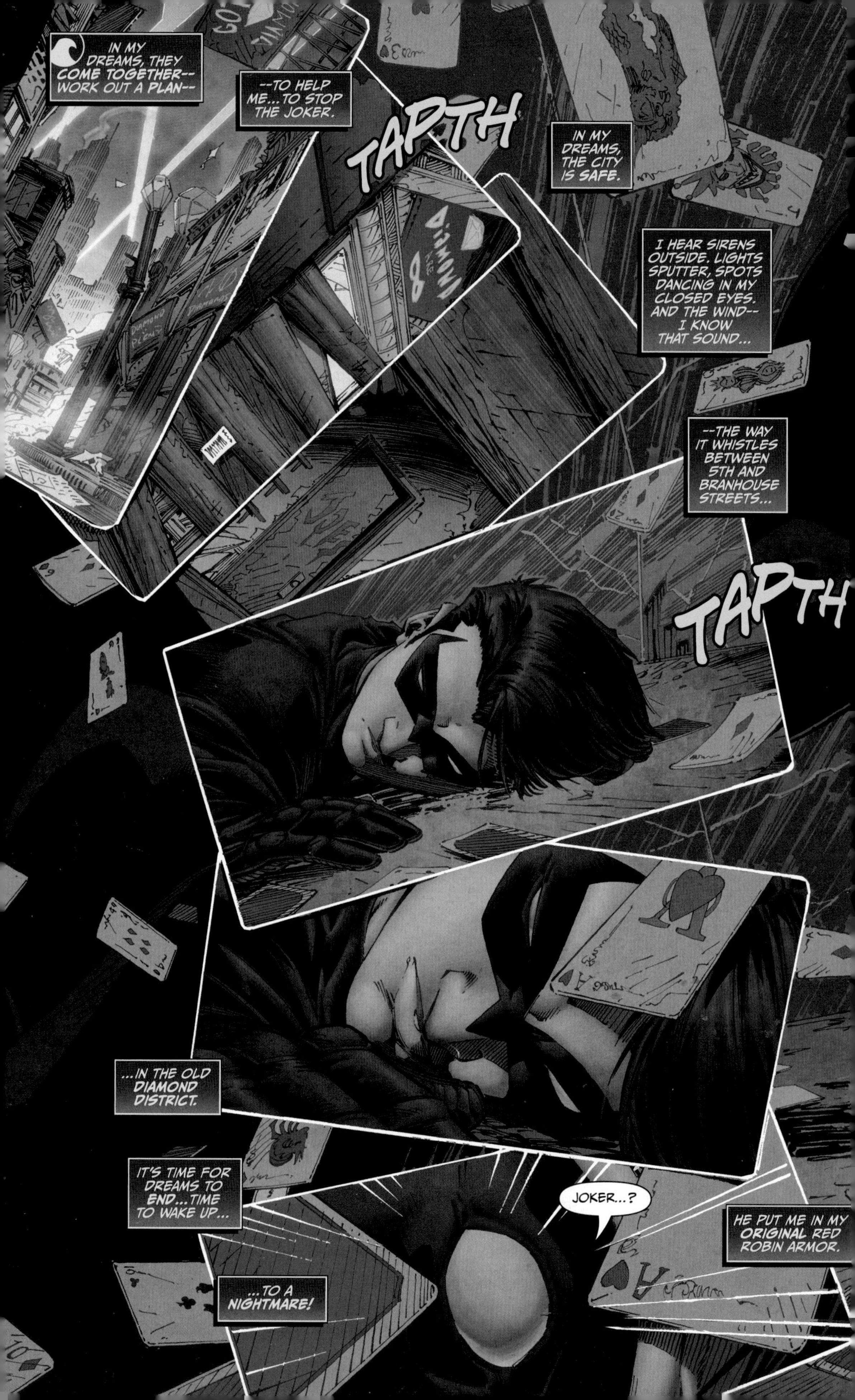
IN MY DREAMS, THEY COME TOGETHER-- WORK OUT A PLAN--
--TO HELP ME...TO STOP THE JOKER.
TAPTH
IN MY DREAMS, THE CITY IS SAFE.
I HEAR SIRENS OUTSIDE. LIGHTS SPUTTER, SPOTS DANCING IN MY CLOSED EYES. AND THE WIND-- I KNOW THAT SOUND...
--THE WAY IT WHISTLES BETWEEN 5TH AND BRANHOUSE STREETS...
TAPTH
...IN THE OLD DIAMOND DISTRICT.
IT'S TIME FOR DREAMS TO END...TIME TO WAKE UP...
JOKER...?
HE PUT ME IN MY ORIGINAL RED ROBIN ARMOR.
...TO A NIGHTMARE!

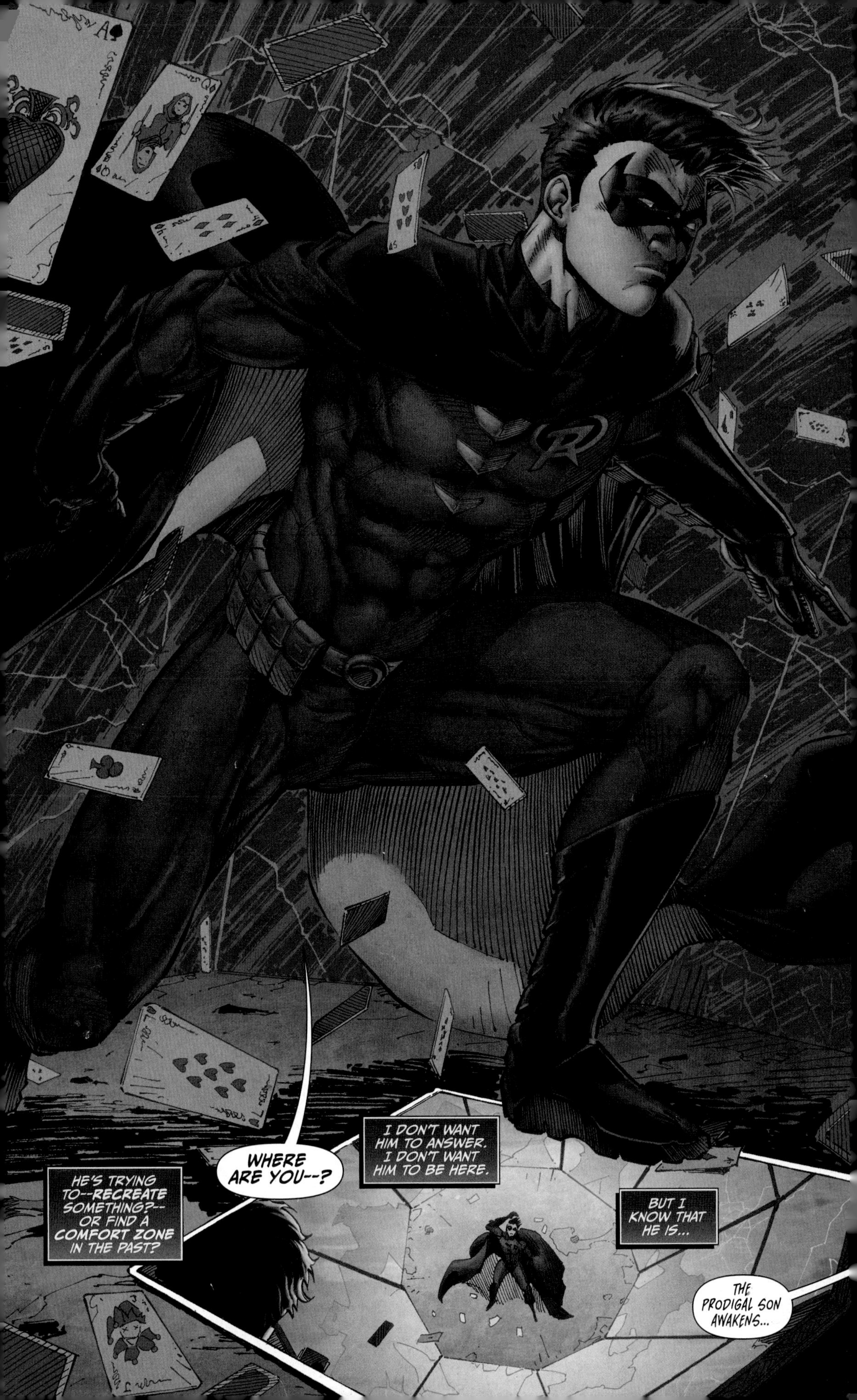
HE'S TRYING TO--RECREATE SOMETHING?-- OR FIND A COMFORT ZONE IN THE PAST?
WHERE ARE YOU--?
I DON'T WANT HIM TO ANSWER. I DON'T WANT HIM TO BE HERE.
BUT I KNOW THAT HE IS...
THE PRODIGAL SON AWAKENS...

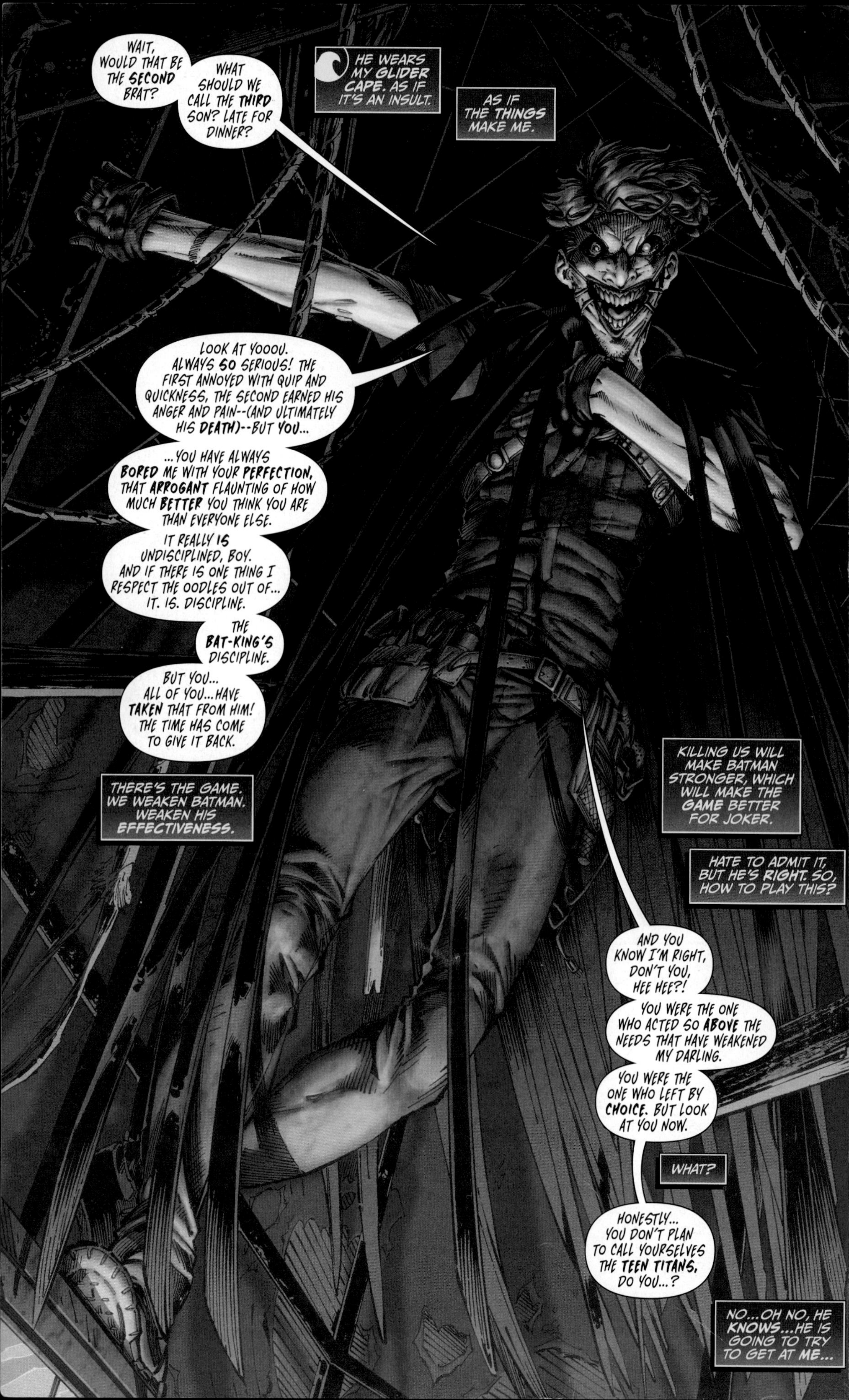

WAIT, WOULD THAT BE THE SECOND BRAT?
WHAT SHOULD WE CALL THE THIRD SON? LATE FOR DINNER?
HE WEARS MY GLIDER CAPE. AS IF IT'S AN INSULT.
AS IF THE THINGS MAKE ME.
LOOK AT YOOOU. ALWAYS SO SERIOUS! THE FIRST ANNOYED WITH QUIP AND QUICKNESS, THE SECOND EARNED HIS ANGER AND PAIN--(AND ULTIMATELY HIS DEATH)--BUT YOU...
...YOU HAVE ALWAYS BORED ME WITH YOUR PERFECTION, THAT ARROGANT FLAUNTING OF HOW MUCH BETTER YOU THINK YOU ARE THAN EVERYONE ELSE.
IT REALLY IS UNDISCIPLINED, BOY. AND IF THERE IS ONE THING I RESPECT THE OODLES OUT OF... IT. IS. DISCIPLINE.
THE BAT-KING'S DISCIPLINE.
BUT YOU... ALL OF YOU...HAVE TAKEN THAT FROM HIM! THE TIME HAS COME TO GIVE IT BACK.
THERE'S THE GAME. WE WEAKEN BATMAN. WEAKEN HIS EFFECTIVENESS.
KILLING US WILL MAKE BATMAN STRONGER, WHICH WILL MAKE THE GAME BETTER FOR JOKER.
HATE TO ADMIT IT, BUT HE'S RIGHT. SO, HOW TO PLAY THIS?
AND YOU KNOW I'M RIGHT, DON'T YOU, HEE HEE?!
YOU WERE THE ONE WHO ACTED SO ABOVE THE NEEDS THAT HAVE WEAKENED MY DARLING.
YOU WERE THE ONE WHO LEFT BY CHOICE. BUT LOOK AT YOU NOW.
WHAT?
HONESTLY... YOU DON'T PLAN TO CALL YOURSELVES THE TEEN TITANS, DO YOU...?
NO...OH NO, HE KNOWS...HE IS GOING TO TRY TO GET AT ME...

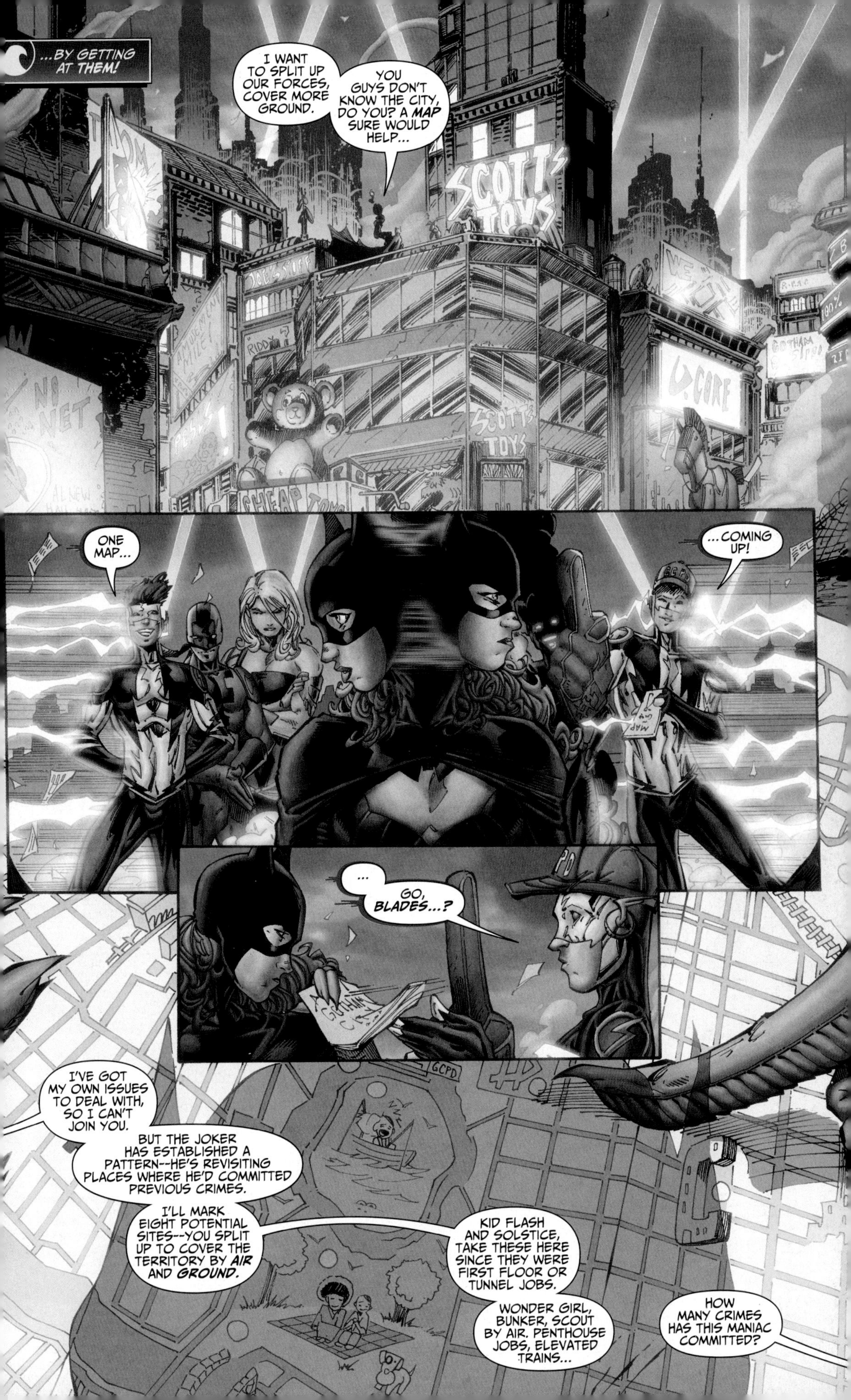
...BY GETTING AT THEM!
I WANT TO SPLIT UP OUR FORCES, COVER MORE GROUND.
YOU GUYS DON'T KNOW THE CITY, DO YOU? A MAP SURE WOULD HELP...
SCOTT'S TOYS
JOE'S STUFF
AMUSEMENT MILE
NO NET
CHEAP TOYS
U.CORE
ONE MAP...
...COMING UP!
... GO, BLADES...?
GCPD
I'VE GOT MY OWN ISSUES TO DEAL WITH, SO I CAN'T JOIN YOU.
BUT THE JOKER HAS ESTABLISHED A PATTERN--HE'S REVISITING PLACES WHERE HE'D COMMITTED PREVIOUS CRIMES.
I'LL MARK EIGHT POTENTIAL SITES--YOU SPLIT UP TO COVER THE TERRITORY BY AIR AND GROUND.
KID FLASH AND SOLSTICE, TAKE THESE HERE SINCE THEY WERE FIRST FLOOR OR TUNNEL JOBS.
WONDER GIRL, BUNKER, SCOUT BY AIR. PENTHOUSE JOBS, ELEVATED TRAINS...
HOW MANY CRIMES HAS THIS MANIAC COMMITTED?

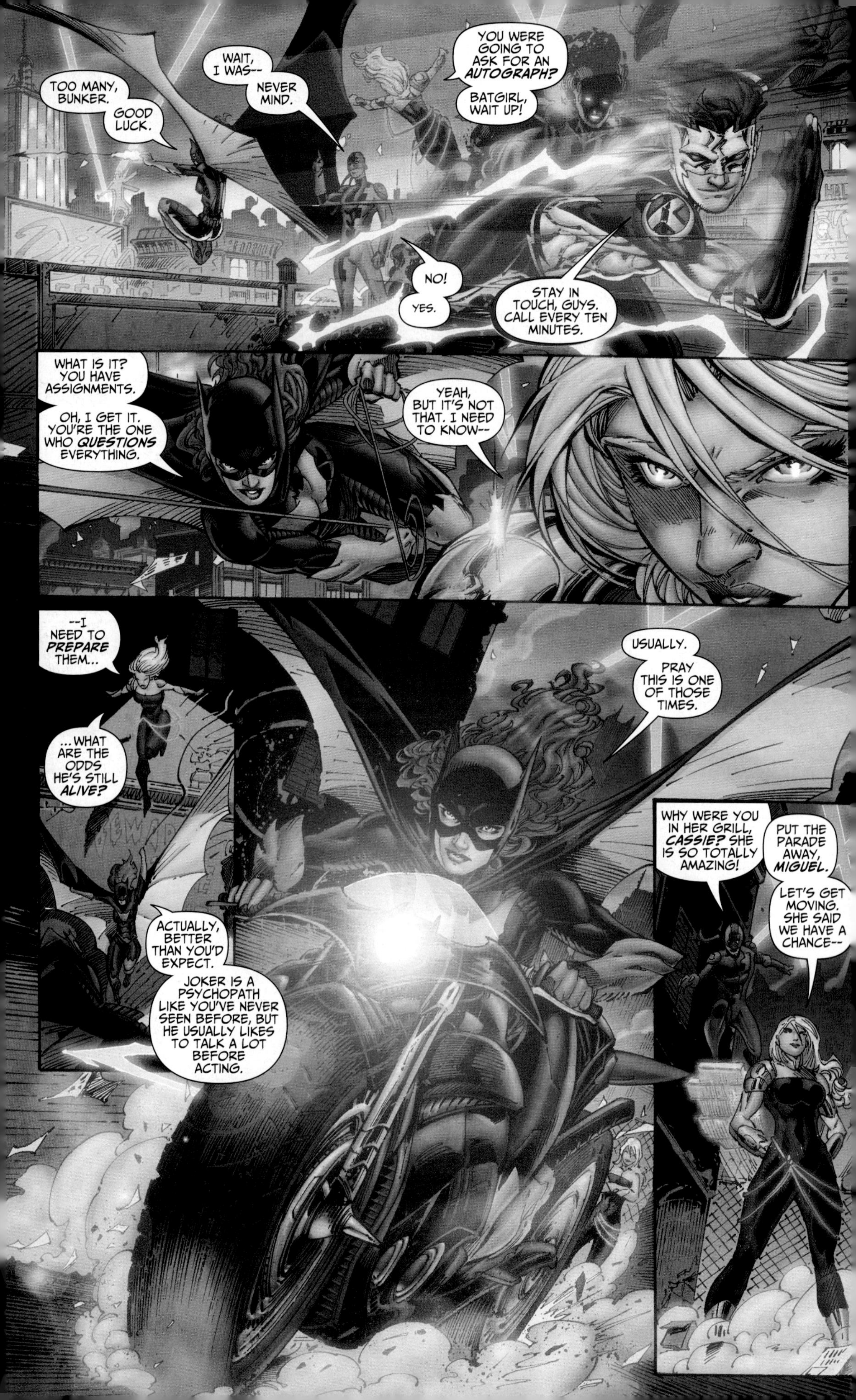
TOO MANY, BUNKER.
GOOD LUCK.
WAIT, I WAS--
NEVER MIND.
YOU WERE GOING TO ASK FOR AN AUTOGRAPH?
BATGIRL, WAIT UP!
NO!
YES.
STAY IN TOUCH, GUYS. CALL EVERY TEN MINUTES.
WHAT IS IT? YOU HAVE ASSIGNMENTS.
OH, I GET IT. YOU'RE THE ONE WHO QUESTIONS EVERYTHING.
YEAH, BUT IT'S NOT THAT. I NEED TO KNOW--
--I NEED TO PREPARE THEM...
...WHAT ARE THE ODDS HE'S STILL ALIVE?
ACTUALLY, BETTER THAN YOU'D EXPECT.
JOKER IS A PSYCHOPATH LIKE YOU'VE NEVER SEEN BEFORE, BUT HE USUALLY LIKES TO TALK A LOT BEFORE ACTING.
USUALLY.
PRAY THIS IS ONE OF THOSE TIMES.
WHY WERE YOU IN HER GRILL, CASSIE? SHE IS SO TOTALLY AMAZING!
PUT THE PARADE AWAY, MIGUEL.
LET'S GET MOVING. SHE SAID WE HAVE A CHANCE--

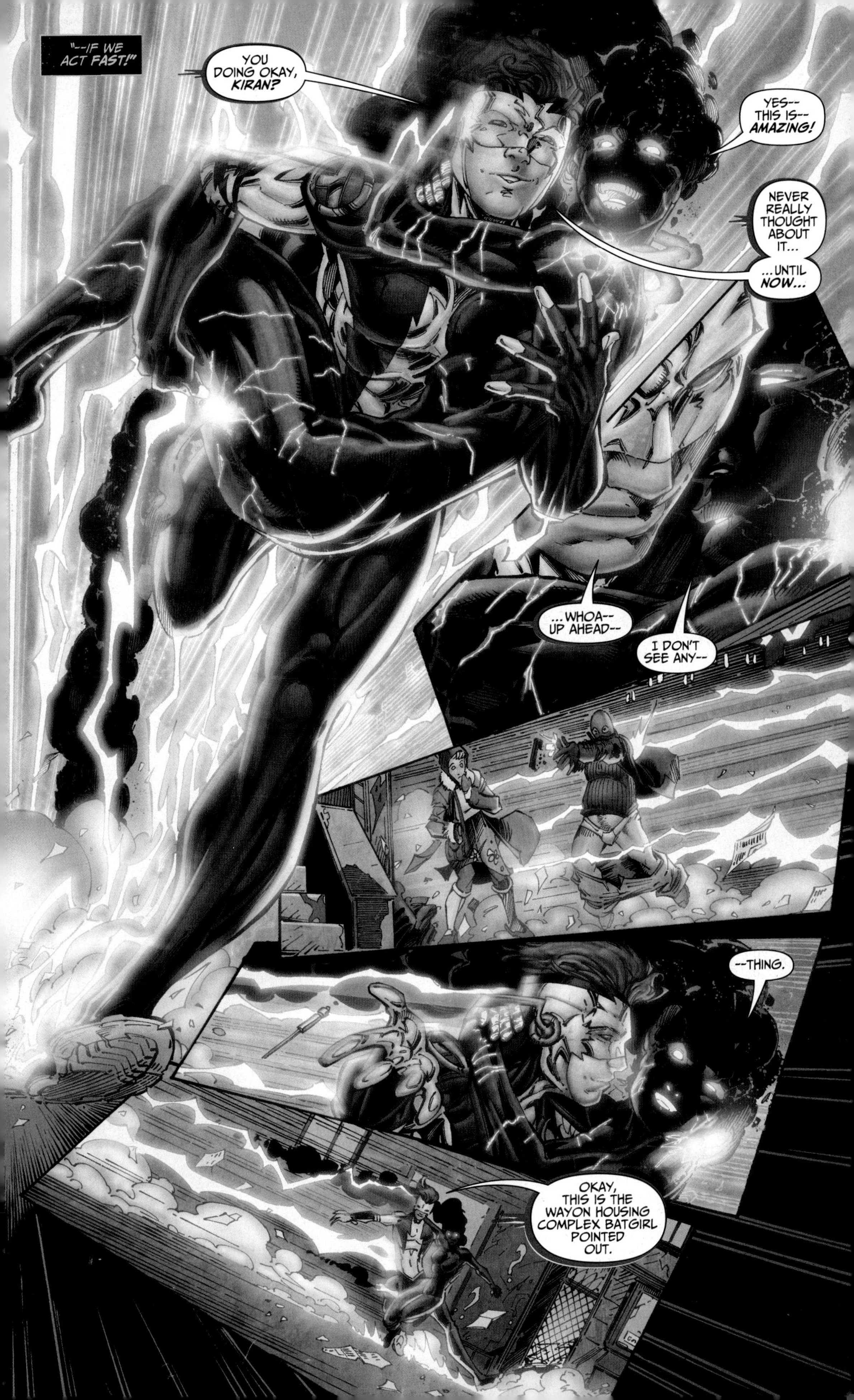
"--IF WE ACT FAST!"
YOU DOING OKAY, KIRAN?
YES-- THIS IS-- AMAZING!
NEVER REALLY THOUGHT ABOUT IT...
...UNTIL NOW...
...WHOA-- UP AHEAD--
I DON'T SEE ANY--
--THING.
OKAY, THIS IS THE WAYON HOUSING COMPLEX BATGIRL POINTED OUT.

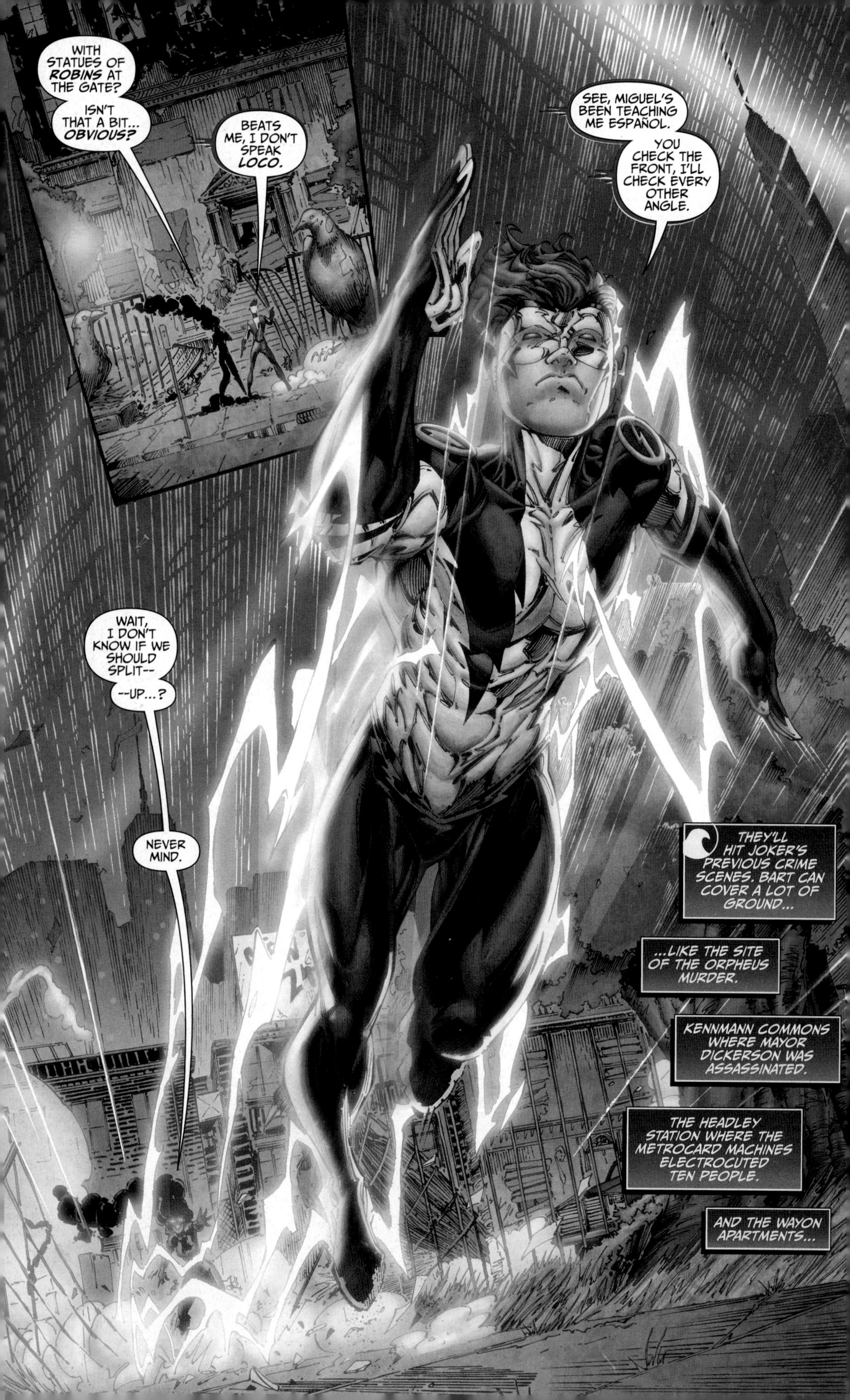

WITH STATUES OF ROBINS AT THE GATE?
ISN'T THAT A BIT... OBVIOUS?
BEATS ME, I DON'T SPEAK LOCO.
SEE, MIGUEL'S BEEN TEACHING ME ESPAÑOL.
YOU CHECK THE FRONT, I'LL CHECK EVERY OTHER ANGLE.
WAIT, I DON'T KNOW IF WE SHOULD SPLIT--
--UP...?
NEVER MIND.
THEY'LL HIT JOKER'S PREVIOUS CRIME SCENES. BART CAN COVER A LOT OF GROUND...
...LIKE THE SITE OF THE ORPHEUS MURDER.
KENNMANN COMMONS WHERE MAYOR DICKERSON WAS ASSASSINATED.
THE HEADLEY STATION WHERE THE METROCARD MACHINES ELECTROCUTED TEN PEOPLE.
AND THE WAYON APARTMENTS...

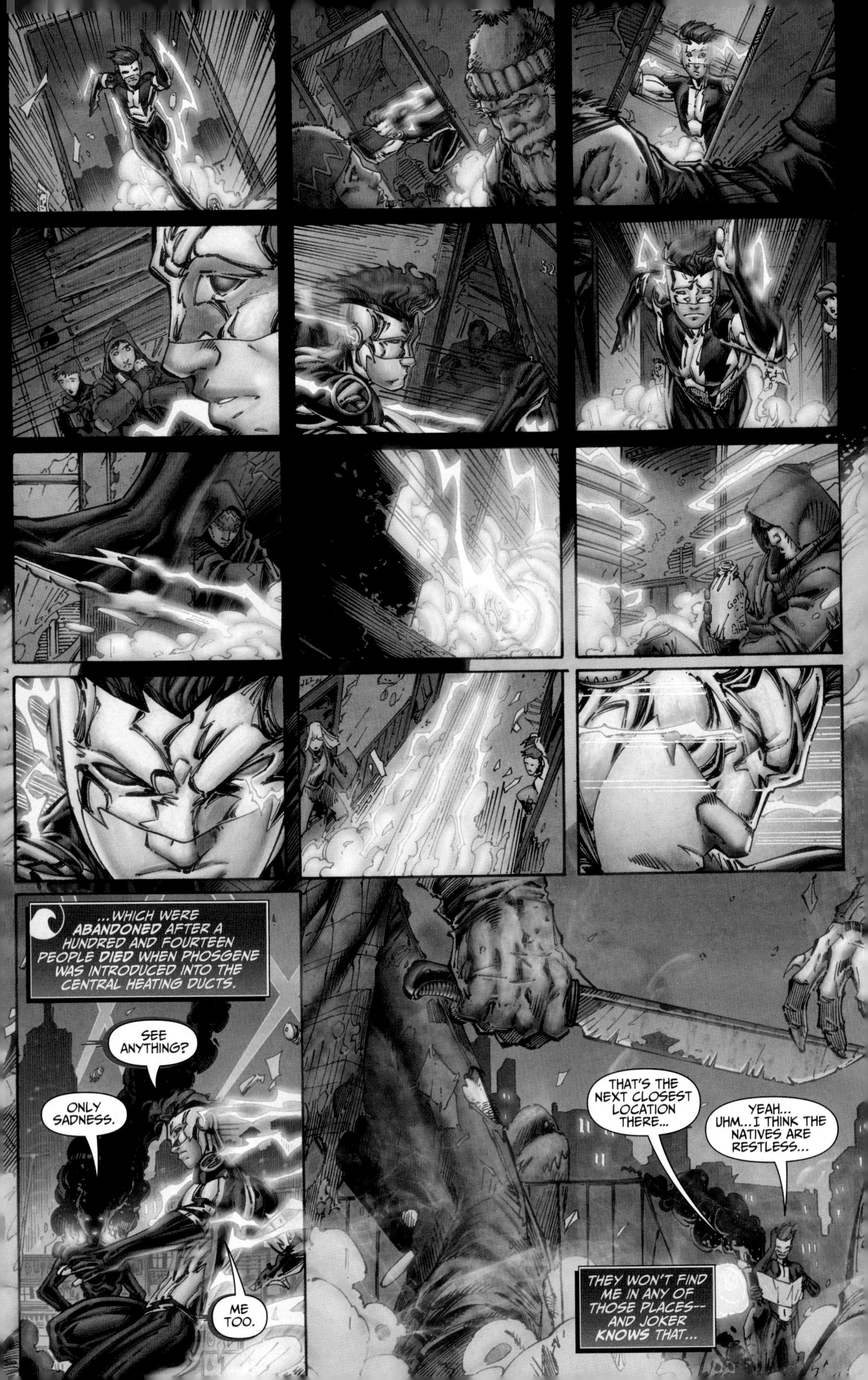
...WHICH WERE ABANDONED AFTER A HUNDRED AND FOURTEEN PEOPLE DIED WHEN PHOSGENE WAS INTRODUCED INTO THE CENTRAL HEATING DUCTS.
SEE ANYTHING?
ONLY SADNESS.
ME TOO.
THAT'S THE NEXT CLOSEST LOCATION THERE...
YEAH... UHM...I THINK THE NATIVES ARE RESTLESS...
THEY WON'T FIND ME IN ANY OF THOSE PLACES-- AND JOKER KNOWS THAT...

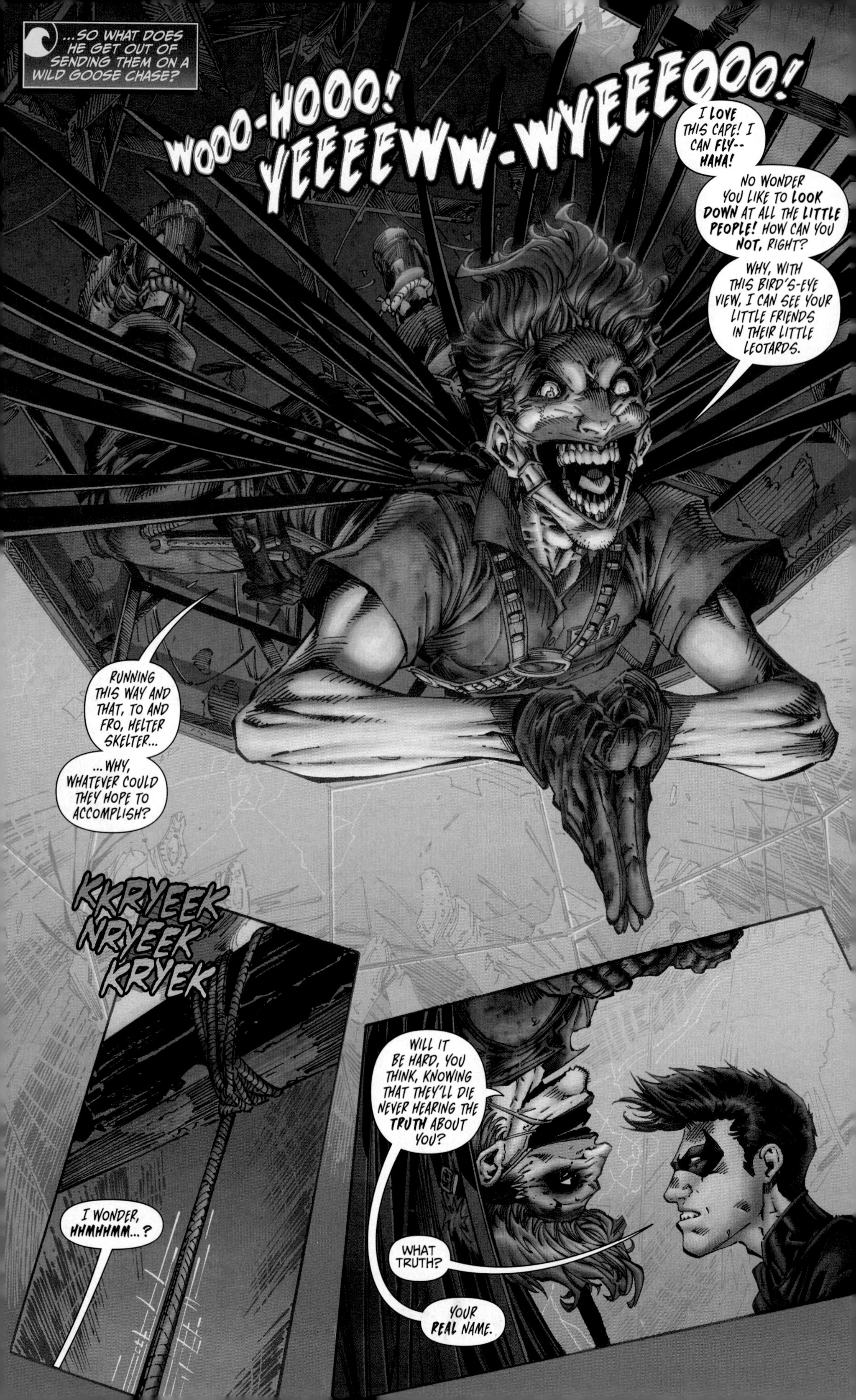

...SO WHAT DOES HE GET OUT OF SENDING THEM ON A WILD GOOSE CHASE?
WOOO-HOOO! YEEEEWW-WYEEEOOO!
I LOVE THIS CAPE! I CAN FLY-- HAHA!
NO WONDER YOU LIKE TO LOOK DOWN AT ALL THE LITTLE PEOPLE! HOW CAN YOU NOT, RIGHT?
WHY, WITH THIS BIRD'S-EYE VIEW, I CAN SEE YOUR LITTLE FRIENDS IN THEIR LITTLE LEOTARDS.
RUNNING THIS WAY AND THAT, TO AND FRO, HELTER SKELTER...
...WHY, WHATEVER COULD THEY HOPE TO ACCOMPLISH?
KKRYEEK NRYEEK KRYEK
WILL IT BE HARD, YOU THINK, KNOWING THAT THEY'LL DIE NEVER HEARING THE TRUTH ABOUT YOU?
I WONDER, HMMHMM...?
WHAT TRUTH?
YOUR REAL NAME.

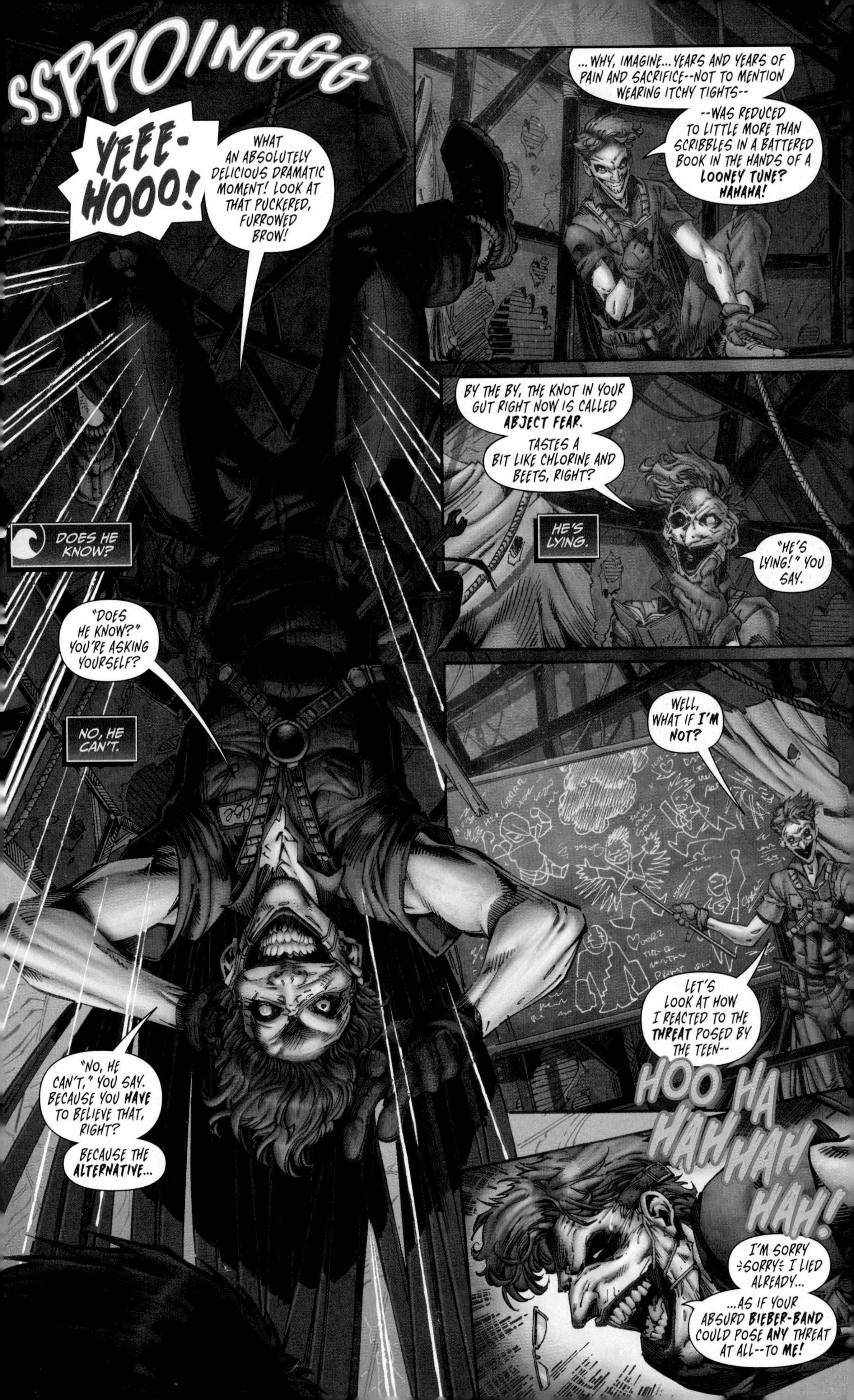
SSPPOINGGG
YEEE-HOOO!
WHAT AN ABSOLUTELY DELICIOUS DRAMATIC MOMENT! LOOK AT THAT PUCKERED, FURROWED BROW!
...WHY, IMAGINE... YEARS AND YEARS OF PAIN AND SACRIFICE--NOT TO MENTION WEARING ITCHY TIGHTS--
--WAS REDUCED TO LITTLE MORE THAN SCRIBBLES IN A BATTERED BOOK IN THE HANDS OF A LOONEY TUNE? HAHAHA!
BY THE BY, THE KNOT IN YOUR GUT RIGHT NOW IS CALLED ABJECT FEAR.
TASTES A BIT LIKE CHLORINE AND BEETS, RIGHT?
DOES HE KNOW?
HE'S LYING.
"HE'S LYING!" YOU SAY.
"DOES HE KNOW?" YOU'RE ASKING YOURSELF?
NO, HE CAN'T.
WELL, WHAT IF I'M NOT?
LET'S LOOK AT HOW I REACTED TO THE THREAT POSED BY THE TEEN--
"NO, HE CAN'T," YOU SAY. BECAUSE YOU HAVE TO BELIEVE THAT, RIGHT?
BECAUSE THE ALTERNATIVE...
HOO HA HAH HAH HAH HAH!
I'M SORRY SORRY I LIED ALREADY...
...AS IF YOUR ABSURD BIEBER-BAND COULD POSE ANY THREAT AT ALL--TO ME!

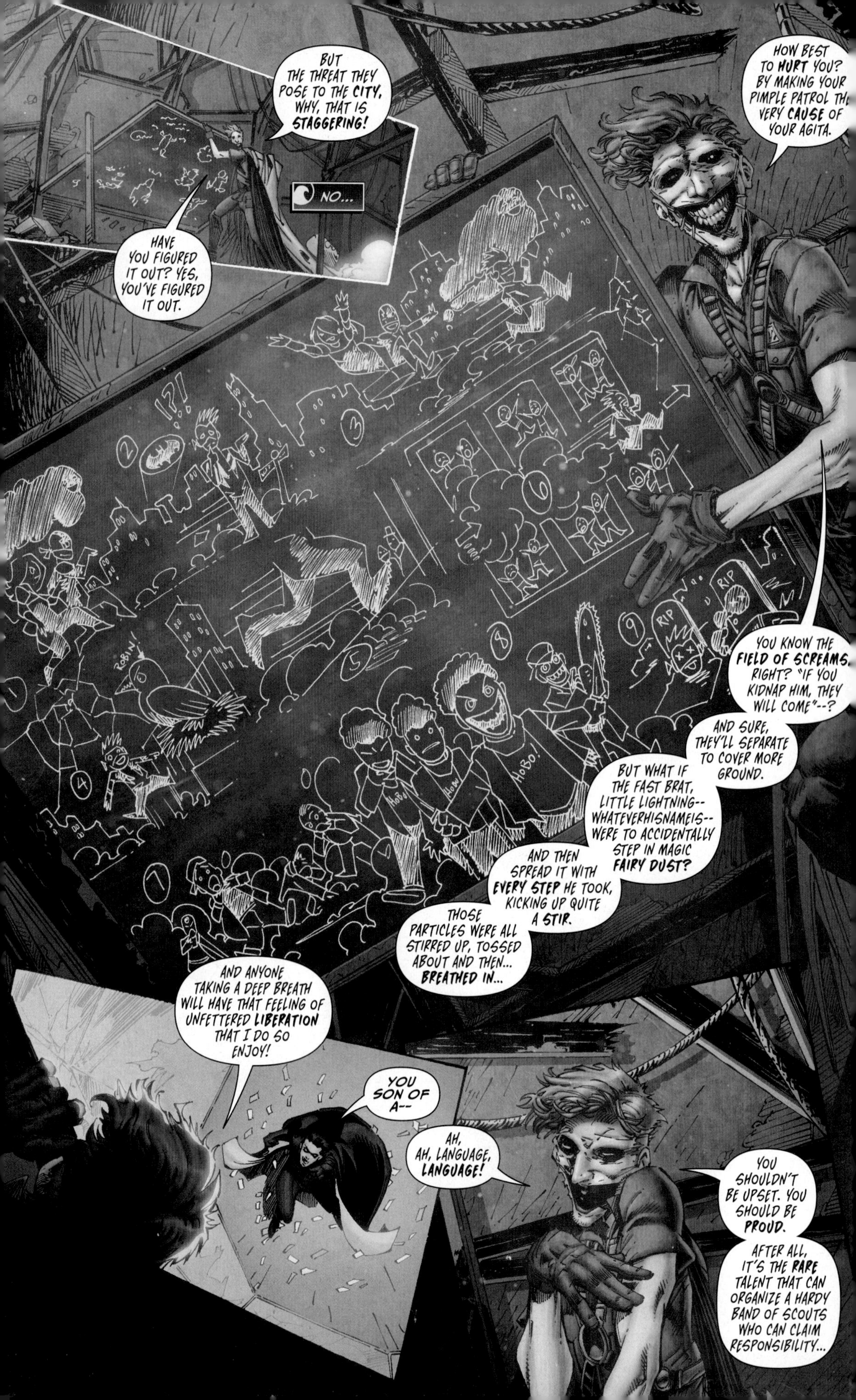

BUT THE THREAT THEY POSE TO THE CITY, WHY, THAT IS STAGGERING!
NO...
HAVE YOU FIGURED IT OUT? YES, YOU'VE FIGURED IT OUT.
HOW BEST TO HURT YOU? BY MAKING YOUR PIMPLE PATROL THE VERY CAUSE OF YOUR AGITA.
!?!
ROBIN!
HOBO!
HOBO
HOW
RIP
RIP
YOU KNOW THE FIELD OF SCREAMS, RIGHT? "IF YOU KIDNAP HIM, THEY WILL COME"--?
AND SURE, THEY'LL SEPARATE TO COVER MORE GROUND.
BUT WHAT IF THE FAST BRAT, LITTLE LIGHTNING--WHATEVERHISNAMEIS--WERE TO ACCIDENTALLY STEP IN MAGIC FAIRY DUST?
AND THEN SPREAD IT WITH EVERY STEP HE TOOK, KICKING UP QUITE A STIR.
THOSE PARTICLES WERE ALL STIRRED UP, TOSSED ABOUT AND THEN... BREATHED IN...
AND ANYONE TAKING A DEEP BREATH WILL HAVE THAT FEELING OF UNFETTERED LIBERATION THAT I DO SO ENJOY!
YOU SON OF A--
AH, AH, LANGUAGE, LANGUAGE!
YOU SHOULDN'T BE UPSET. YOU SHOULD BE PROUD.
AFTER ALL, IT'S THE RARE TALENT THAT CAN ORGANIZE A HARDY BAND OF SCOUTS WHO CAN CLAIM RESPONSIBILITY...

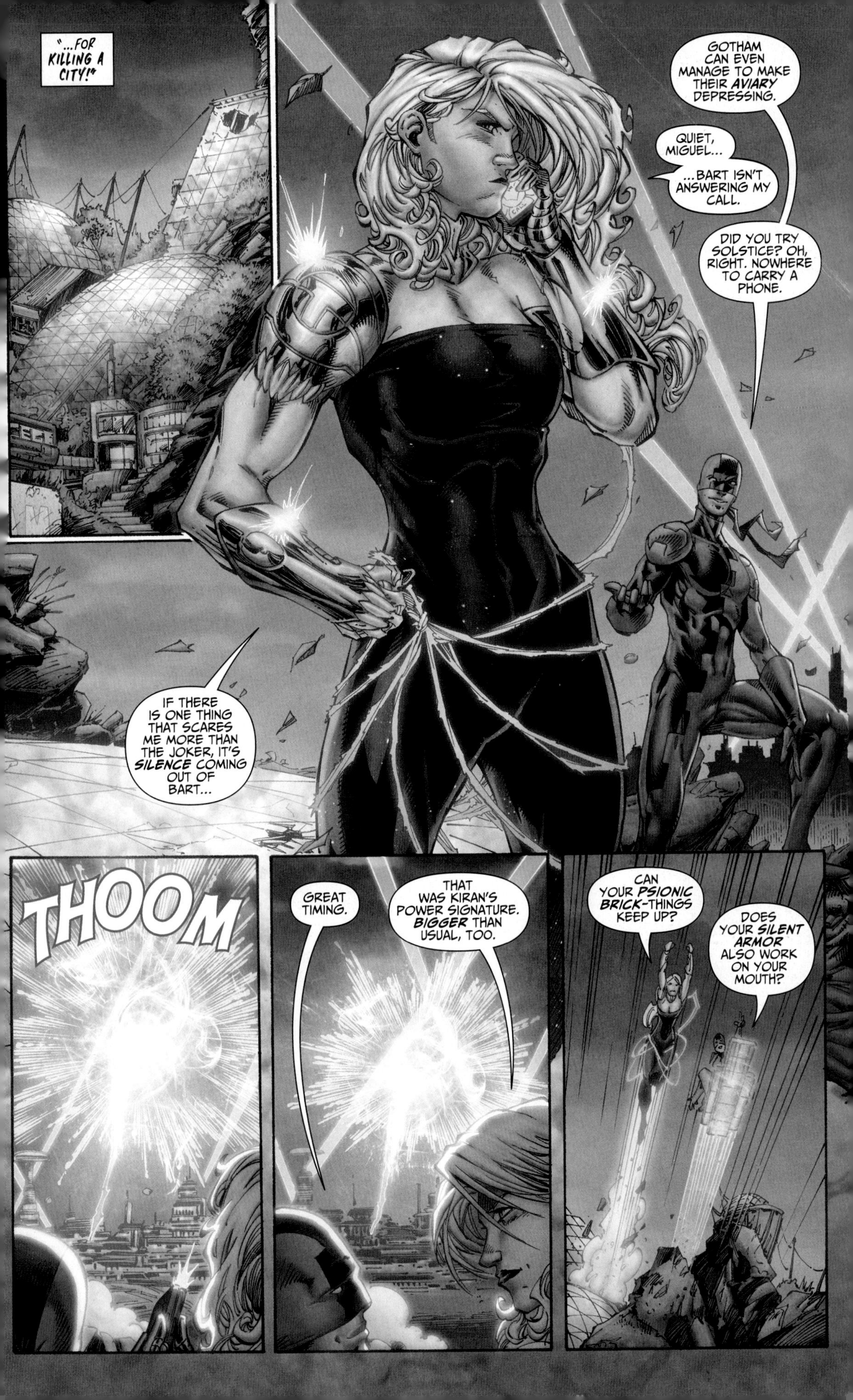
"...FOR KILLING A CITY!"
GOTHAM CAN EVEN MANAGE TO MAKE THEIR AVIARY DEPRESSING.
QUIET, MIGUEL...
...BART ISN'T ANSWERING MY CALL.
DID YOU TRY SOLSTICE? OH, RIGHT. NOWHERE TO CARRY A PHONE.
IF THERE IS ONE THING THAT SCARES ME MORE THAN THE JOKER, IT'S SILENCE COMING OUT OF BART...
THOOM
GREAT TIMING.
THAT WAS KIRAN'S POWER SIGNATURE. BIGGER THAN USUAL, TOO.
CAN YOUR PSIONIC BRICK-THINGS KEEP UP?
DOES YOUR SILENT ARMOR ALSO WORK ON YOUR MOUTH?

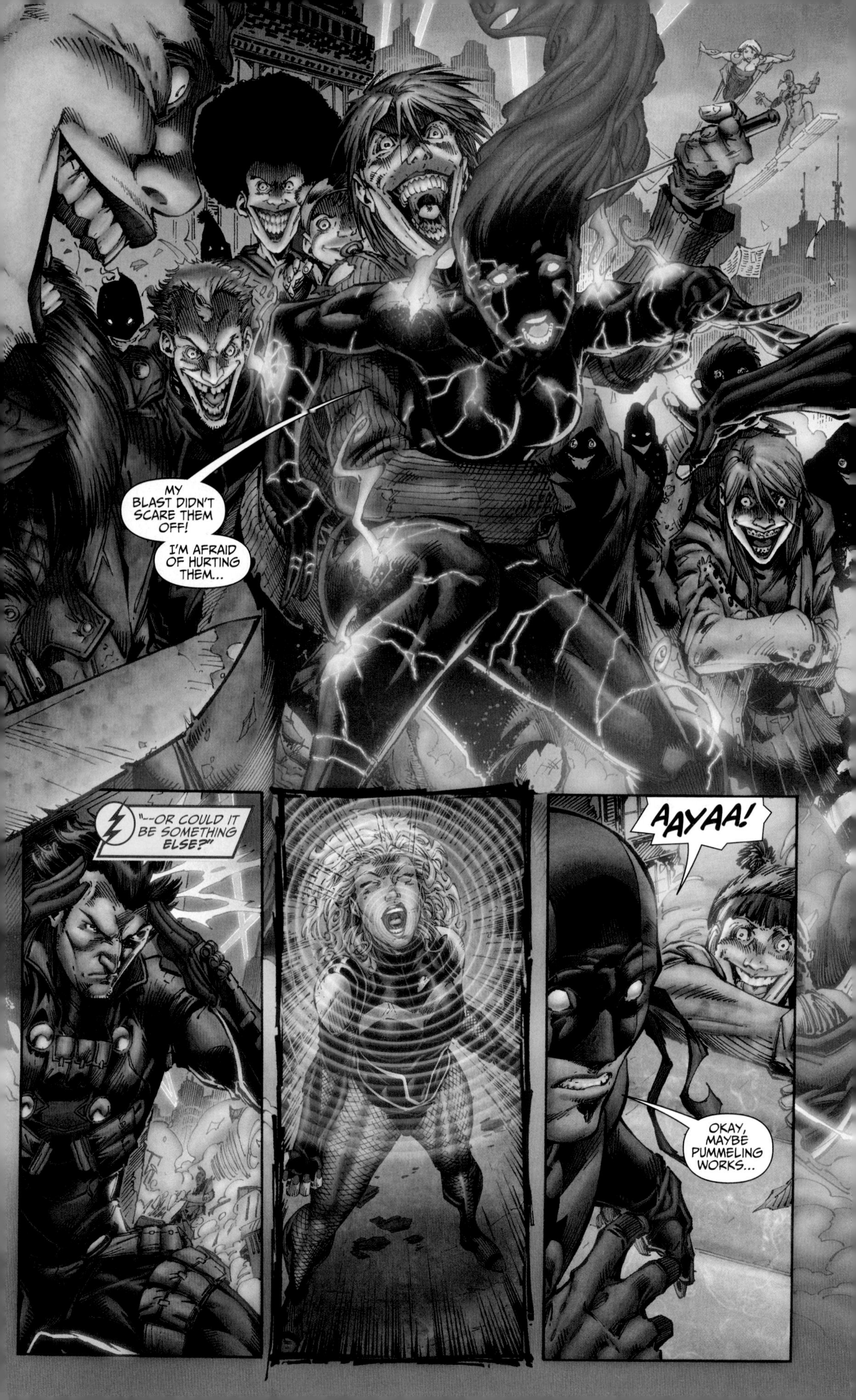
MY BLAST DIDN'T SCARE THEM OFF!
I'M AFRAID OF HURTING THEM...
"--OR COULD IT BE SOMETHING ELSE?"
AAYAA!
OKAY, MAYBE PUMMELING WORKS...

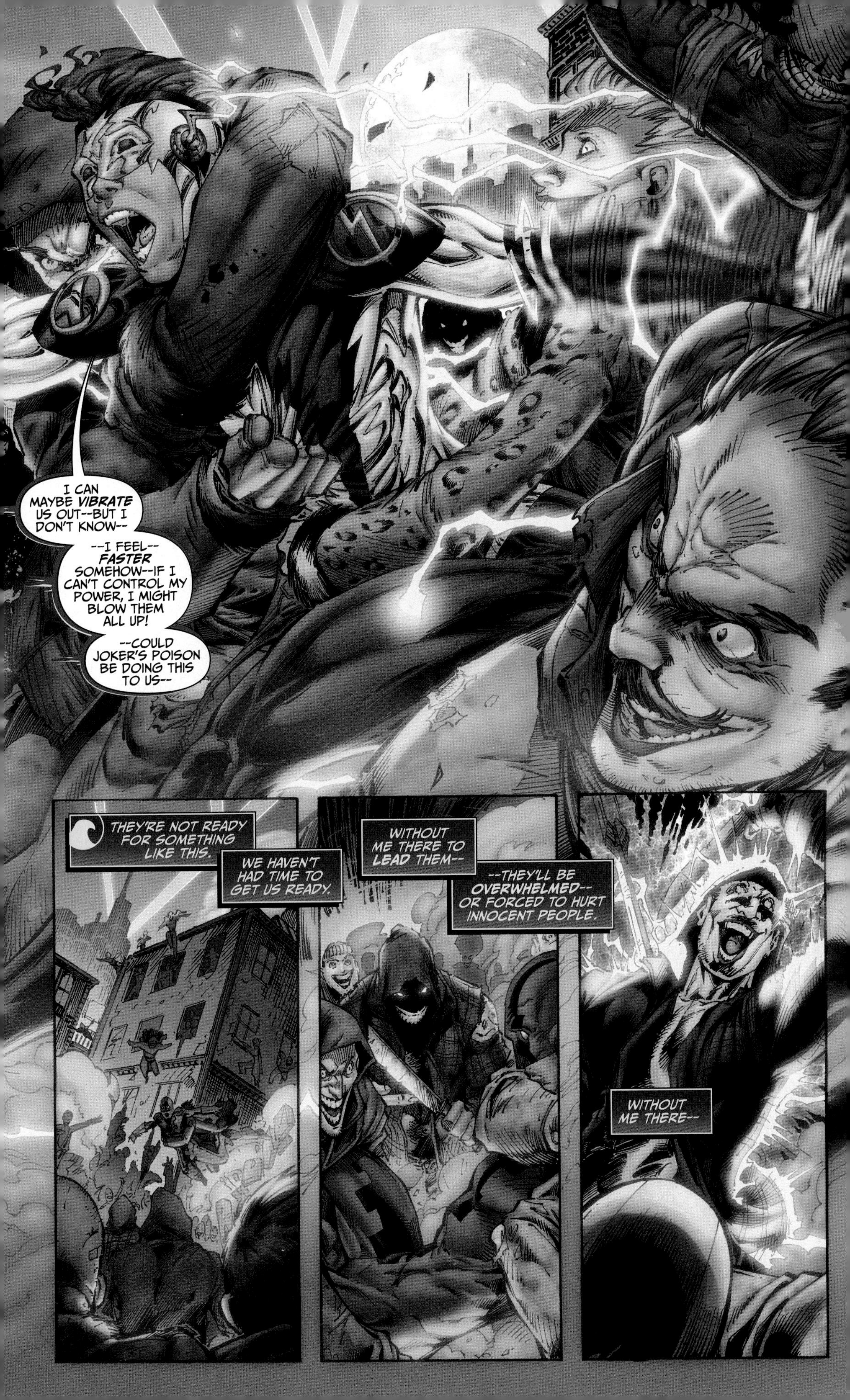
I CAN MAYBE VIBRATE US OUT--BUT I DON'T KNOW--
--I FEEL--FASTER SOMEHOW--IF I CAN'T CONTROL MY POWER, I MIGHT BLOW THEM ALL UP!
--COULD JOKER'S POISON BE DOING THIS TO US--
THEY'RE NOT READY FOR SOMETHING LIKE THIS.
WE HAVEN'T HAD TIME TO GET US READY.
WITHOUT ME THERE TO LEAD THEM--
--THEY'LL BE OVERWHELMED--OR FORCED TO HURT INNOCENT PEOPLE.
WITHOUT ME THERE--

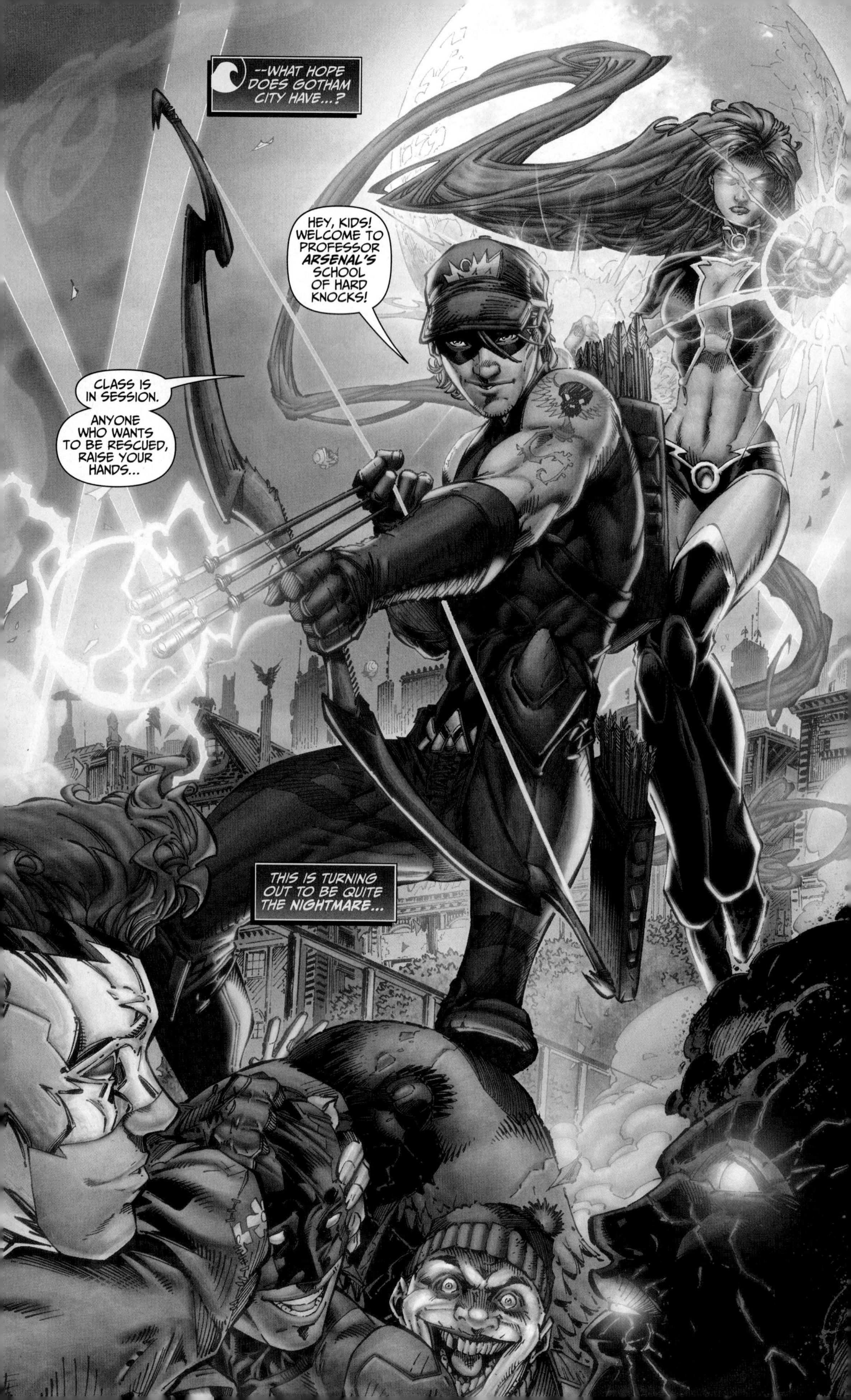
--WHAT HOPE DOES GOTHAM CITY HAVE...?
HEY, KIDS! WELCOME TO PROFESSOR ARSENAL'S SCHOOL OF HARD KNOCKS!
CLASS IS IN SESSION.
ANYONE WHO WANTS TO BE RESCUED, RAISE YOUR HANDS...
THIS IS TURNING OUT TO BE QUITE THE NIGHTMARE...

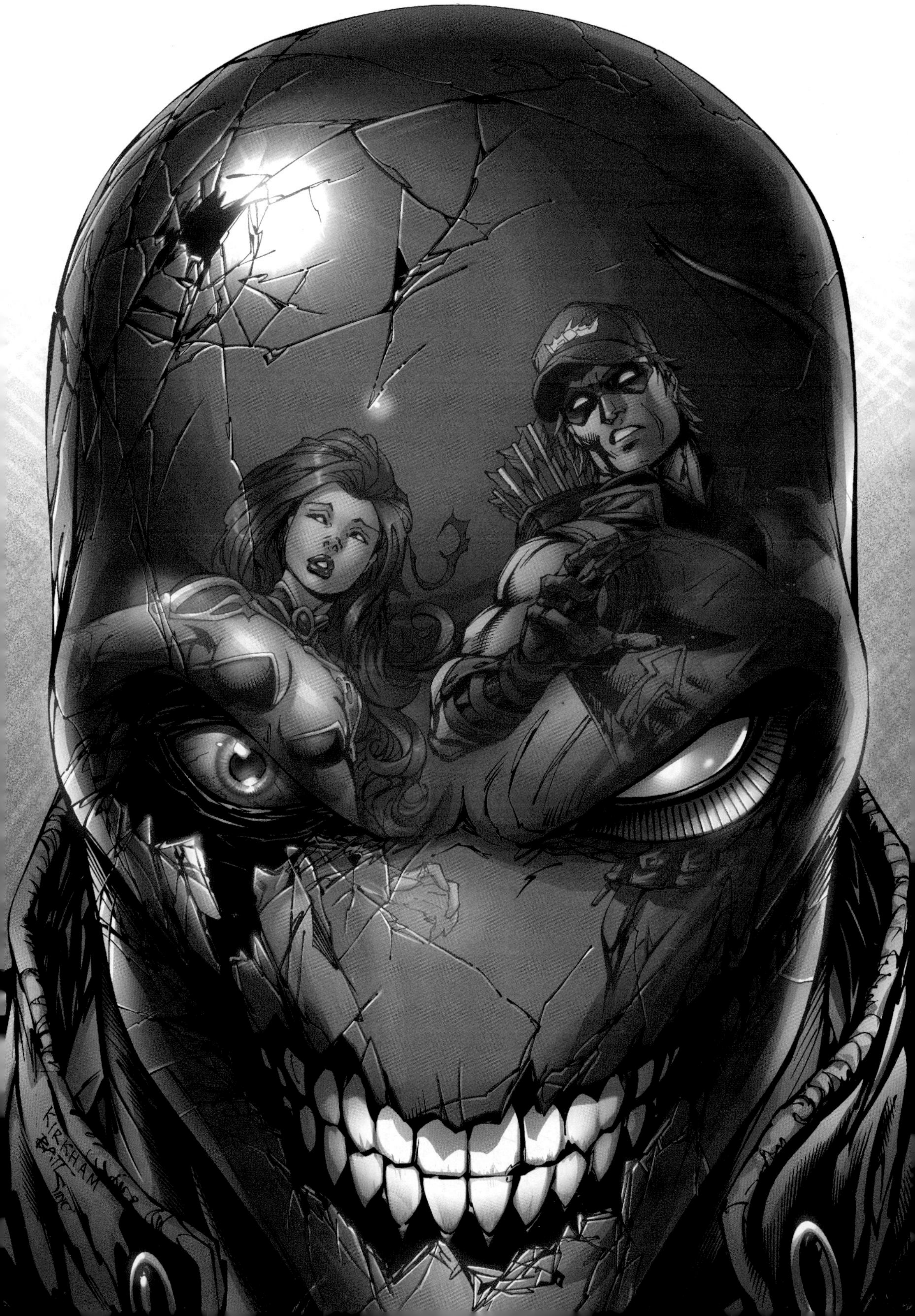
KIRKHAM

FAMILY MATTERS!

SCOTT LOBDELL writer TIMOTHY GREEN II penciller WAYNE FAUCHER inker
cover art by TYLER KIRKHAM, BATT & ALEX SINCLAIR

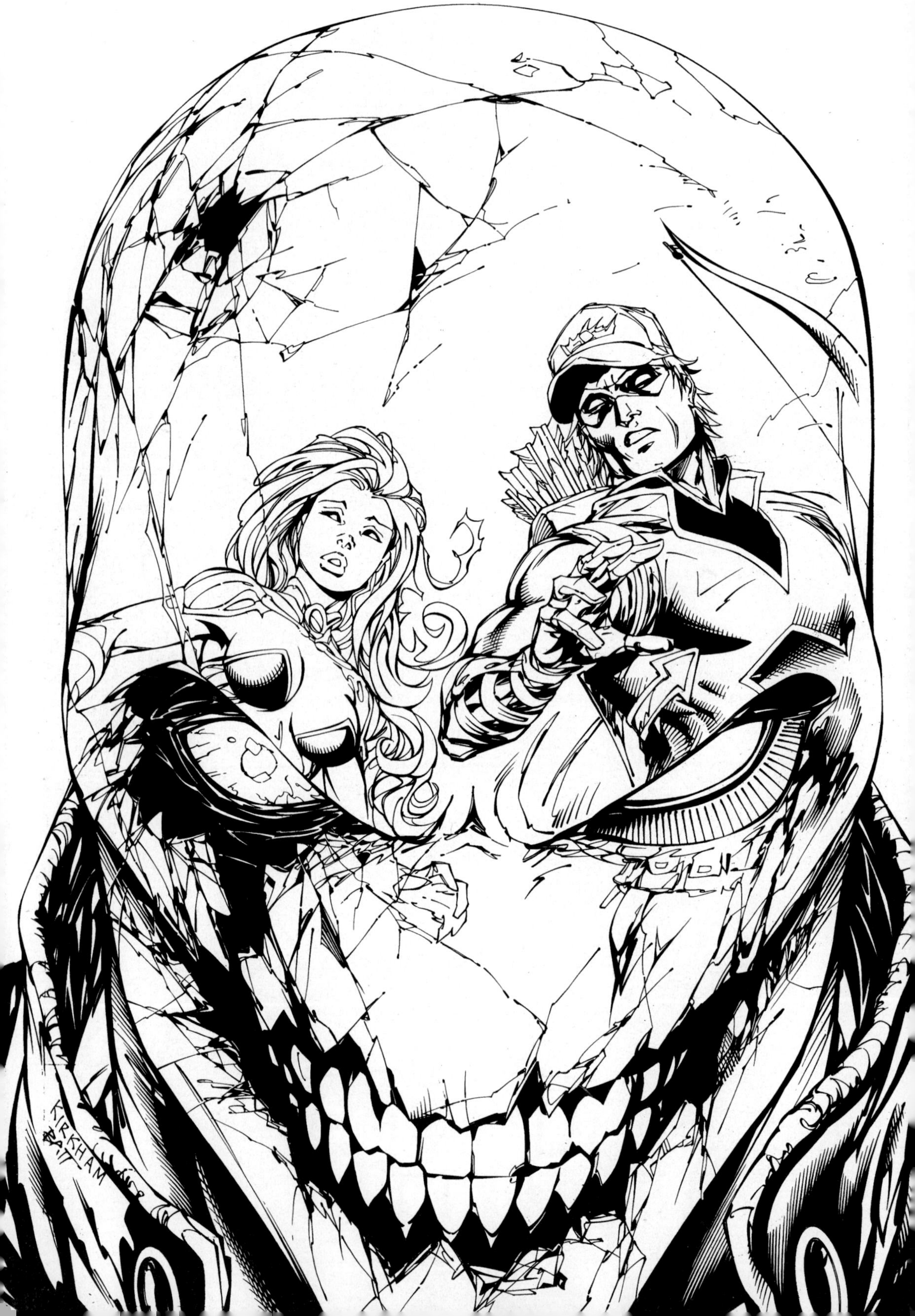

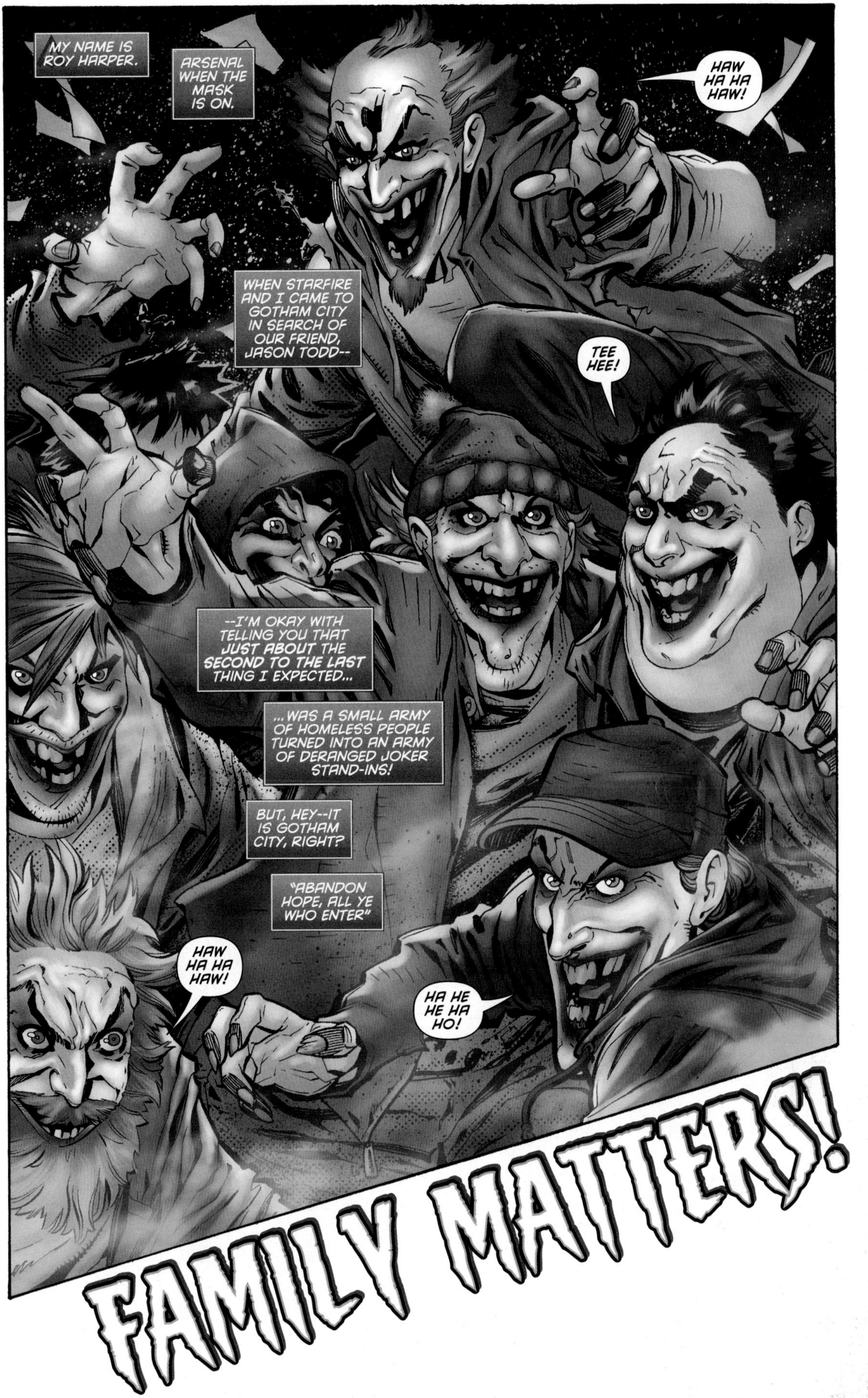
MY NAME IS ROY HARPER.
ARSENAL WHEN THE MASK IS ON.
HAW HA HA HAW!
WHEN STARFIRE AND I CAME TO GOTHAM CITY IN SEARCH OF OUR FRIEND, JASON TODD--
TEE HEE!
--I'M OKAY WITH TELLING YOU THAT JUST ABOUT THE SECOND TO THE LAST THING I EXPECTED...
...WAS A SMALL ARMY OF HOMELESS PEOPLE TURNED INTO AN ARMY OF DERANGED JOKER STAND-INS!
BUT, HEY--IT IS GOTHAM CITY, RIGHT?
"ABANDON HOPE, ALL YE WHO ENTER"
HAW HA HA HAW!
HA HE HE HA HO!
FAMILY MATTERS!

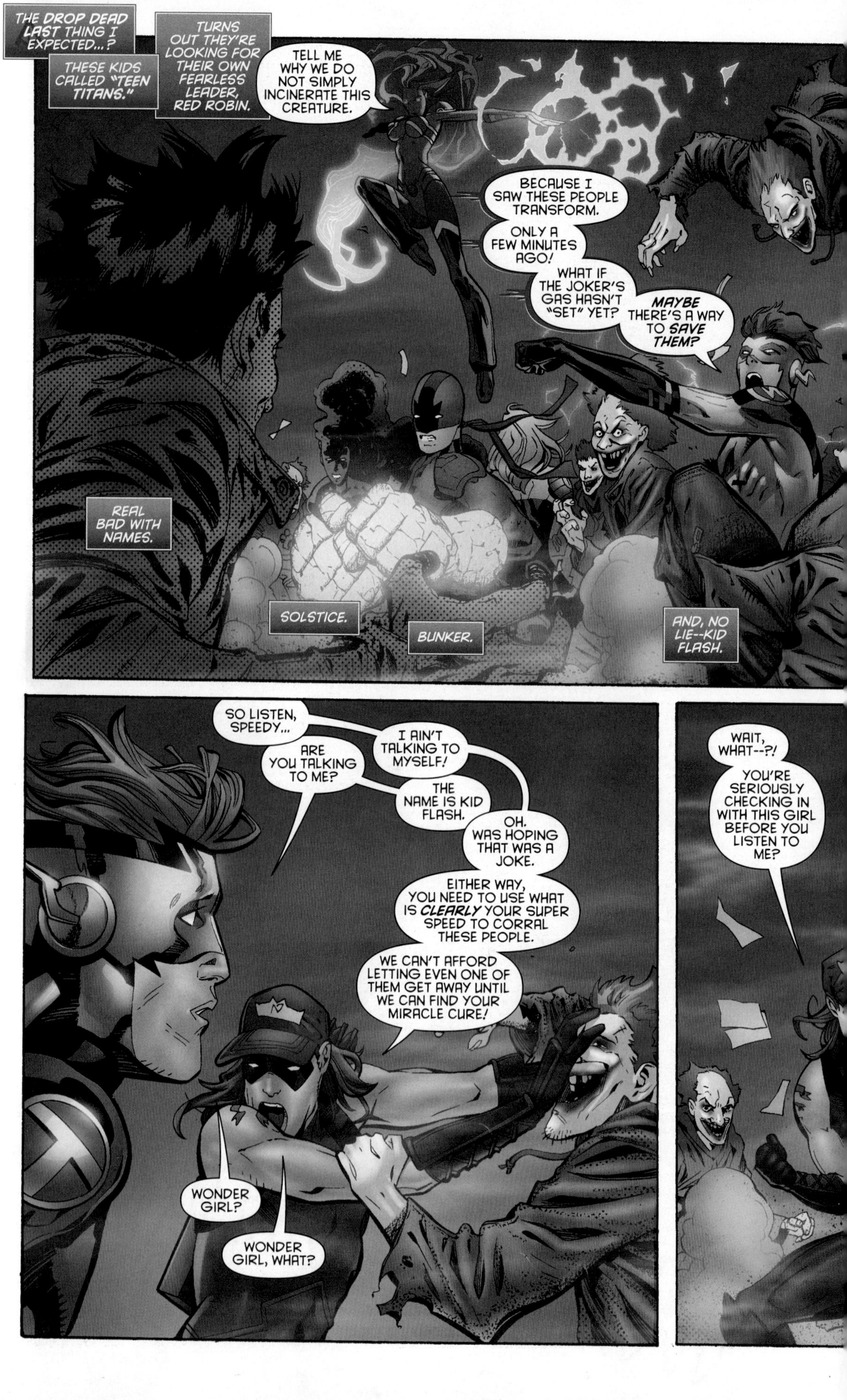
THE DROP DEAD LAST THING I EXPECTED...?
THESE KIDS CALLED "TEEN TITANS."
TURNS OUT THEY'RE LOOKING FOR THEIR OWN FEARLESS LEADER, RED ROBIN.
TELL ME WHY WE DO NOT SIMPLY INCINERATE THIS CREATURE.
BECAUSE I SAW THESE PEOPLE TRANSFORM.
ONLY A FEW MINUTES AGO!
WHAT IF THE JOKER'S GAS HASN'T "SET" YET?
MAYBE THERE'S A WAY TO SAVE THEM?
REAL BAD WITH NAMES.
SOLSTICE.
BUNKER.
AND, NO LIE--KID FLASH.
SO LISTEN, SPEEDY...
ARE YOU TALKING TO ME?
I AIN'T TALKING TO MYSELF!
THE NAME IS KID FLASH.
OH. WAS HOPING THAT WAS A JOKE.
EITHER WAY, YOU NEED TO USE WHAT IS CLEARLY YOUR SUPER SPEED TO CORRAL THESE PEOPLE.
WE CAN'T AFFORD LETTING EVEN ONE OF THEM GET AWAY UNTIL WE CAN FIND YOUR MIRACLE CURE!
WONDER GIRL?
WONDER GIRL, WHAT?
WAIT, WHAT--?!
YOU'RE SERIOUSLY CHECKING IN WITH THIS GIRL BEFORE YOU LISTEN TO ME?

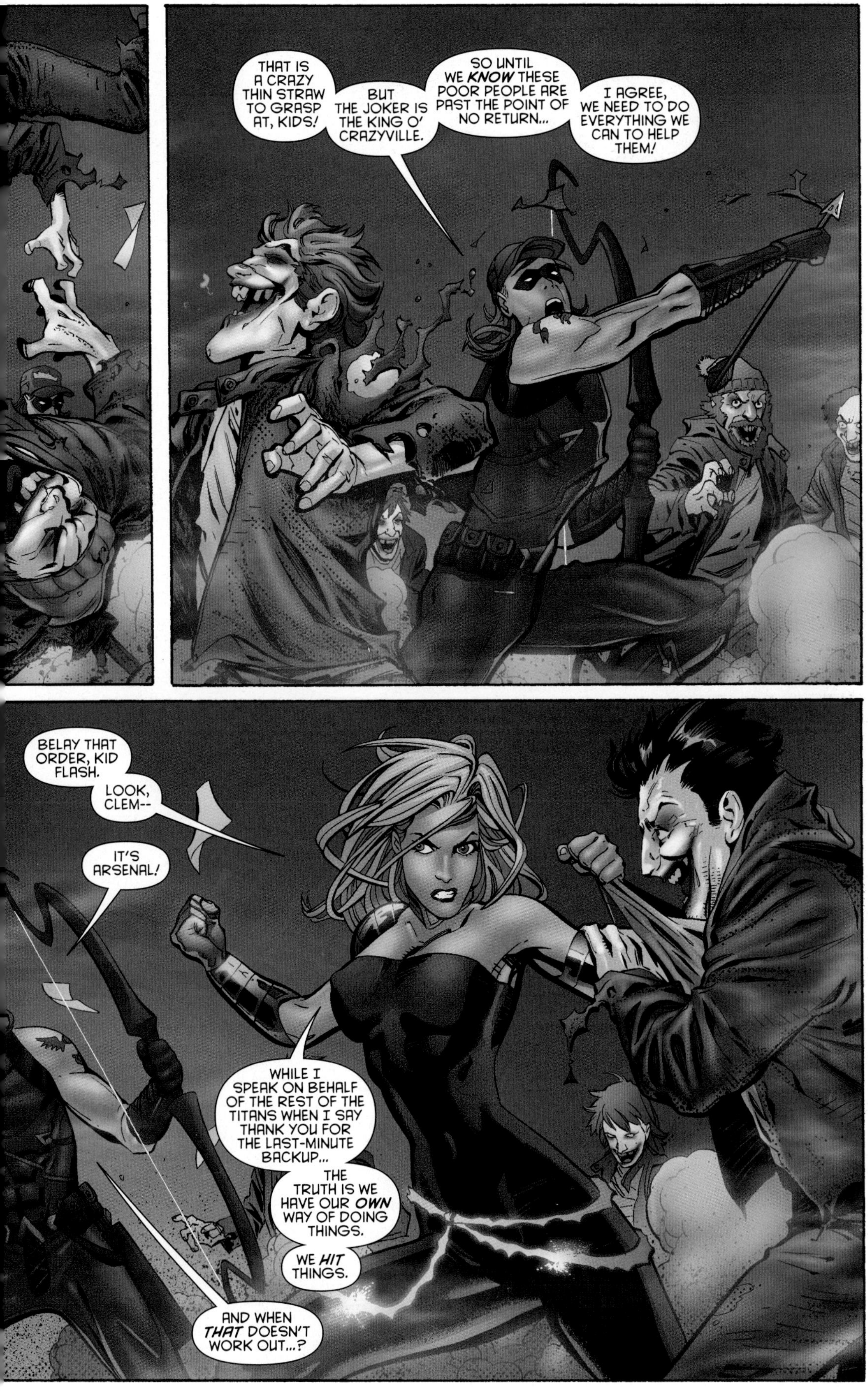
THAT IS A CRAZY THIN STRAW TO GRASP AT, KIDS!
BUT THE JOKER IS THE KING O' CRAZYVILLE.
SO UNTIL WE KNOW THESE POOR PEOPLE ARE PAST THE POINT OF NO RETURN...
I AGREE, WE NEED TO DO EVERYTHING WE CAN TO HELP THEM!
BELAY THAT ORDER, KID FLASH.
LOOK, CLEM--
IT'S ARSENAL!
WHILE I SPEAK ON BEHALF OF THE REST OF THE TITANS WHEN I SAY THANK YOU FOR THE LAST-MINUTE BACKUP...
THE TRUTH IS WE HAVE OUR OWN WAY OF DOING THINGS.
WE HIT THINGS.
AND WHEN THAT DOESN'T WORK OUT...?

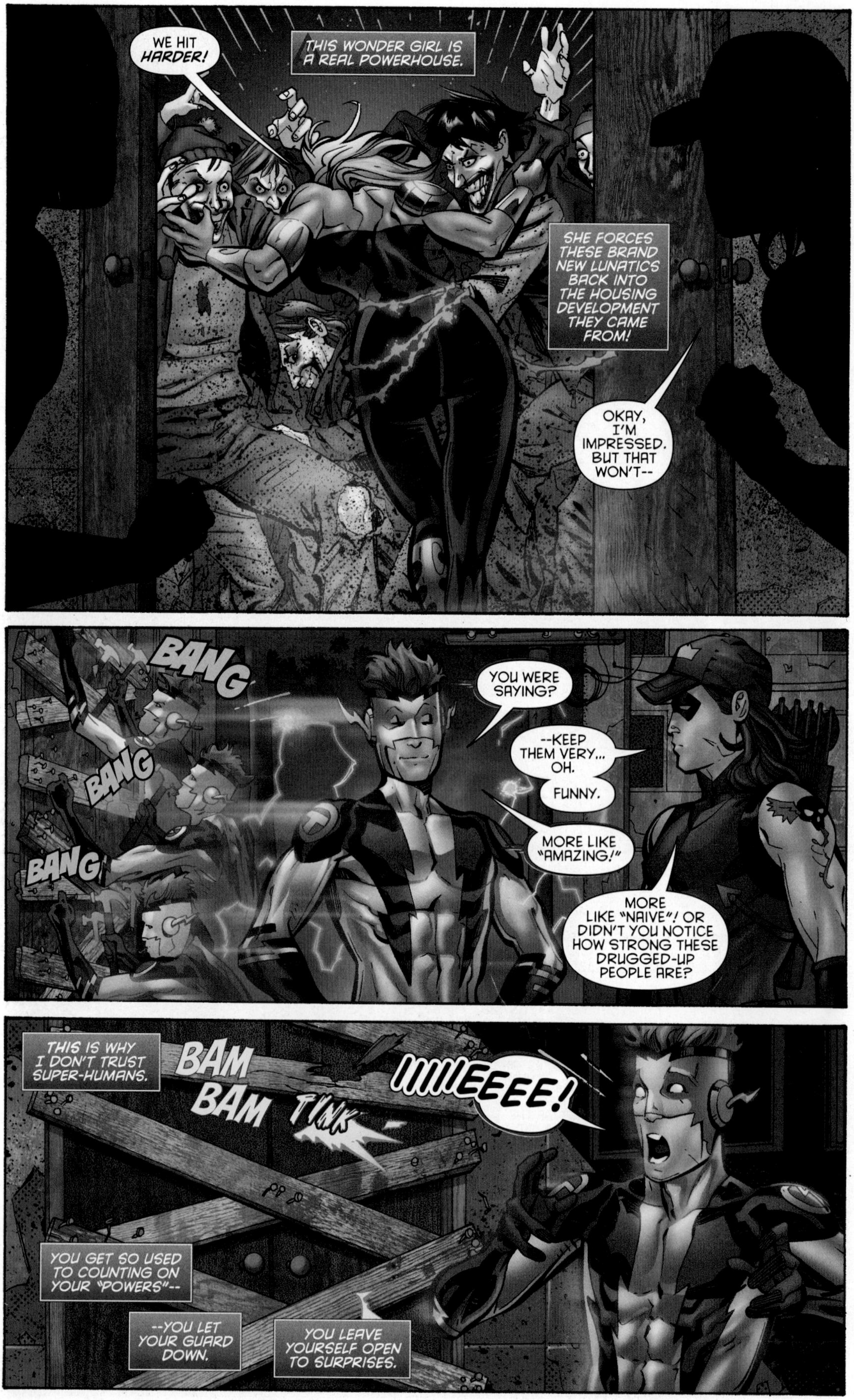
WE HIT HARDER!
THIS WONDER GIRL IS A REAL POWERHOUSE.
SHE FORCES THESE BRAND NEW LUNATICS BACK INTO THE HOUSING DEVELOPMENT THEY CAME FROM!
OKAY, I'M IMPRESSED. BUT THAT WON'T--
BANG
BANG
BANG
YOU WERE SAYING?
--KEEP THEM VERY... OH.
FUNNY.
MORE LIKE "AMAZING!"
MORE LIKE "NAIVE"! OR DIDN'T YOU NOTICE HOW STRONG THESE DRUGGED-UP PEOPLE ARE?
THIS IS WHY I DON'T TRUST SUPER-HUMANS.
BAM
BAM
TINK
IIIIIEEEEE!
YOU GET SO USED TO COUNTING ON YOUR "POWERS"--
--YOU LET YOUR GUARD DOWN.
YOU LEAVE YOURSELF OPEN TO SURPRISES.

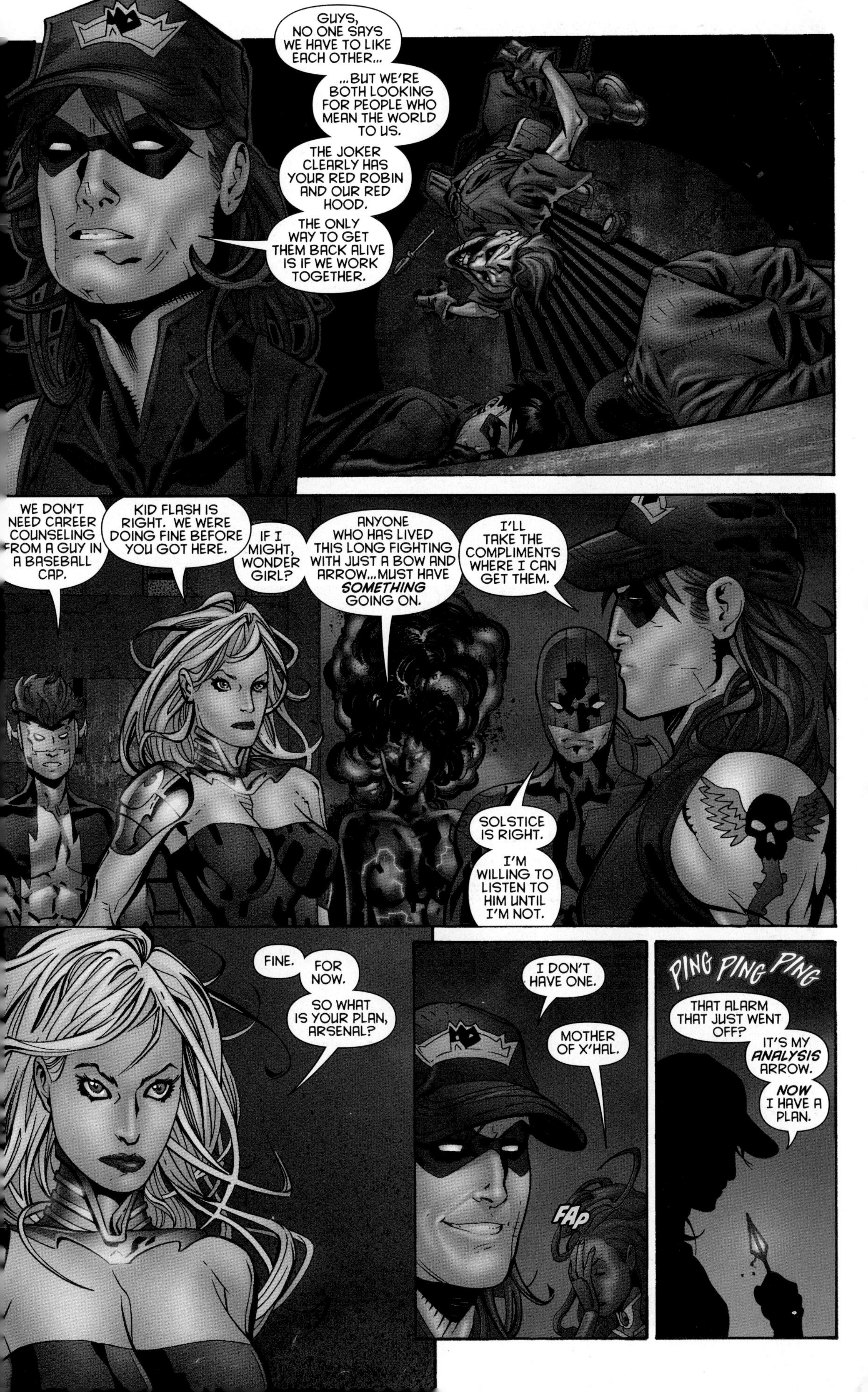
GUYS, NO ONE SAYS WE HAVE TO LIKE EACH OTHER...
...BUT WE'RE BOTH LOOKING FOR PEOPLE WHO MEAN THE WORLD TO US.
THE JOKER CLEARLY HAS YOUR RED ROBIN AND OUR RED HOOD.
THE ONLY WAY TO GET THEM BACK ALIVE IS IF WE WORK TOGETHER.
WE DON'T NEED CAREER COUNSELING FROM A GUY IN A BASEBALL CAP.
KID FLASH IS RIGHT. WE WERE DOING FINE BEFORE YOU GOT HERE.
IF I MIGHT, WONDER GIRL?
ANYONE WHO HAS LIVED THIS LONG FIGHTING WITH JUST A BOW AND ARROW...MUST HAVE *SOMETHING* GOING ON.
I'LL TAKE THE COMPLIMENTS WHERE I CAN GET THEM.
SOLSTICE IS RIGHT.
I'M WILLING TO LISTEN TO HIM UNTIL I'M NOT.
FINE.
FOR NOW.
SO WHAT IS YOUR PLAN, ARSENAL?
I DON'T HAVE ONE.
MOTHER OF X'HAL.
FAP
PING PING PING
THAT ALARM THAT JUST WENT OFF?
IT'S MY *ANALYSIS* ARROW.
NOW I HAVE A PLAN.

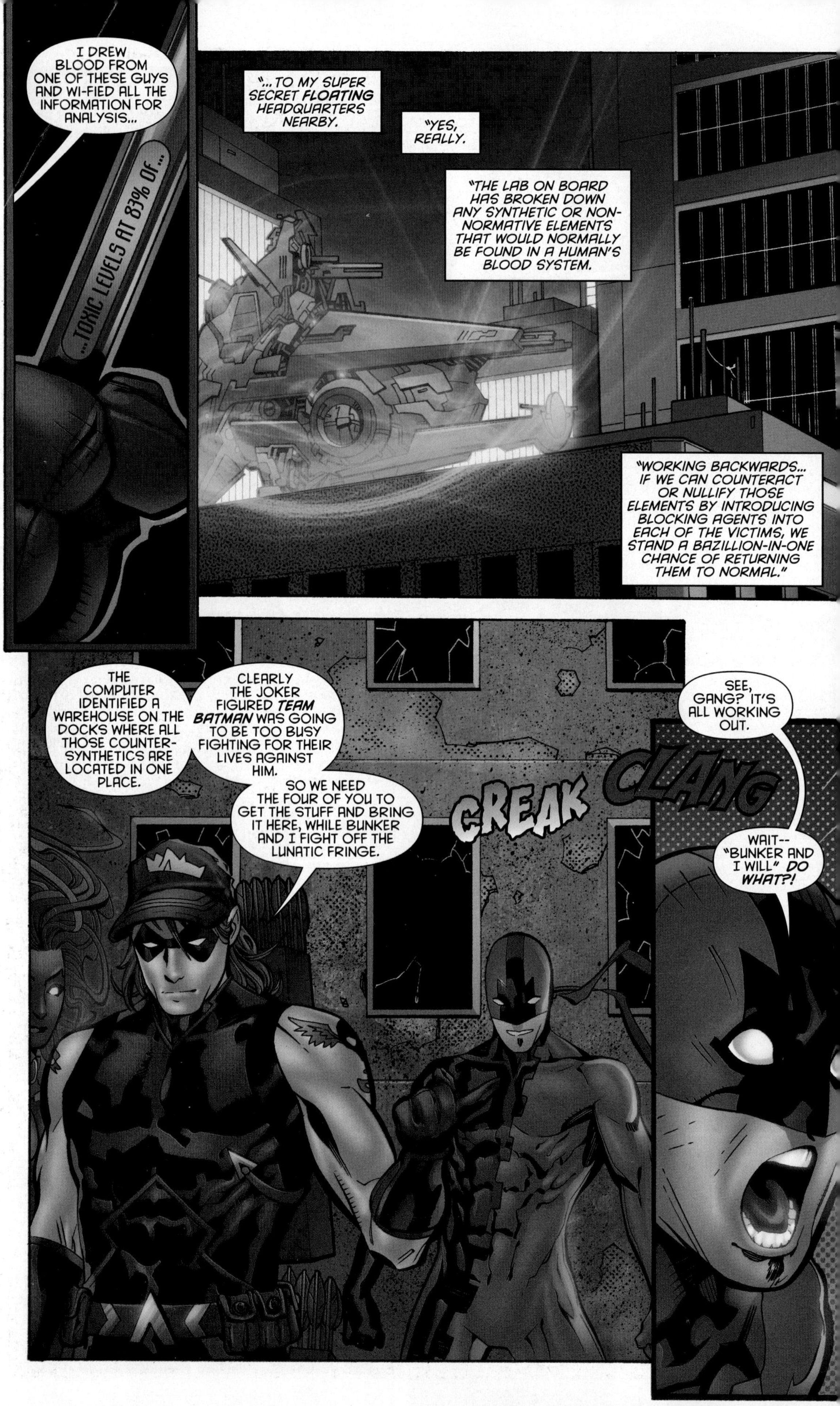
I DREW BLOOD FROM ONE OF THESE GUYS AND WI-FIED ALL THE INFORMATION FOR ANALYSIS...
...TOXIC LEVELS AT 83% OF...
"...TO MY SUPER SECRET *FLOATING* HEADQUARTERS NEARBY.
"YES, REALLY.
"THE LAB ON BOARD HAS BROKEN DOWN ANY SYNTHETIC OR NON-NORMATIVE ELEMENTS THAT WOULD NORMALLY BE FOUND IN A HUMAN'S BLOOD SYSTEM.
"WORKING BACKWARDS... IF WE CAN COUNTERACT OR NULLIFY THOSE ELEMENTS BY INTRODUCING BLOCKING AGENTS INTO EACH OF THE VICTIMS, WE STAND A BAZILLION-IN-ONE CHANCE OF RETURNING THEM TO NORMAL."
THE COMPUTER IDENTIFIED A WAREHOUSE ON THE DOCKS WHERE ALL THOSE COUNTER-SYNTHETICS ARE LOCATED IN ONE PLACE.
CLEARLY THE JOKER FIGURED *TEAM BATMAN* WAS GOING TO BE TOO BUSY FIGHTING FOR THEIR LIVES AGAINST HIM.
SO WE NEED THE FOUR OF YOU TO GET THE STUFF AND BRING IT HERE, WHILE BUNKER AND I FIGHT OFF THE LUNATIC FRINGE.
CREAK
CLANG
SEE, GANG? IT'S ALL WORKING OUT.
WAIT-- "BUNKER AND I WILL" *DO WHAT?!*

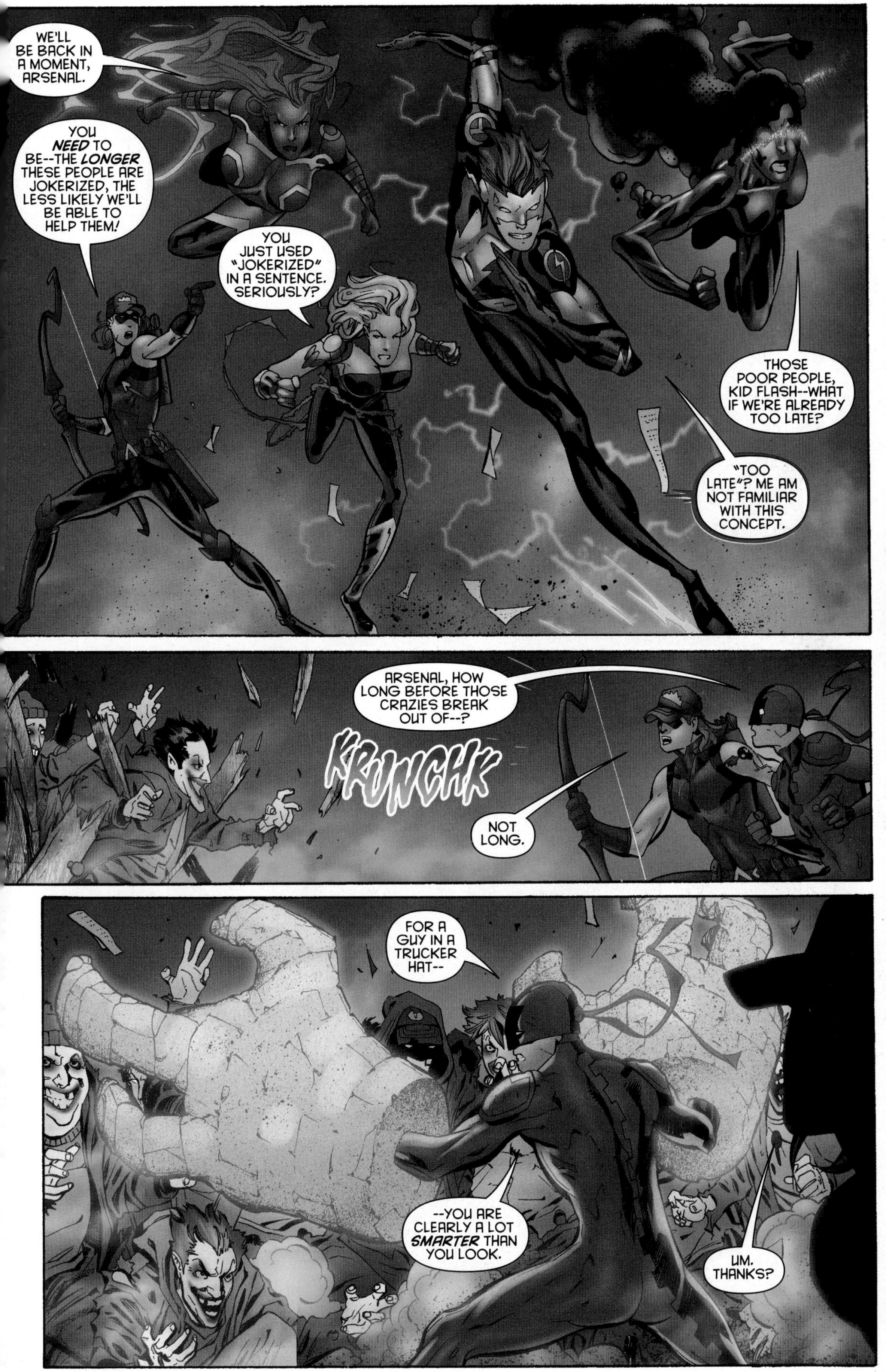
WE'LL BE BACK IN A MOMENT, ARSENAL.
YOU *NEED* TO BE--THE *LONGER* THESE PEOPLE ARE JOKERIZED, THE LESS LIKELY WE'LL BE ABLE TO HELP THEM!
YOU JUST USED "JOKERIZED" IN A SENTENCE. SERIOUSLY?
THOSE POOR PEOPLE, KID FLASH--WHAT IF WE'RE ALREADY TOO LATE?
"TOO LATE"? ME AM NOT FAMILIAR WITH THIS CONCEPT.
ARSENAL, HOW LONG BEFORE THOSE CRAZIES BREAK OUT OF--?
KRUNCHK
NOT LONG.
FOR A GUY IN A TRUCKER HAT--
--YOU ARE CLEARLY A LOT *SMARTER* THAN YOU LOOK.
UM. THANKS?

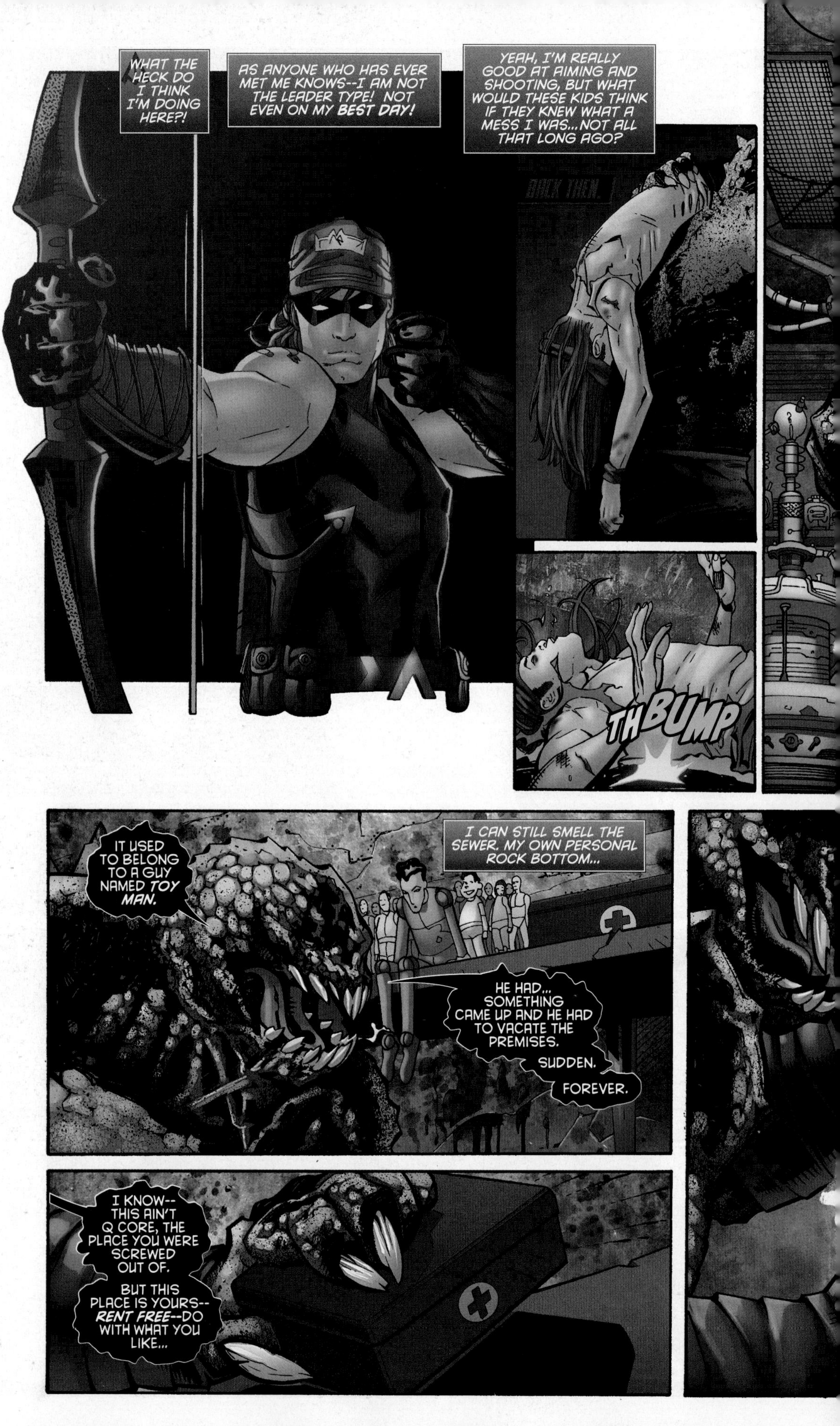

WHAT THE HECK DO I THINK I'M DOING HERE?!
AS ANYONE WHO HAS EVER MET ME KNOWS--I AM NOT THE LEADER TYPE! NOT EVEN ON MY BEST DAY!
YEAH, I'M REALLY GOOD AT AIMING AND SHOOTING, BUT WHAT WOULD THESE KIDS THINK IF THEY KNEW WHAT A MESS I WAS...NOT ALL THAT LONG AGO?
BACK THEN.
THBUMP
I CAN STILL SMELL THE SEWER. MY OWN PERSONAL ROCK BOTTOM...
IT USED TO BELONG TO A GUY NAMED TOY MAN.
HE HAD... SOMETHING CAME UP AND HE HAD TO VACATE THE PREMISES.
SUDDEN.
FOREVER.
I KNOW-- THIS AIN'T Q CORE, THE PLACE YOU WERE SCREWED OUT OF.
BUT THIS PLACE IS YOURS-- RENT FREE--DO WITH WHAT YOU LIKE...

HOLY SPIT--WHAT THE *HELL* IS THIS *PLACE?!*

...SO LONG AS YOU STAY IN THE PROGRAM.

"THE PROG--" YOU MEAN, A.A.?

SERIOUSLY? KILLER CROC IS BADGERING ME INTO GOING TO A.A.?

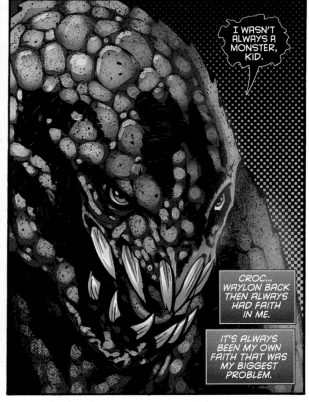

I WASN'T ALWAYS A MONSTER, KID.

CROC... WAYLON BACK THEN ALWAYS HAD FAITH IN ME.

IT'S ALWAYS BEEN MY OWN FAITH THAT WAS MY BIGGEST PROBLEM.

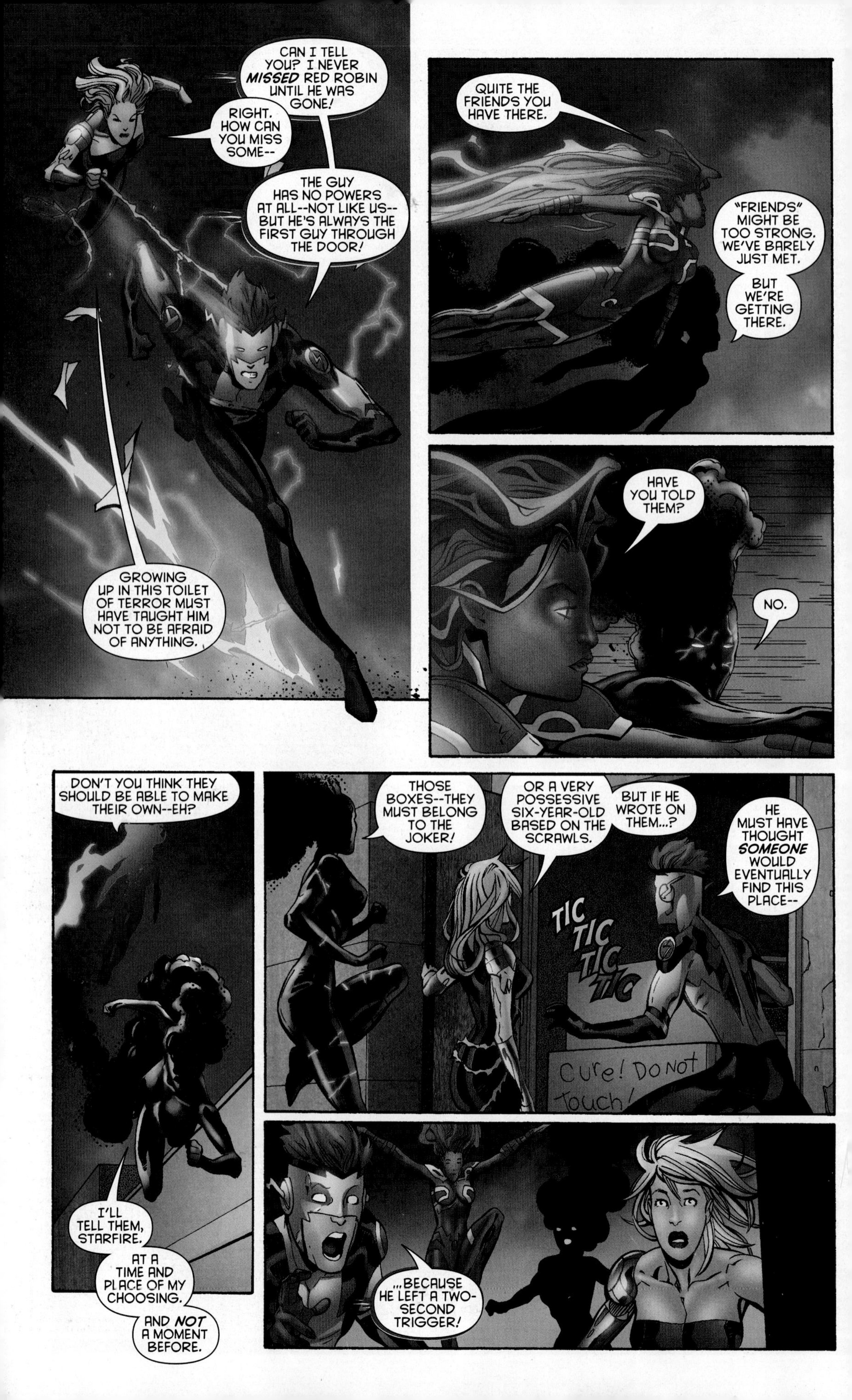
CAN I TELL YOU? I NEVER MISSED RED ROBIN UNTIL HE WAS GONE!
RIGHT. HOW CAN YOU MISS SOME--
THE GUY HAS NO POWERS AT ALL--NOT LIKE US--BUT HE'S ALWAYS THE FIRST GUY THROUGH THE DOOR!
GROWING UP IN THIS TOILET OF TERROR MUST HAVE TAUGHT HIM NOT TO BE AFRAID OF ANYTHING.
QUITE THE FRIENDS YOU HAVE THERE.
"FRIENDS" MIGHT BE TOO STRONG. WE'VE BARELY JUST MET.
BUT WE'RE GETTING THERE.
HAVE YOU TOLD THEM?
NO.
DON'T YOU THINK THEY SHOULD BE ABLE TO MAKE THEIR OWN--EH?
I'LL TELL THEM, STARFIRE.
AT A TIME AND PLACE OF MY CHOOSING.
AND NOT A MOMENT BEFORE.
THOSE BOXES--THEY MUST BELONG TO THE JOKER!
OR A VERY POSSESSIVE SIX-YEAR-OLD BASED ON THE SCRAWLS.
BUT IF HE WROTE ON THEM...?
HE MUST HAVE THOUGHT SOMEONE WOULD EVENTUALLY FIND THIS PLACE--
TIC TIC TIC TIC
Cure! Do Not Touch!
...BECAUSE HE LEFT A TWO-SECOND TRIGGER!

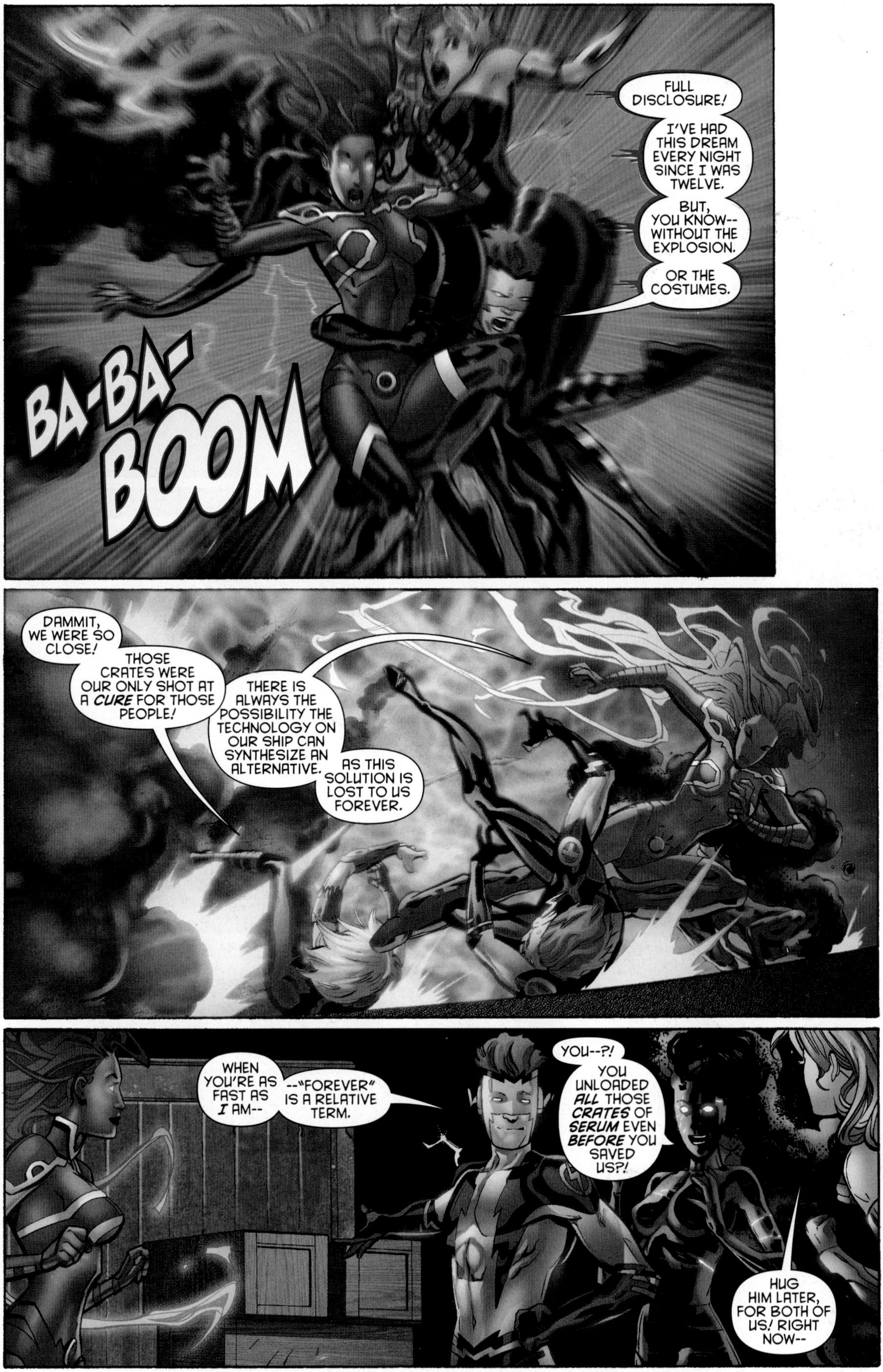
FULL DISCLOSURE!
I'VE HAD THIS DREAM EVERY NIGHT SINCE I WAS TWELVE.
BUT, YOU KNOW-- WITHOUT THE EXPLOSION.
OR THE COSTUMES.
BA-BA-BOOM
DAMMIT, WE WERE SO CLOSE!
THOSE CRATES WERE OUR ONLY SHOT AT A *CURE* FOR THOSE PEOPLE!
THERE IS ALWAYS THE POSSIBILITY THE TECHNOLOGY ON OUR SHIP CAN SYNTHESIZE AN ALTERNATIVE.
AS THIS SOLUTION IS LOST TO US FOREVER.
WHEN YOU'RE AS FAST AS *I* AM--
--"FOREVER" IS A RELATIVE TERM.
YOU--?!
YOU UNLOADED *ALL* THOSE *CRATES* OF *SERUM* EVEN *BEFORE* YOU SAVED US?!
HUG HIM LATER, FOR BOTH OF US! RIGHT NOW--

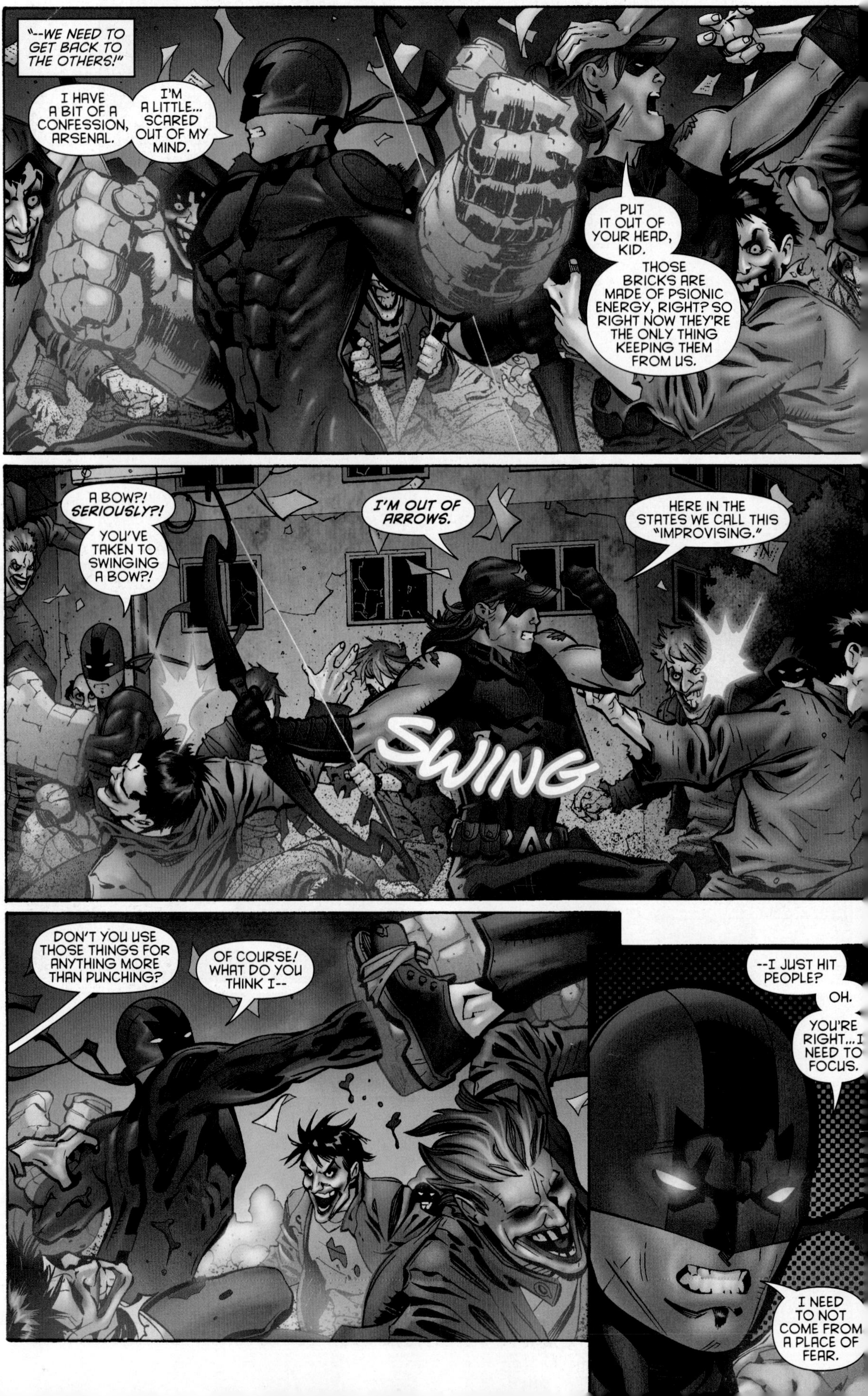
"--WE NEED TO GET BACK TO THE OTHERS!"
I HAVE A BIT OF A CONFESSION, ARSENAL.
I'M A LITTLE... SCARED OUT OF MY MIND.
PUT IT OUT OF YOUR HEAD, KID.
THOSE BRICKS ARE MADE OF PSIONIC ENERGY, RIGHT? SO RIGHT NOW THEY'RE THE ONLY THING KEEPING THEM FROM US.
A BOW?! SERIOUSLY?!
YOU'VE TAKEN TO SWINGING A BOW?!
I'M OUT OF ARROWS.
HERE IN THE STATES WE CALL THIS "IMPROVISING."
SWING
DON'T YOU USE THOSE THINGS FOR ANYTHING MORE THAN PUNCHING?
OF COURSE! WHAT DO YOU THINK I--
--I JUST HIT PEOPLE?
OH.
YOU'RE RIGHT...I NEED TO FOCUS.
I NEED TO NOT COME FROM A PLACE OF FEAR.

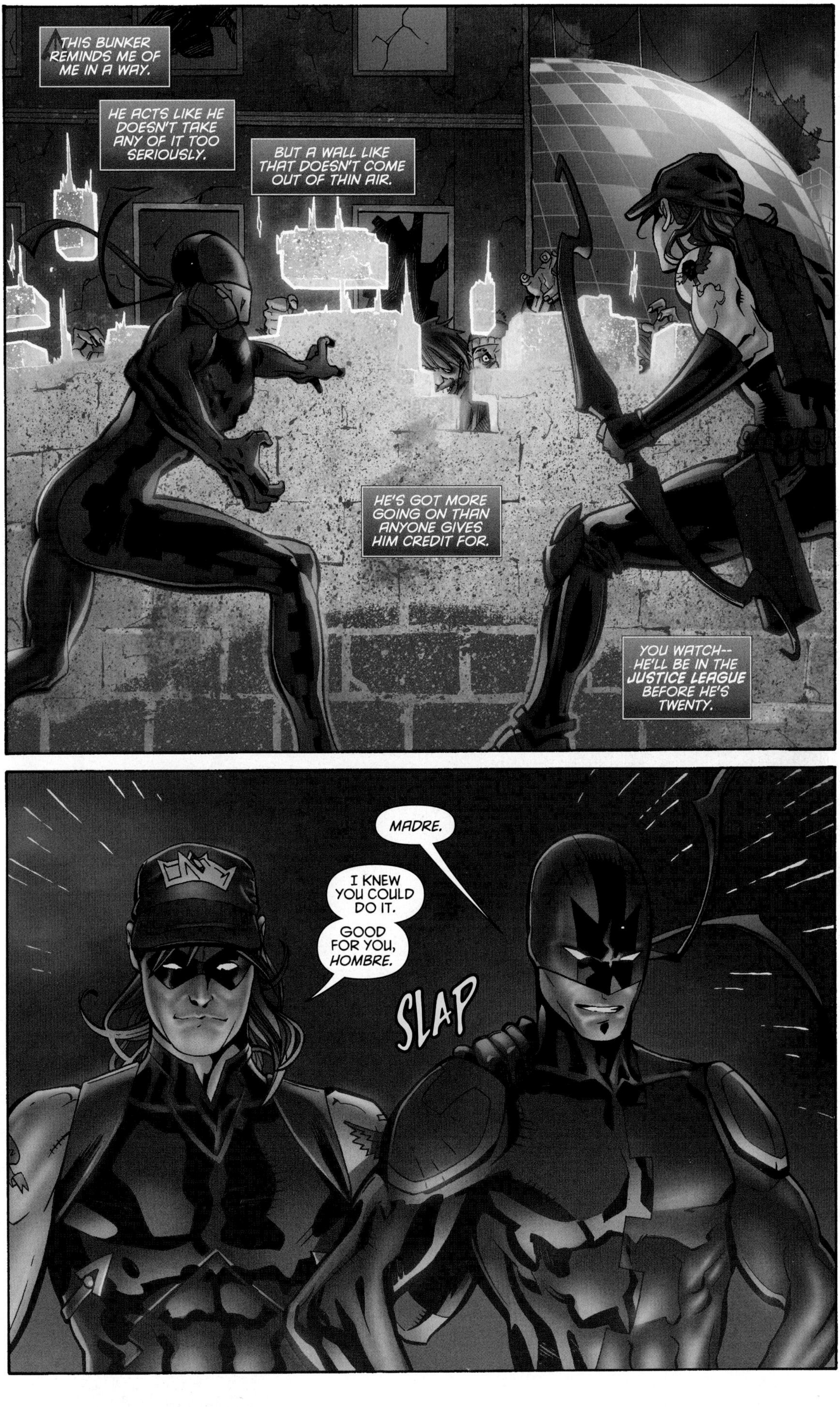
THIS BUNKER REMINDS ME OF ME IN A WAY.
HE ACTS LIKE HE DOESN'T TAKE ANY OF IT TOO SERIOUSLY.
BUT A WALL LIKE THAT DOESN'T COME OUT OF THIN AIR.
HE'S GOT MORE GOING ON THAN ANYONE GIVES HIM CREDIT FOR.
YOU WATCH-- HE'LL BE IN THE JUSTICE LEAGUE BEFORE HE'S TWENTY.
MADRE.
I KNEW YOU COULD DO IT.
GOOD FOR YOU, HOMBRE.
SLAP

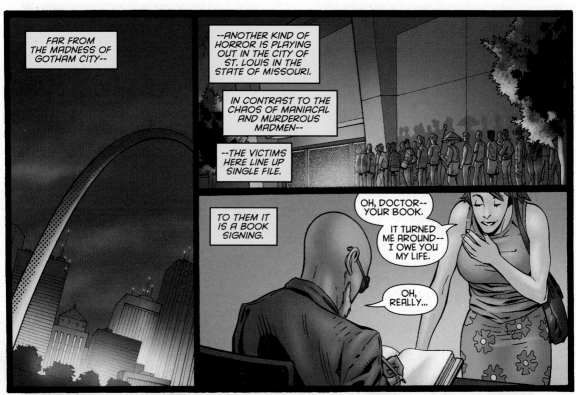

FAR FROM THE MADNESS OF GOTHAM CITY--

--ANOTHER KIND OF HORROR IS PLAYING OUT IN THE CITY OF ST. LOUIS IN THE STATE OF MISSOURI.

IN CONTRAST TO THE CHAOS OF MANIACAL AND MURDEROUS MADMEN--

--THE VICTIMS HERE LINE UP SINGLE FILE.

TO THEM IT IS A BOOK SIGNING.

OH, DOCTOR-- YOUR BOOK.

IT TURNED ME AROUND-- I OWE YOU MY LIFE.

OH, REALLY...

BUT TO THIS AUTHOR, IT IS AN OPPORTUNITY.

THAT'S GOOD TO KNOW.

PERHAPS SOME DAY I'LL HAVE TO STOP BY...AND COLLECT IT.

A CHANCE TO LOOK INTO THE EYE OF THE HOPELESS, THE FOOLISH.

A CHANCE TO LOOK THEM DIRECTLY IN THE EYES AND TELL THEM THEIR FATE FROM BEHIND HIS EMPTY SMILE.

HIS NAME IS DR. HUGO STRANGE.

IT HAS NEVER BEEN ENOUGH FOR THE MAN TO DEVOUR HIS VICTIMS.

HE HAS ALWAYS NEEDED TO TOY WITH THEM.

TO SAVOR THEM.

WHAT'S SO STRANGE ABOUT BEING HAPPY?

BY DR. HUGO STRANGE

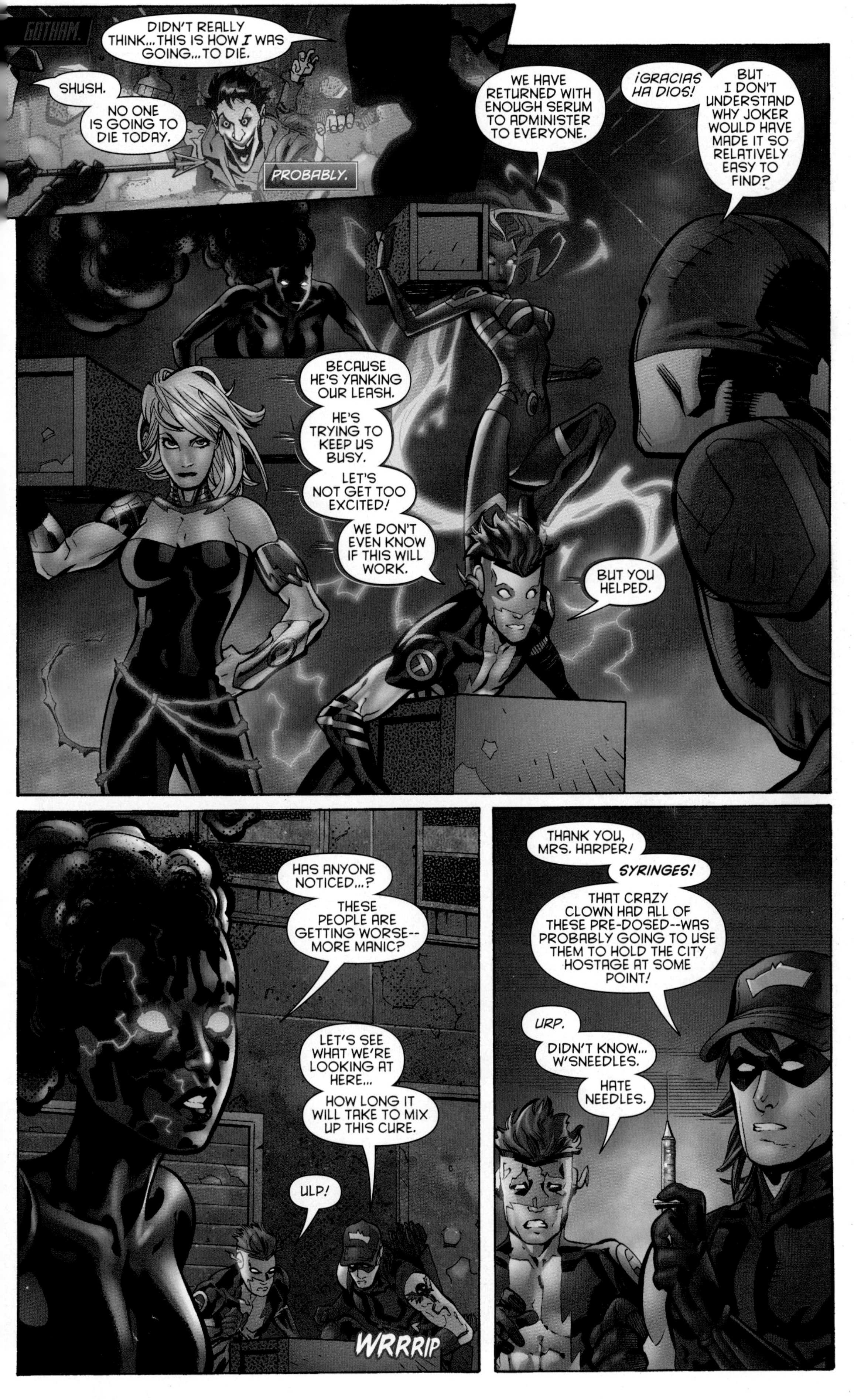
GOTHAM.
DIDN'T REALLY THINK...THIS IS HOW I WAS GOING...TO DIE.
SHUSH.
NO ONE IS GOING TO DIE TODAY.
PROBABLY.
WE HAVE RETURNED WITH ENOUGH SERUM TO ADMINISTER TO EVERYONE.
¡GRACIAS HA DIOS!
BUT I DON'T UNDERSTAND WHY JOKER WOULD HAVE MADE IT SO RELATIVELY EASY TO FIND?
BECAUSE HE'S YANKING OUR LEASH.
HE'S TRYING TO KEEP US BUSY.
LET'S NOT GET TOO EXCITED!
WE DON'T EVEN KNOW IF THIS WILL WORK.
BUT YOU HELPED.
HAS ANYONE NOTICED...?
THESE PEOPLE ARE GETTING WORSE-- MORE MANIC?
LET'S SEE WHAT WE'RE LOOKING AT HERE...
HOW LONG IT WILL TAKE TO MIX UP THIS CURE.
ULP!
WRRRIP
THANK YOU, MRS. HARPER!
SYRINGES!
THAT CRAZY CLOWN HAD ALL OF THESE PRE-DOSED--WAS PROBABLY GOING TO USE THEM TO HOLD THE CITY HOSTAGE AT SOME POINT!
URP.
DIDN'T KNOW... W'SNEEDLES.
HATE NEEDLES.

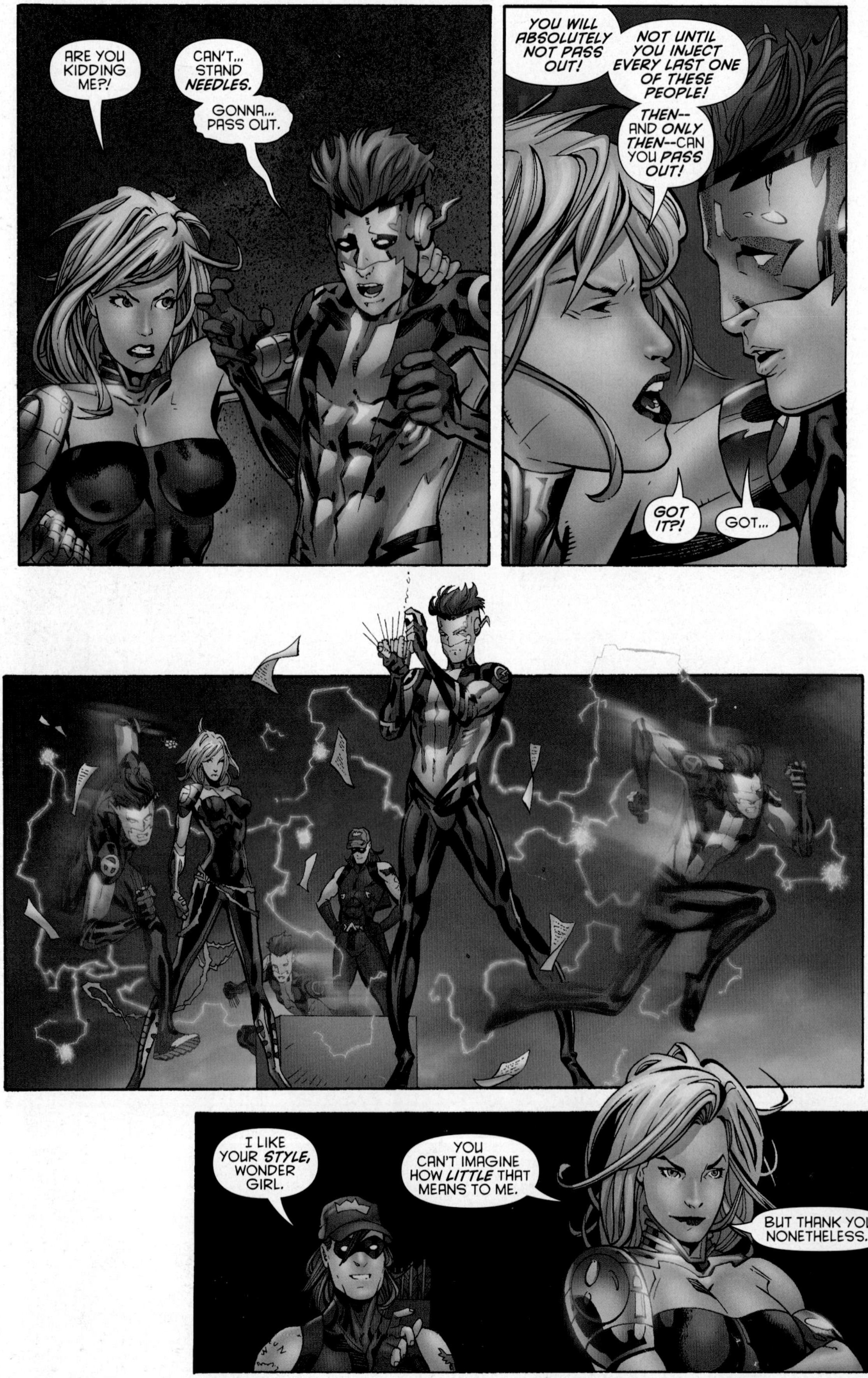
ARE YOU KIDDING ME?!
CAN'T... STAND NEEDLES.
GONNA... PASS OUT.
YOU WILL ABSOLUTELY NOT PASS OUT!
NOT UNTIL YOU INJECT EVERY LAST ONE OF THESE PEOPLE!
THEN-- AND ONLY THEN--CAN YOU PASS OUT!
GOT IT?!
GOT...
I LIKE YOUR STYLE, WONDER GIRL.
YOU CAN'T IMAGINE HOW LITTLE THAT MEANS TO ME.
BUT THANK YOU NONETHELESS.

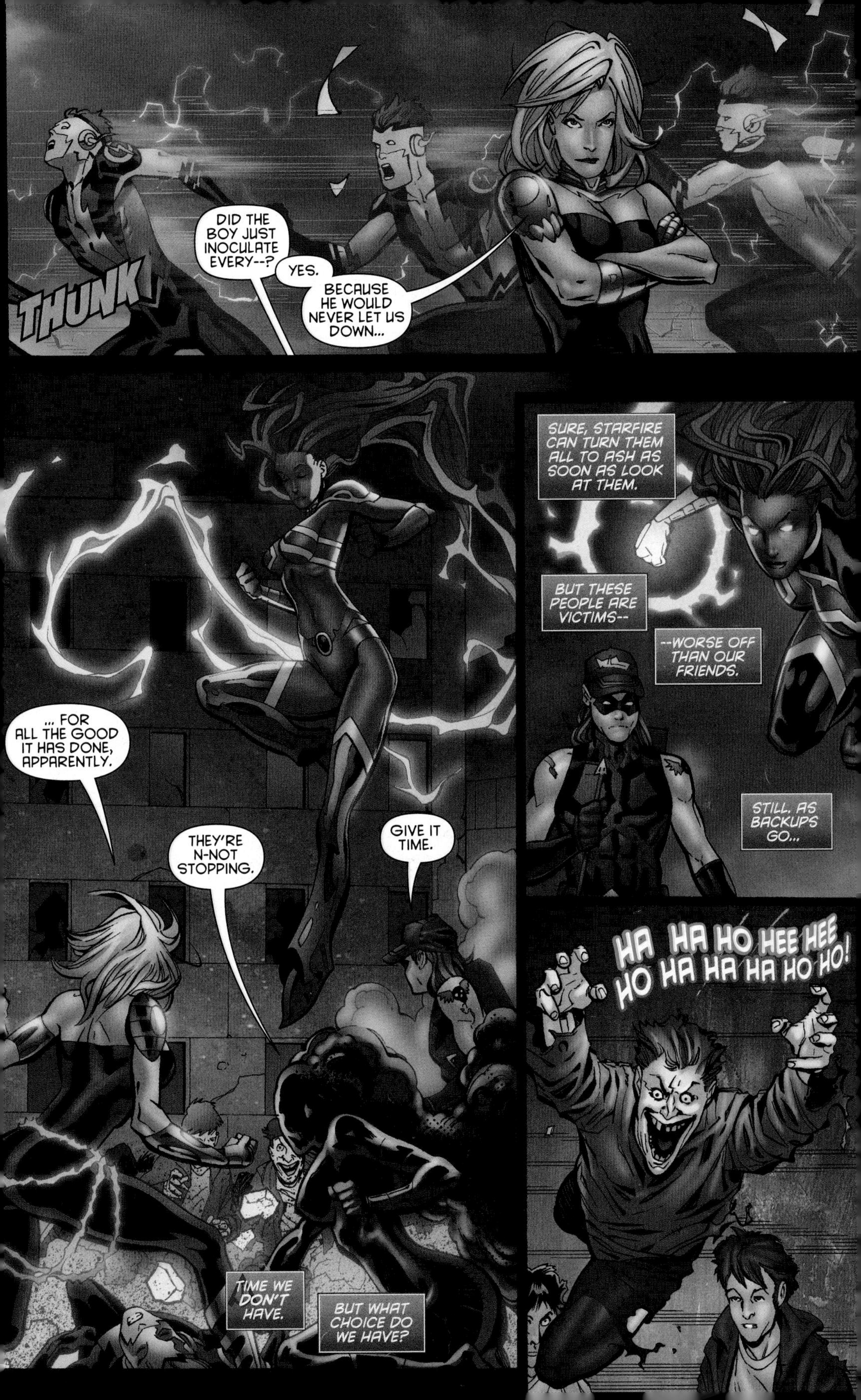
THUNK
DID THE BOY JUST INOCULATE EVERY--?
YES.
BECAUSE HE WOULD NEVER LET US DOWN...
... FOR ALL THE GOOD IT HAS DONE, APPARENTLY.
THEY'RE N-NOT STOPPING.
GIVE IT TIME.
TIME WE DON'T HAVE.
BUT WHAT CHOICE DO WE HAVE?
SURE, STARFIRE CAN TURN THEM ALL TO ASH AS SOON AS LOOK AT THEM.
BUT THESE PEOPLE ARE VICTIMS--
--WORSE OFF THAN OUR FRIENDS.
STILL. AS BACKUPS GO...
HA HA HO HEE HEE HO HA HA HA HO HO!

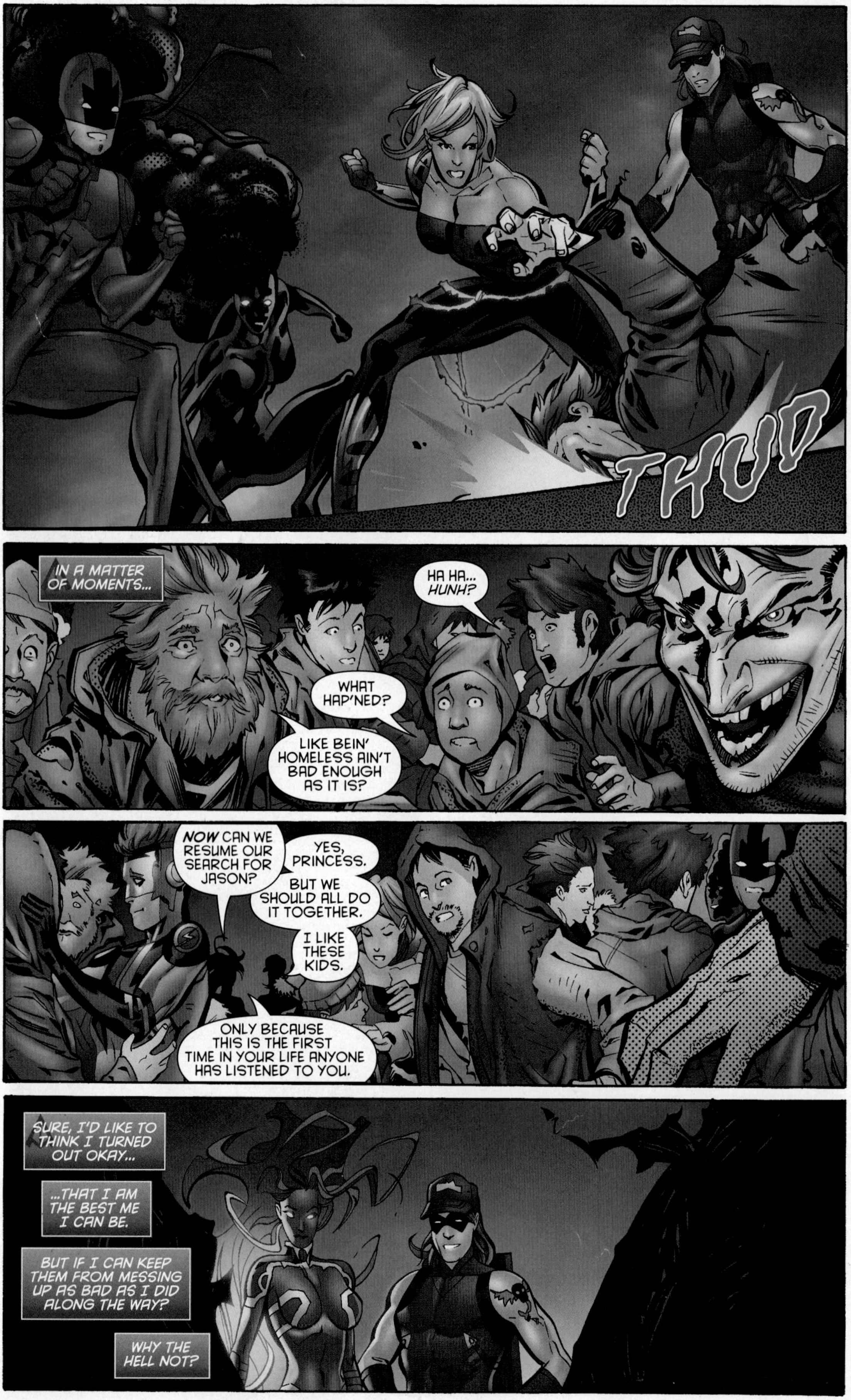
THUD
IN A MATTER OF MOMENTS...
HA HA... HUNH?
WHAT HAP'NED?
LIKE BEIN' HOMELESS AIN'T BAD ENOUGH AS IT IS?
NOW CAN WE RESUME OUR SEARCH FOR JASON?
YES, PRINCESS.
BUT WE SHOULD ALL DO IT TOGETHER.
I LIKE THESE KIDS.
ONLY BECAUSE THIS IS THE FIRST TIME IN YOUR LIFE ANYONE HAS LISTENED TO YOU.
SURE, I'D LIKE TO THINK I TURNED OUT OKAY...
...THAT I AM THE BEST ME I CAN BE.
BUT IF I CAN KEEP THEM FROM MESSING UP AS BAD AS I DID ALONG THE WAY?
WHY THE HELL NOT?

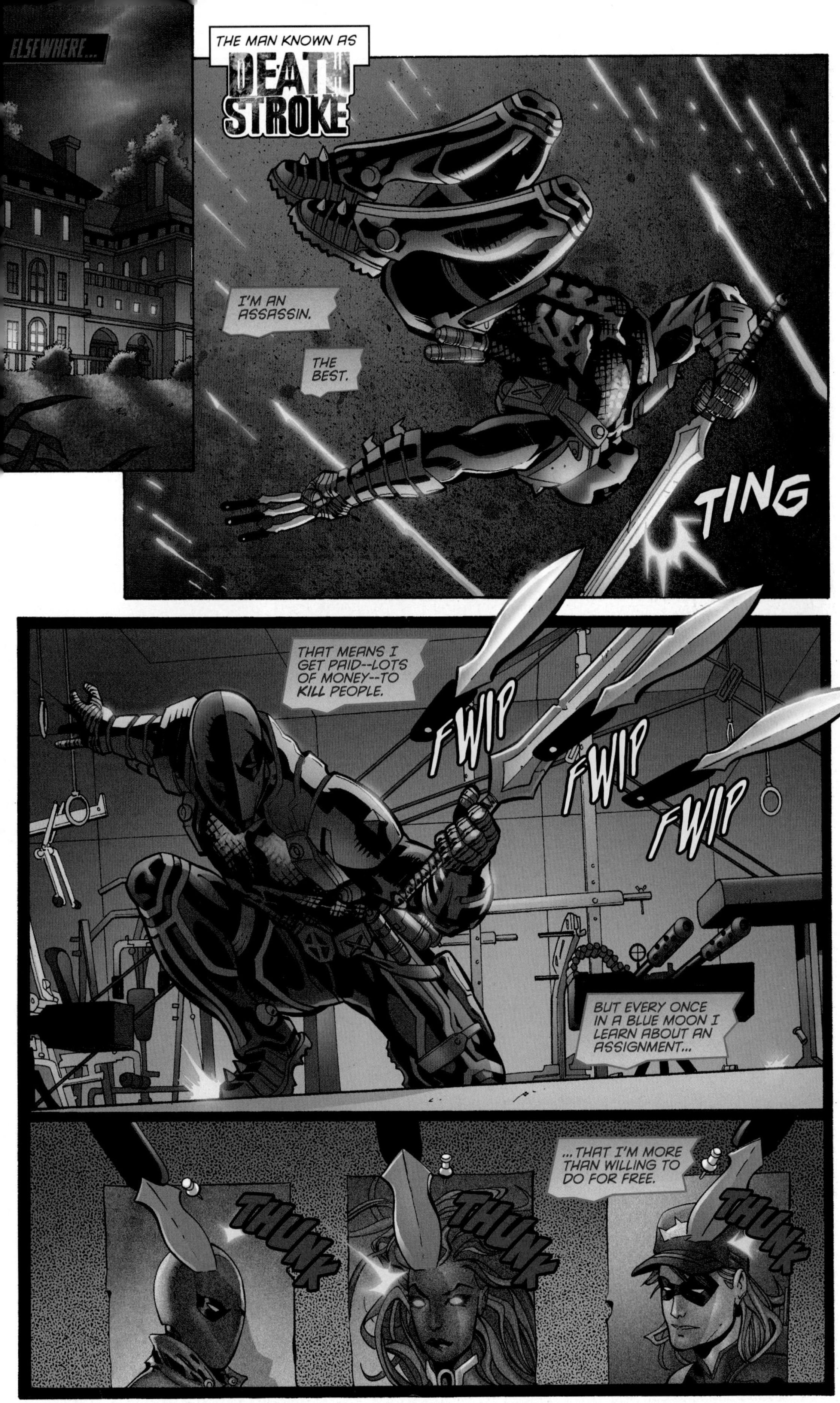
ELSEWHERE...
THE MAN KNOWN AS
DEATHSTROKE
I'M AN ASSASSIN.
THE BEST.
TING
THAT MEANS I GET PAID--LOTS OF MONEY--TO KILL PEOPLE.
FWIP
FWIP
FWIP
BUT EVERY ONCE IN A BLUE MOON I LEARN ABOUT AN ASSIGNMENT...
...THAT I'M MORE THAN WILLING TO DO FOR FREE.
THUNK
THUNK
THUNK

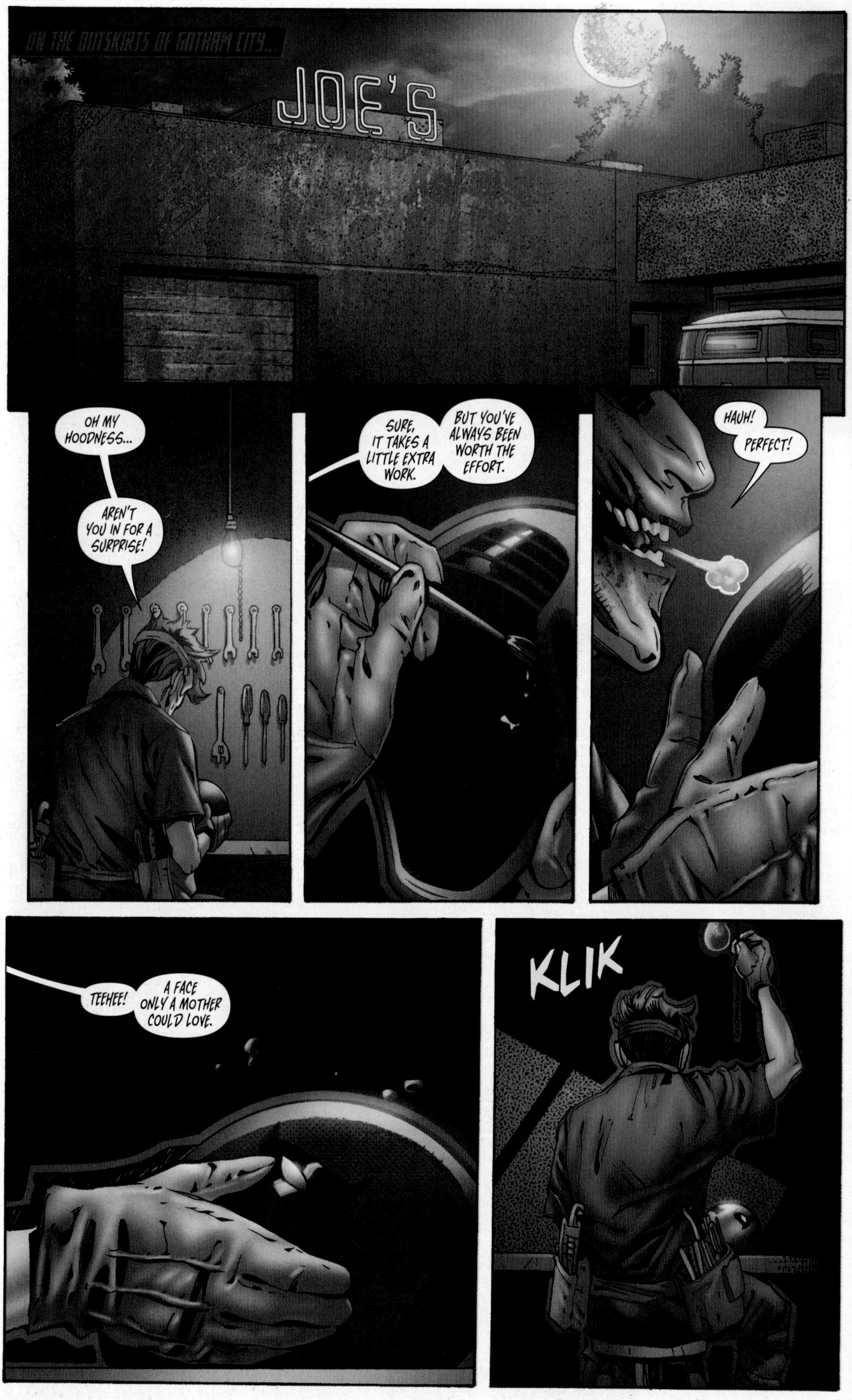
ON THE OUTSKIRTS OF GOTHAM CITY...
JOE'S
OH MY HOODNESS...
AREN'T YOU IN FOR A SURPRISE!
SURE, IT TAKES A LITTLE EXTRA WORK.
BUT YOU'VE ALWAYS BEEN WORTH THE EFFORT.
HAUH!
PERFECT!
TEEHEE!
A FACE ONLY A MOTHER COULD LOVE.
KLIK

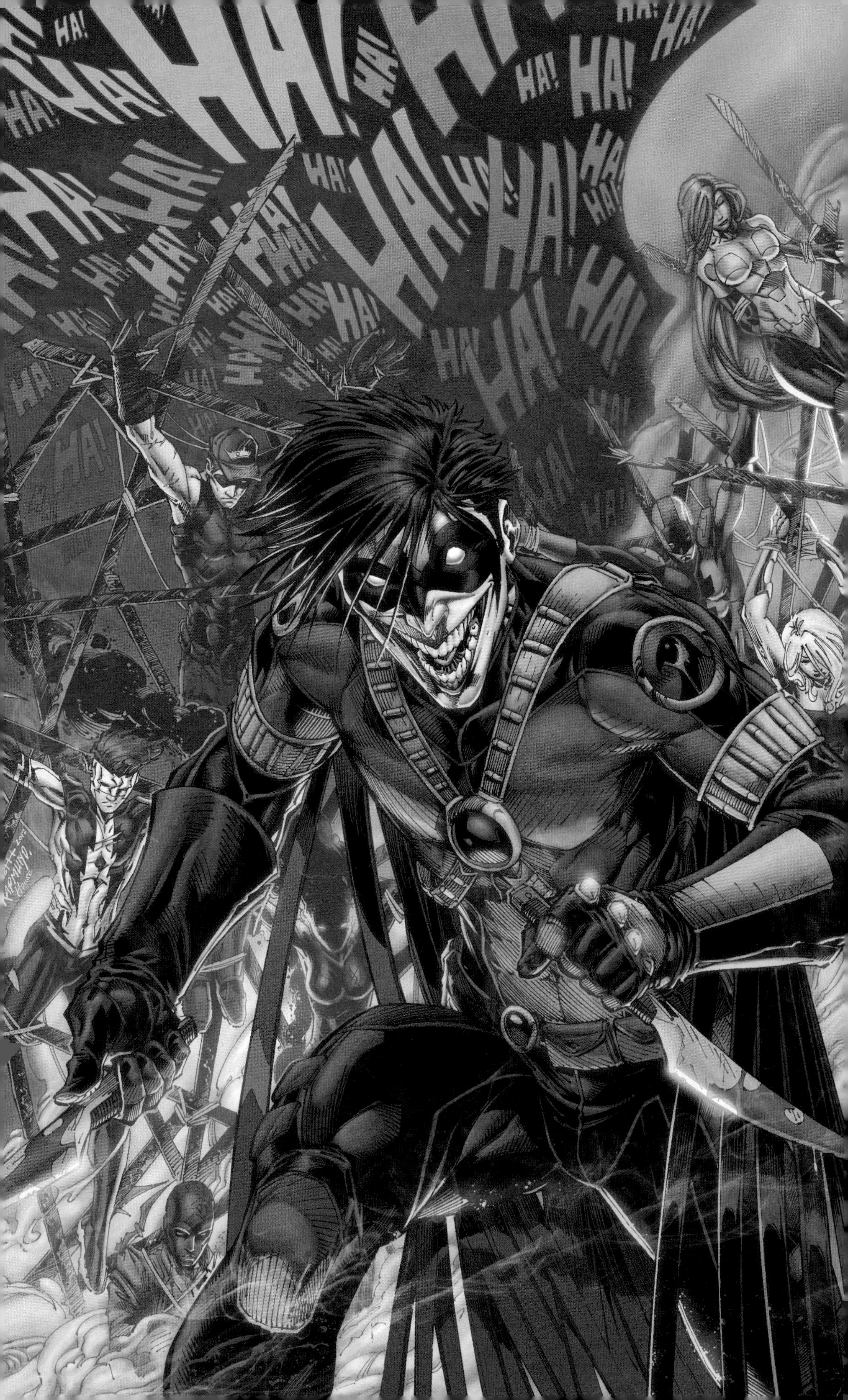
HA! HA! HA! HA! HA! HA! HA! HA! HA! HA! HA! HA!
HA! HA! HA! HA! HA! HA! HA! HA! HA! HA! HA! HA!
HA! HA! HA! HA! HA! HA! HA! HA! HA! HA! HA! HA!

GOTHAM RUNS RED!

SCOTT LOBDELL & FABIAN NICIEZA writers **BRETT BOOTH** penciller **NORM RAPMUND** inker

cover art by **BRETT BOOTH, NORM RAPMUND & ANDREW DALHOUSE**

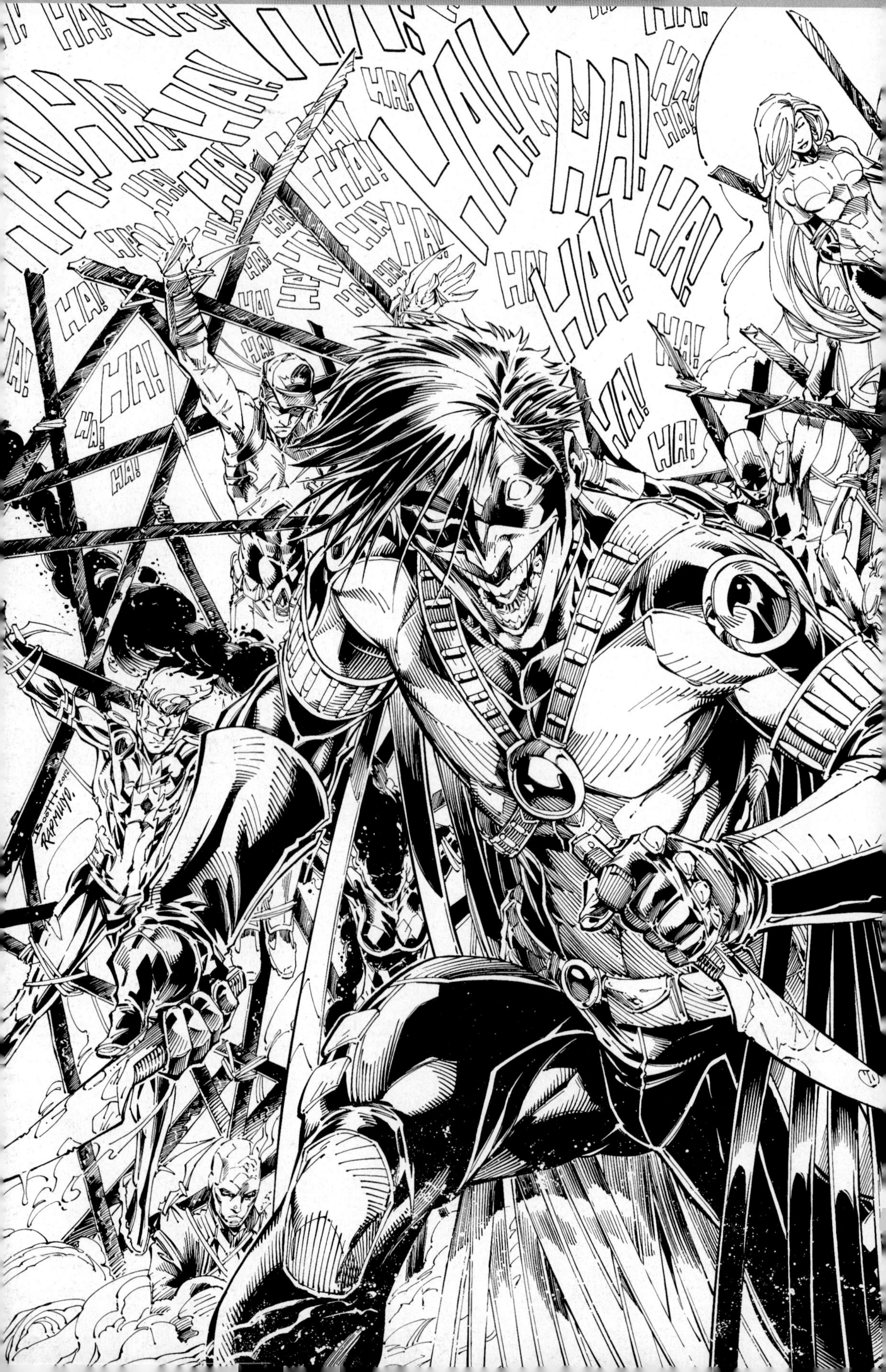
HA!
HA!
HA!
HA!
HA!
HA!
HA!
HA!
HA!
HA!
HA!
HA!

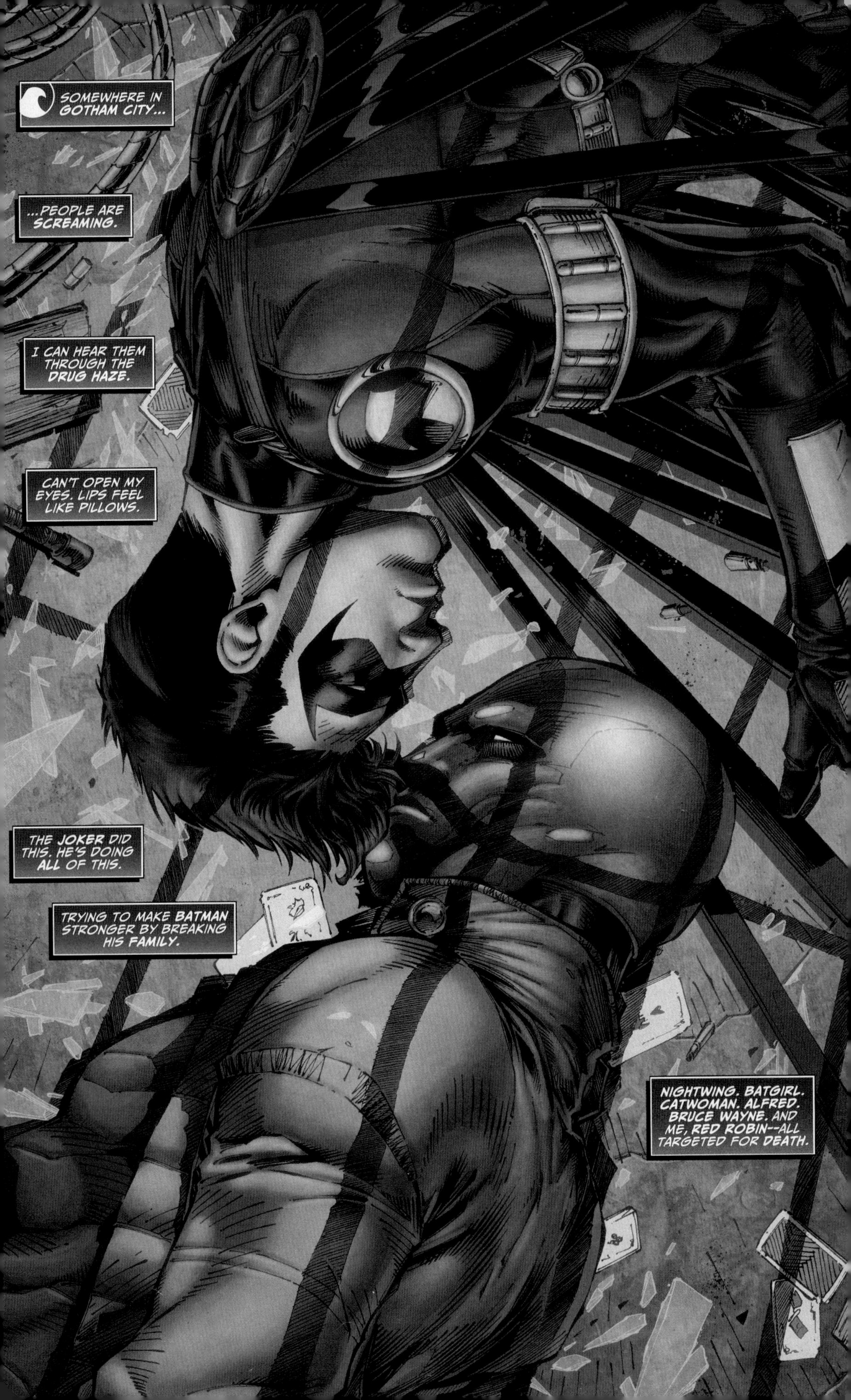
SOMEWHERE IN GOTHAM CITY...
...PEOPLE ARE SCREAMING.
I CAN HEAR THEM THROUGH THE DRUG HAZE.
CAN'T OPEN MY EYES. LIPS FEEL LIKE PILLOWS.
THE JOKER DID THIS. HE'S DOING ALL OF THIS.
TRYING TO MAKE BATMAN STRONGER BY BREAKING HIS FAMILY.
NIGHTWING. BATGIRL. CATWOMAN. ALFRED. BRUCE WAYNE. AND ME, RED ROBIN--ALL TARGETED FOR DEATH.

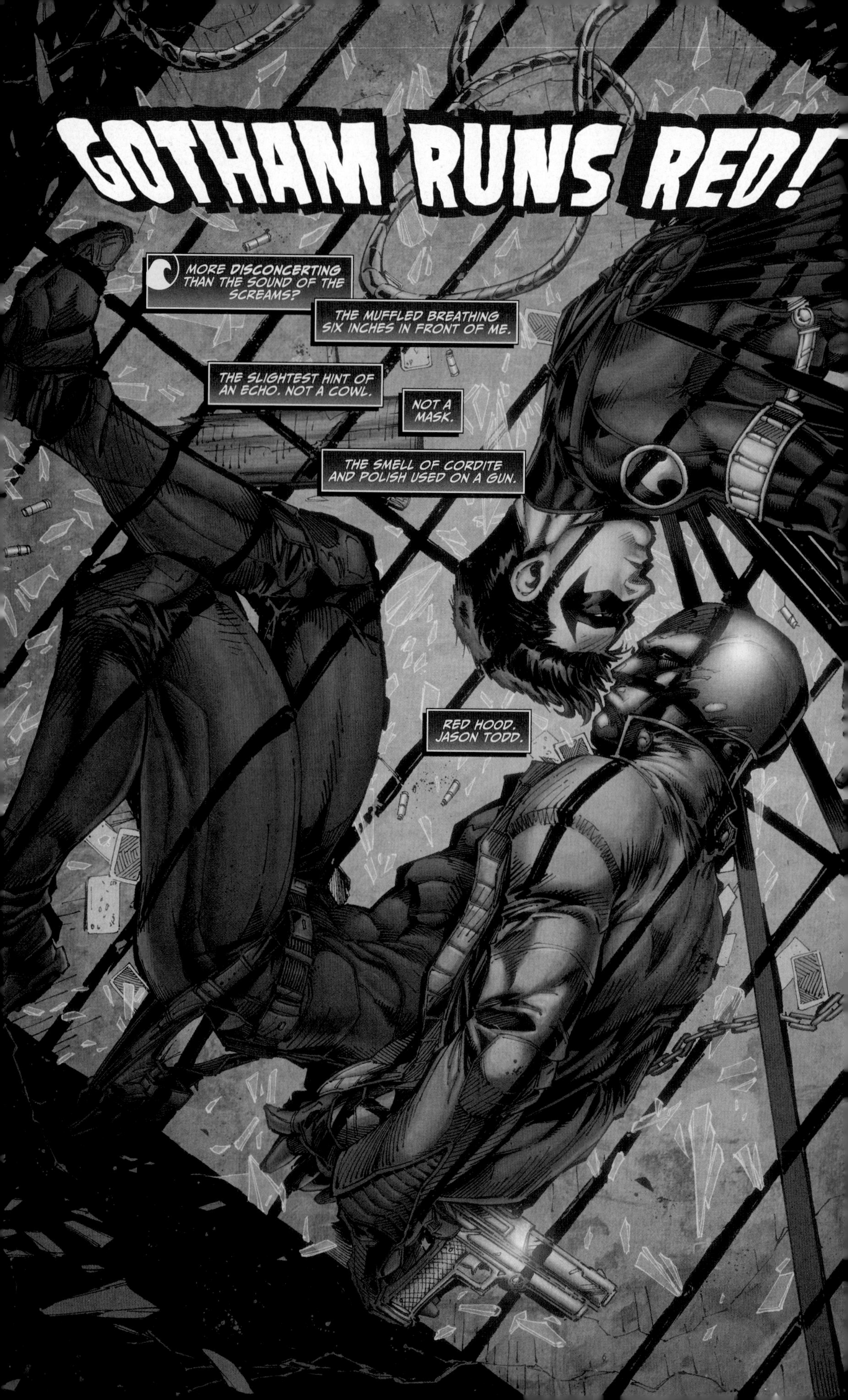

GOTHAM RUNS RED!
MORE DISCONCERTING THAN THE SOUND OF THE SCREAMS?
THE MUFFLED BREATHING SIX INCHES IN FRONT OF ME.
THE SLIGHTEST HINT OF AN ECHO. NOT A COWL.
NOT A MASK.
THE SMELL OF CORDITE AND POLISH USED ON A GUN.
RED HOOD. JASON TODD.

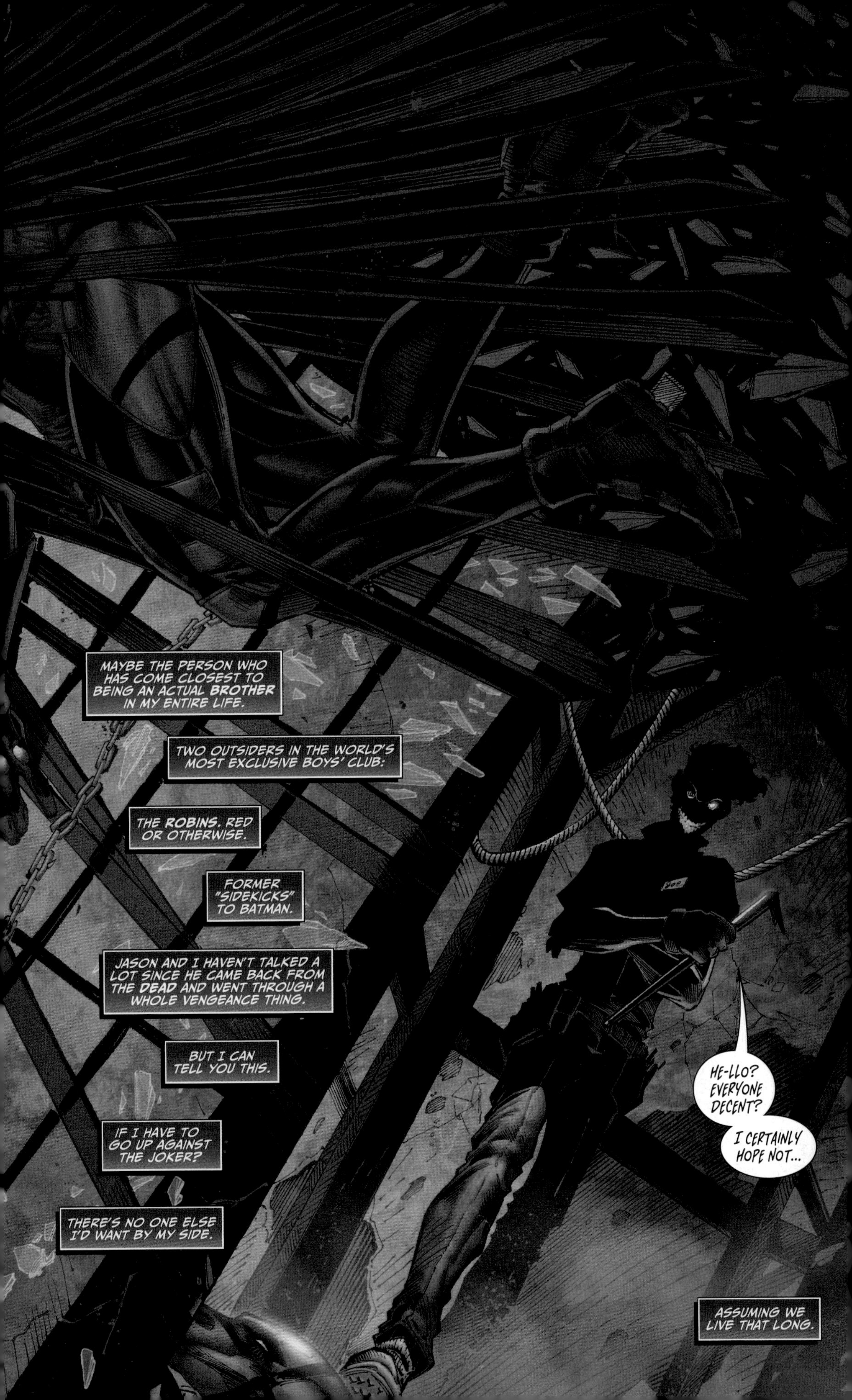
MAYBE THE PERSON WHO HAS COME CLOSEST TO BEING AN ACTUAL BROTHER IN MY ENTIRE LIFE.
TWO OUTSIDERS IN THE WORLD'S MOST EXCLUSIVE BOYS' CLUB:
THE ROBINS. RED OR OTHERWISE.
FORMER "SIDEKICKS" TO BATMAN.
JASON AND I HAVEN'T TALKED A LOT SINCE HE CAME BACK FROM THE DEAD AND WENT THROUGH A WHOLE VENGEANCE THING.
BUT I CAN TELL YOU THIS.
IF I HAVE TO GO UP AGAINST THE JOKER?
THERE'S NO ONE ELSE I'D WANT BY MY SIDE.
HE-LLO? EVERYONE DECENT?
I CERTAINLY HOPE NOT...
ASSUMING WE LIVE THAT LONG.

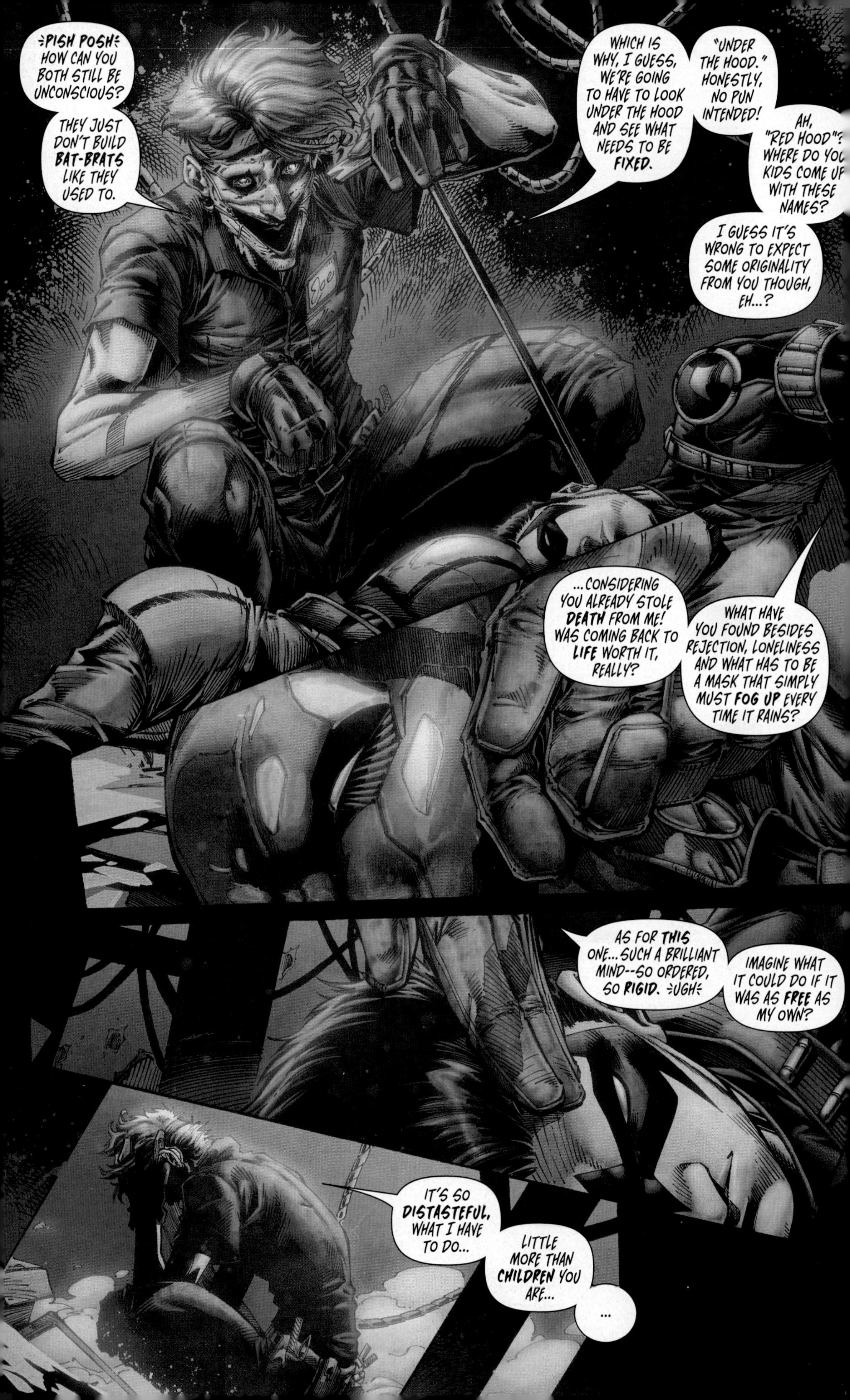

PISH POSH HOW CAN YOU BOTH STILL BE UNCONSCIOUS?
THEY JUST DON'T BUILD BAT-BRATS LIKE THEY USED TO.
WHICH IS WHY, I GUESS, WE'RE GOING TO HAVE TO LOOK UNDER THE HOOD AND SEE WHAT NEEDS TO BE FIXED.
"UNDER THE HOOD." HONESTLY, NO PUN INTENDED!
AH, "RED HOOD"? WHERE DO YOU KIDS COME UP WITH THESE NAMES?
I GUESS IT'S WRONG TO EXPECT SOME ORIGINALITY FROM YOU THOUGH, EH...?
...CONSIDERING YOU ALREADY STOLE DEATH FROM ME! WAS COMING BACK TO LIFE WORTH IT, REALLY?
WHAT HAVE YOU FOUND BESIDES REJECTION, LONELINESS AND WHAT HAS TO BE A MASK THAT SIMPLY MUST FOG UP EVERY TIME IT RAINS?
AS FOR THIS ONE... SUCH A BRILLIANT MIND--SO ORDERED, SO RIGID. UGH
IMAGINE WHAT IT COULD DO IF IT WAS AS FREE AS MY OWN?
IT'S SO DISTASTEFUL, WHAT I HAVE TO DO...
LITTLE MORE THAN CHILDREN YOU ARE...
...

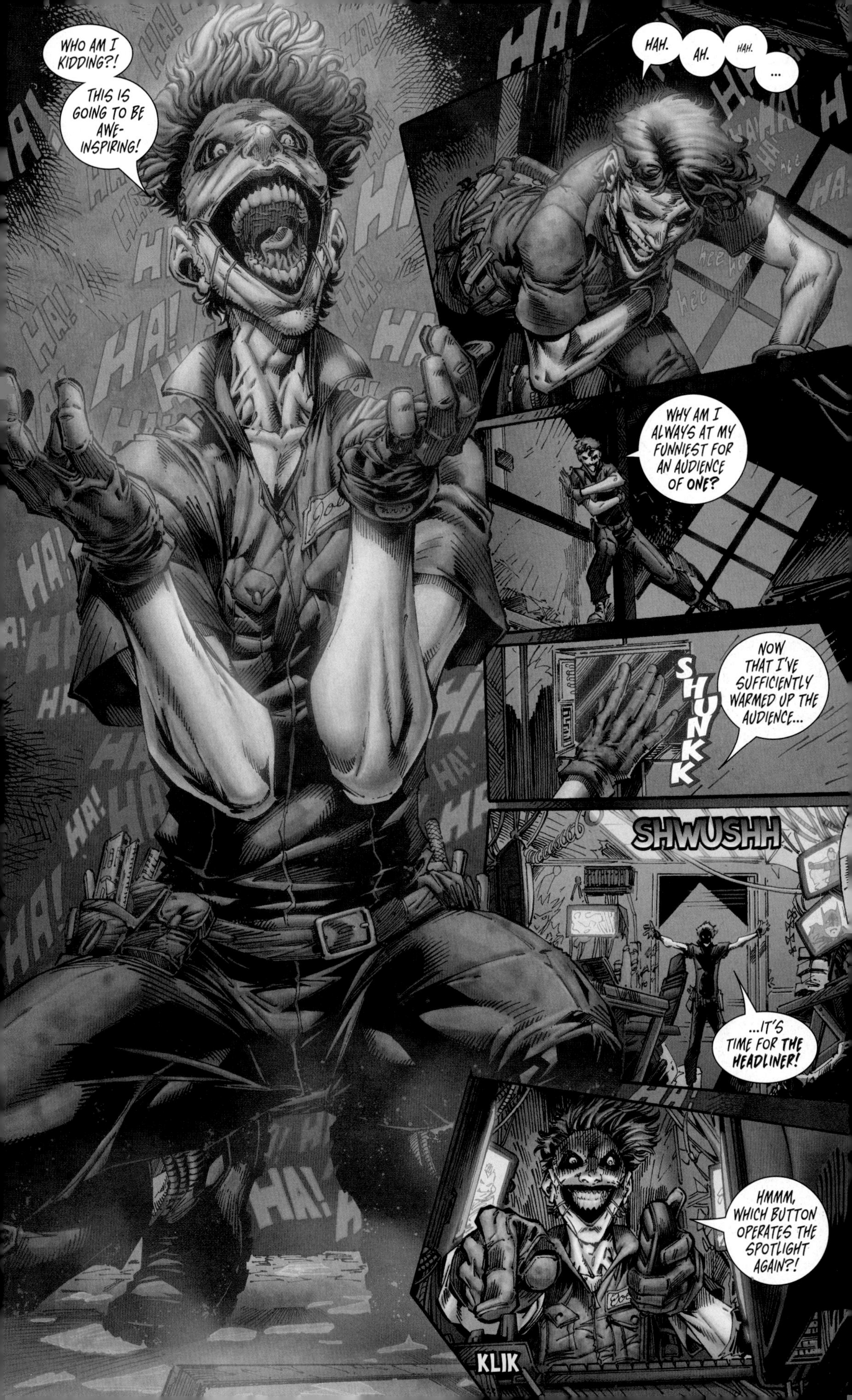

WHO AM I KIDDING?!
THIS IS GOING TO BE AWE-INSPIRING!
HA! HA! HA!
HAH.
AH.
HAH.
...
WHY AM I ALWAYS AT MY FUNNIEST FOR AN AUDIENCE OF ONE?
SHUNKK
NOW THAT I'VE SUFFICIENTLY WARMED UP THE AUDIENCE...
SHWUSHH
...IT'S TIME FOR THE HEADLINER!
HMMM, WHICH BUTTON OPERATES THE SPOTLIGHT AGAIN?!
KLIK

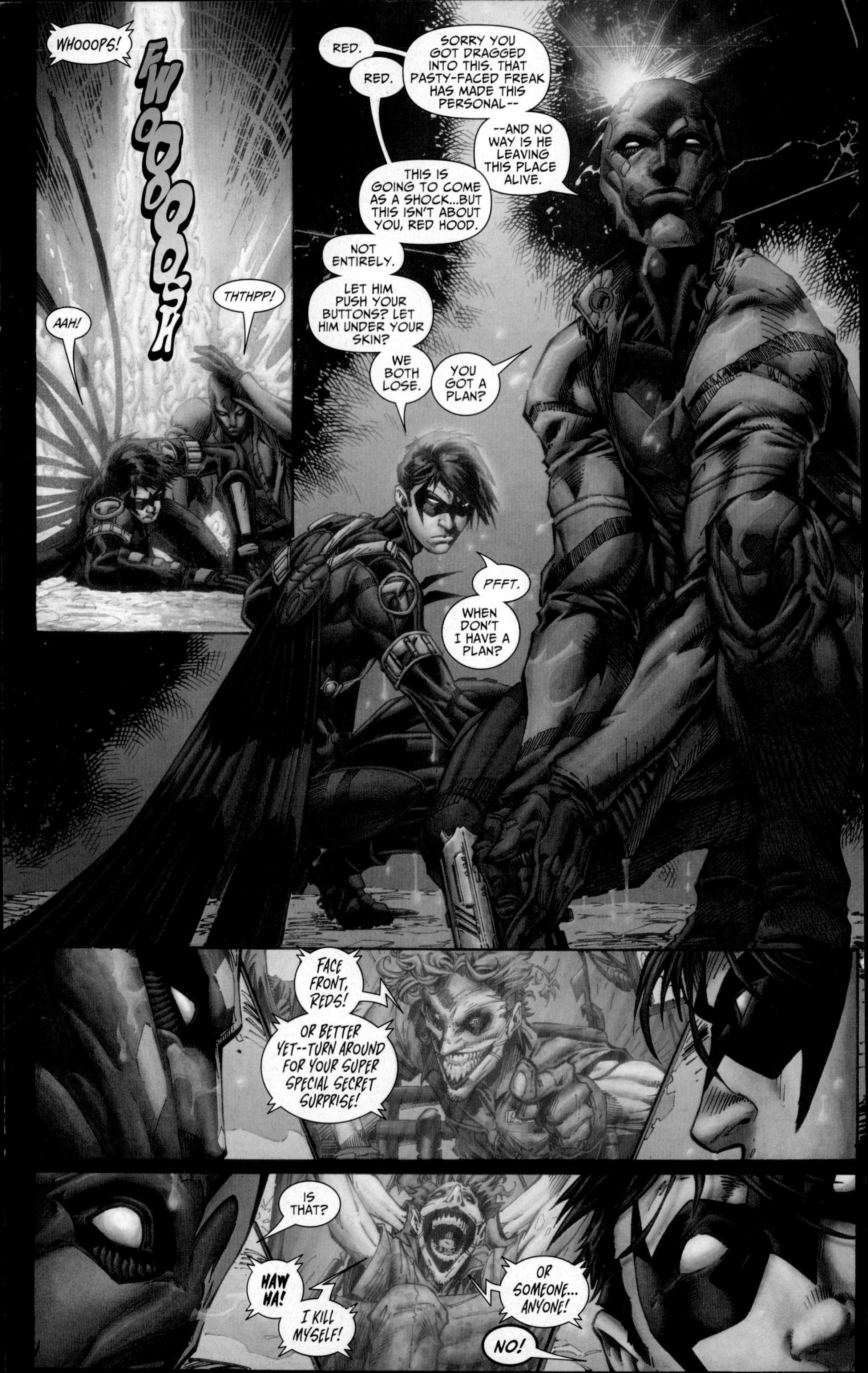

WHOOOPS!
FWOOOOOOSH
AAH!
THTHPP!
RED.
SORRY YOU GOT DRAGGED INTO THIS. THAT PASTY-FACED FREAK HAS MADE THIS PERSONAL--
--AND NO WAY IS HE LEAVING THIS PLACE ALIVE.
RED.
THIS IS GOING TO COME AS A SHOCK...BUT THIS ISN'T ABOUT YOU, RED HOOD.
NOT ENTIRELY.
LET HIM PUSH YOUR BUTTONS? LET HIM UNDER YOUR SKIN?
WE BOTH LOSE.
YOU GOT A PLAN?
PFFT.
WHEN DON'T I HAVE A PLAN?
FACE FRONT, REDS!
OR BETTER YET--TURN AROUND FOR YOUR SUPER SPECIAL SECRET SURPRISE!
IS THAT?
HAW HA!
I KILL MYSELF!
OR SOMEONE... ANYONE!
NO!

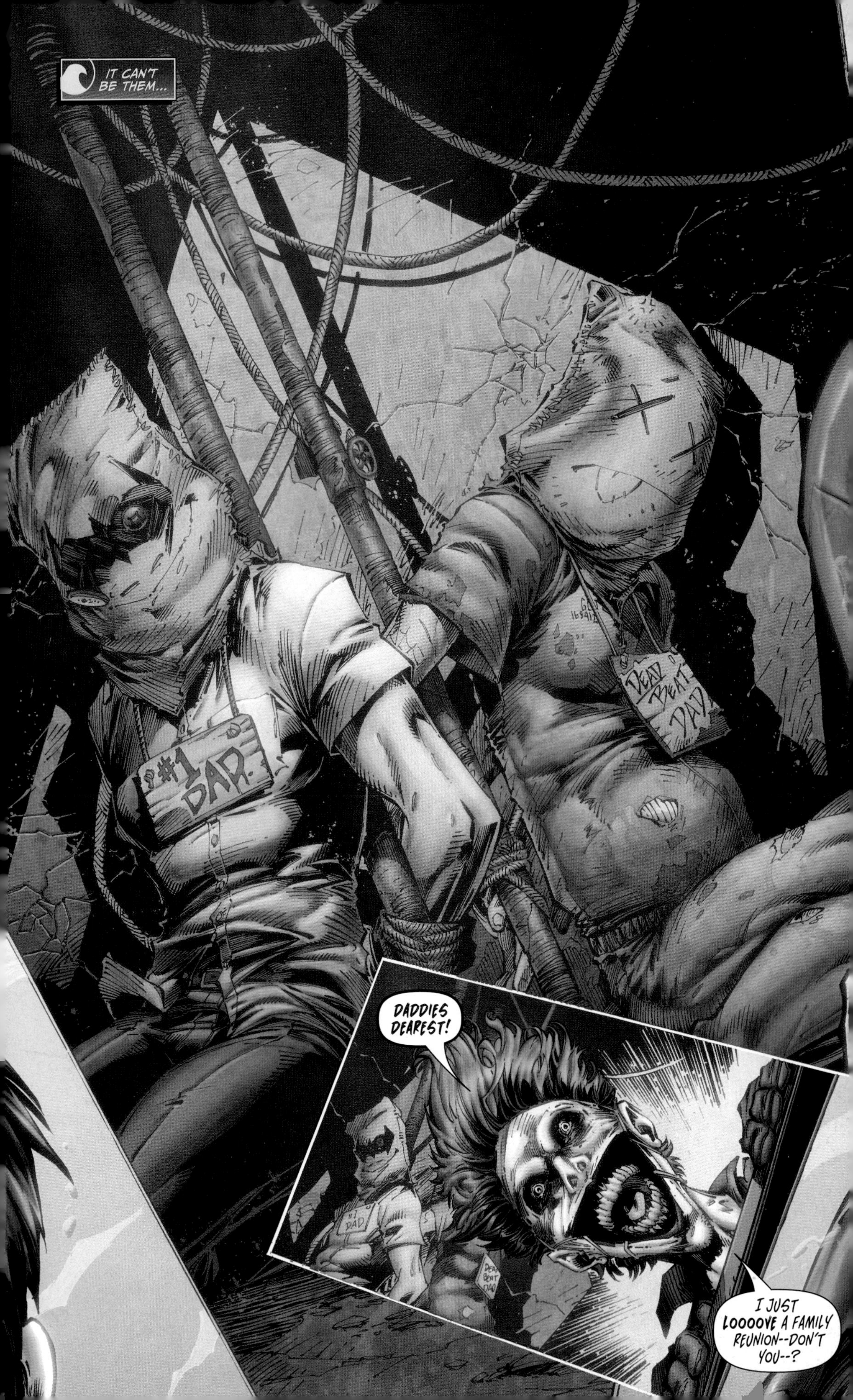
IT CAN'T BE THEM...
#1 DAD.
DEAD BEAT DAD
DADDIES DEAREST!
I JUST LOOOOVE A FAMILY REUNION--DON'T YOU--?

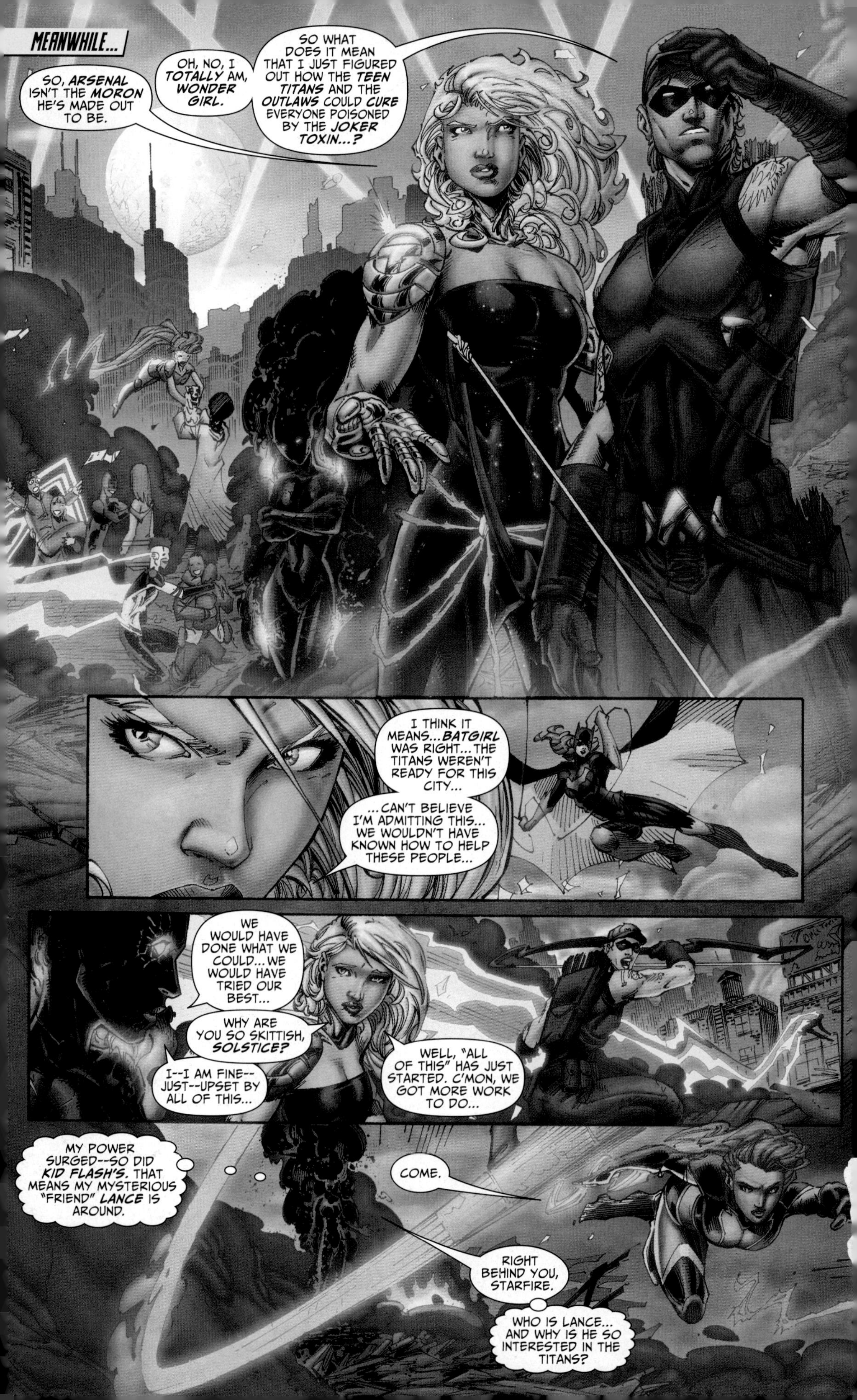
MEANWHILE...
SO, ARSENAL ISN'T THE MORON HE'S MADE OUT TO BE.
OH, NO, I TOTALLY AM, WONDER GIRL.
SO WHAT DOES IT MEAN THAT I JUST FIGURED OUT HOW THE TEEN TITANS AND THE OUTLAWS COULD CURE EVERYONE POISONED BY THE JOKER TOXIN...?
I THINK IT MEANS...BATGIRL WAS RIGHT...THE TITANS WEREN'T READY FOR THIS CITY...
...CAN'T BELIEVE I'M ADMITTING THIS... WE WOULDN'T HAVE KNOWN HOW TO HELP THESE PEOPLE...
WE WOULD HAVE DONE WHAT WE COULD...WE WOULD HAVE TRIED OUR BEST...
WHY ARE YOU SO SKITTISH, SOLSTICE?
I--I AM FINE-- JUST--UPSET BY ALL OF THIS...
WELL, "ALL OF THIS" HAS JUST STARTED. C'MON, WE GOT MORE WORK TO DO...
MY POWER SURGED--SO DID KID FLASH'S. THAT MEANS MY MYSTERIOUS "FRIEND" LANCE IS AROUND.
COME.
RIGHT BEHIND YOU, STARFIRE.
WHO IS LANCE... AND WHY IS HE SO INTERESTED IN THE TITANS?

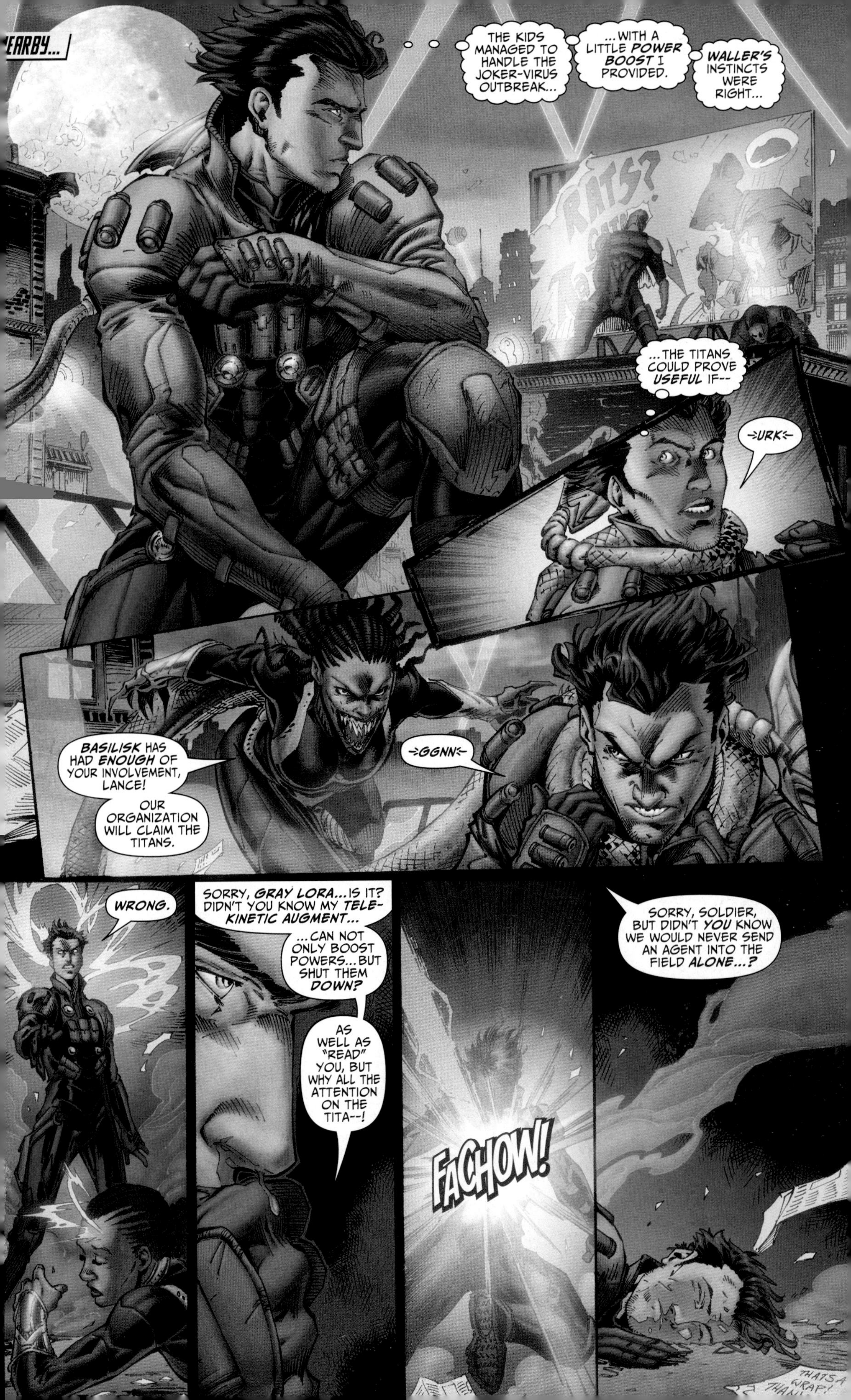
EARBY...
THE KIDS MANAGED TO HANDLE THE JOKER-VIRUS OUTBREAK...
...WITH A LITTLE POWER BOOST I PROVIDED.
WALLER'S INSTINCTS WERE RIGHT...
...THE TITANS COULD PROVE USEFUL IF--
URK
BASILISK HAS HAD ENOUGH OF YOUR INVOLVEMENT, LANCE!
OUR ORGANIZATION WILL CLAIM THE TITANS.
GGNN
WRONG.
SORRY, GRAY LORA...IS IT? DIDN'T YOU KNOW MY TELE-KINETIC AUGMENT...
...CAN NOT ONLY BOOST POWERS...BUT SHUT THEM DOWN?
AS WELL AS "READ" YOU, BUT WHY ALL THE ATTENTION ON THE TITA--!
FACHOW!
SORRY, SOLDIER, BUT DIDN'T YOU KNOW WE WOULD NEVER SEND AN AGENT INTO THE FIELD ALONE...?

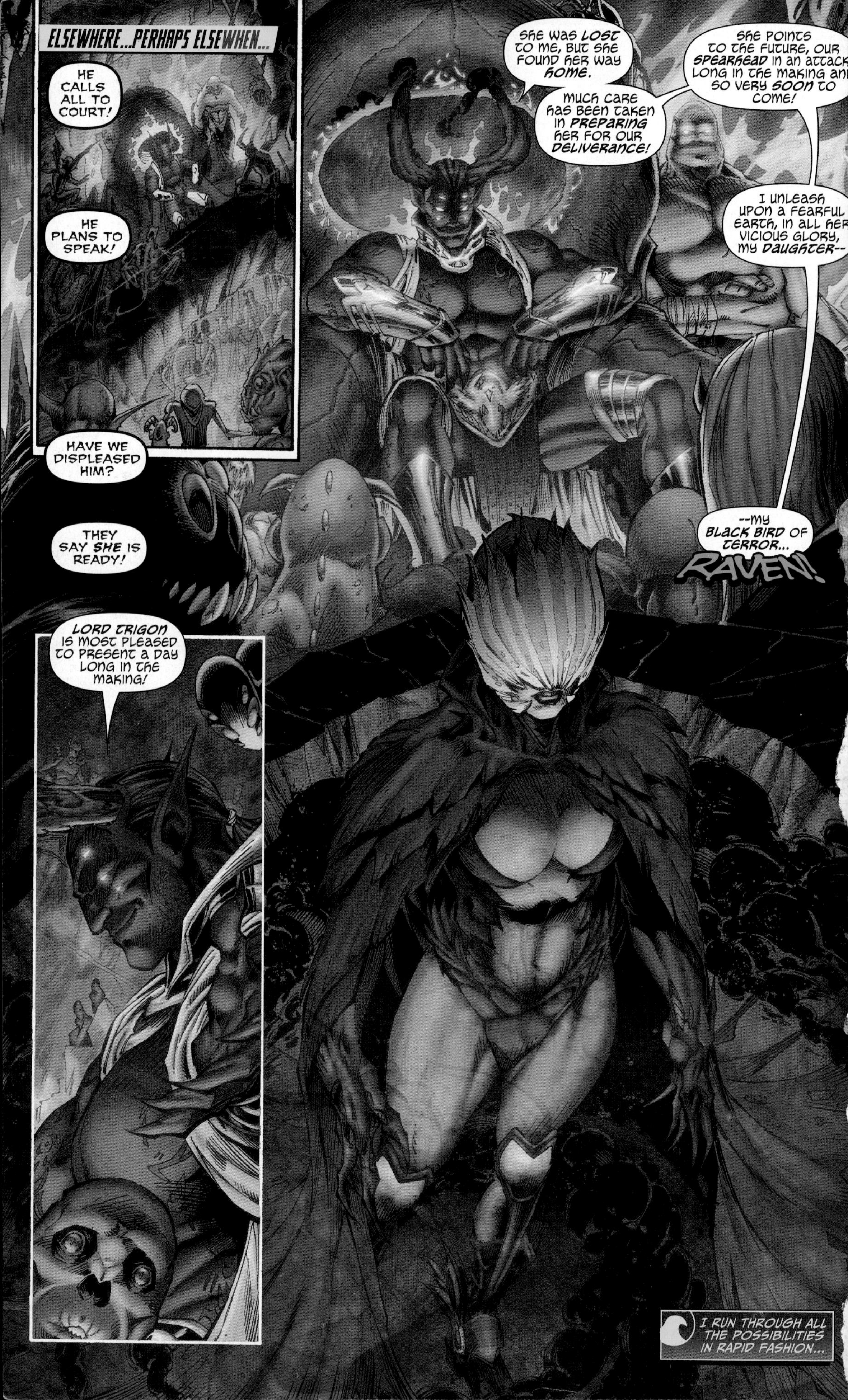

ELSEWHERE...PERHAPS ELSEWHEN...
HE CALLS ALL TO COURT!
HE PLANS TO SPEAK!
HAVE WE DISPLEASED HIM?
THEY SAY SHE IS READY!
SHE WAS LOST TO ME, BUT SHE FOUND HER WAY HOME.
MUCH CARE HAS BEEN TAKEN IN PREPARING HER FOR OUR DELIVERANCE!
SHE POINTS TO THE FUTURE, OUR SPEARHEAD IN AN ATTACK LONG IN THE MAKING AND SO VERY SOON TO COME!
I UNLEASH UPON A FEARFUL EARTH, IN ALL HER VICIOUS GLORY, MY DAUGHTER--
LORD TRIGON IS MOST PLEASED TO PRESENT A DAY LONG IN THE MAKING!
--MY BLACK BIRD OF TERROR...
RAVEN!
I RUN THROUGH ALL THE POSSIBILITIES IN RAPID FASHION...

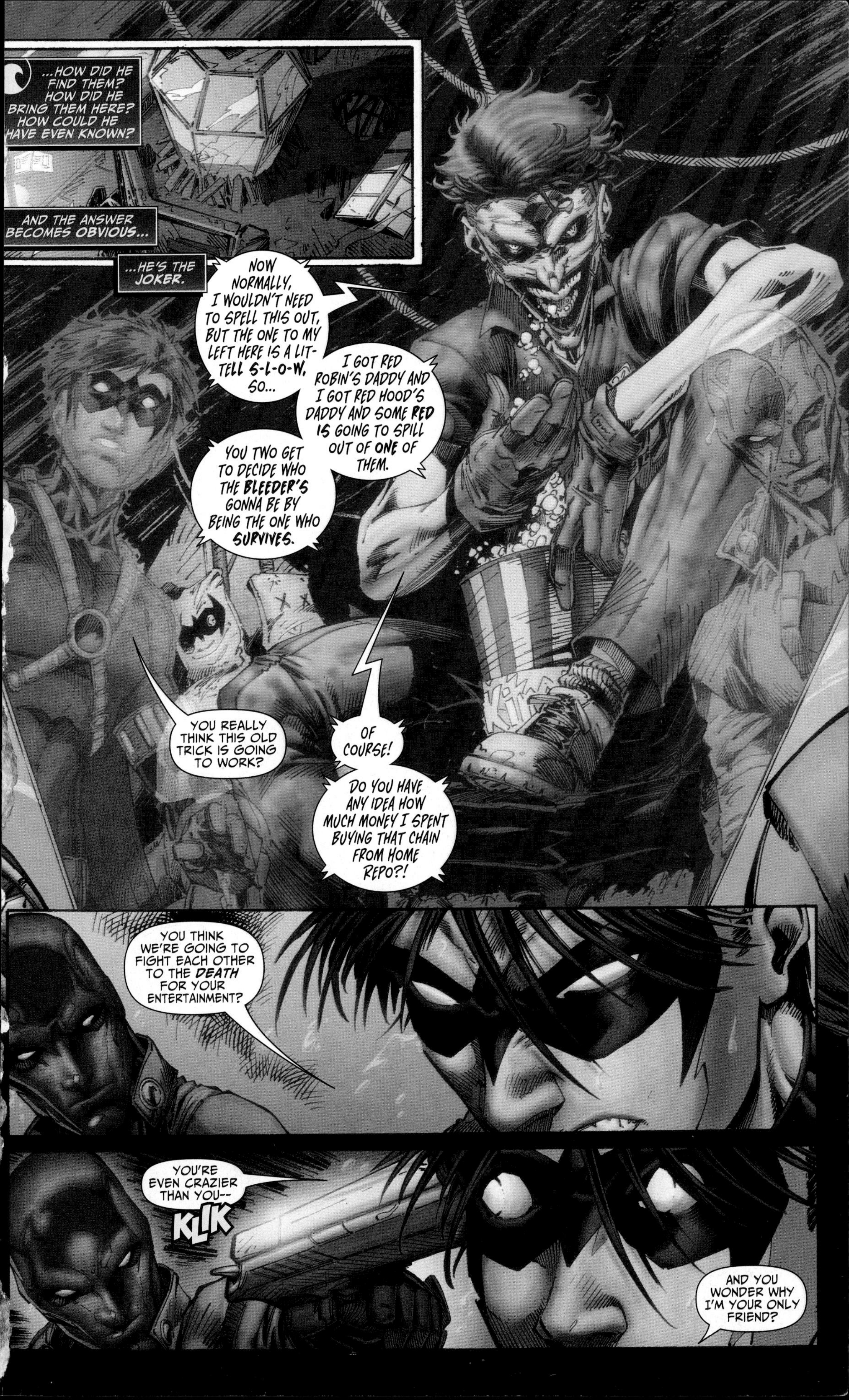
...HOW DID HE FIND THEM? HOW DID HE BRING THEM HERE? HOW COULD HE HAVE EVEN KNOWN?
AND THE ANSWER BECOMES OBVIOUS...
...HE'S THE JOKER.
NOW NORMALLY, I WOULDN'T NEED TO SPELL THIS OUT, BUT THE ONE TO MY LEFT HERE IS A LIT-TELL S-L-O-W, SO...
I GOT RED ROBIN'S DADDY AND I GOT RED HOOD'S DADDY AND SOME RED IS GOING TO SPILL OUT OF ONE OF THEM.
YOU TWO GET TO DECIDE WHO THE BLEEDER'S GONNA BE BY BEING THE ONE WHO SURVIVES.
YOU REALLY THINK THIS OLD TRICK IS GOING TO WORK?
OF COURSE!
DO YOU HAVE ANY IDEA HOW MUCH MONEY I SPENT BUYING THAT CHAIN FROM HOME REPO?!
YOU THINK WE'RE GOING TO FIGHT EACH OTHER TO THE DEATH FOR YOUR ENTERTAINMENT?
YOU'RE EVEN CRAZIER THAN YOU--
KLIK
AND YOU WONDER WHY I'M YOUR ONLY FRIEND?

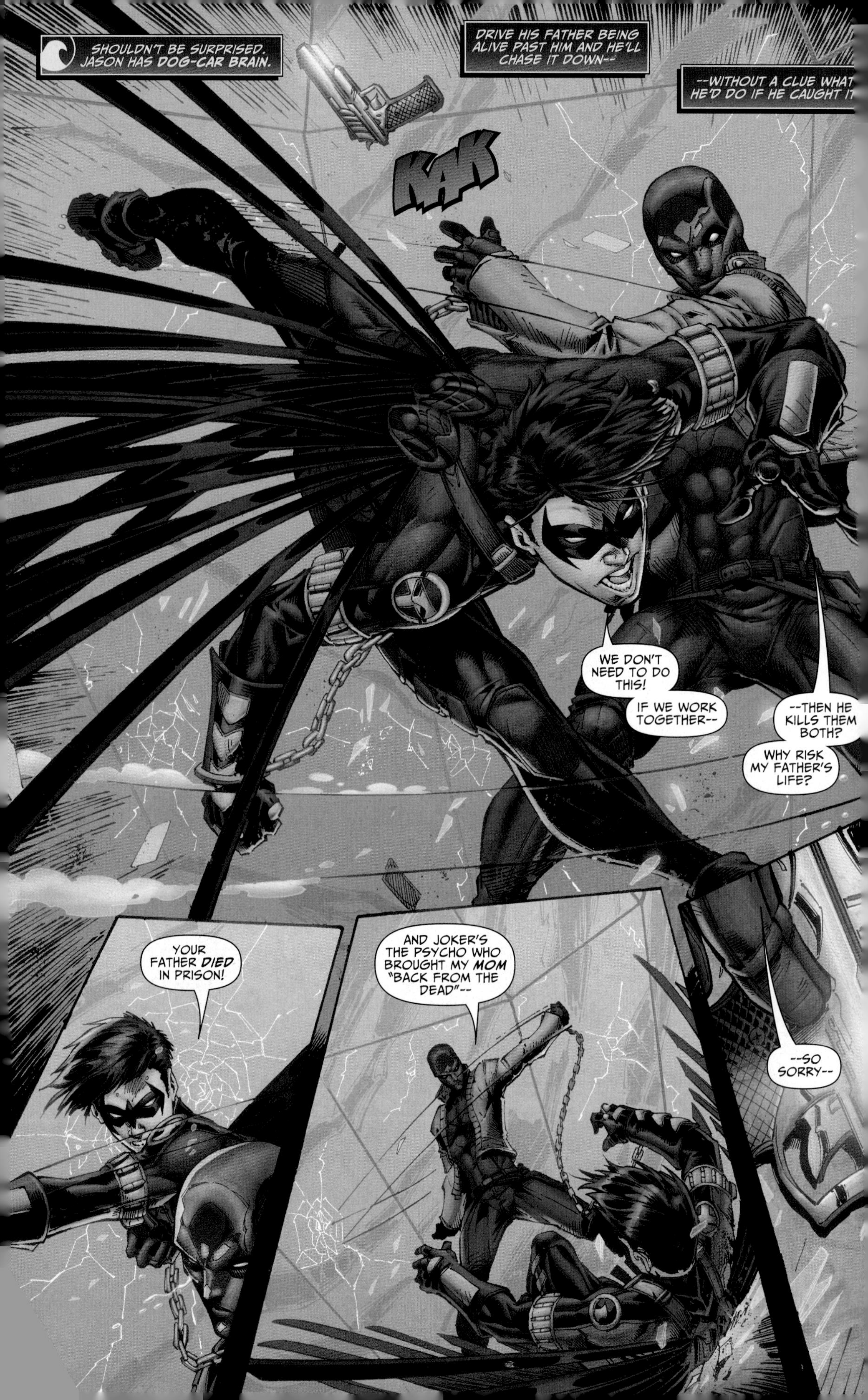
SHOULDN'T BE SURPRISED. JASON HAS DOG-CAR BRAIN.
DRIVE HIS FATHER BEING ALIVE PAST HIM AND HE'LL CHASE IT DOWN--
--WITHOUT A CLUE WHAT HE'D DO IF HE CAUGHT IT.
KAK
WE DON'T NEED TO DO THIS!
IF WE WORK TOGETHER--
--THEN HE KILLS THEM BOTH?
WHY RISK MY FATHER'S LIFE?
YOUR FATHER DIED IN PRISON!
AND JOKER'S THE PSYCHO WHO BROUGHT MY MOM "BACK FROM THE DEAD"--
--SO SORRY--

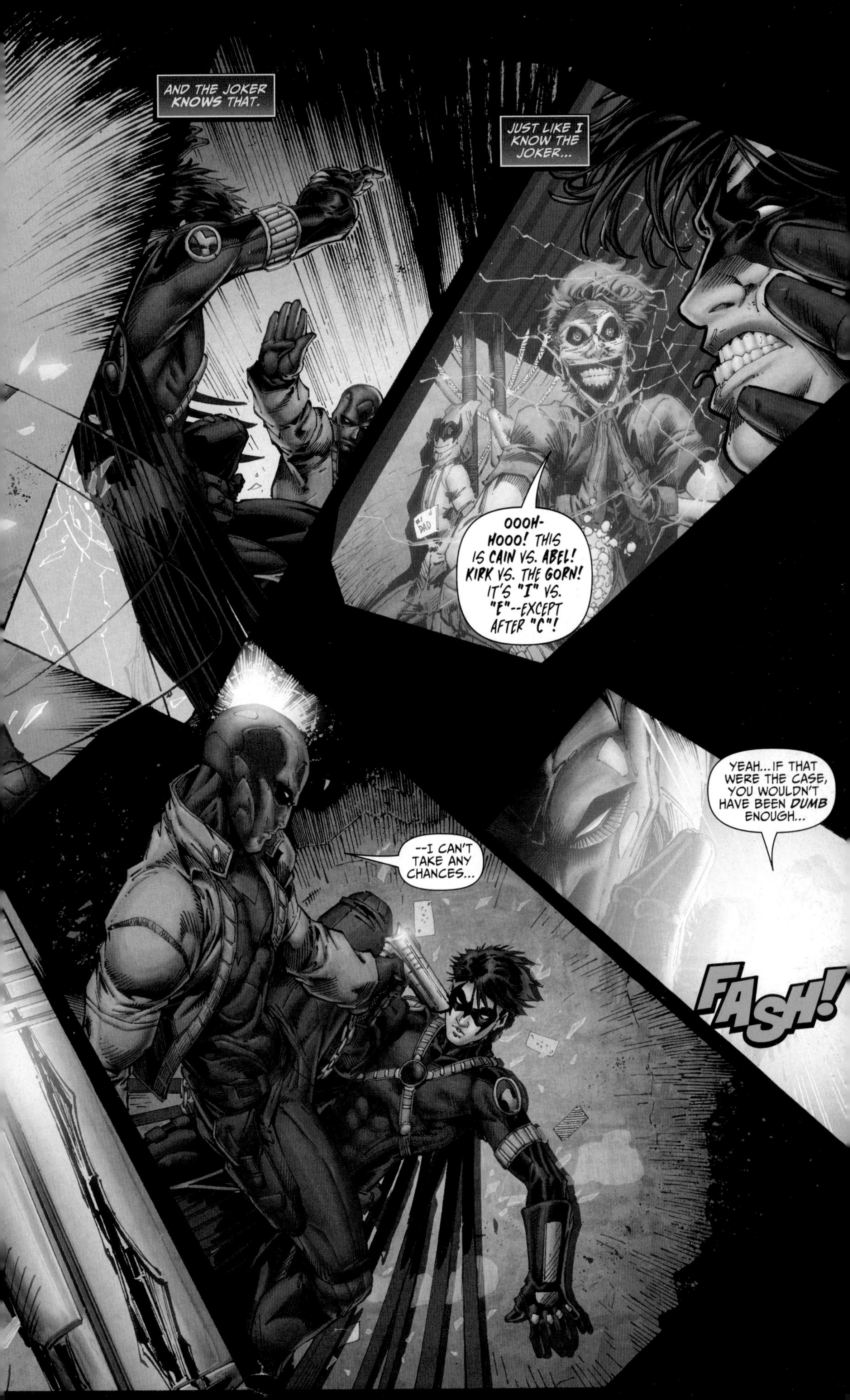
AND THE JOKER KNOWS THAT.
JUST LIKE I KNOW THE JOKER...
OOOH-HOOO! THIS IS CAIN VS. ABEL! KIRK VS. THE GORN! IT'S "I" VS. "E"--EXCEPT AFTER "C"!
#1 DAD
--I CAN'T TAKE ANY CHANCES...
YEAH...IF THAT WERE THE CASE, YOU WOULDN'T HAVE BEEN DUMB ENOUGH...
FASH!

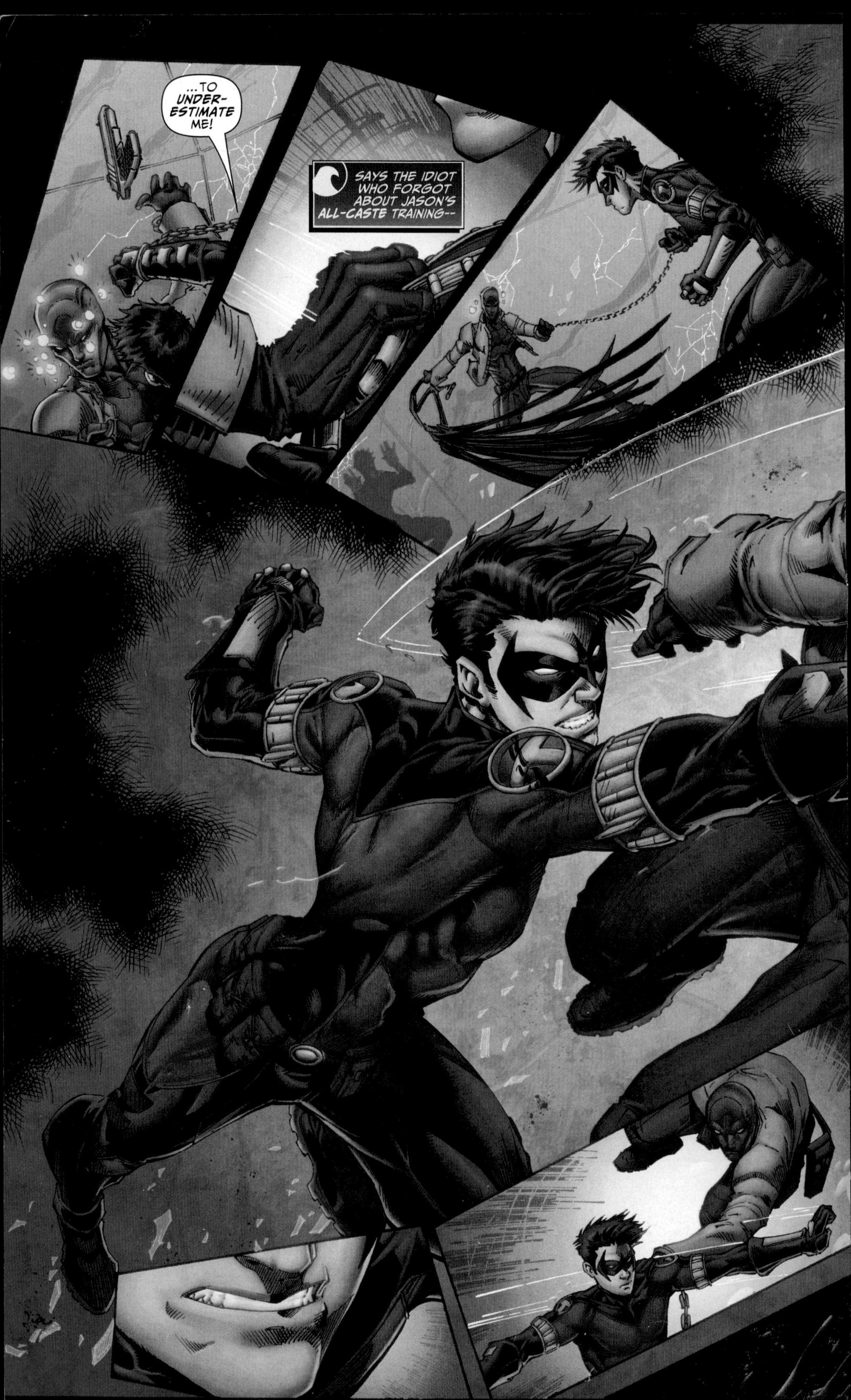
...TO UNDER-ESTIMATE ME!
SAYS THE IDIOT WHO FORGOT ABOUT JASON'S ALL-CASTE TRAINING--

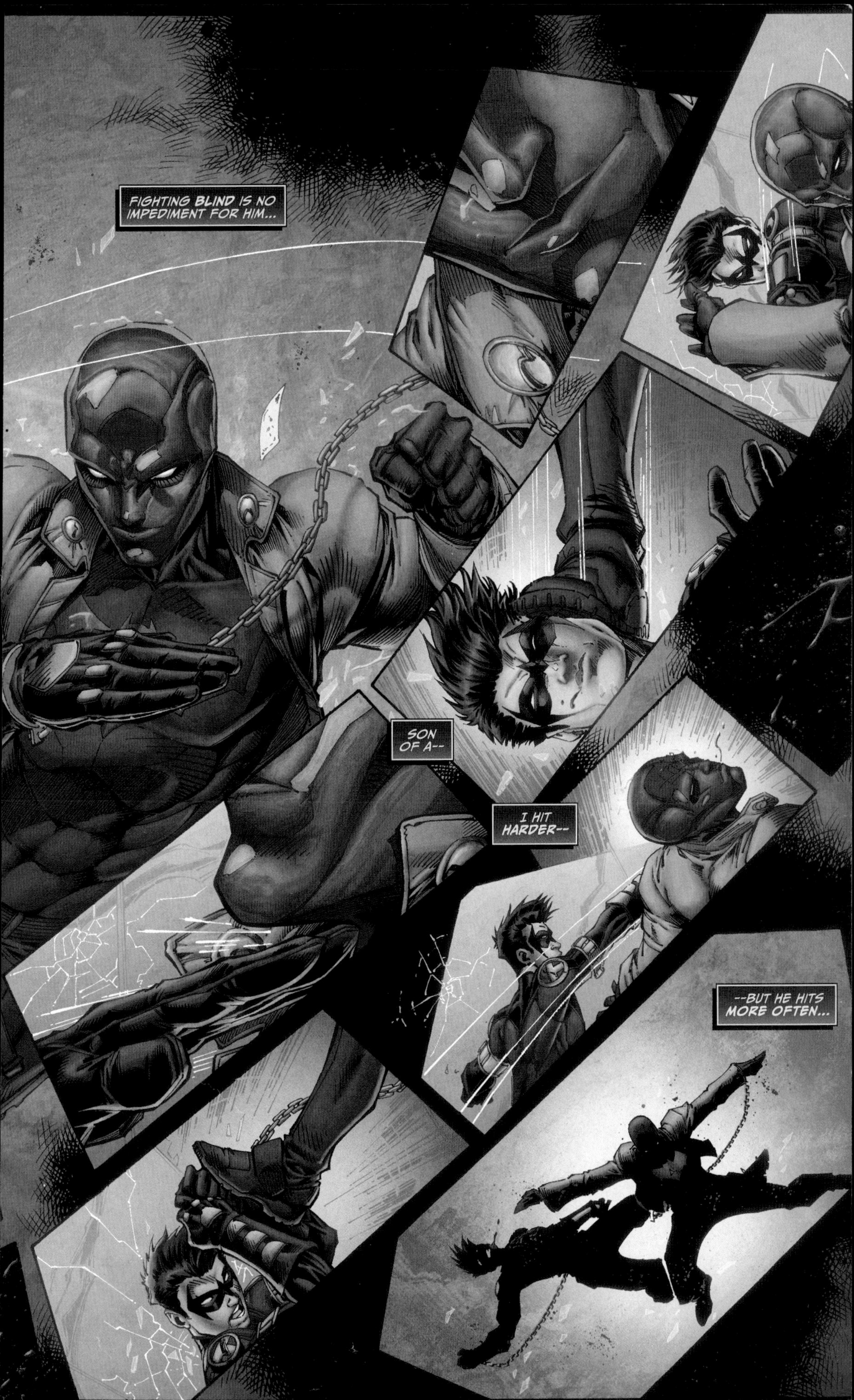
FIGHTING BLIND IS NO IMPEDIMENT FOR HIM...
SON OF A--
I HIT HARDER--
--BUT HE HITS MORE OFTEN...

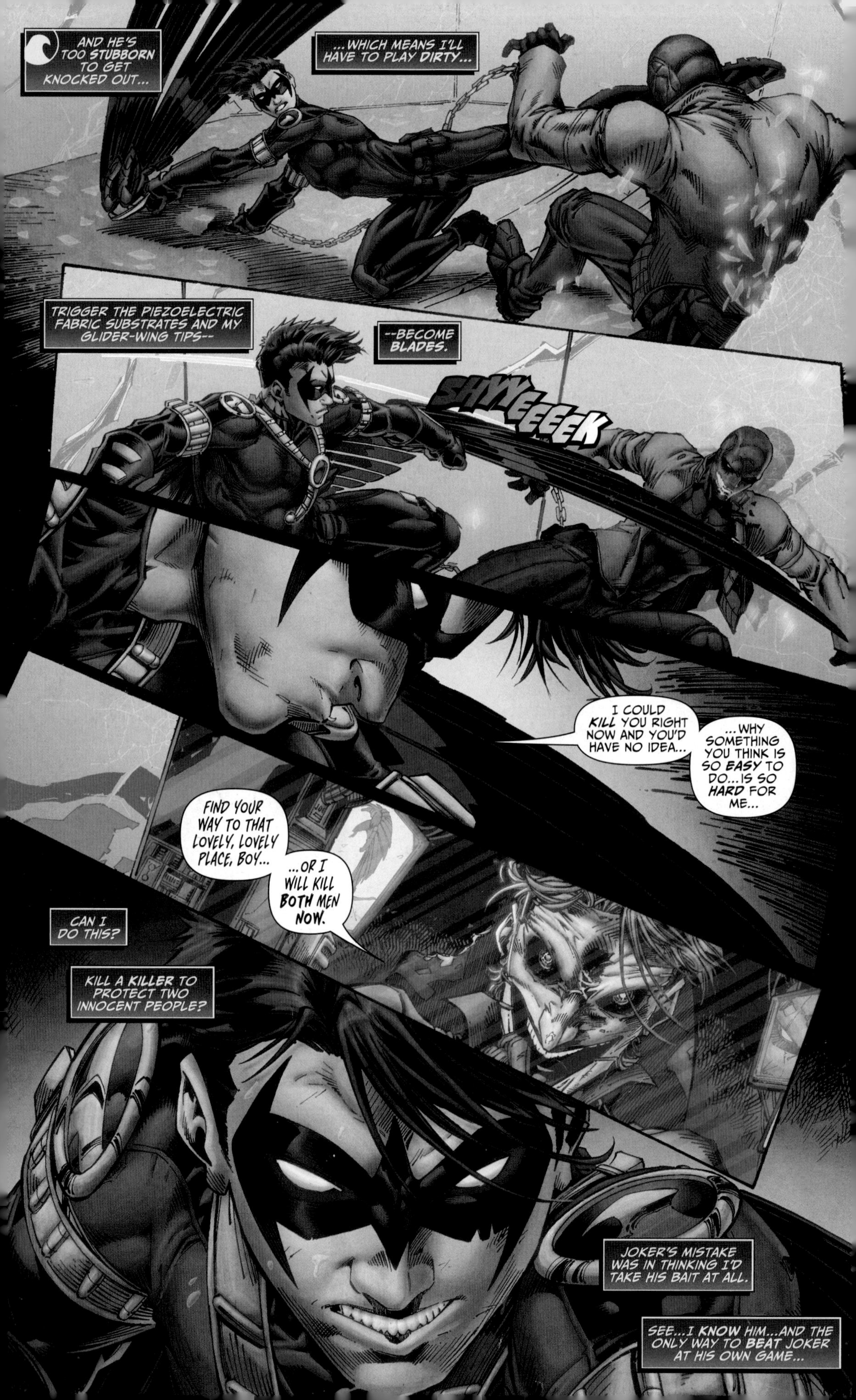
AND HE'S TOO STUBBORN TO GET KNOCKED OUT...
...WHICH MEANS I'LL HAVE TO PLAY DIRTY...
TRIGGER THE PIEZOELECTRIC FABRIC SUBSTRATES AND MY GLIDER-WING TIPS--
--BECOME BLADES.
SHYYEEEEK
I COULD KILL YOU RIGHT NOW AND YOU'D HAVE NO IDEA...
...WHY SOMETHING YOU THINK IS SO EASY TO DO...IS SO HARD FOR ME...
FIND YOUR WAY TO THAT LOVELY, LOVELY PLACE, BOY...
...OR I WILL KILL BOTH MEN NOW.
CAN I DO THIS?
KILL A KILLER TO PROTECT TWO INNOCENT PEOPLE?
JOKER'S MISTAKE WAS IN THINKING I'D TAKE HIS BAIT AT ALL.
SEE...I KNOW HIM...AND THE ONLY WAY TO BEAT JOKER AT HIS OWN GAME...

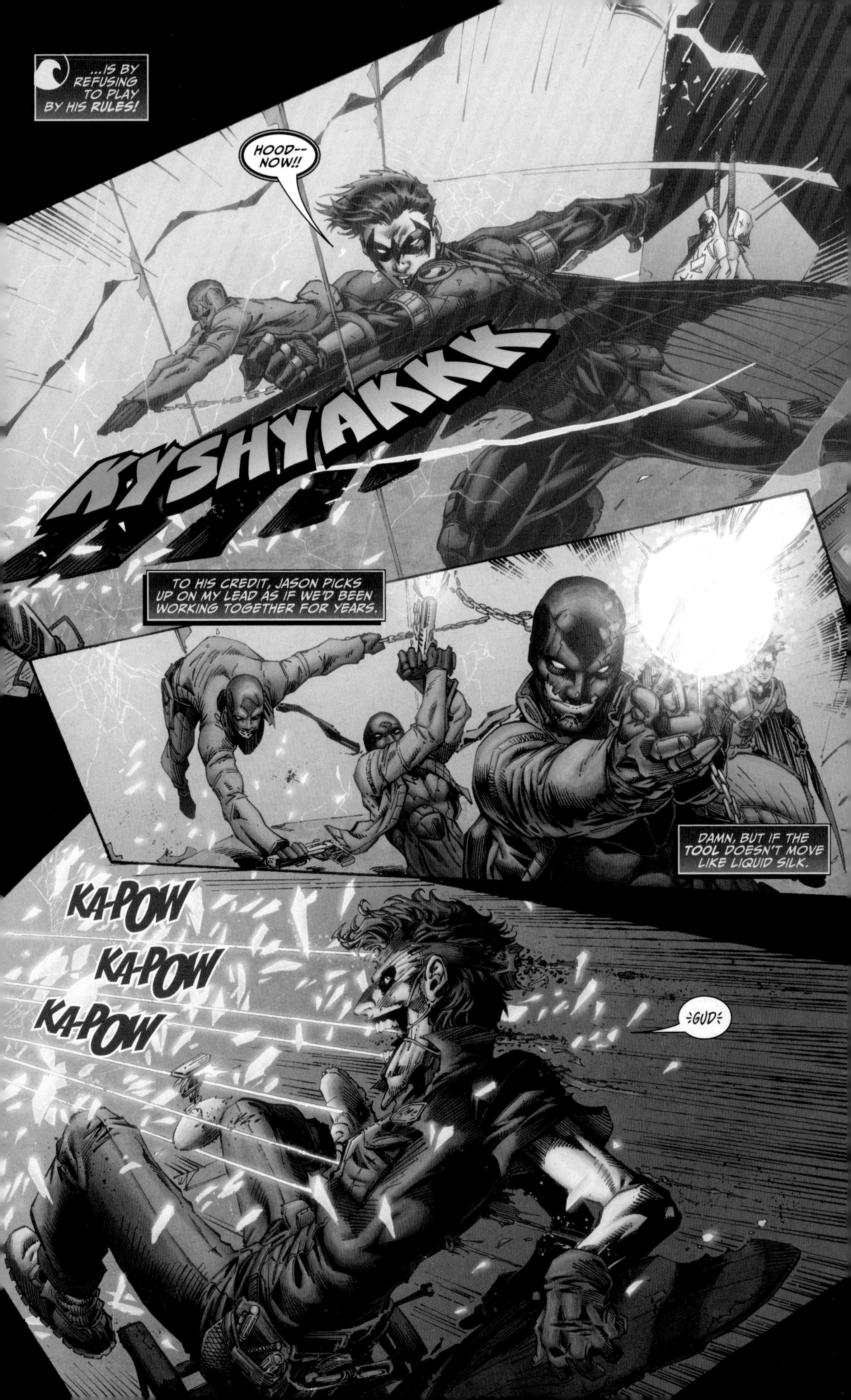
...IS BY REFUSING TO PLAY BY HIS RULES!
HOOD-- NOW!!
KYSHYAKKK
TO HIS CREDIT, JASON PICKS UP ON MY LEAD AS IF WE'D BEEN WORKING TOGETHER FOR YEARS.
DAMN, BUT IF THE TOOL DOESN'T MOVE LIKE LIQUID SILK.
KA-POW
KA-POW
KA-POW
GUD

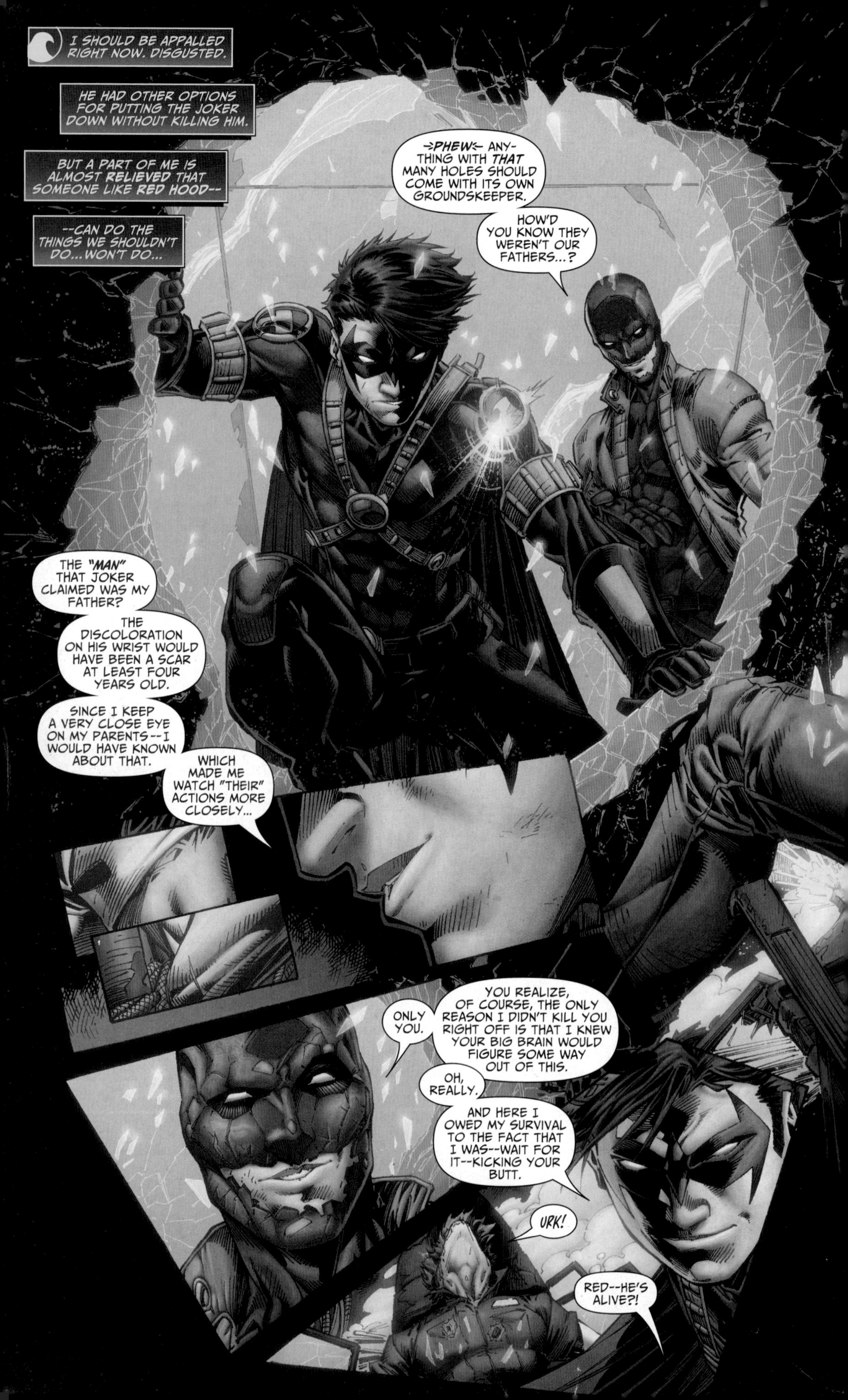
I SHOULD BE APPALLED RIGHT NOW. DISGUSTED.
HE HAD OTHER OPTIONS FOR PUTTING THE JOKER DOWN WITHOUT KILLING HIM.
BUT A PART OF ME IS ALMOST RELIEVED THAT SOMEONE LIKE RED HOOD--
--CAN DO THE THINGS WE SHOULDN'T DO...WON'T DO...
-PHEW- ANYTHING WITH THAT MANY HOLES SHOULD COME WITH ITS OWN GROUNDSKEEPER.
HOW'D YOU KNOW THEY WEREN'T OUR FATHERS...?
THE "MAN" THAT JOKER CLAIMED WAS MY FATHER?
THE DISCOLORATION ON HIS WRIST WOULD HAVE BEEN A SCAR AT LEAST FOUR YEARS OLD.
SINCE I KEEP A VERY CLOSE EYE ON MY PARENTS--I WOULD HAVE KNOWN ABOUT THAT.
WHICH MADE ME WATCH "THEIR" ACTIONS MORE CLOSELY...
YOU REALIZE, OF COURSE, THE ONLY REASON I DIDN'T KILL YOU RIGHT OFF IS THAT I KNEW YOUR BIG BRAIN WOULD FIGURE SOME WAY OUT OF THIS.
ONLY YOU.
OH, REALLY.
AND HERE I OWED MY SURVIVAL TO THE FACT THAT I WAS--WAIT FOR IT--KICKING YOUR BUTT.
URK!
RED--HE'S ALIVE?!

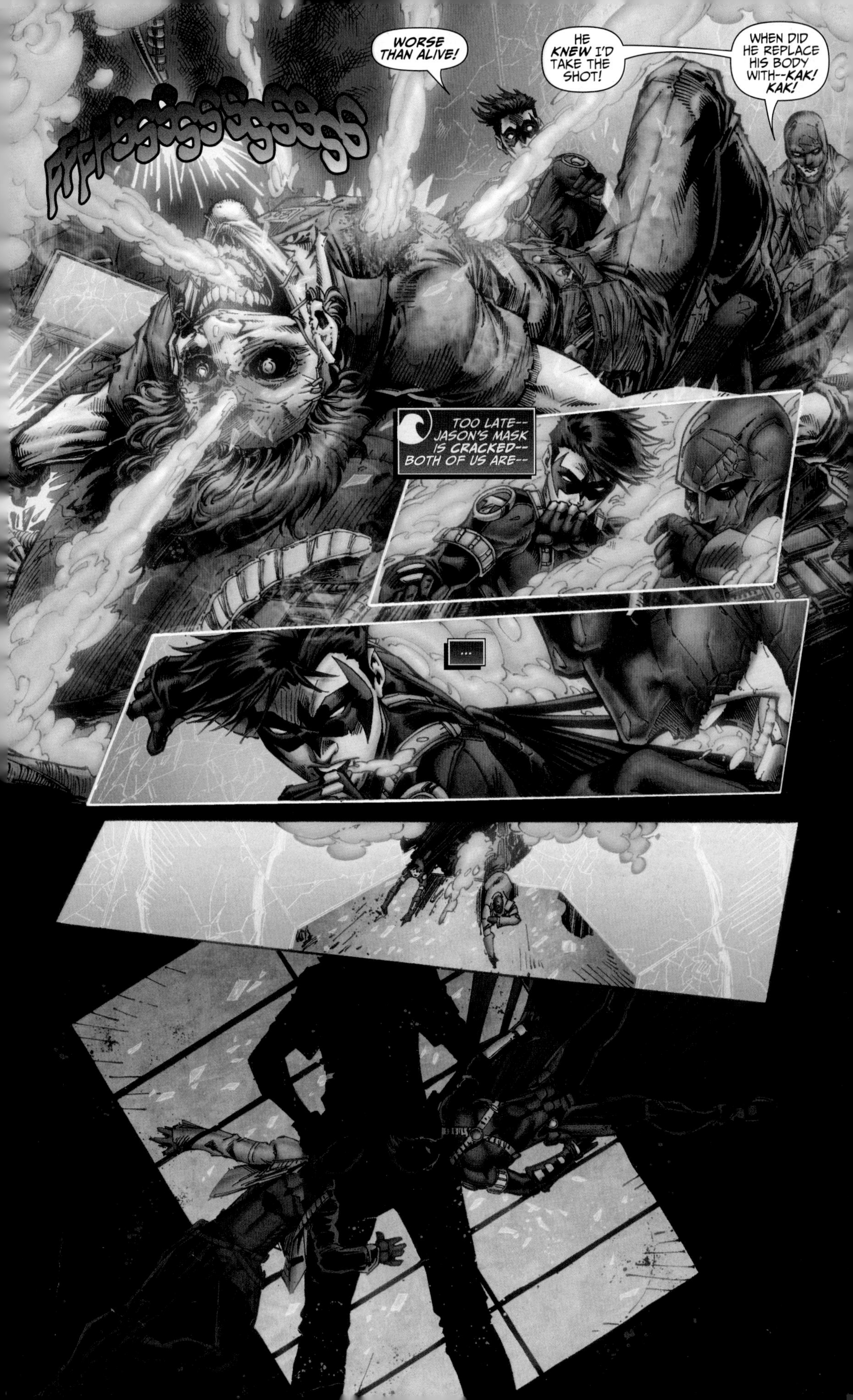
WORSE THAN ALIVE!
HE KNEW I'D TAKE THE SHOT!
WHEN DID HE REPLACE HIS BODY WITH--KAK! KAK!
TOO LATE--JASON'S MASK IS CRACKED--BOTH OF US ARE--
...

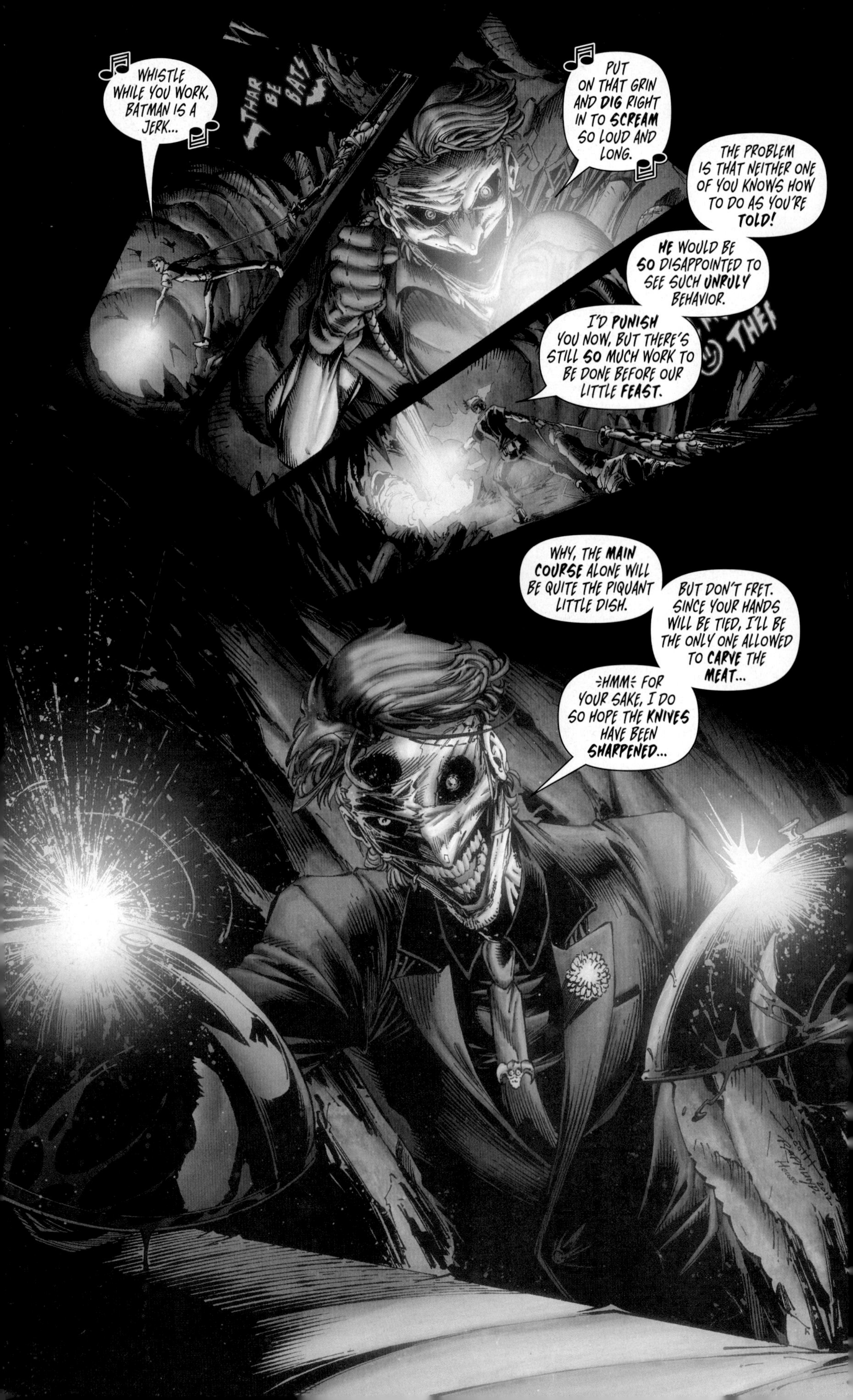

WHISTLE WHILE YOU WORK, BATMAN IS A JERK...
THAR BE BATS
PUT ON THAT GRIN AND DIG RIGHT IN TO SCREAM SO LOUD AND LONG.
THE PROBLEM IS THAT NEITHER ONE OF YOU KNOWS HOW TO DO AS YOU'RE TOLD!
HE WOULD BE SO DISAPPOINTED TO SEE SUCH UNRULY BEHAVIOR.
I'D PUNISH YOU NOW, BUT THERE'S STILL SO MUCH WORK TO BE DONE BEFORE OUR LITTLE FEAST.
WHY, THE MAIN COURSE ALONE WILL BE QUITE THE PIQUANT LITTLE DISH.
BUT DON'T FRET. SINCE YOUR HANDS WILL BE TIED, I'LL BE THE ONLY ONE ALLOWED TO CARVE THE MEAT...
HMM FOR YOUR SAKE, I DO SO HOPE THE KNIVES HAVE BEEN SHARPENED...

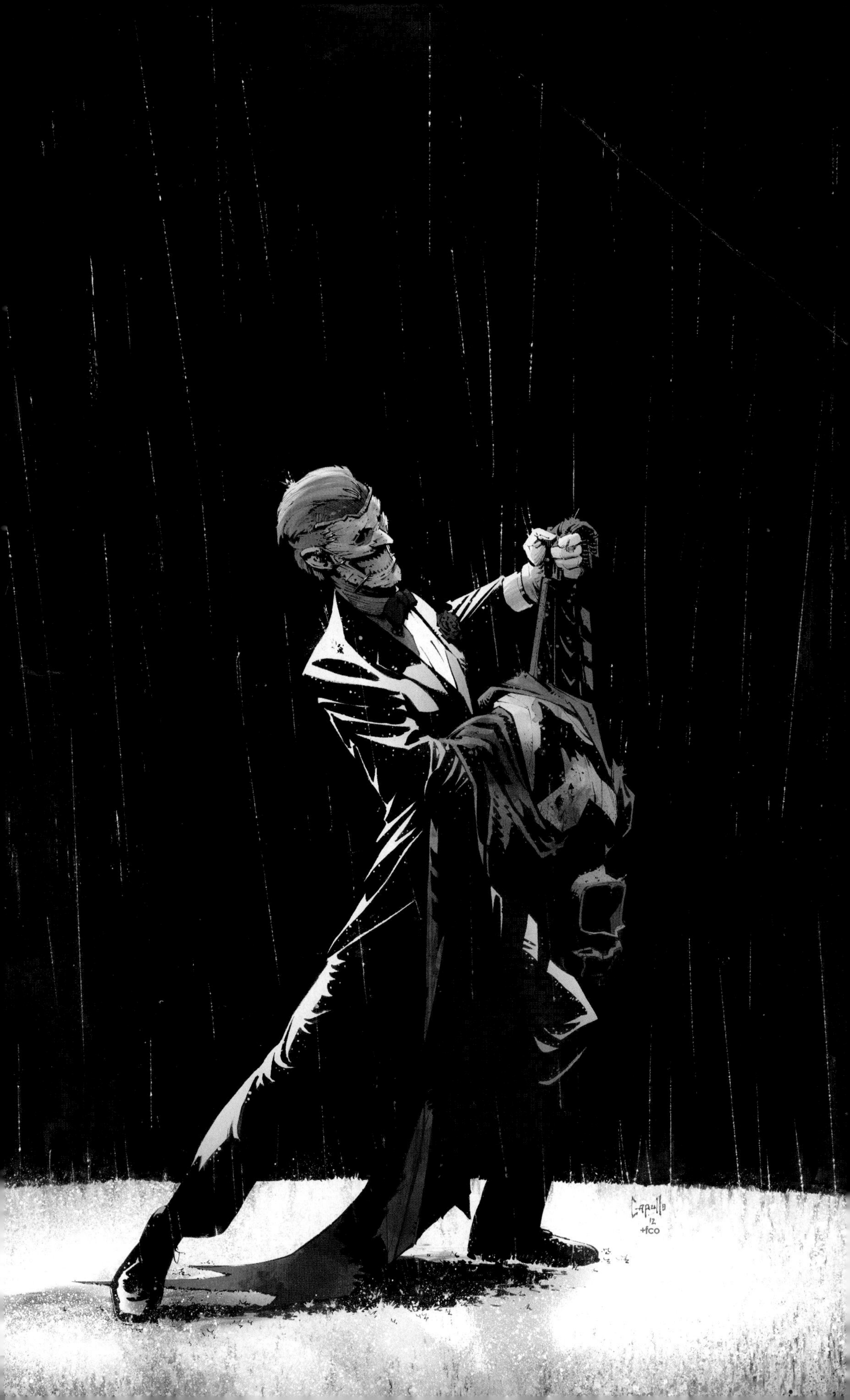
Capullo
'12
+fco

THE PUNCHLINE

SCOTT SNYDER writer **GREG CAPULLO** penciller **JONATHAN GLAPION** inker cover art by **GREG CAPULLO & FCO PLASCENCIA**

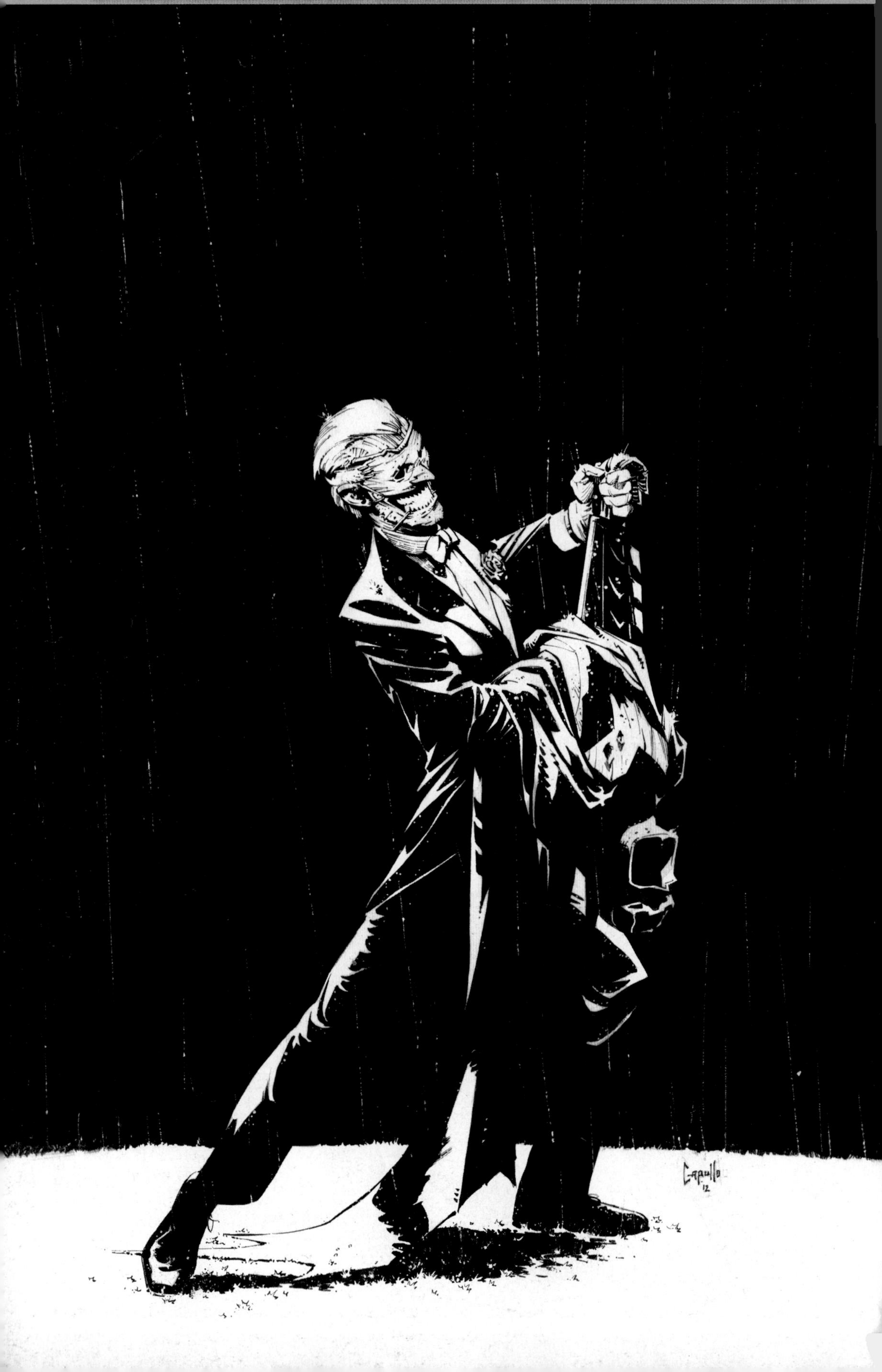

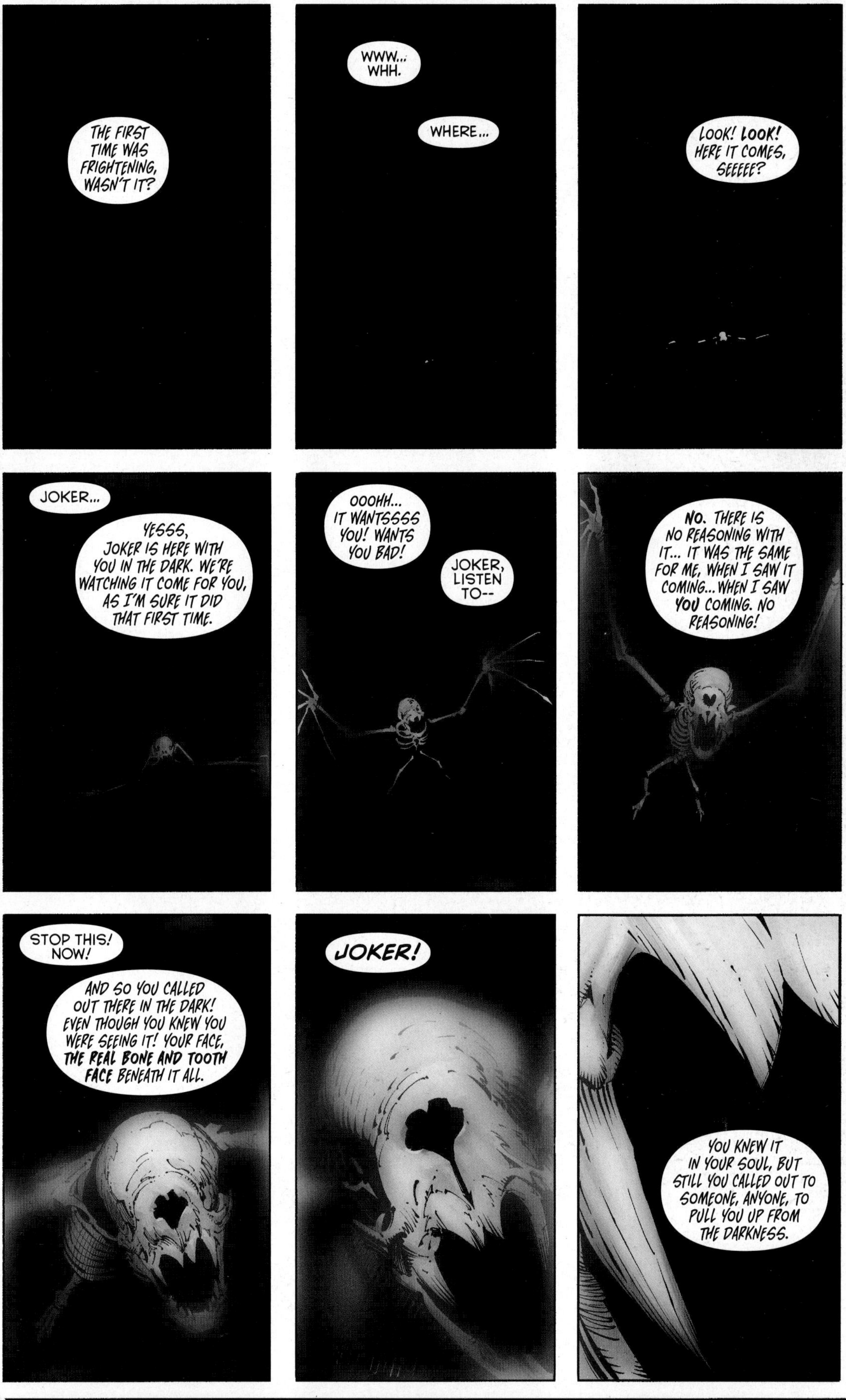
THE FIRST TIME WAS FRIGHTENING, WASN'T IT?
WWW... WHH.
WHERE...
LOOK! LOOK! HERE IT COMES, SEEEEE?
JOKER...
YESSS, JOKER IS HERE WITH YOU IN THE DARK. WE'RE WATCHING IT COME FOR YOU, AS I'M SURE IT DID THAT FIRST TIME.
OOOHH... IT WANTSSSS YOU! WANTS YOU BAD!
JOKER, LISTEN TO--
NO. THERE IS NO REASONING WITH IT... IT WAS THE SAME FOR ME, WHEN I SAW IT COMING... WHEN I SAW YOU COMING. NO REASONING!
STOP THIS! NOW!
AND SO YOU CALLED OUT THERE IN THE DARK! EVEN THOUGH YOU KNEW YOU WERE SEEING IT! YOUR FACE, THE REAL BONE AND TOOTH FACE BENEATH IT ALL.
JOKER!
YOU KNEW IT IN YOUR SOUL, BUT STILL YOU CALLED OUT TO SOMEONE, ANYONE, TO PULL YOU UP FROM THE DARKNESS.

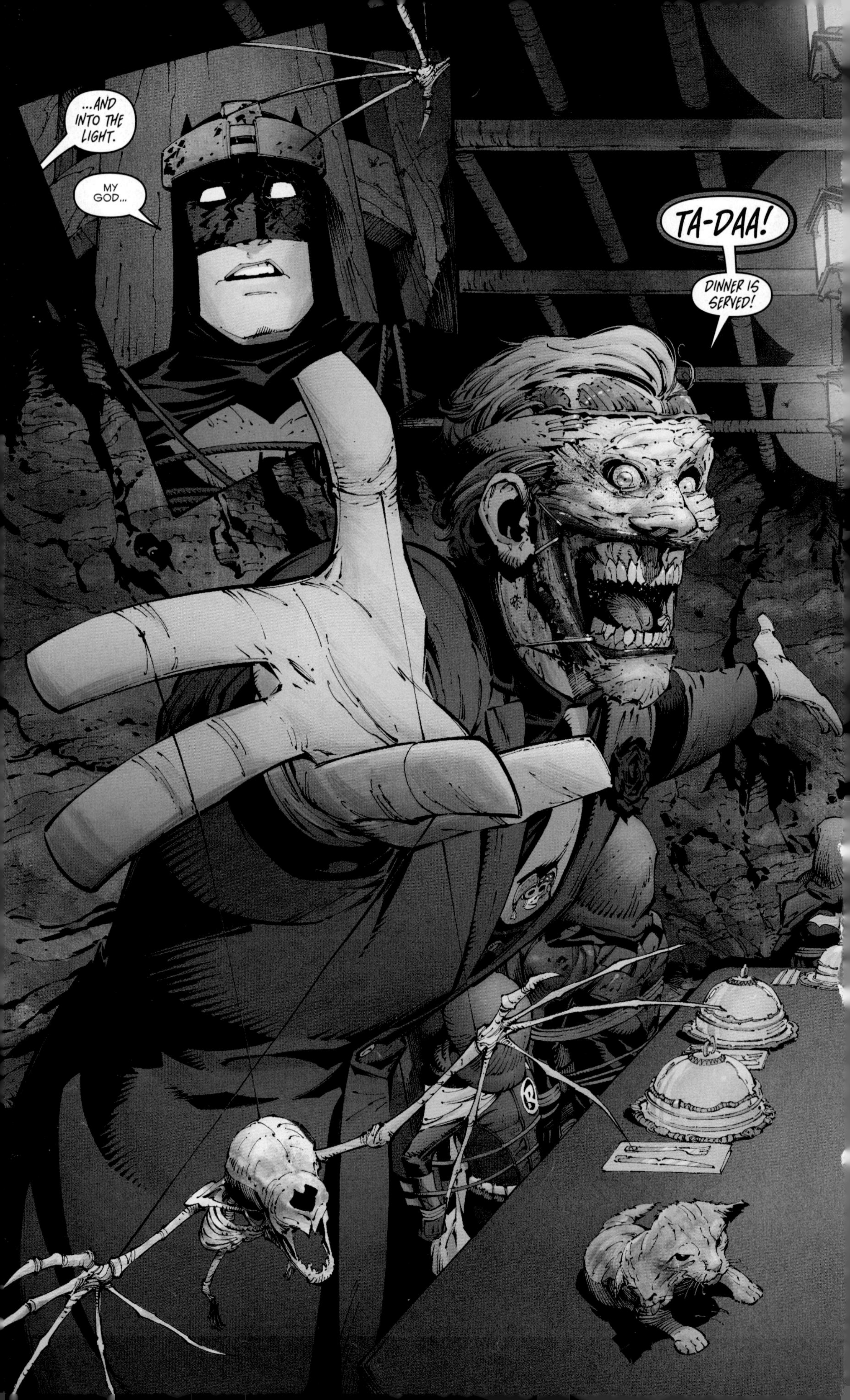
...AND INTO THE LIGHT.
MY GOD...
TA-DAA!
DINNER IS SERVED!

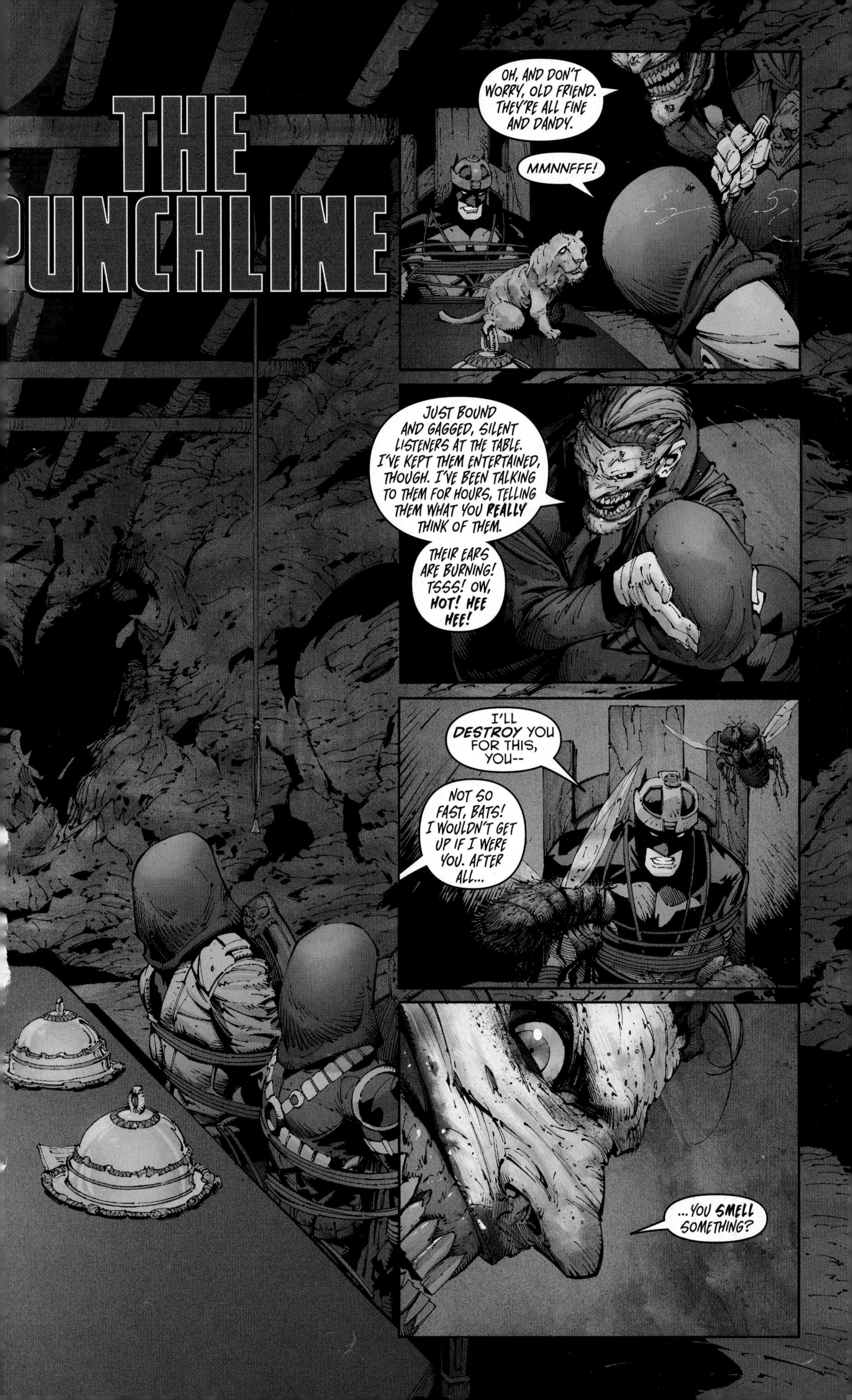
THE PUNCHLINE
OH, AND DON'T WORRY, OLD FRIEND. THEY'RE ALL FINE AND DANDY.
MMNNFFF!
JUST BOUND AND GAGGED, SILENT LISTENERS AT THE TABLE. I'VE KEPT THEM ENTERTAINED, THOUGH. I'VE BEEN TALKING TO THEM FOR HOURS, TELLING THEM WHAT YOU REALLY THINK OF THEM.
THEIR EARS ARE BURNING! TSSS! OW, HOT! HEE HEE!
I'LL DESTROY YOU FOR THIS, YOU--
NOT SO FAST, BATS! I WOULDN'T GET UP IF I WERE YOU. AFTER ALL...
...YOU SMELL SOMETHING?

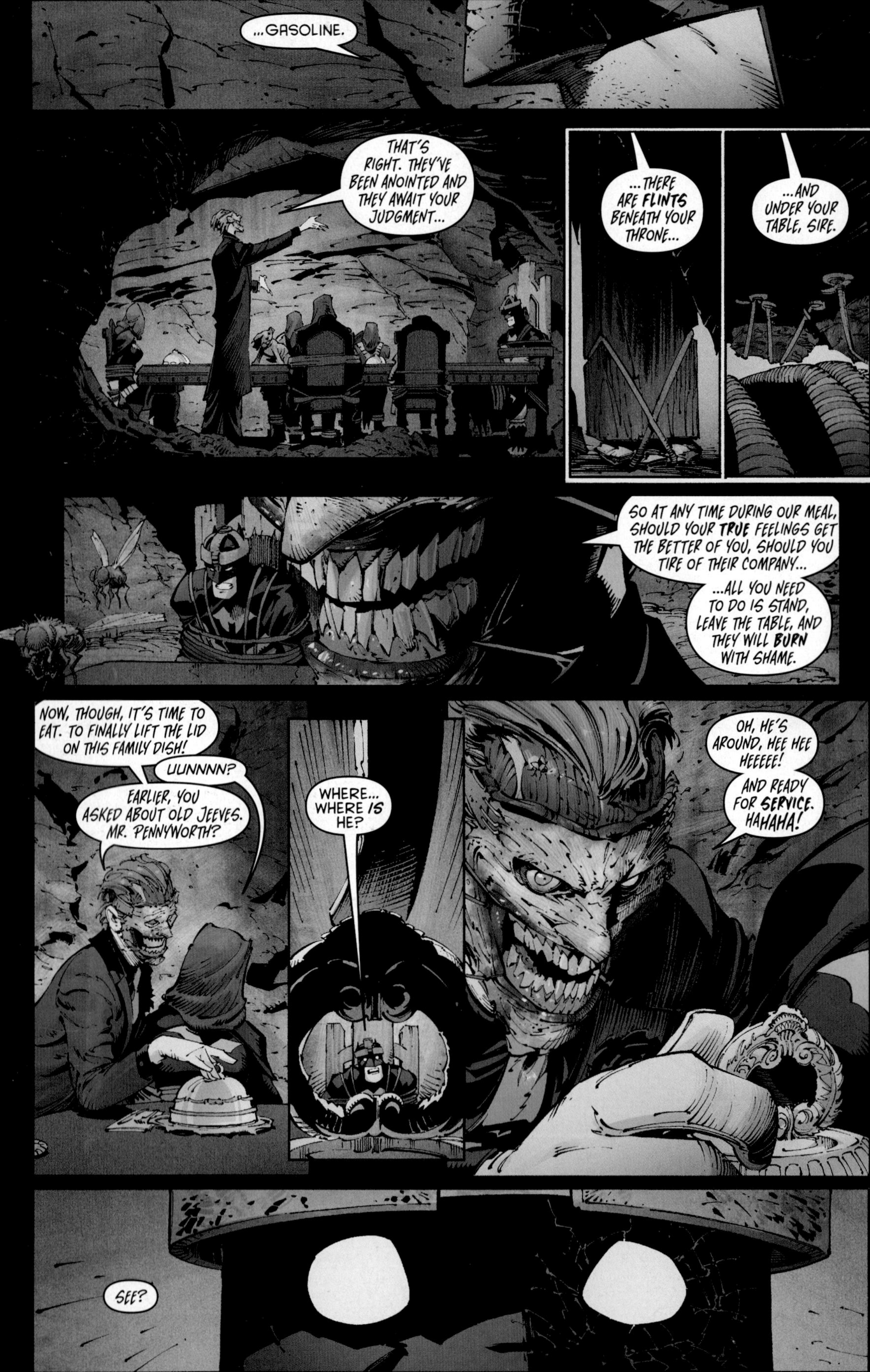
...GASOLINE.
THAT'S RIGHT. THEY'VE BEEN ANOINTED AND THEY AWAIT YOUR JUDGMENT...
...THERE ARE FLINTS BENEATH YOUR THRONE...
...AND UNDER YOUR TABLE, SIRE.
SO AT ANY TIME DURING OUR MEAL, SHOULD YOUR TRUE FEELINGS GET THE BETTER OF YOU, SHOULD YOU TIRE OF THEIR COMPANY...
...ALL YOU NEED TO DO IS STAND, LEAVE THE TABLE, AND THEY WILL BURN WITH SHAME.
NOW, THOUGH, IT'S TIME TO EAT. TO FINALLY LIFT THE LID ON THIS FAMILY DISH!
UUNNNN?
EARLIER, YOU ASKED ABOUT OLD JEEVES. MR. PENNYWORTH?
WHERE... WHERE IS HE?
OH, HE'S AROUND, HEE HEE HEEEEE!
AND READY FOR SERVICE. HAHAHA!
SEE?

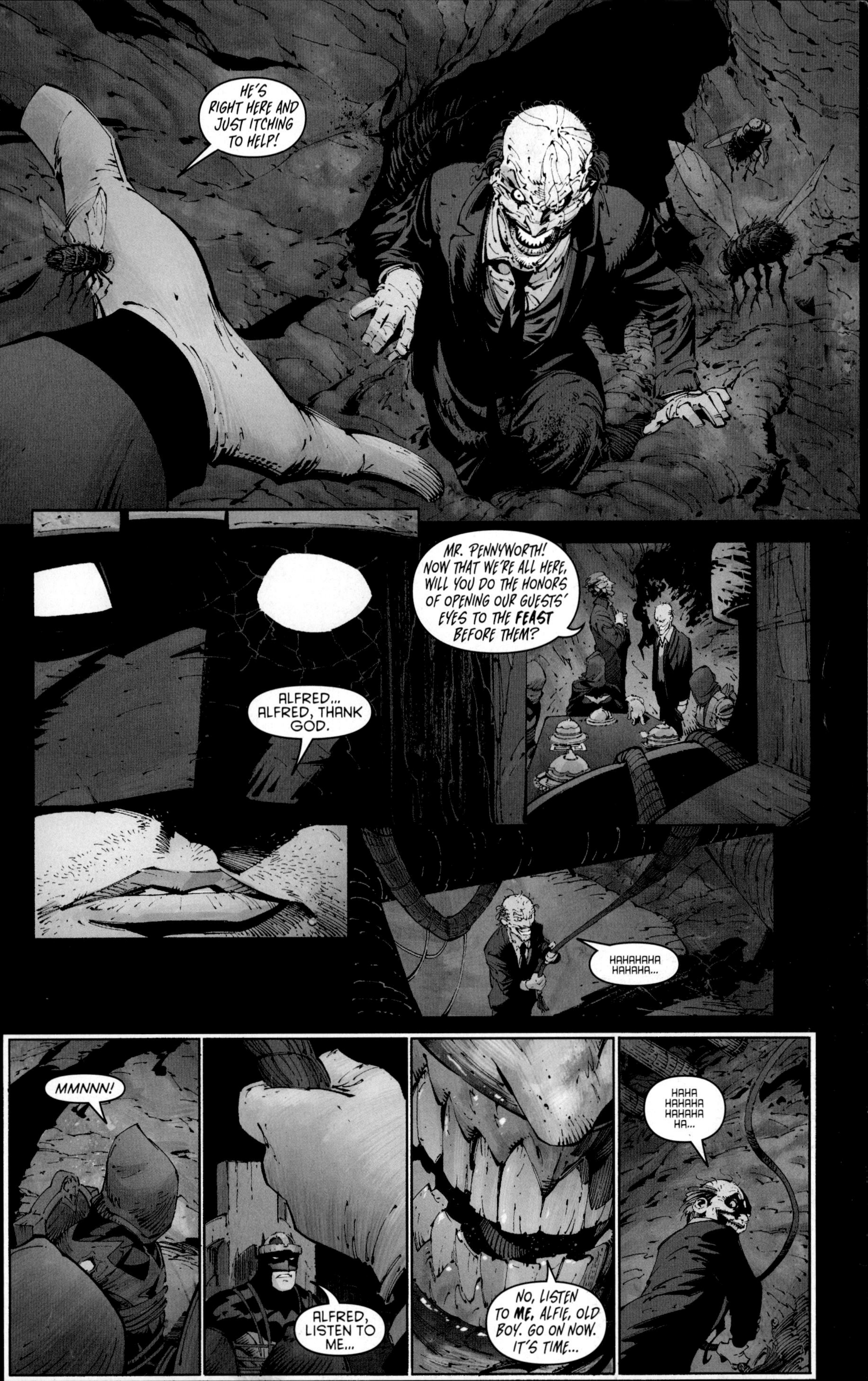
HE'S RIGHT HERE AND JUST ITCHING TO HELP!
MR. PENNYWORTH! NOW THAT WE'RE ALL HERE, WILL YOU DO THE HONORS OF OPENING OUR GUESTS' EYES TO THE **FEAST** BEFORE THEM?
ALFRED... ALFRED, THANK GOD.
HAHAHAHA HAHAHA...
MMNNN!
ALFRED, LISTEN TO ME...
NO, LISTEN TO **ME**, ALFIE, OLD BOY. GO ON NOW. IT'S TIME...
HAHA HAHAHA HAHAHA HA...

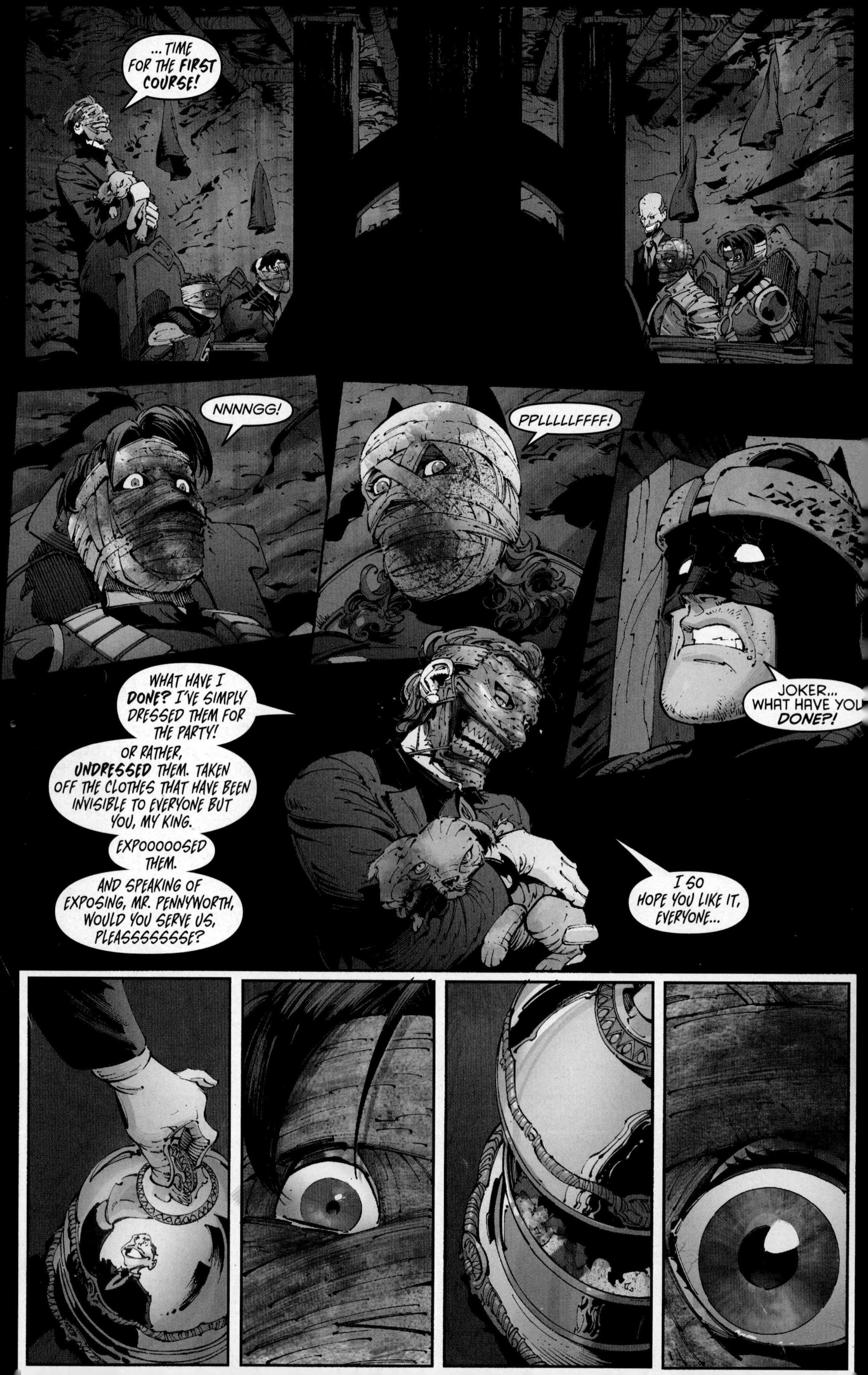
...TIME FOR THE FIRST COURSE!
NNNNGG!
PPLLLLLLFFFF!
JOKER... WHAT HAVE YOU DONE?!
WHAT HAVE I DONE? I'VE SIMPLY DRESSED THEM FOR THE PARTY!
OR RATHER, UNDRESSED THEM. TAKEN OFF THE CLOTHES THAT HAVE BEEN INVISIBLE TO EVERYONE BUT YOU, MY KING.
EXPOOOOOSED THEM.
AND SPEAKING OF EXPOSING, MR. PENNYWORTH, WOULD YOU SERVE US, PLEASSSSSSSE?
I SO HOPE YOU LIKE IT, EVERYONE...

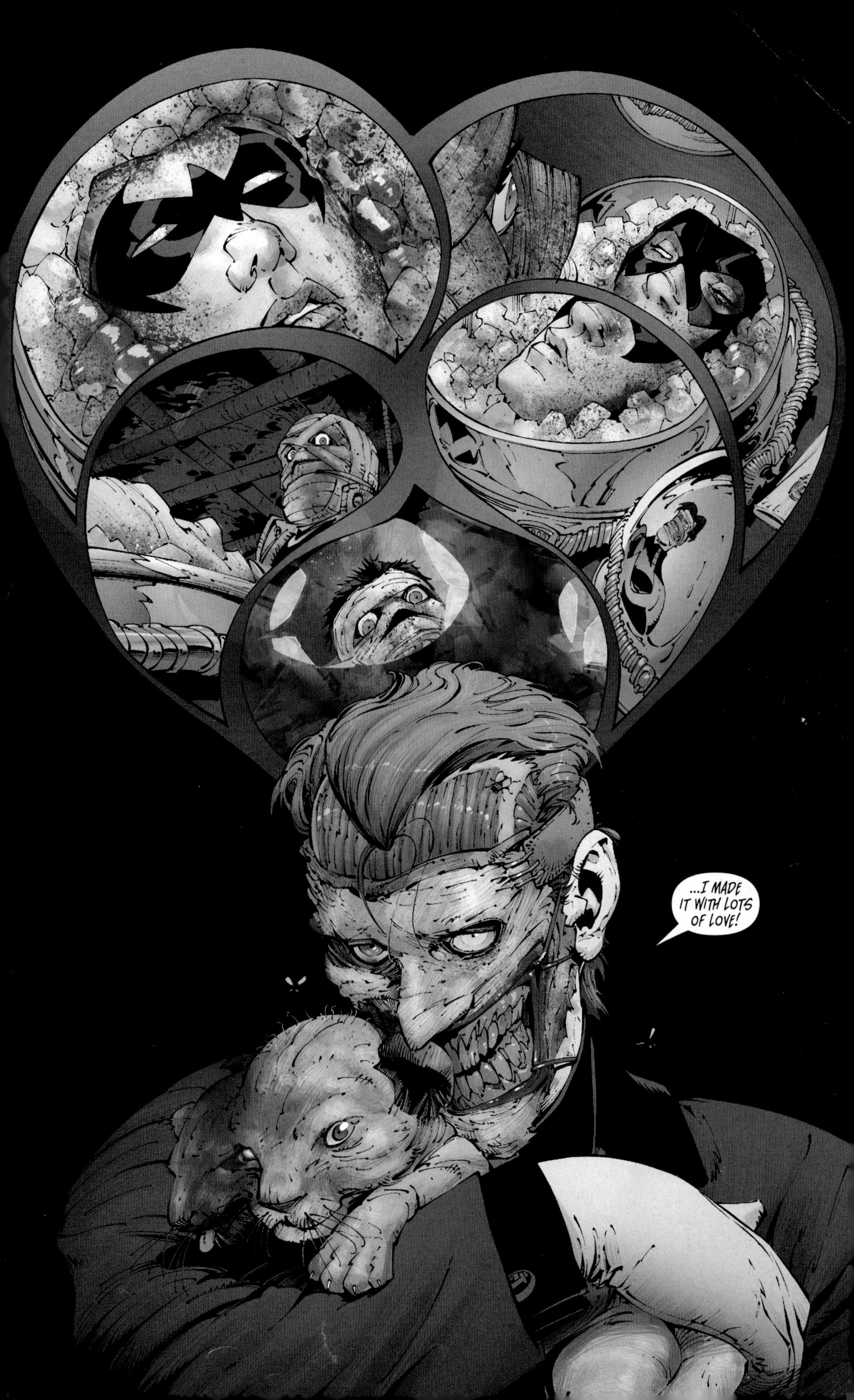
...I MADE IT WITH LOTS OF LOVE!

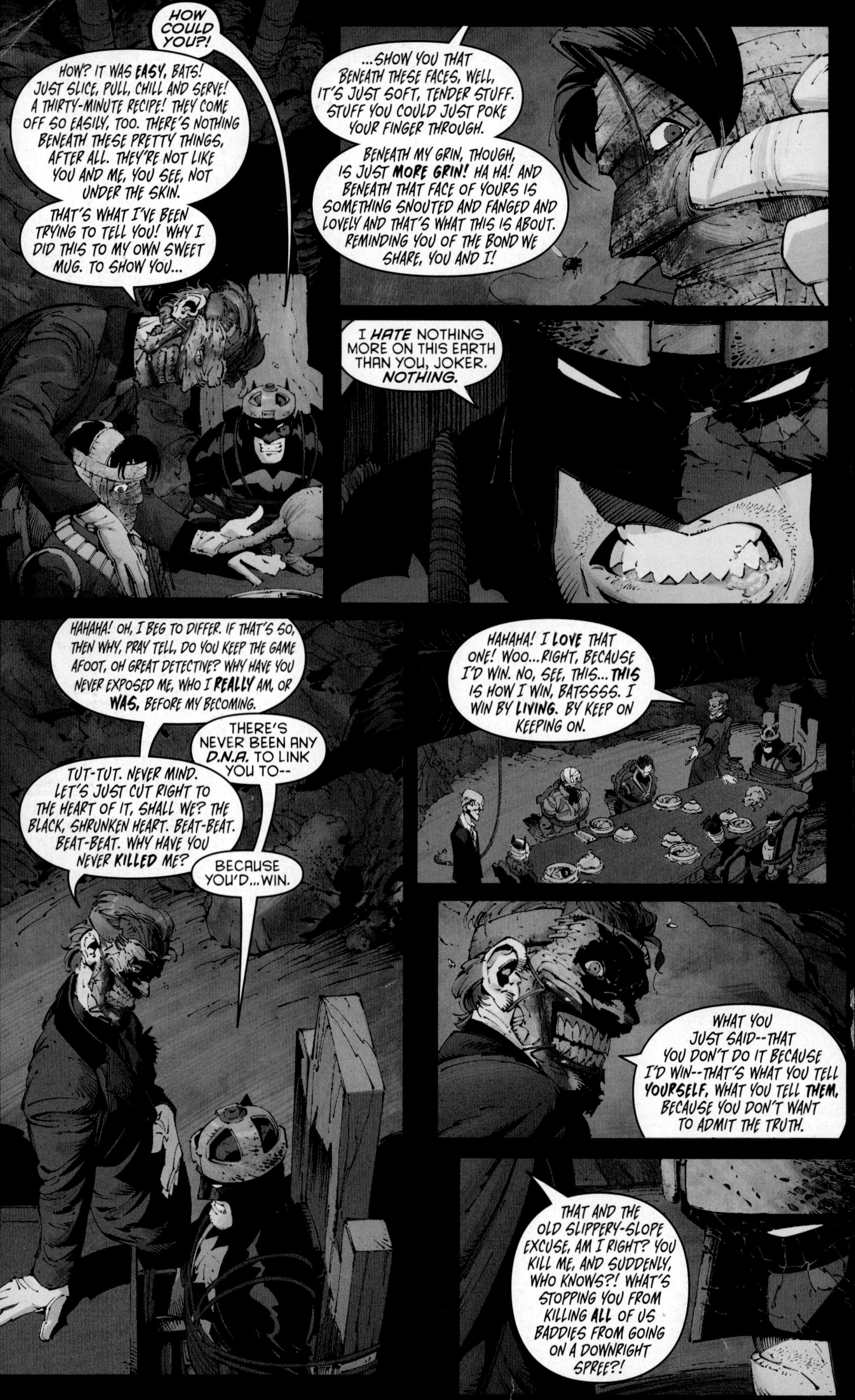
HOW COULD YOU?!
HOW? IT WAS EASY, BATS! JUST SLICE, PULL, CHILL AND SERVE! A THIRTY-MINUTE RECIPE! THEY COME OFF SO EASILY, TOO. THERE'S NOTHING BENEATH THESE PRETTY THINGS, AFTER ALL. THEY'RE NOT LIKE YOU AND ME, YOU SEE, NOT UNDER THE SKIN.
THAT'S WHAT I'VE BEEN TRYING TO TELL YOU! WHY I DID THIS TO MY OWN SWEET MUG. TO SHOW YOU...
...SHOW YOU THAT BENEATH THESE FACES, WELL, IT'S JUST SOFT, TENDER STUFF. STUFF YOU COULD JUST POKE YOUR FINGER THROUGH.
BENEATH MY GRIN, THOUGH, IS JUST MORE GRIN! HA HA! AND BENEATH THAT FACE OF YOURS IS SOMETHING SNOUTED AND FANGED AND LOVELY AND THAT'S WHAT THIS IS ABOUT. REMINDING YOU OF THE BOND WE SHARE, YOU AND I!
I HATE NOTHING MORE ON THIS EARTH THAN YOU, JOKER. NOTHING.
HAHAHA! OH, I BEG TO DIFFER. IF THAT'S SO, THEN WHY, PRAY TELL, DO YOU KEEP THE GAME AFOOT, OH GREAT DETECTIVE? WHY HAVE YOU NEVER EXPOSED ME, WHO I REALLY AM, OR WAS, BEFORE MY BECOMING.
THERE'S NEVER BEEN ANY D.N.A. TO LINK YOU TO--
TUT-TUT. NEVER MIND. LET'S JUST CUT RIGHT TO THE HEART OF IT, SHALL WE? THE BLACK, SHRUNKEN HEART. BEAT-BEAT. BEAT-BEAT. WHY HAVE YOU NEVER KILLED ME?
BECAUSE YOU'D...WIN.
HAHAHA! I LOVE THAT ONE! WOO...RIGHT, BECAUSE I'D WIN. NO, SEE, THIS...THIS IS HOW I WIN, BATSSSS. I WIN BY LIVING. BY KEEP ON KEEPING ON.
WHAT YOU JUST SAID--THAT YOU DON'T DO IT BECAUSE I'D WIN--THAT'S WHAT YOU TELL YOURSELF, WHAT YOU TELL THEM, BECAUSE YOU DON'T WANT TO ADMIT THE TRUTH.
THAT AND THE OLD SLIPPERY-SLOPE EXCUSE, AM I RIGHT? YOU KILL ME, AND SUDDENLY, WHO KNOWS?! WHAT'S STOPPING YOU FROM KILLING ALL OF US BADDIES FROM GOING ON A DOWNRIGHT SPREE?!

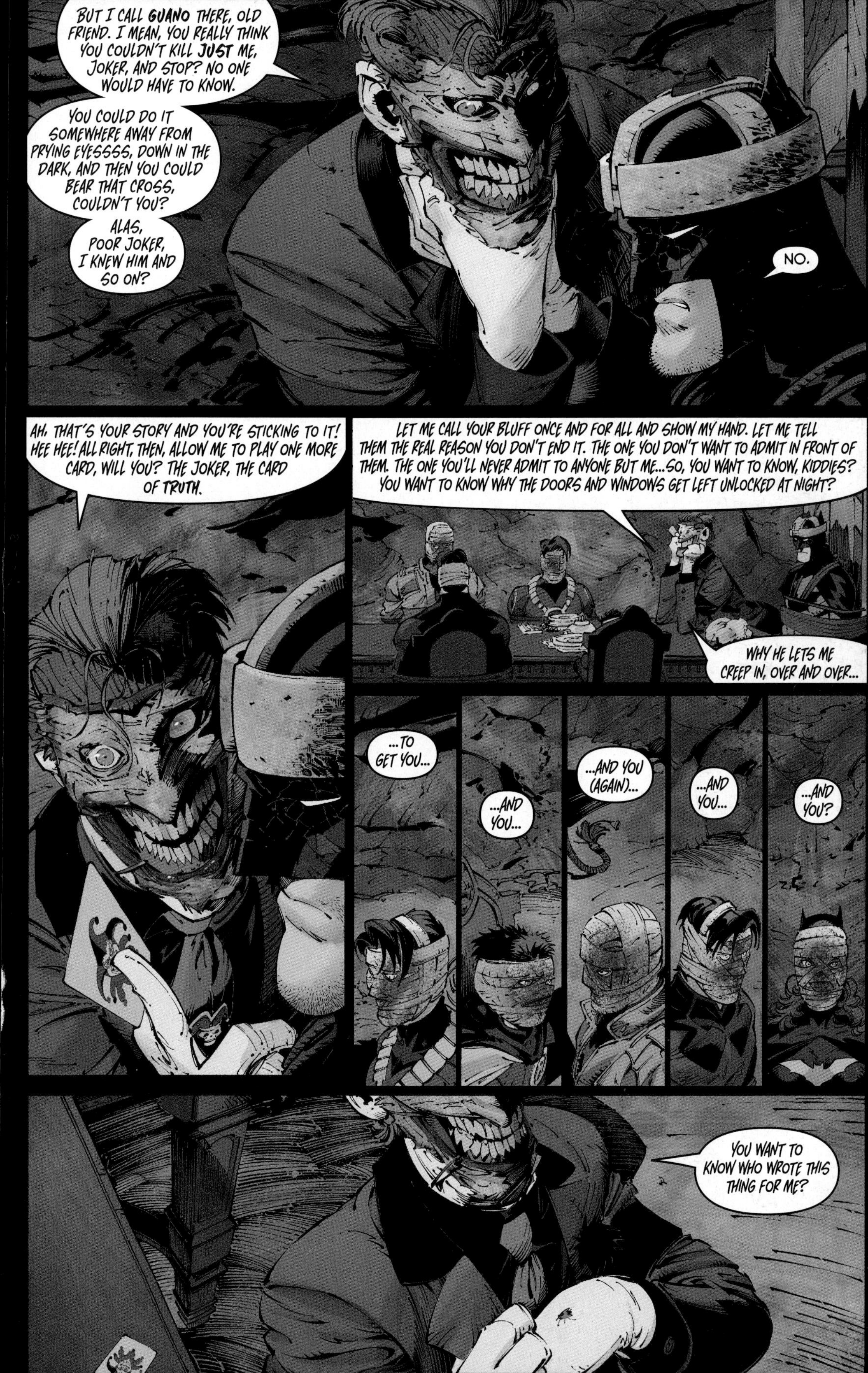
BUT I CALL GUANO THERE, OLD FRIEND. I MEAN, YOU REALLY THINK YOU COULDN'T KILL JUST ME, JOKER, AND STOP? NO ONE WOULD HAVE TO KNOW.
YOU COULD DO IT SOMEWHERE AWAY FROM PRYING EYESSSS, DOWN IN THE DARK, AND THEN YOU COULD BEAR THAT CROSS, COULDN'T YOU?
ALAS, POOR JOKER, I KNEW HIM AND SO ON?
NO.
AH, THAT'S YOUR STORY AND YOU'RE STICKING TO IT! HEE HEE! ALL RIGHT, THEN, ALLOW ME TO PLAY ONE MORE CARD, WILL YOU? THE JOKER, THE CARD OF TRUTH.
LET ME CALL YOUR BLUFF ONCE AND FOR ALL AND SHOW MY HAND. LET ME TELL THEM THE REAL REASON YOU DON'T END IT. THE ONE YOU DON'T WANT TO ADMIT IN FRONT OF THEM. THE ONE YOU'LL NEVER ADMIT TO ANYONE BUT ME...SO, YOU WANT TO KNOW, KIDDIES? YOU WANT TO KNOW WHY THE DOORS AND WINDOWS GET LEFT UNLOCKED AT NIGHT?
WHY HE LETS ME CREEP IN, OVER AND OVER...
...TO GET YOU...
...AND YOU...
...AND YOU (AGAIN)...
...AND YOU...
...AND YOU?
YOU WANT TO KNOW WHO WROTE THIS THING FOR ME?

...IT WAS YOU, BATS.

YOU WROTE THIS LITTLE LOVE LETTER, THIS BACKWARDS MAP, THIS HIT LIST...AND YOU WRITE IT AGAIN AND AGAIN, EVERY TIME YOU KEEP ONE OF US ALIVE, BUT LET ONE OF THEM FALL. AND THEY WILL FALL, MAYBE ONE BY ONE, MAYBE TOGETHER...BUT LOOK TO THE FUTURE, REALLY LOOK, AND YOU KNOW IT'S COMING...

...THAT DAY WHEN THEY'RE ALL DEAD AND BURIED, IN THEIR COLD BAT-GRAVES (HEE-HEE). BUT LOOK! THERE'S ME AND MY FRIENDS, AND...WHY, WE'RE STILL ALIVE AND KICKING! AND THERE YOU ARE, BATSSS...CHASING US, FOREVER CHASING!

AND WHY? BECAUSE IT'S WHAT YOU WANT TO HAPPEN. IT'S WHAT YOU NEEEEED. BECAUSE YOU SEE, WITH US YOU'RE MORE! WITH US, YOU TRANSSSCEND! WITH US, YOU'RE ALWAYS.

BUT THEM, THEY MAKE YOU EVERYTHING YOU WANT TO FORGET THAT YOU ARE, EVERYTHING YOU'RE AFRAID OF. AND YOU WERE AFRAID, WHEN YOU TOOK THEM IN. I KNOW. IT'S OKAY, OLD FRIEND. IT WAS A MOMENT OF WEAKNESSSS... THE DIRT WAS PULLING.

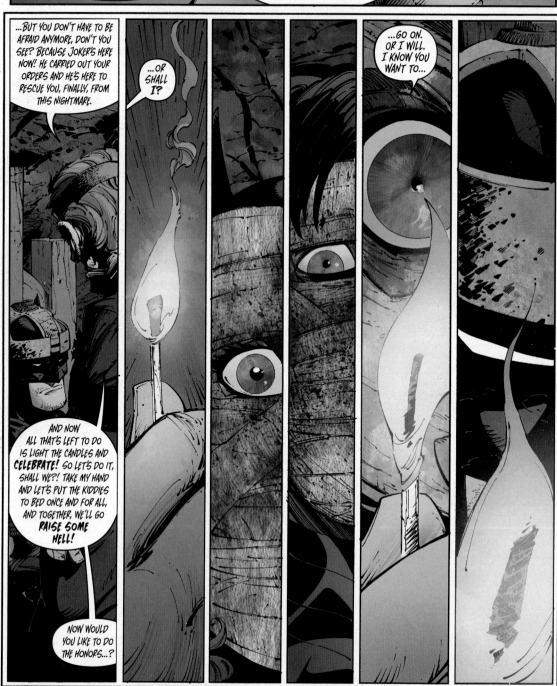

...BUT YOU DON'T HAVE TO BE AFRAID ANYMORE, DON'T YOU SEE? BECAUSE JOKER'S HERE NOW! HE CARRIED OUT YOUR ORDERS AND HE'S HERE TO RESCUE YOU, FINALLY, FROM THIS NIGHTMARE.

...OR SHALL I?

...GO ON. OR I WILL. I KNOW YOU WANT TO...

AND NOW ALL THAT'S LEFT TO DO IS LIGHT THE CANDLES AND CELEBRATE! SO LET'S DO IT, SHALL WE?! TAKE MY HAND AND LET'S PUT THE KIDDIES TO BED ONCE AND FOR ALL, AND TOGETHER, WE'LL GO RAISE SOME HELL!

NOW WOULD YOU LIKE TO DO THE HONORS...?

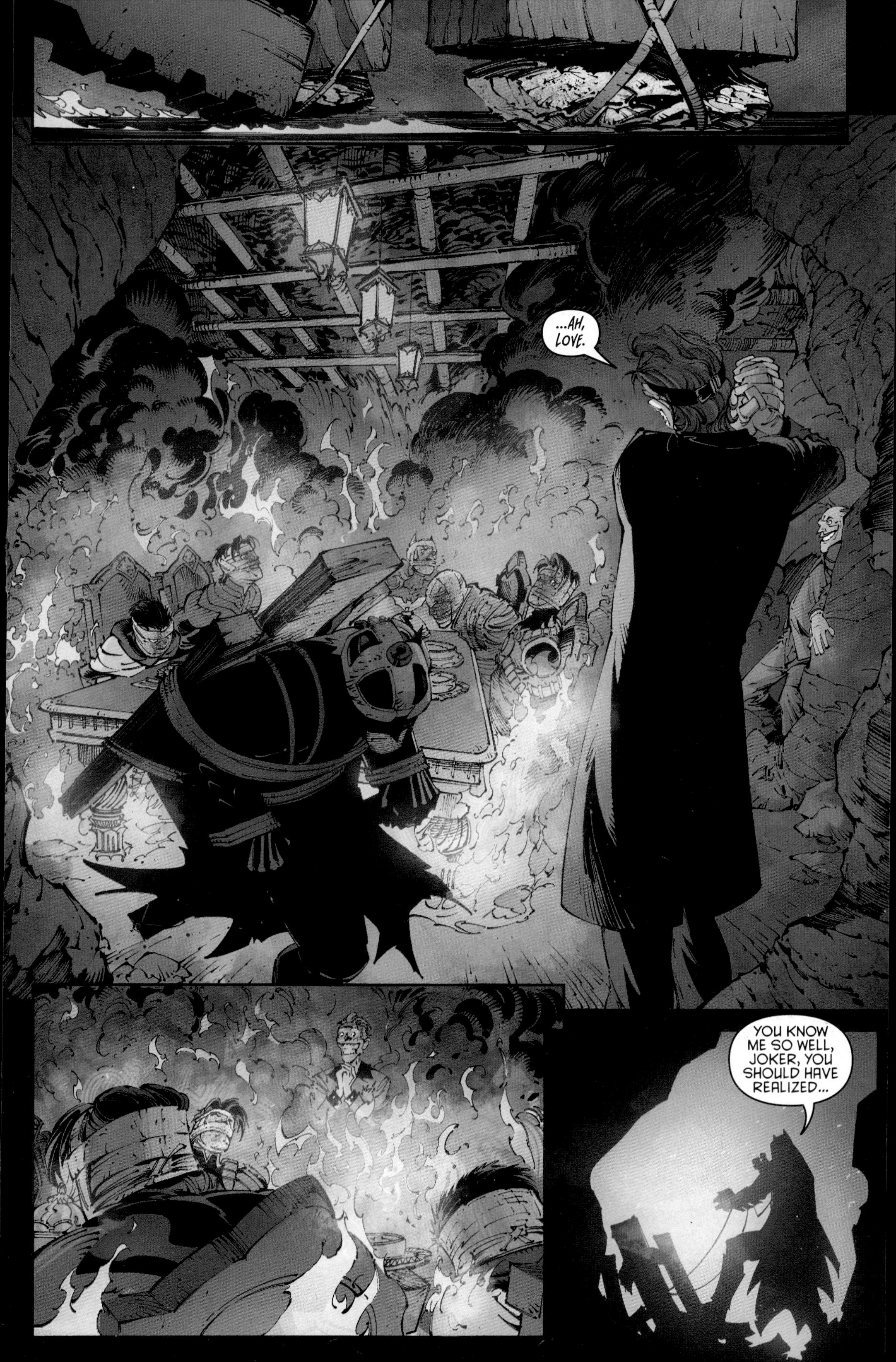
...AH, LOVE.
YOU KNOW ME SO WELL, JOKER, YOU SHOULD HAVE REALIZED...

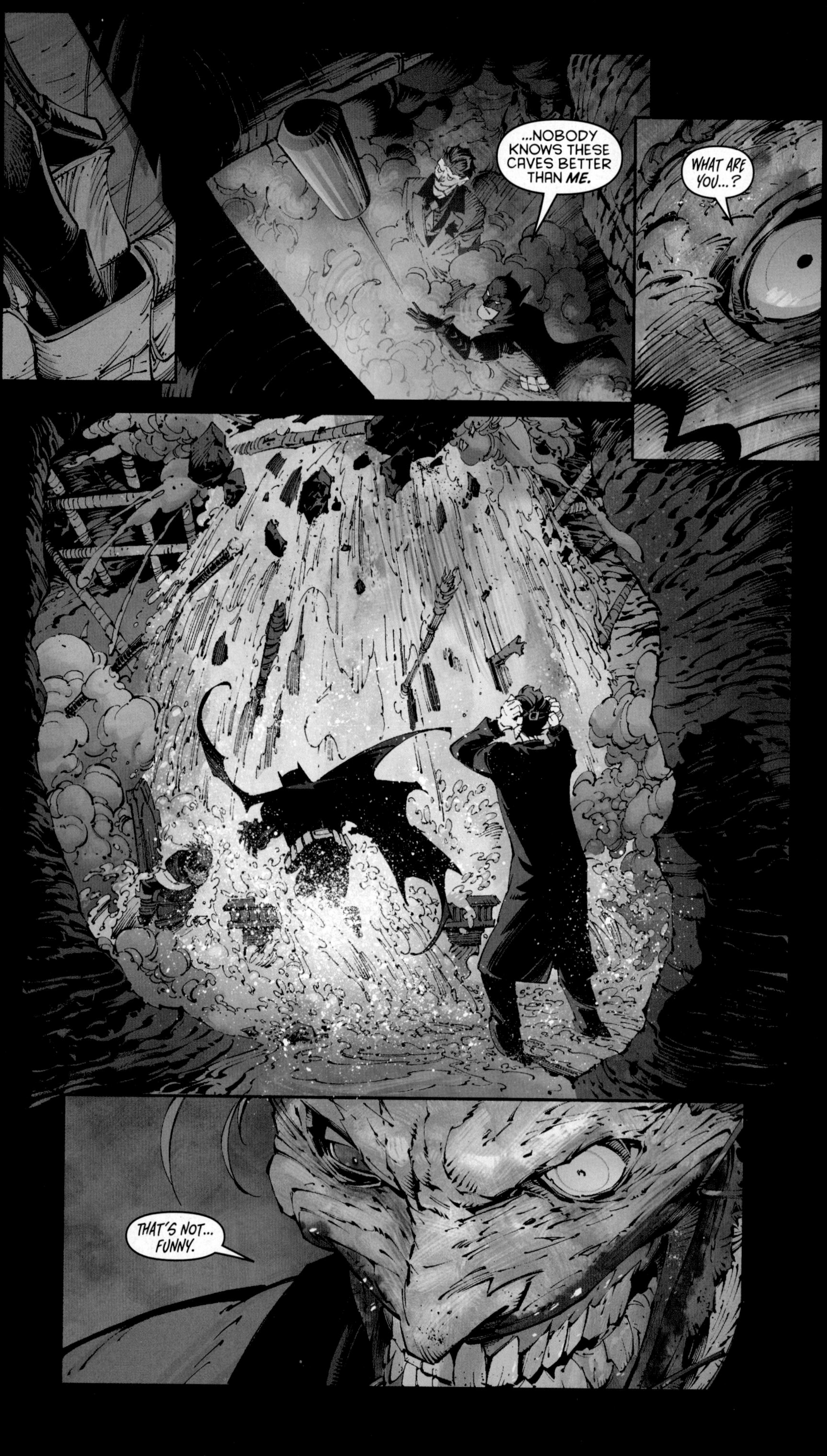
...NOBODY KNOWS THESE CAVES BETTER THAN ME.
WHAT ARE YOU...?
THAT'S NOT... FUNNY.

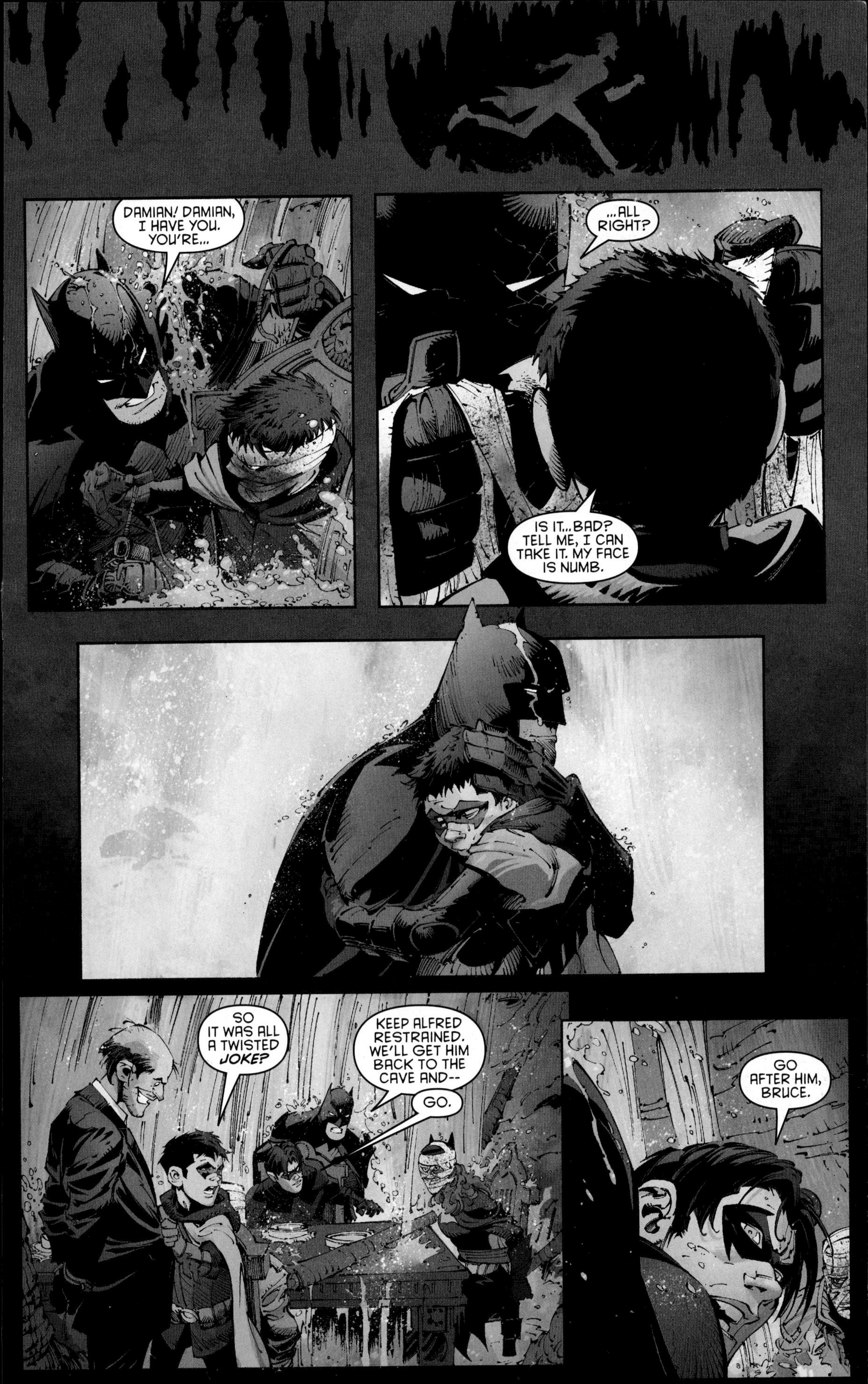
DAMIAN! DAMIAN, I HAVE YOU. YOU'RE...
...ALL RIGHT?
IS IT...BAD? TELL ME, I CAN TAKE IT. MY FACE IS NUMB.
SO IT WAS ALL A TWISTED *JOKE?*
KEEP ALFRED RESTRAINED. WE'LL GET HIM BACK TO THE CAVE AND--
GO.
GO AFTER HIM, BRUCE.

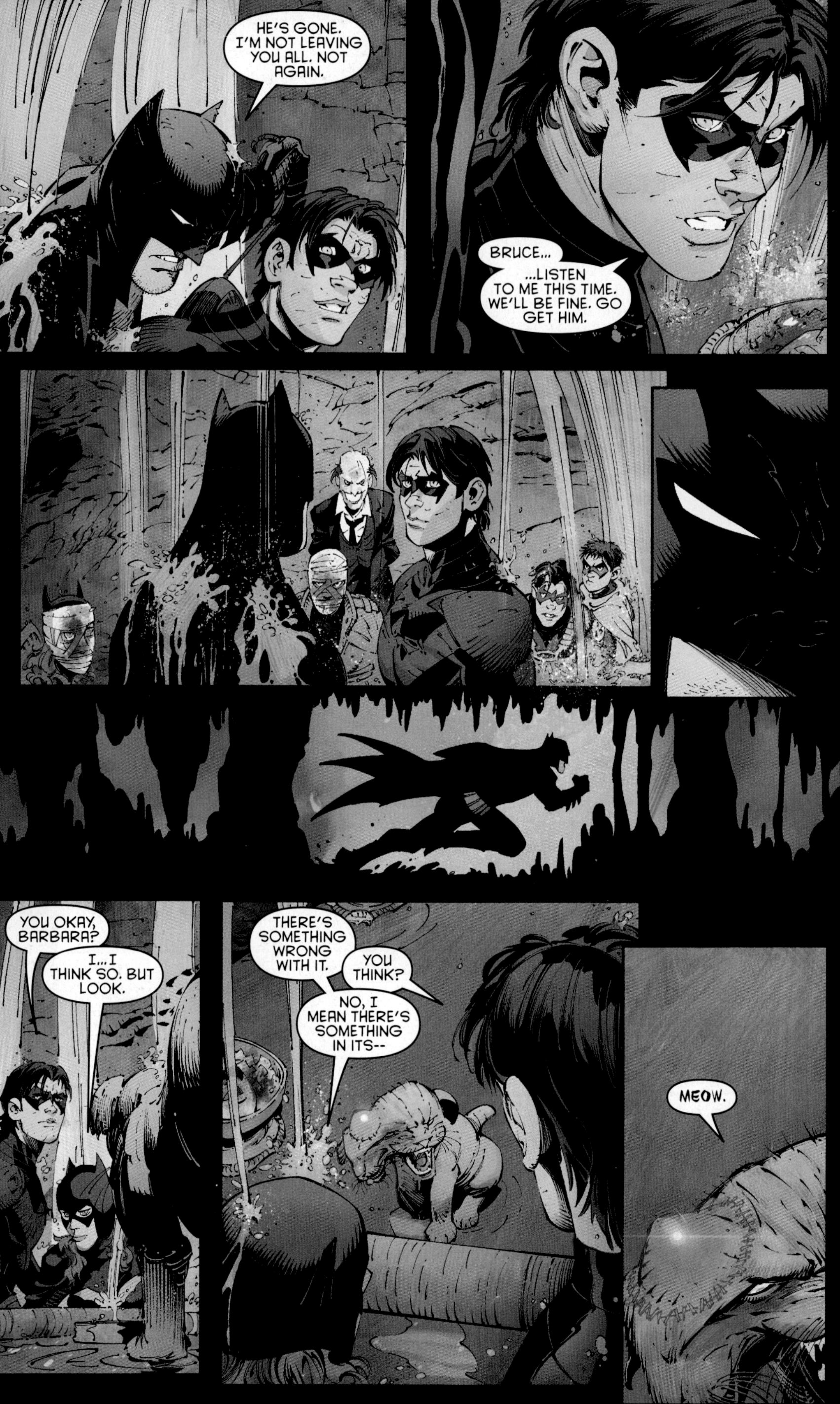
HE'S GONE. I'M NOT LEAVING YOU ALL. NOT AGAIN.
BRUCE...
...LISTEN TO ME THIS TIME. WE'LL BE FINE. GO GET HIM.
YOU OKAY, BARBARA?
I...I THINK SO. BUT LOOK.
THERE'S SOMETHING WRONG WITH IT.
YOU THINK?
NO, I MEAN THERE'S SOMETHING IN ITS--
MEOW.

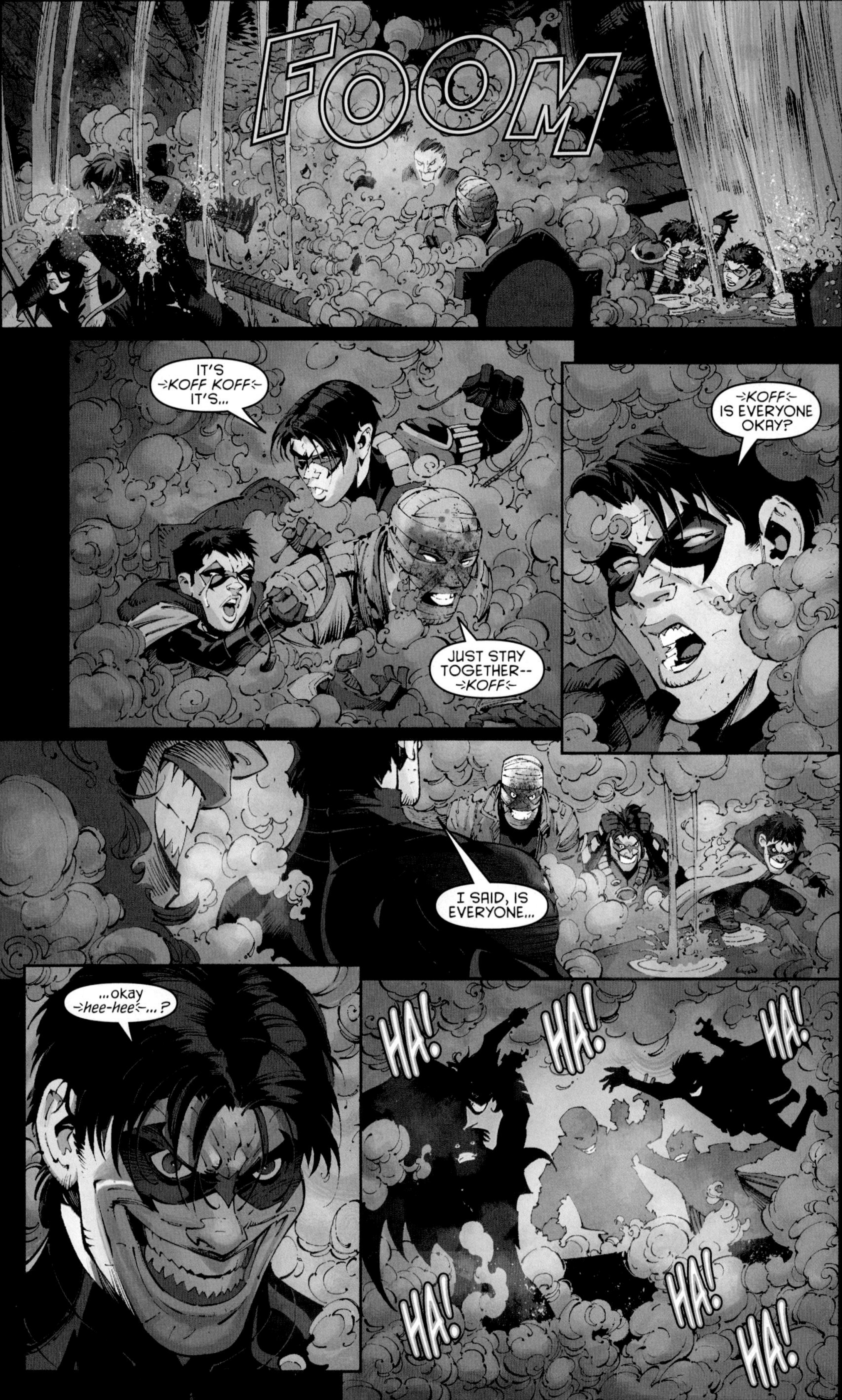
FOOM
IT'S -KOFF KOFF- IT'S...
JUST STAY TOGETHER-- -KOFF-
-KOFF- IS EVERYONE OKAY?
I SAID, IS EVERYONE...
...okay -hee-hee-...?
HA!
HA!
HA!
HA!
HA!
HA!

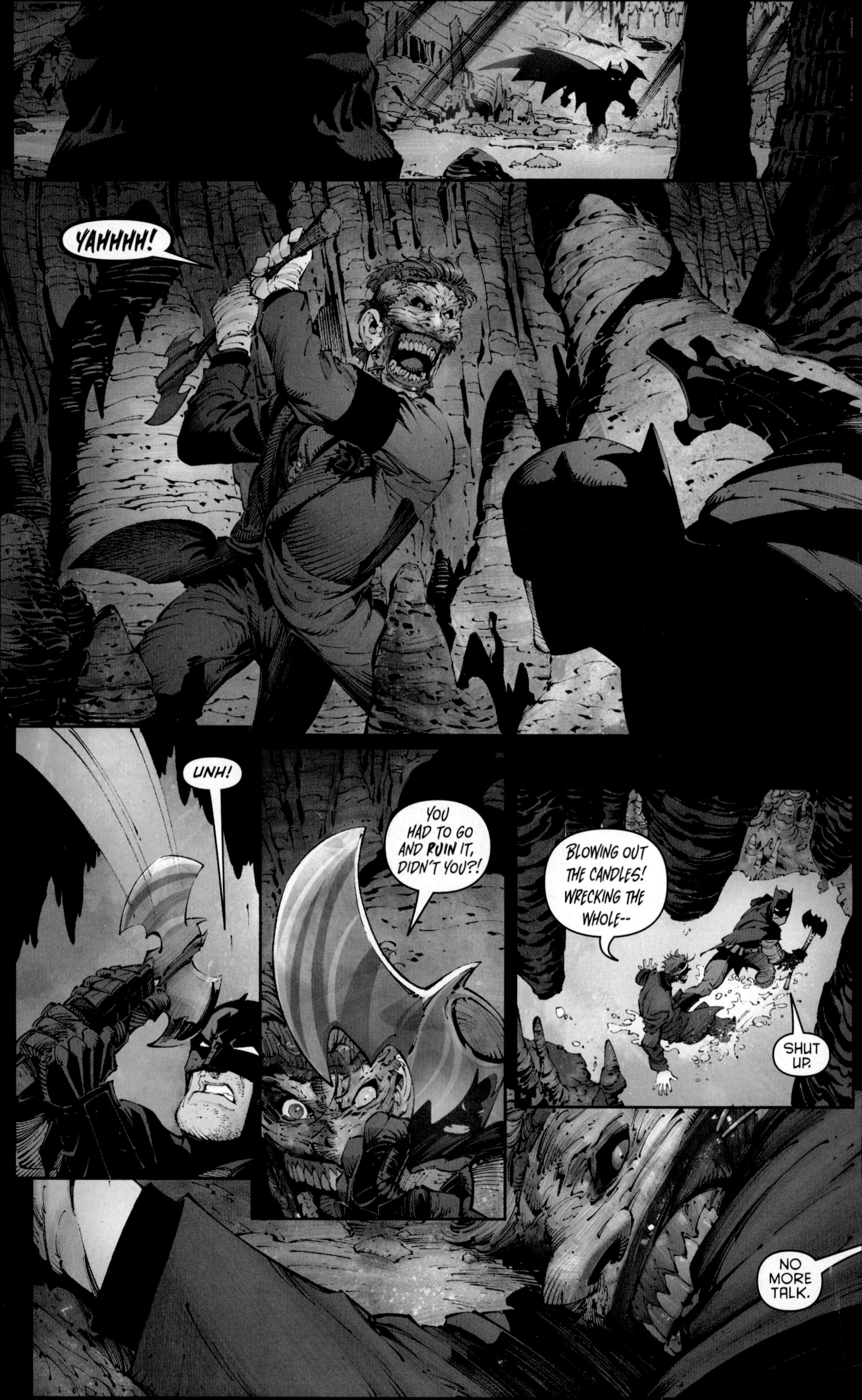
YAHHHH!
UNH!
YOU HAD TO GO AND RUIN IT, DIDN'T YOU?!
BLOWING OUT THE CANDLES! WRECKING THE WHOLE--
SHUT UP.
NO MORE TALK.

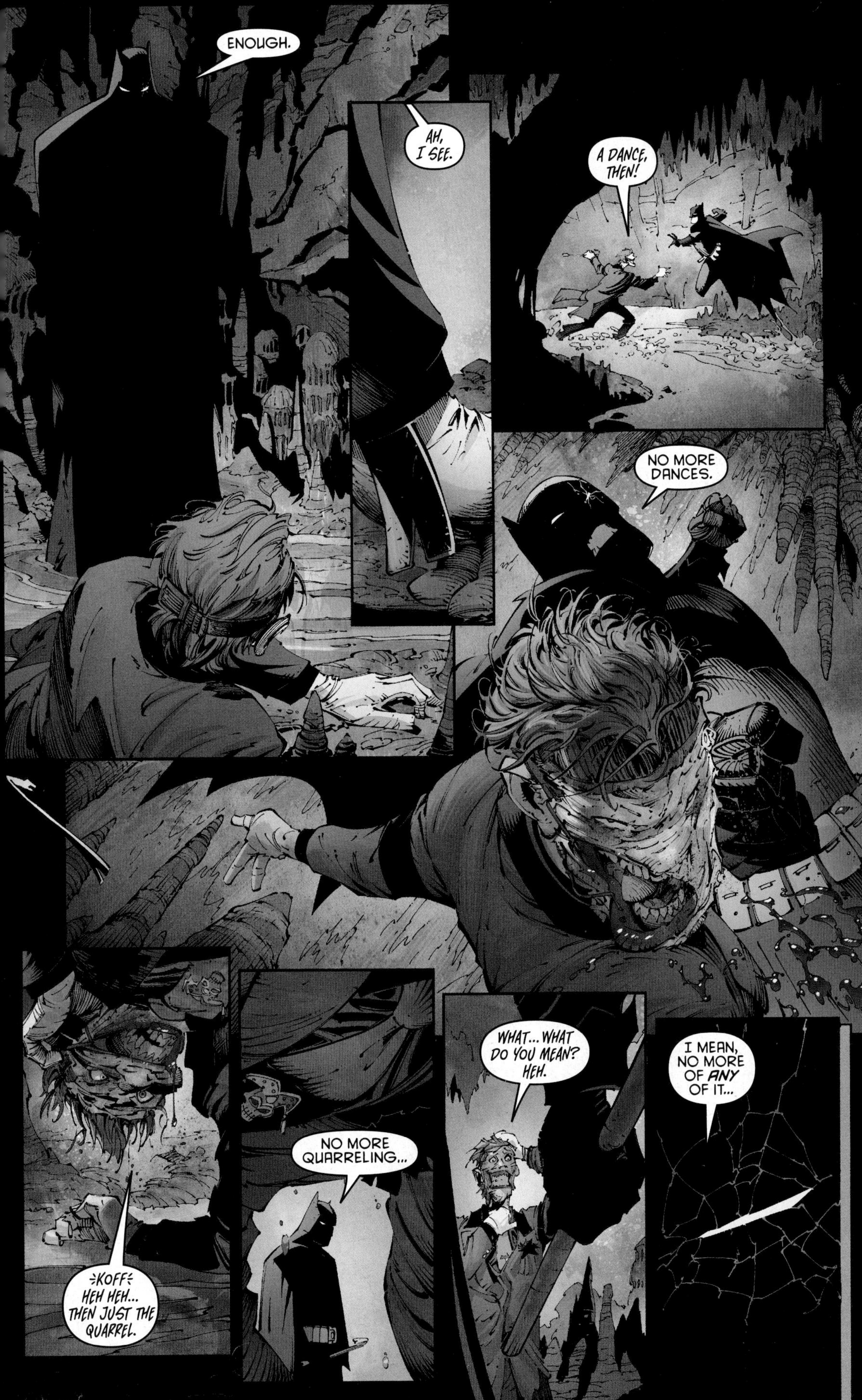
ENOUGH.
AH, I SEE.
A DANCE, THEN!
NO MORE DANCES.
KOFF HEH HEH... THEN JUST THE QUARREL.
NO MORE QUARRELING...
WHAT... WHAT DO YOU MEAN? HEH.
I MEAN, NO MORE OF ANY OF IT...

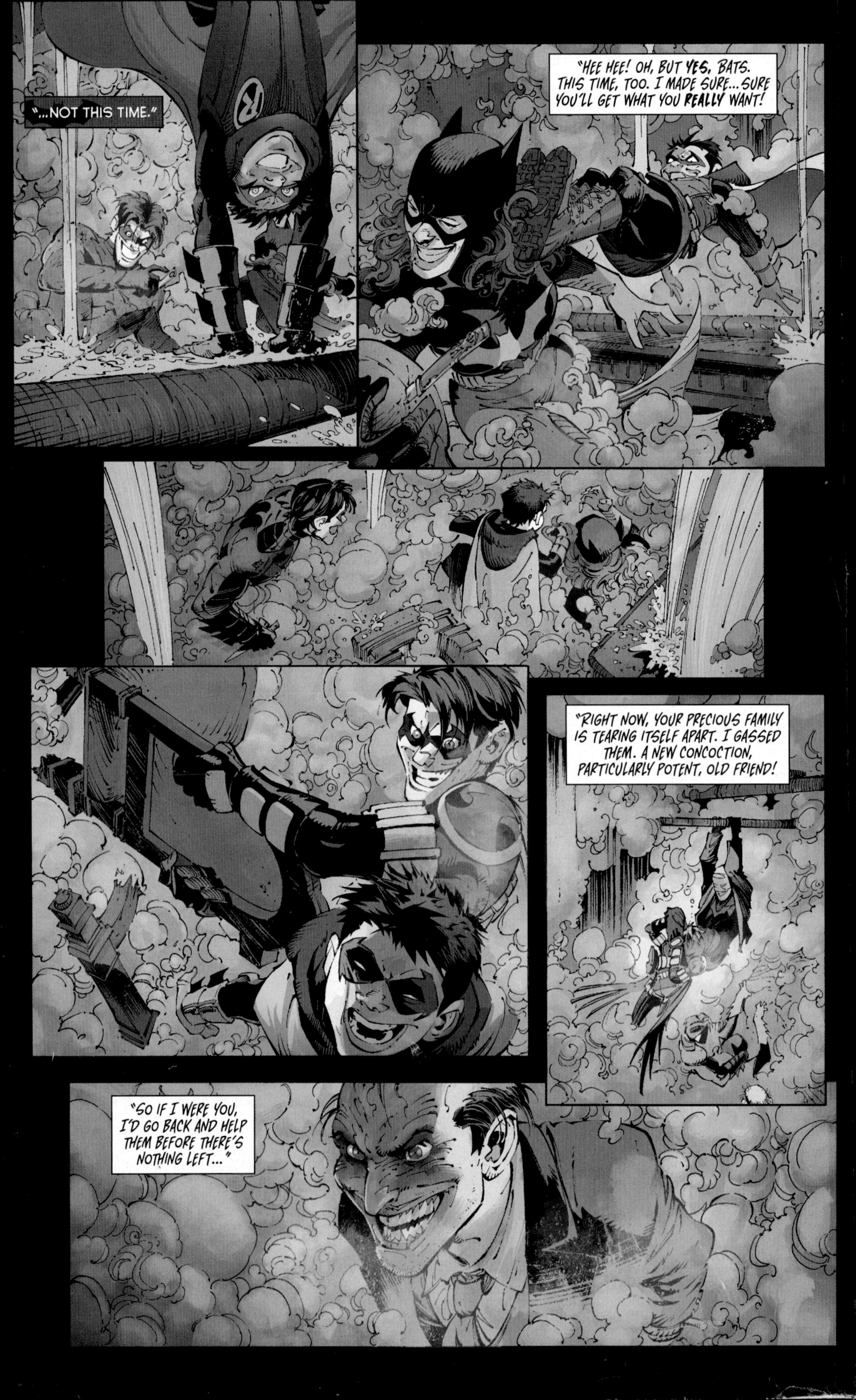
"...NOT THIS TIME."
"HEE HEE! OH, BUT YES, BATS. THIS TIME, TOO. I MADE SURE...SURE YOU'LL GET WHAT YOU REALLY WANT!
"RIGHT NOW, YOUR PRECIOUS FAMILY IS TEARING ITSELF APART. I GASSED THEM. A NEW CONCOCTION, PARTICULARLY POTENT, OLD FRIEND!
"SO IF I WERE YOU, I'D GO BACK AND HELP THEM BEFORE THERE'S NOTHING LEFT..."

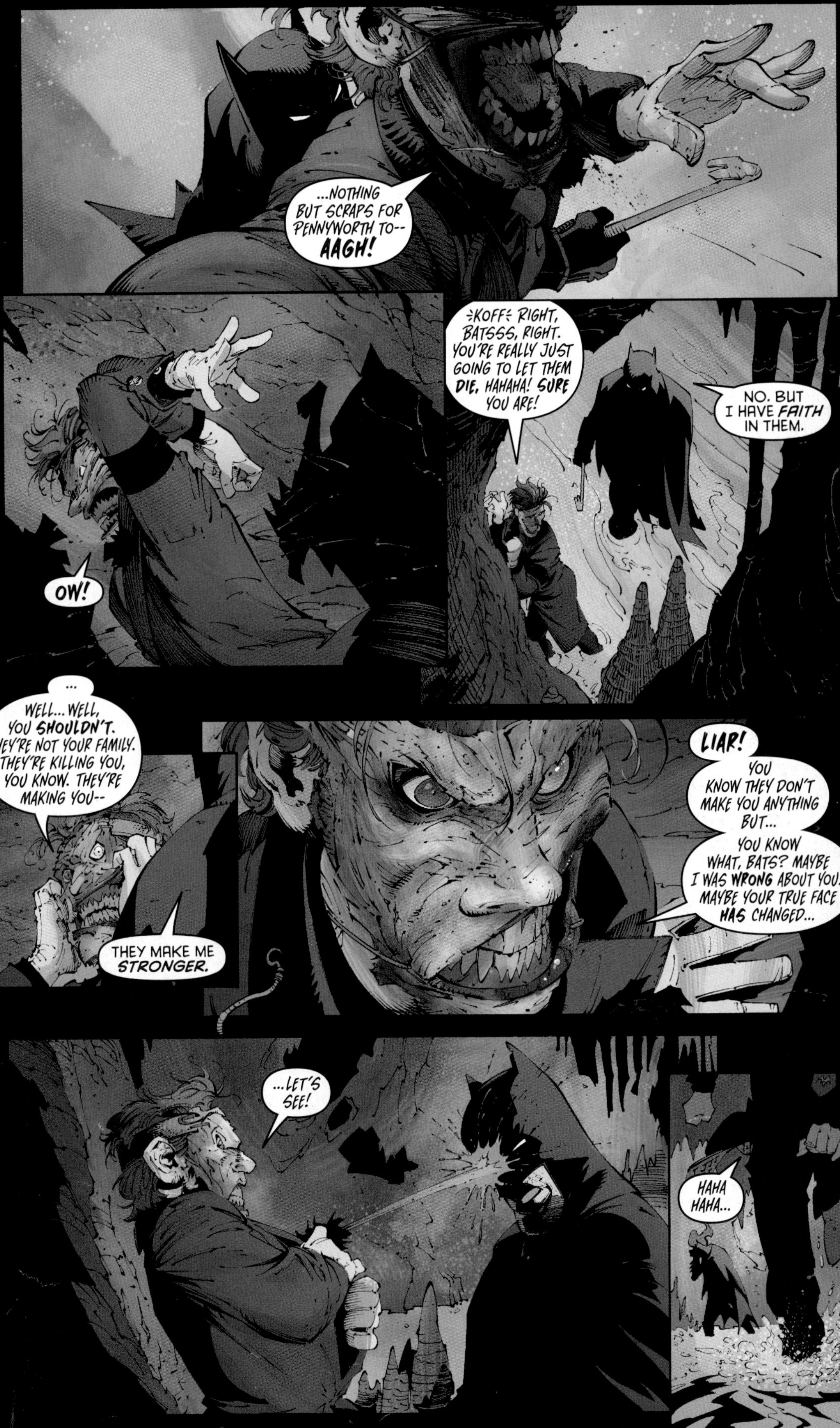
...NOTHING BUT SCRAPS FOR PENNYWORTH TO-- AAGH!
OW!
KOFF RIGHT, BATSSS, RIGHT. YOU'RE REALLY JUST GOING TO LET THEM DIE, HAHAHA! SURE YOU ARE!
NO. BUT I HAVE FAITH IN THEM.
...
WELL... WELL, YOU SHOULDN'T. THEY'RE NOT YOUR FAMILY. THEY'RE KILLING YOU, YOU KNOW. THEY'RE MAKING YOU--
THEY MAKE ME STRONGER.
LIAR!
YOU KNOW THEY DON'T MAKE YOU ANYTHING BUT...
YOU KNOW WHAT, BATS? MAYBE I WAS WRONG ABOUT YOU! MAYBE YOUR TRUE FACE HAS CHANGED...
...LET'S SEE!
HAHA HAHA...

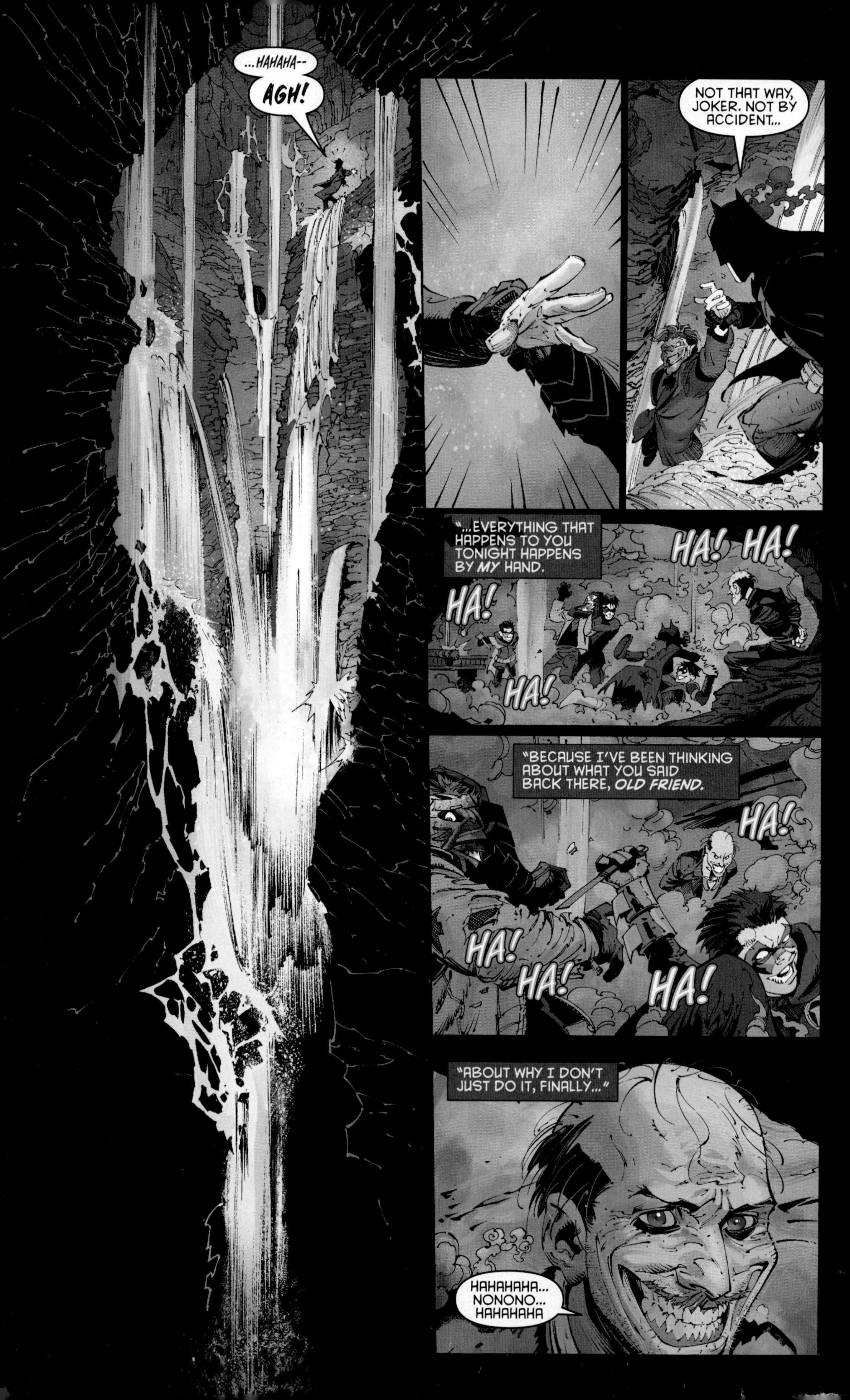
...HAHAHA--
AGH!
NOT THAT WAY, JOKER. NOT BY ACCIDENT...
"...EVERYTHING THAT HAPPENS TO YOU TONIGHT HAPPENS BY MY HAND.
HA! HA!
HA!
HA!
"BECAUSE I'VE BEEN THINKING ABOUT WHAT YOU SAID BACK THERE, OLD FRIEND.
HA!
HA!
HA!
HA!
"ABOUT WHY I DON'T JUST DO IT, FINALLY..."
HAHAHAHA... NONONO... HAHAHAHA

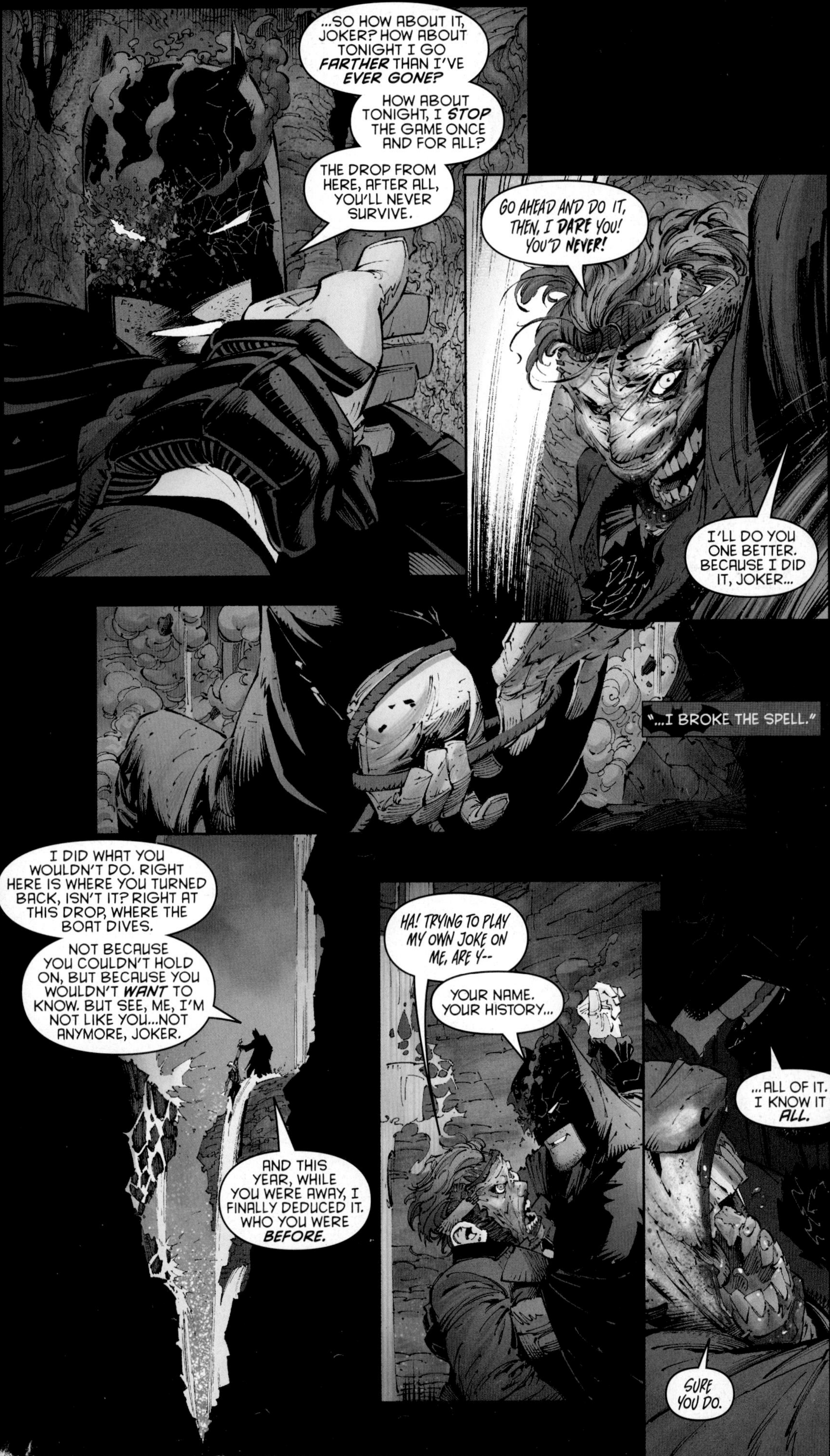

...SO HOW ABOUT IT, JOKER? HOW ABOUT TONIGHT I GO *FARTHER* THAN I'VE *EVER GONE?*
HOW ABOUT TONIGHT, I *STOP* THE GAME ONCE AND FOR ALL?
THE DROP FROM HERE, AFTER ALL, YOU'LL NEVER SURVIVE.
GO AHEAD AND DO IT, THEN, I *DARE* YOU! YOU'D *NEVER!*
I'LL DO YOU ONE BETTER. BECAUSE I DID IT, JOKER...
"...I BROKE THE SPELL."
I DID WHAT YOU WOULDN'T DO. RIGHT HERE IS WHERE YOU TURNED BACK, ISN'T IT? RIGHT AT THIS DROP, WHERE THE BOAT DIVES.
NOT BECAUSE YOU COULDN'T HOLD ON, BUT BECAUSE YOU WOULDN'T *WANT* TO KNOW. BUT SEE, ME, I'M NOT LIKE YOU...NOT ANYMORE, JOKER.
AND THIS YEAR, WHILE YOU WERE AWAY, I FINALLY DEDUCED IT. WHO YOU WERE *BEFORE.*
HA! TRYING TO PLAY MY OWN JOKE ON ME, ARE Y--
YOUR NAME. YOUR HISTORY...
...ALL OF IT. I KNOW IT *ALL.*
SURE YOU DO.

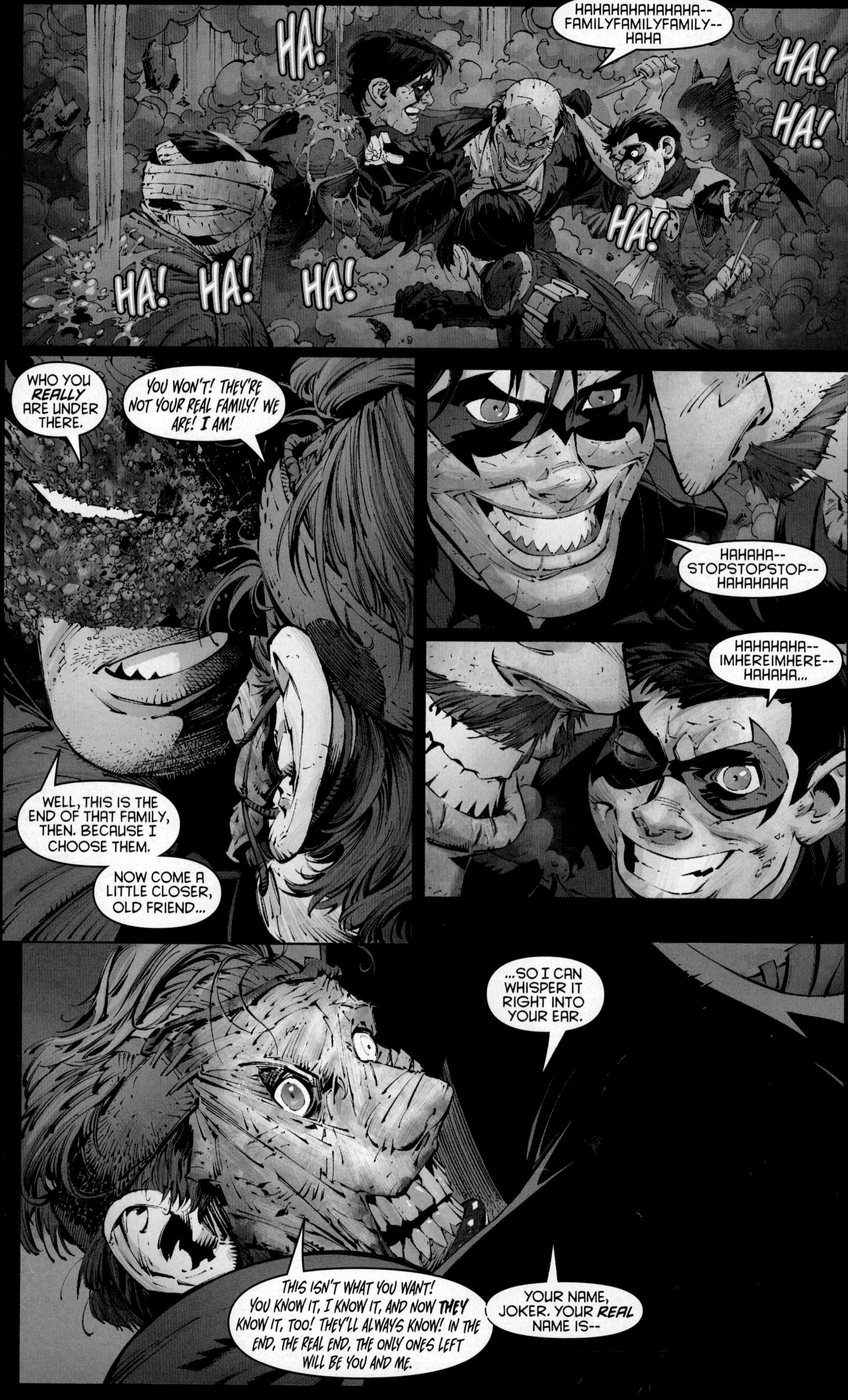
HA!
HAHAHAHAHAHAHA-- FAMILYFAMILYFAMILY-- HAHA
HA!
HA!
HA!
HA! HA!
HA!
WHO YOU REALLY ARE UNDER THERE.
YOU WON'T! THEY'RE NOT YOUR REAL FAMILY! WE ARE! I AM!
HAHAHA-- STOPSTOPSTOP-- HAHAHAHA
WELL, THIS IS THE END OF THAT FAMILY, THEN. BECAUSE I CHOOSE THEM.
NOW COME A LITTLE CLOSER, OLD FRIEND...
HAHAHAHA-- IMHEREIMHERE-- HAHAHA...
...SO I CAN WHISPER IT RIGHT INTO YOUR EAR.
THIS ISN'T WHAT YOU WANT! YOU KNOW IT, I KNOW IT, AND NOW THEY KNOW IT, TOO! THEY'LL ALWAYS KNOW! IN THE END, THE REAL END, THE ONLY ONES LEFT WILL BE YOU AND ME.
YOUR NAME, JOKER. YOUR REAL NAME IS--

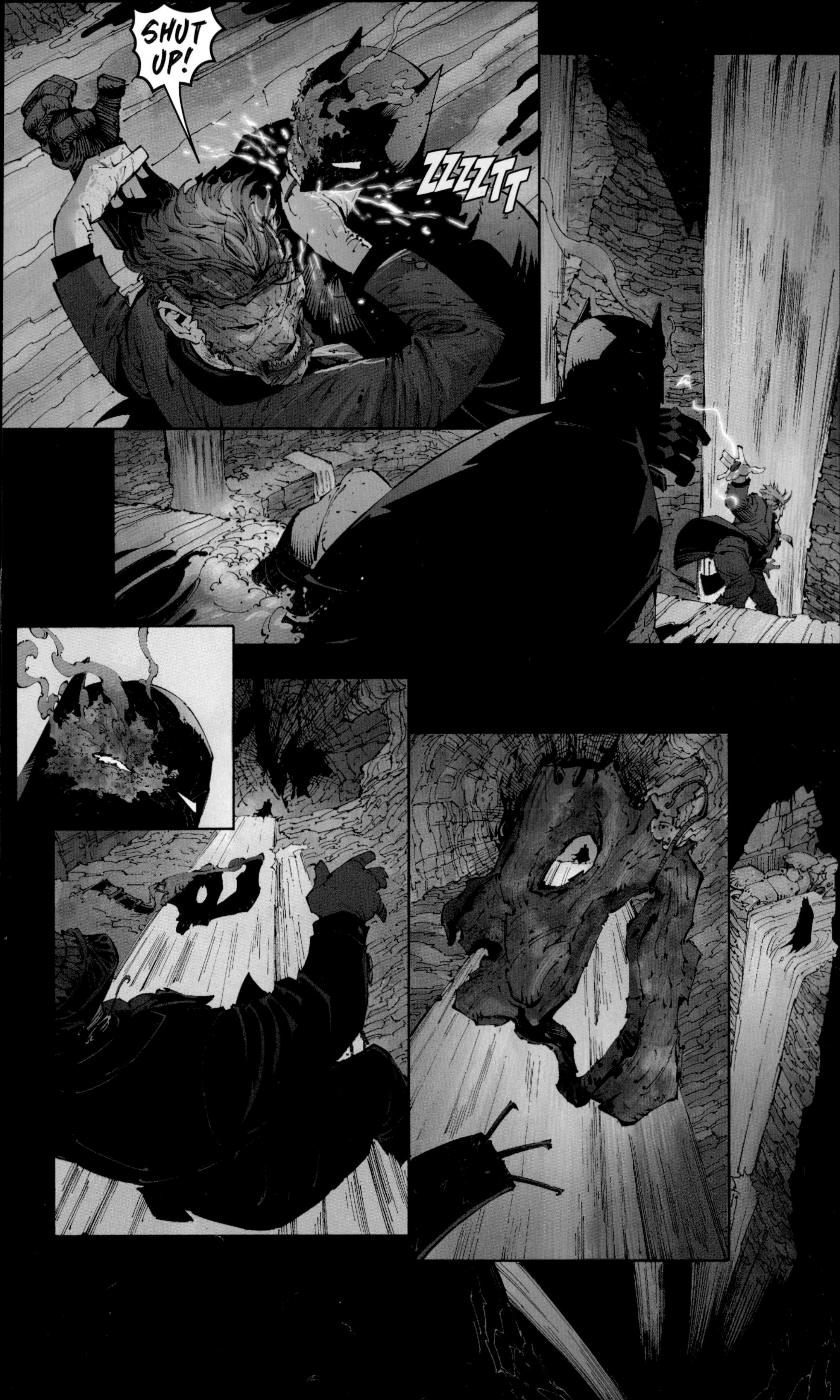
SHUT UP!
ZZZZTT

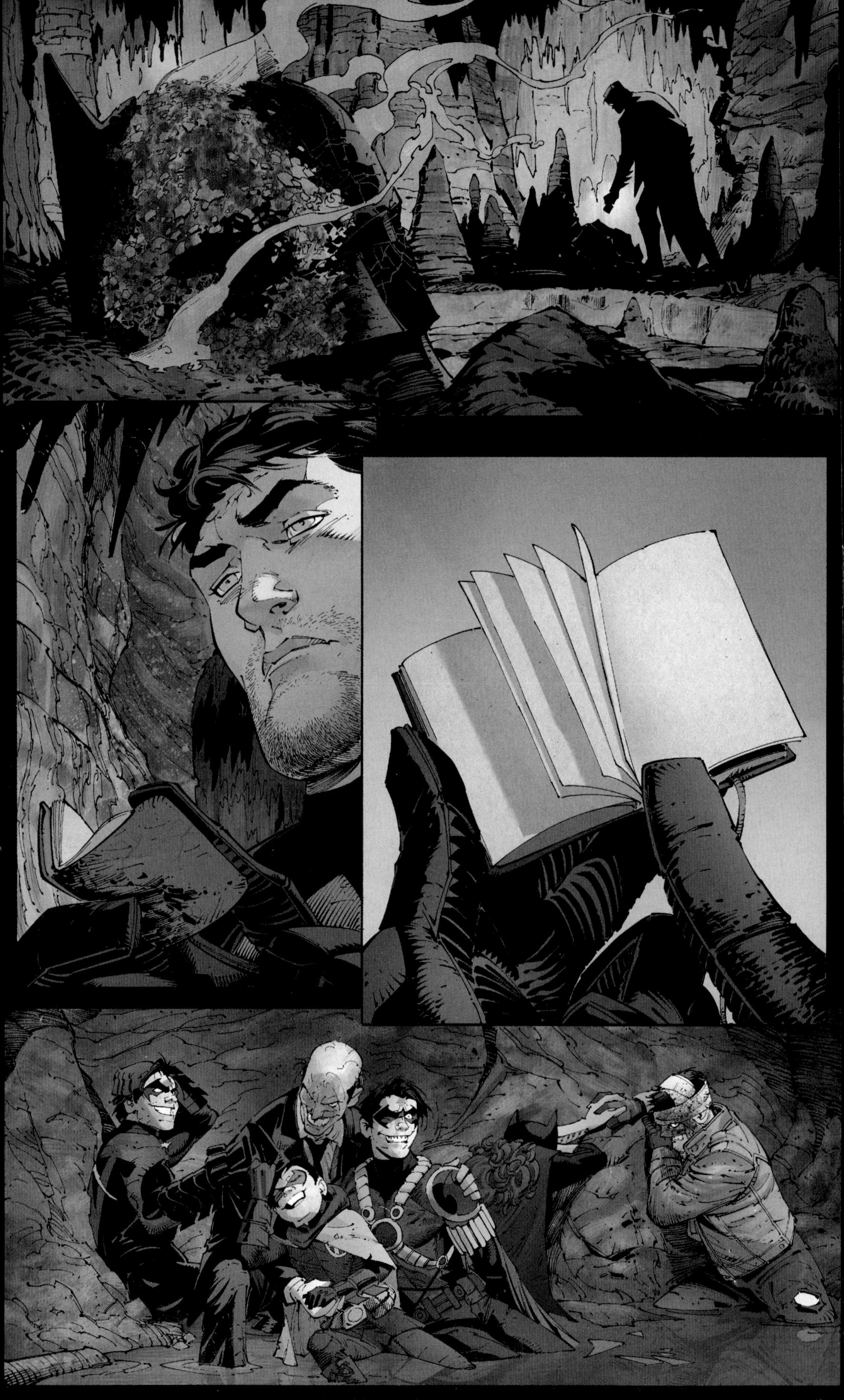

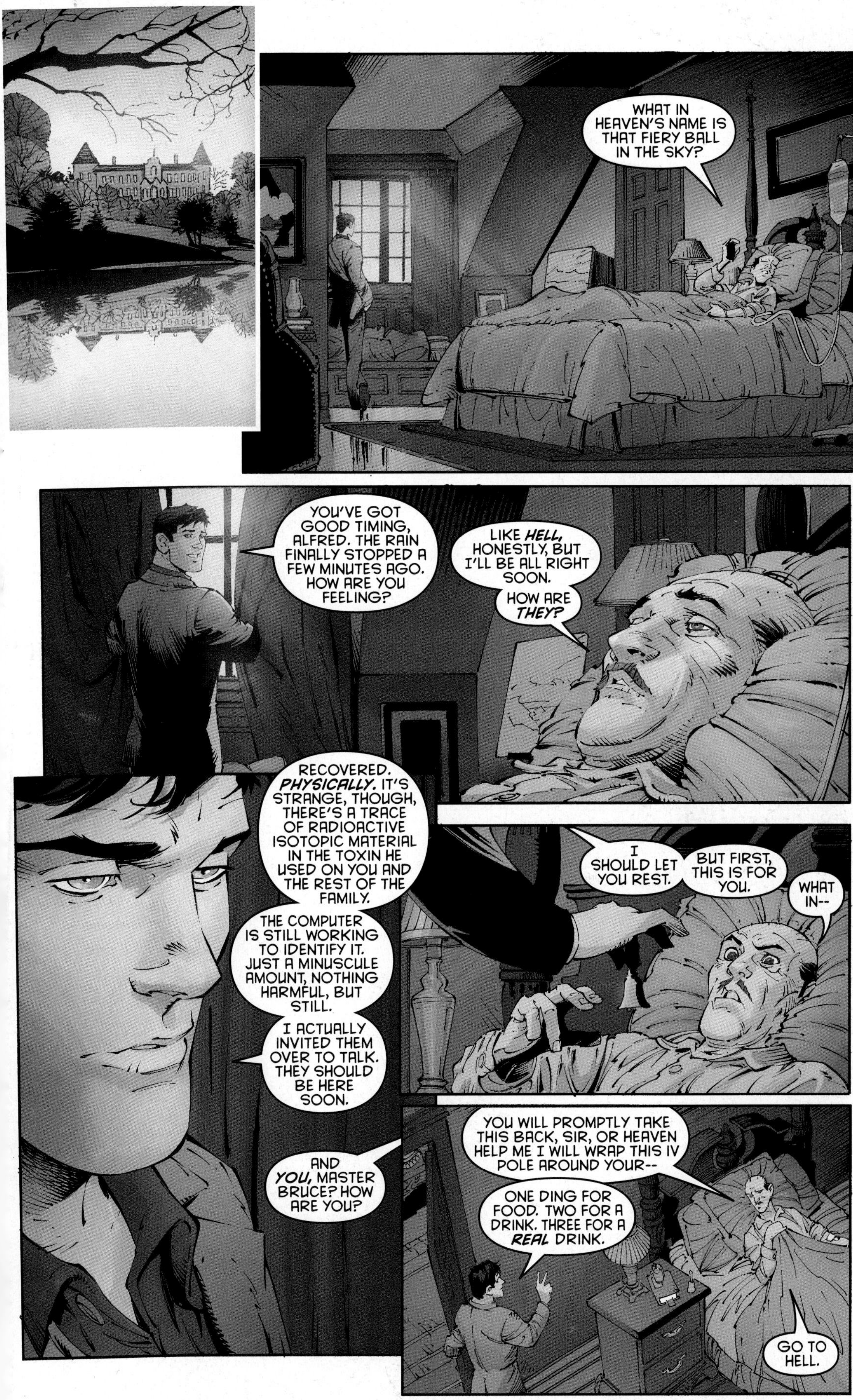
WHAT IN HEAVEN'S NAME IS THAT FIERY BALL IN THE SKY?
YOU'VE GOT GOOD TIMING, ALFRED. THE RAIN FINALLY STOPPED A FEW MINUTES AGO. HOW ARE YOU FEELING?
LIKE HELL, HONESTLY, BUT I'LL BE ALL RIGHT SOON.
HOW ARE THEY?
RECOVERED. PHYSICALLY. IT'S STRANGE, THOUGH, THERE'S A TRACE OF RADIOACTIVE ISOTOPIC MATERIAL IN THE TOXIN HE USED ON YOU AND THE REST OF THE FAMILY.
THE COMPUTER IS STILL WORKING TO IDENTIFY IT. JUST A MINUSCULE AMOUNT, NOTHING HARMFUL, BUT STILL.
I ACTUALLY INVITED THEM OVER TO TALK. THEY SHOULD BE HERE SOON.
AND YOU, MASTER BRUCE? HOW ARE YOU?
I SHOULD LET YOU REST.
BUT FIRST, THIS IS FOR YOU.
WHAT IN--
YOU WILL PROMPTLY TAKE THIS BACK, SIR, OR HEAVEN HELP ME I WILL WRAP THIS IV POLE AROUND YOUR--
ONE DING FOR FOOD. TWO FOR A DRINK. THREE FOR A REAL DRINK.
GO TO HELL.

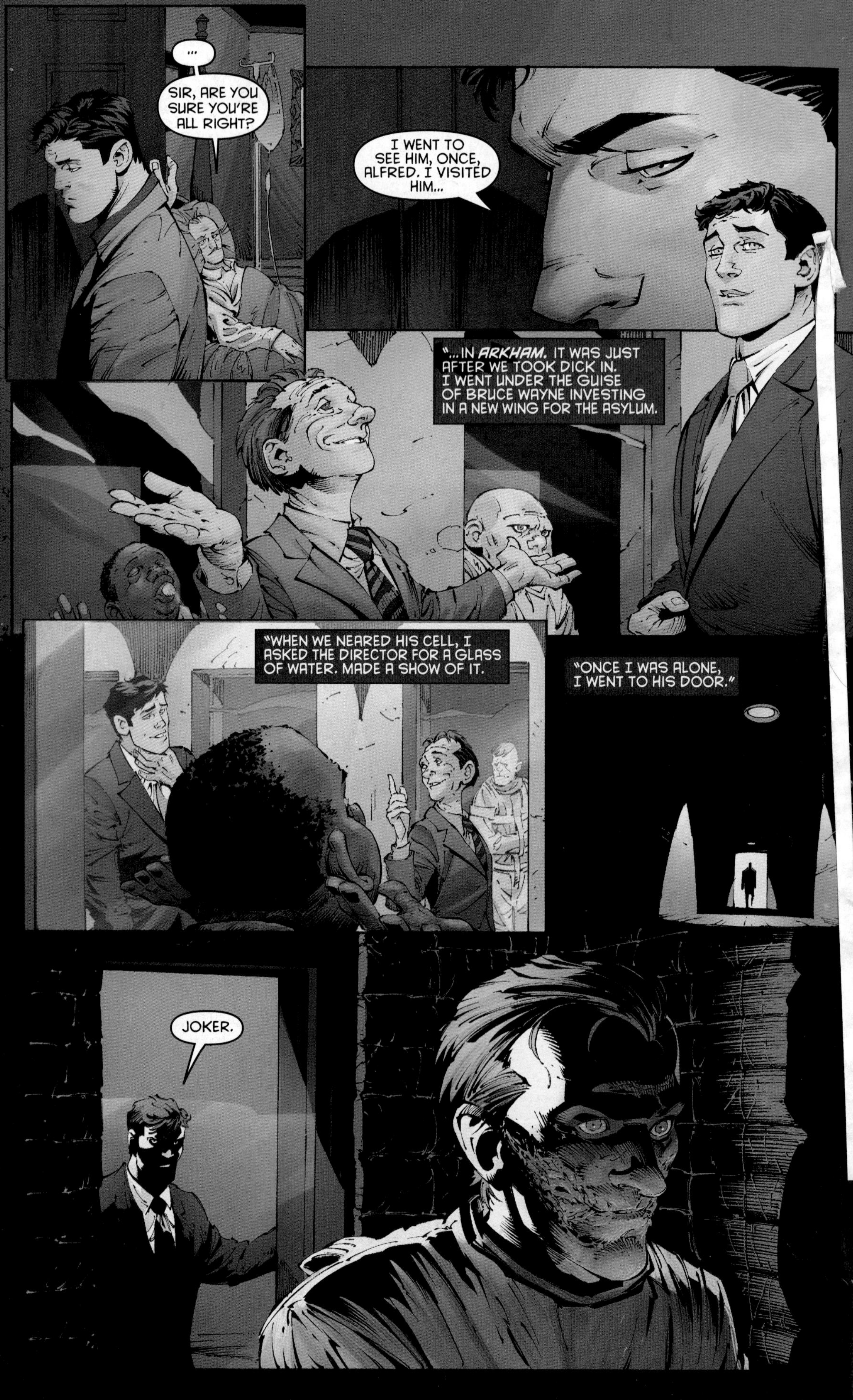
...
SIR, ARE YOU SURE YOU'RE ALL RIGHT?
I WENT TO SEE HIM, ONCE, ALFRED. I VISITED HIM...
"...IN ARKHAM. IT WAS JUST AFTER WE TOOK DICK IN. I WENT UNDER THE GUISE OF BRUCE WAYNE INVESTING IN A NEW WING FOR THE ASYLUM.
"WHEN WE NEARED HIS CELL, I ASKED THE DIRECTOR FOR A GLASS OF WATER. MADE A SHOW OF IT.
"ONCE I WAS ALONE, I WENT TO HIS DOOR."
JOKER.

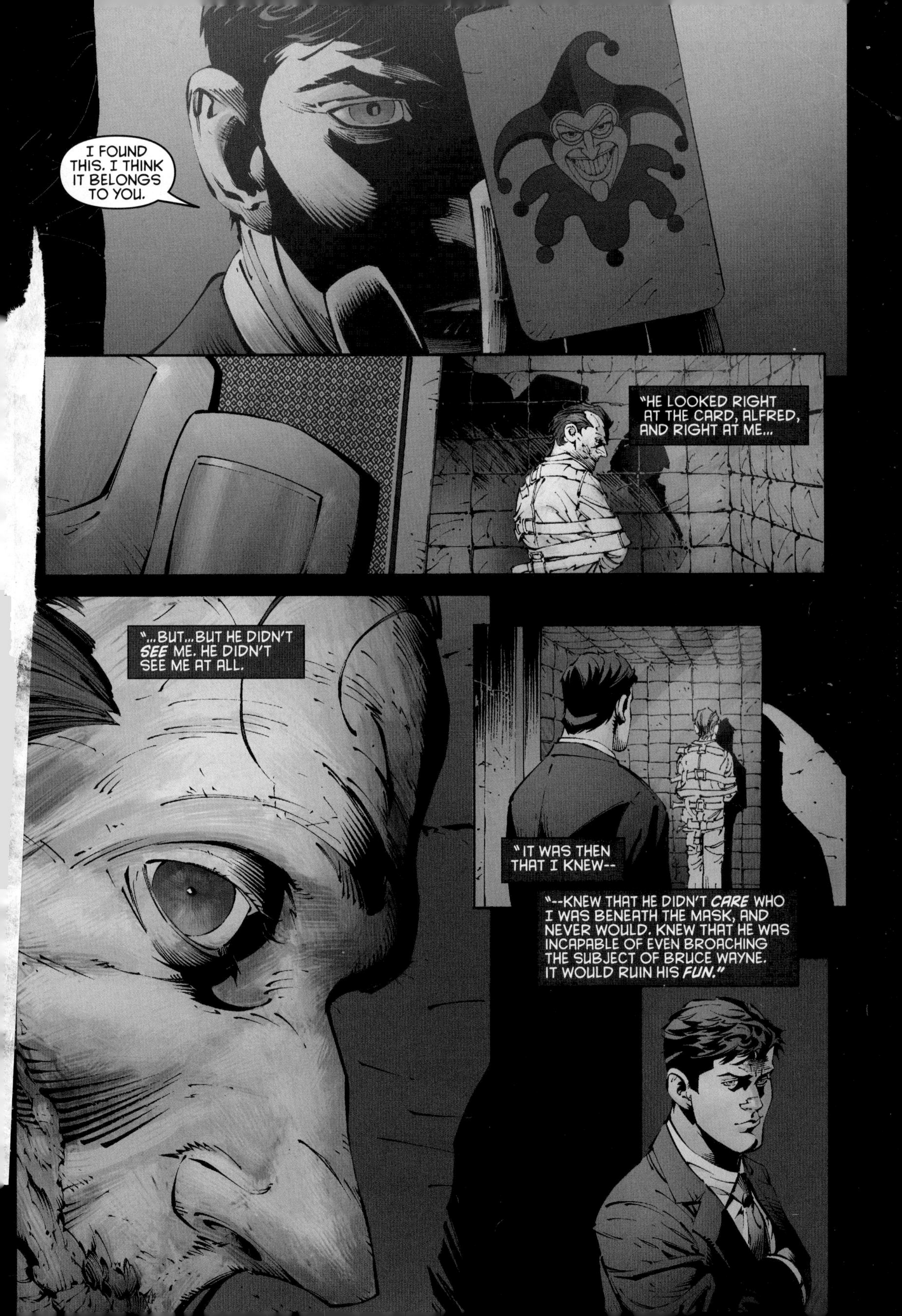
I FOUND THIS. I THINK IT BELONGS TO YOU.
"HE LOOKED RIGHT AT THE CARD, ALFRED, AND RIGHT AT ME...
"...BUT...BUT HE DIDN'T *SEE* ME. HE DIDN'T SEE ME AT ALL.
"IT WAS THEN THAT I KNEW--
"--KNEW THAT HE DIDN'T *CARE* WHO I WAS BENEATH THE MASK, AND NEVER WOULD. KNEW THAT HE WAS INCAPABLE OF EVEN BROACHING THE SUBJECT OF BRUCE WAYNE. IT WOULD RUIN HIS *FUN*."

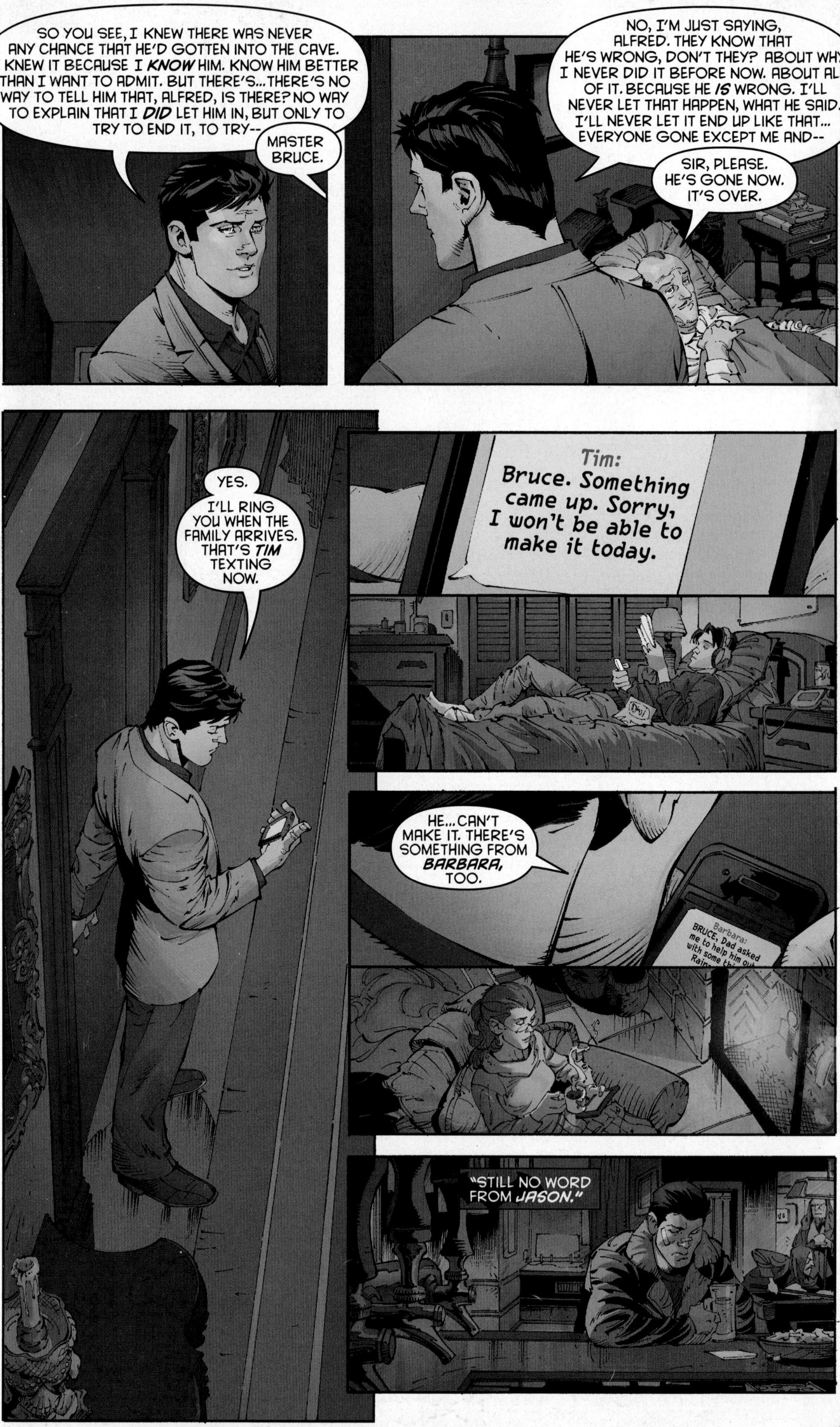
SO YOU SEE, I KNEW THERE WAS NEVER ANY CHANCE THAT HE'D GOTTEN INTO THE CAVE. I KNEW IT BECAUSE I *KNOW* HIM. KNOW HIM BETTER THAN I WANT TO ADMIT. BUT THERE'S...THERE'S NO WAY TO TELL HIM THAT, ALFRED, IS THERE? NO WAY TO EXPLAIN THAT I *DID* LET HIM IN, BUT ONLY TO TRY TO END IT, TO TRY--
MASTER BRUCE.
NO, I'M JUST SAYING, ALFRED. THEY KNOW THAT HE'S WRONG, DON'T THEY? ABOUT WHY I NEVER DID IT BEFORE NOW. ABOUT ALL OF IT. BECAUSE HE *IS* WRONG. I'LL NEVER LET THAT HAPPEN, WHAT HE SAID. I'LL NEVER LET IT END UP LIKE THAT... EVERYONE GONE EXCEPT ME AND--
SIR, PLEASE. HE'S GONE NOW. IT'S OVER.
YES.
I'LL RING YOU WHEN THE FAMILY ARRIVES. THAT'S *TIM* TEXTING NOW.
Tim:
Bruce. Something came up. Sorry, I won't be able to make it today.
HE...CAN'T MAKE IT. THERE'S SOMETHING FROM *BARBARA,* TOO.
Barbara:
BRUCE, Dad asked me to help him out with some
"STILL NO WORD FROM *JASON.*"

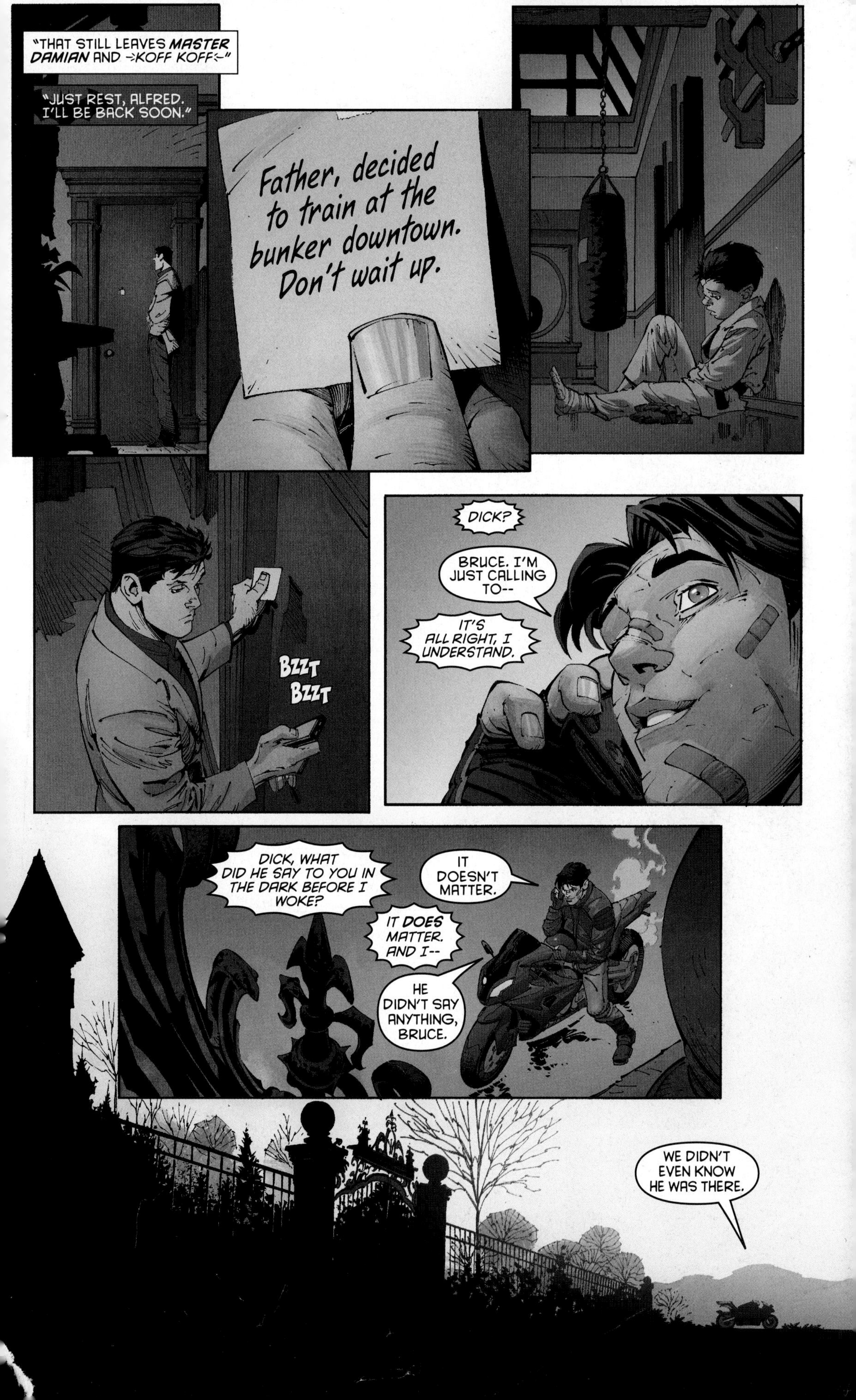
"THAT STILL LEAVES MASTER DAMIAN AND ⪢KOFF KOFF⪡"
"JUST REST, ALFRED. I'LL BE BACK SOON."
Father, decided to train at the bunker downtown. Don't wait up.
BZZT BZZT
DICK?
BRUCE. I'M JUST CALLING TO--
IT'S ALL RIGHT, I UNDERSTAND.
DICK, WHAT DID HE SAY TO YOU IN THE DARK BEFORE I WOKE?
IT DOESN'T MATTER.
IT DOES MATTER. AND I--
HE DIDN'T SAY ANYTHING, BRUCE.
WE DIDN'T EVEN KNOW HE WAS THERE.

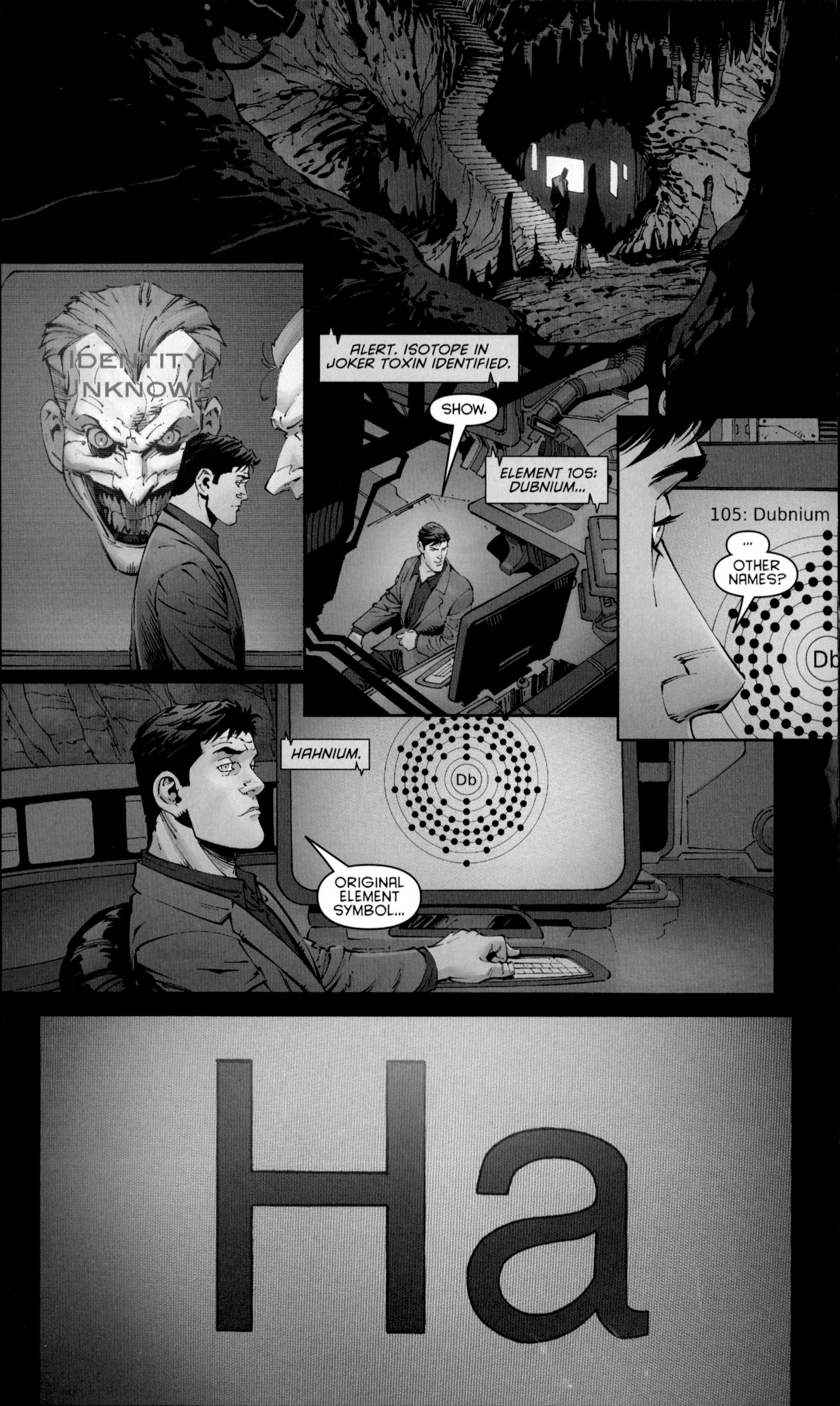
IDENTITY UNKNOWN
ALERT. ISOTOPE IN JOKER TOXIN IDENTIFIED.
SHOW.
ELEMENT 105: DUBNIUM...
105: Dubnium
... OTHER NAMES?
Db
HAHNIUM.
Db
ORIGINAL ELEMENT SYMBOL...
Ha

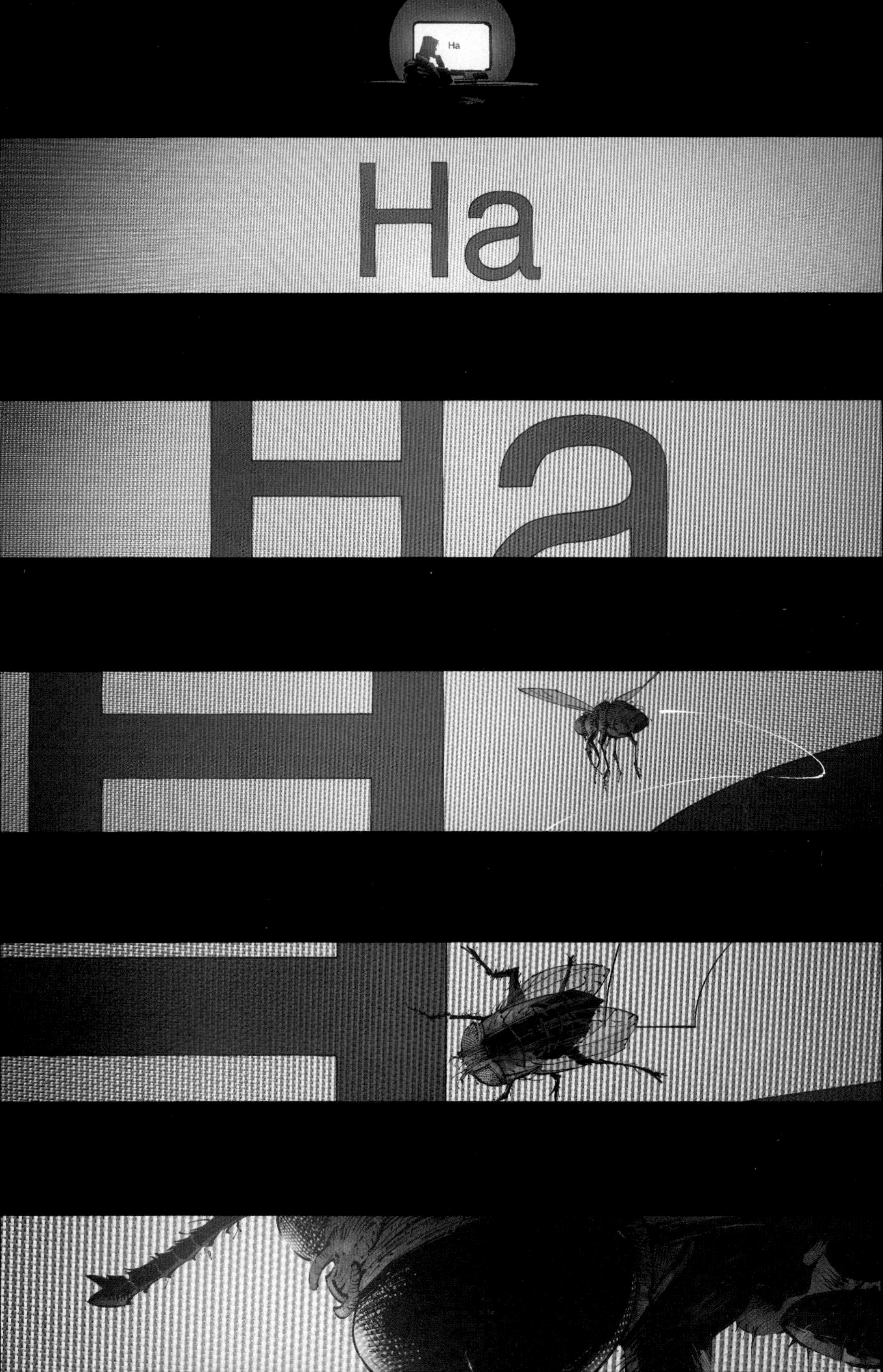
Ha
Ha

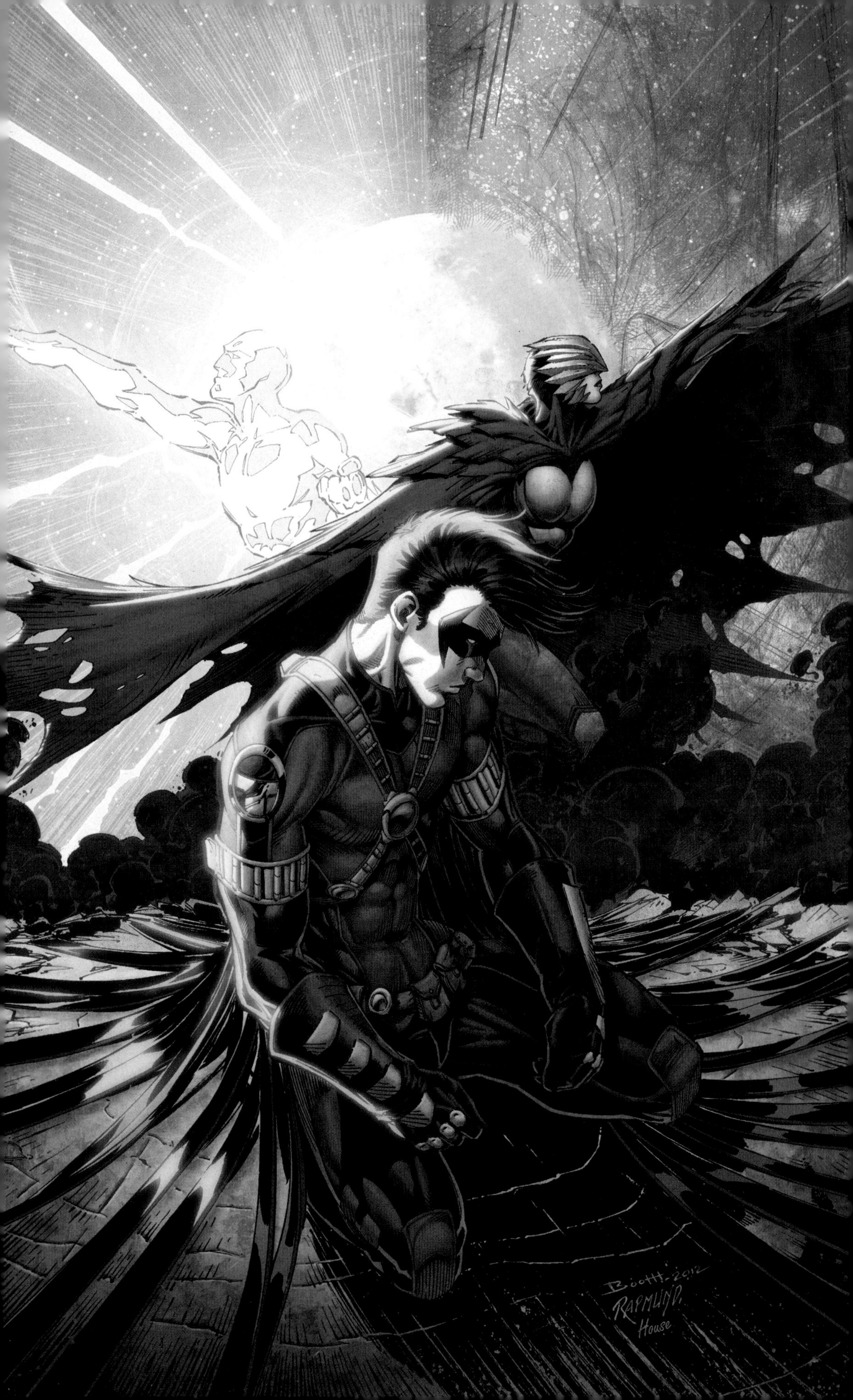
Booth-2012
RAPMUND.
House

GREY MATTERS: A TALE OF LIGHT AND DARK

SCOTT LOBDELL & FABIAN NICIEZA writers **EDDY BARROWS** penciller **EBER FERREIRA** inker

cover art by **BRETT BOOTH, NORM RAPMUND & ANDREW DALHOUSE**

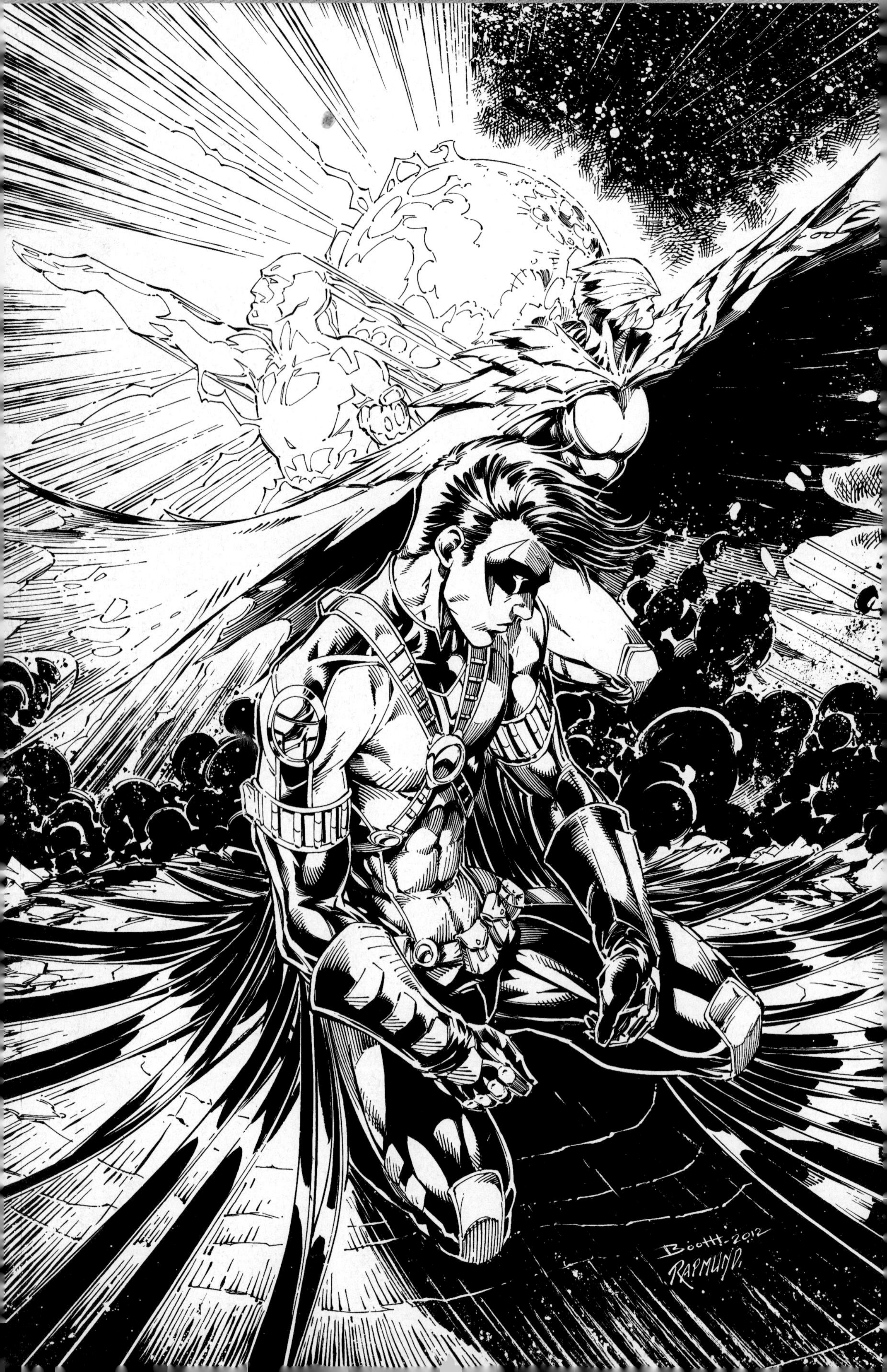
BOOTH-2012
RAPMUND

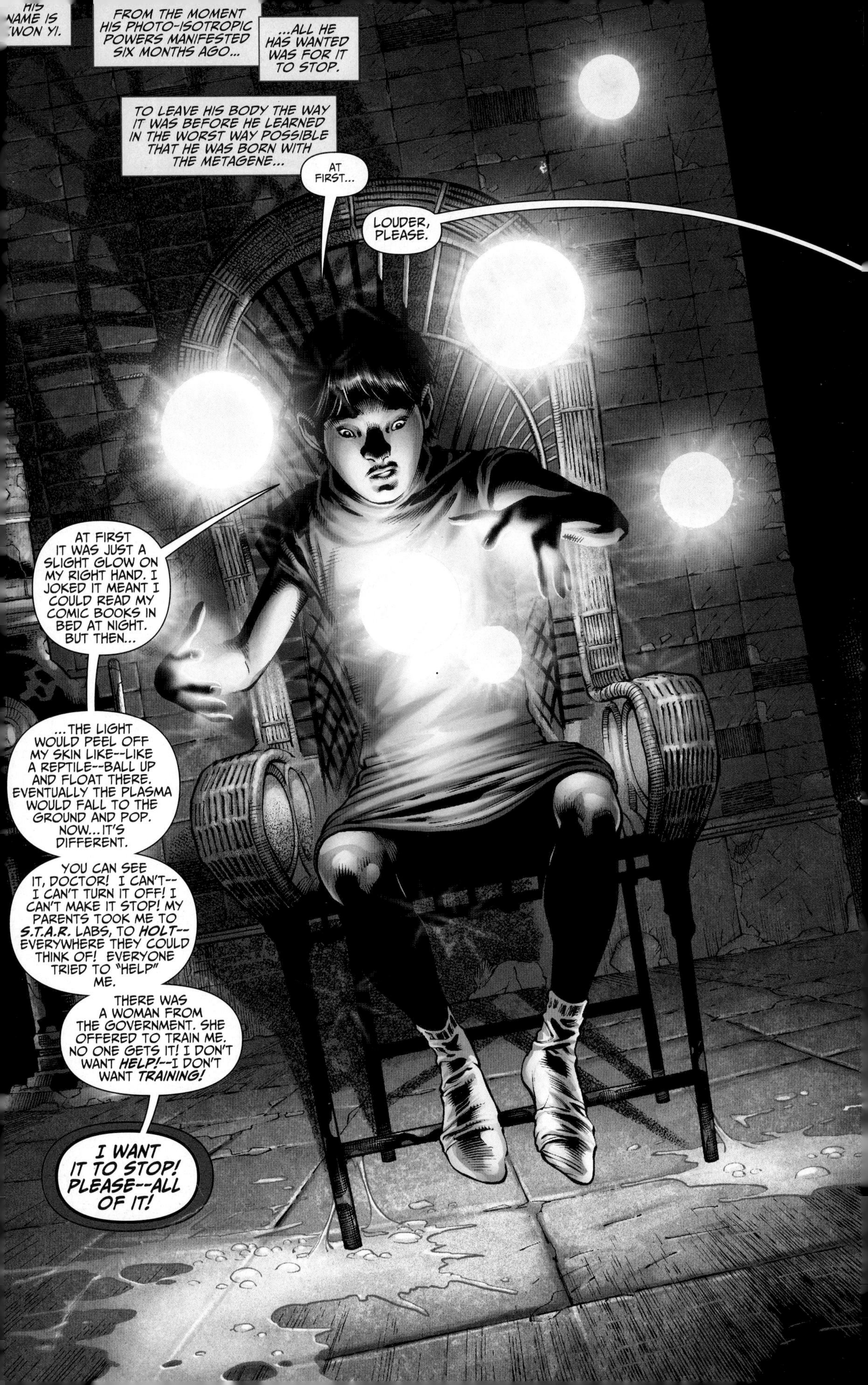
HIS NAME IS KWON YI.
FROM THE MOMENT HIS PHOTO-ISOTROPIC POWERS MANIFESTED SIX MONTHS AGO...
...ALL HE HAS WANTED WAS FOR IT TO STOP.
TO LEAVE HIS BODY THE WAY IT WAS BEFORE HE LEARNED IN THE WORST WAY POSSIBLE THAT HE WAS BORN WITH THE METAGENE...
AT FIRST...
LOUDER, PLEASE.
AT FIRST IT WAS JUST A SLIGHT GLOW ON MY RIGHT HAND. I JOKED IT MEANT I COULD READ MY COMIC BOOKS IN BED AT NIGHT. BUT THEN...
...THE LIGHT WOULD PEEL OFF MY SKIN LIKE--LIKE A REPTILE--BALL UP AND FLOAT THERE. EVENTUALLY THE PLASMA WOULD FALL TO THE GROUND AND POP. NOW...IT'S DIFFERENT.
YOU CAN SEE IT, DOCTOR! I CAN'T--I CAN'T TURN IT OFF! I CAN'T MAKE IT STOP! MY PARENTS TOOK ME TO S.T.A.R. LABS, TO HOLT--EVERYWHERE THEY COULD THINK OF! EVERYONE TRIED TO "HELP" ME.
THERE WAS A WOMAN FROM THE GOVERNMENT. SHE OFFERED TO TRAIN ME. NO ONE GETS IT! I DON'T WANT HELP!--I DON'T WANT TRAINING!
I WANT IT TO STOP! PLEASE--ALL OF IT!

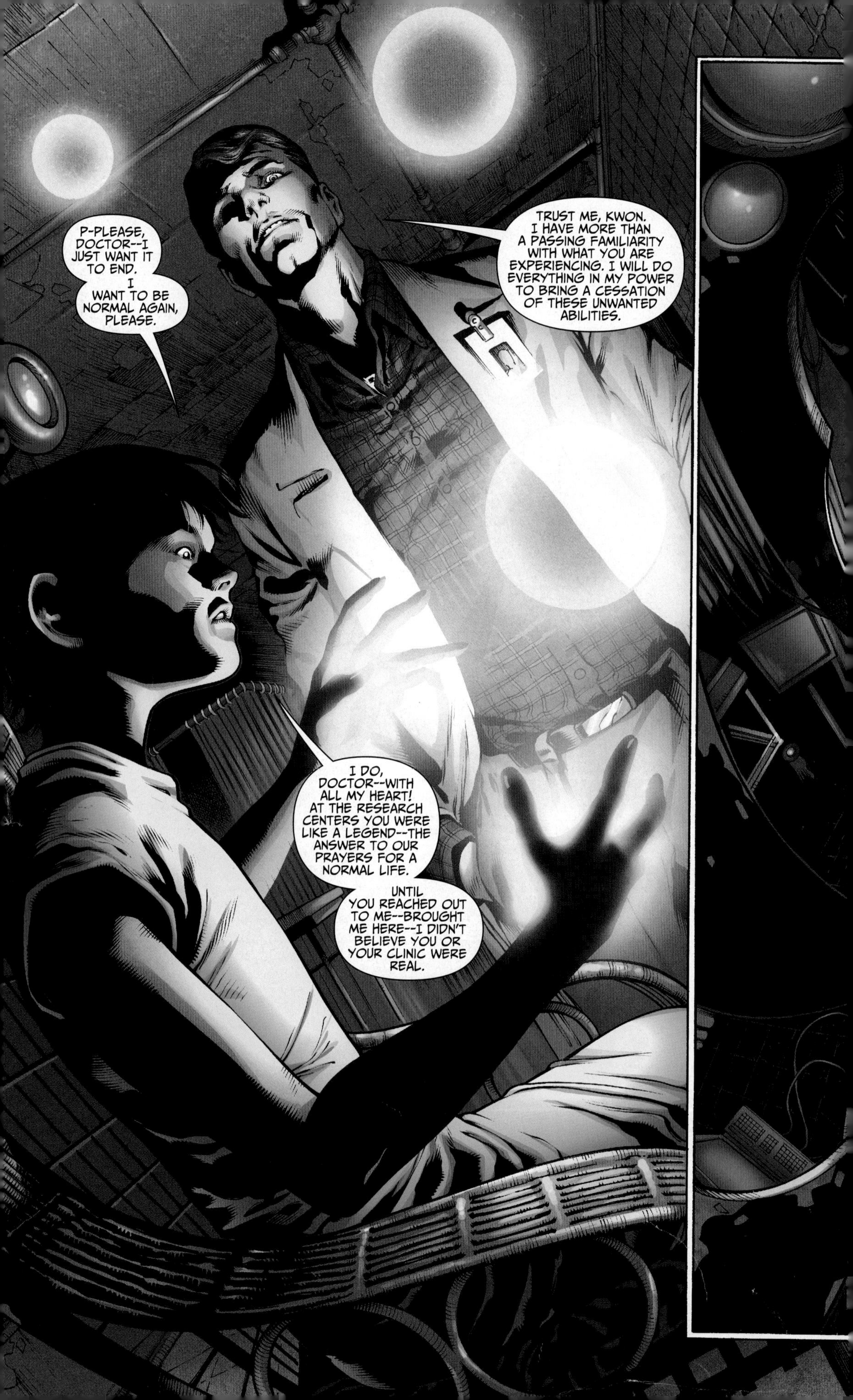
P-PLEASE, DOCTOR--I JUST WANT IT TO END.
I WANT TO BE NORMAL AGAIN, PLEASE.
TRUST ME, KWON. I HAVE MORE THAN A PASSING FAMILIARITY WITH WHAT YOU ARE EXPERIENCING. I WILL DO EVERYTHING IN MY POWER TO BRING A CESSATION OF THESE UNWANTED ABILITIES.
I DO, DOCTOR--WITH ALL MY HEART! AT THE RESEARCH CENTERS YOU WERE LIKE A LEGEND--THE ANSWER TO OUR PRAYERS FOR A NORMAL LIFE.
UNTIL YOU REACHED OUT TO ME--BROUGHT ME HERE--I DIDN'T BELIEVE YOU OR YOUR CLINIC WERE REAL.

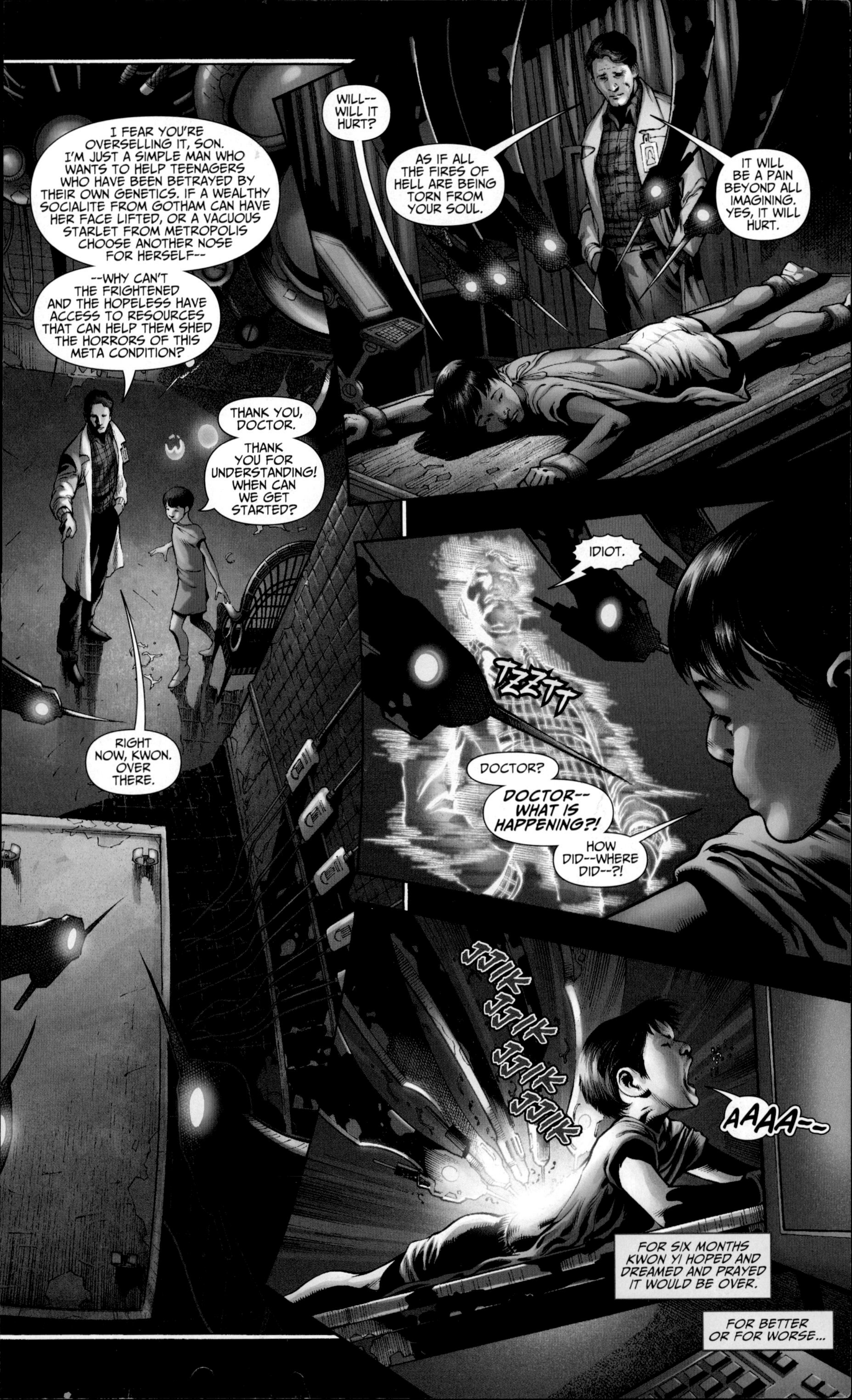
I FEAR YOU'RE OVERSELLING IT, SON. I'M JUST A SIMPLE MAN WHO WANTS TO HELP TEENAGERS WHO HAVE BEEN BETRAYED BY THEIR OWN GENETICS. IF A WEALTHY SOCIALITE FROM GOTHAM CAN HAVE HER FACE LIFTED, OR A VACUOUS STARLET FROM METROPOLIS CHOOSE ANOTHER NOSE FOR HERSELF--
--WHY CAN'T THE FRIGHTENED AND THE HOPELESS HAVE ACCESS TO RESOURCES THAT CAN HELP THEM SHED THE HORRORS OF THIS META CONDITION?
THANK YOU, DOCTOR.
THANK YOU FOR UNDERSTANDING! WHEN CAN WE GET STARTED?
RIGHT NOW, KWON. OVER THERE.
WILL-- WILL IT HURT?
AS IF ALL THE FIRES OF HELL ARE BEING TORN FROM YOUR SOUL.
IT WILL BE A PAIN BEYOND ALL IMAGINING. YES, IT WILL HURT.
IDIOT.
TZZTT
DOCTOR?
DOCTOR-- WHAT IS HAPPENING?!
HOW DID--WHERE DID--?!
JJIK JJIK JJIK JJIK
AAAA--
FOR SIX MONTHS KWON YI HOPED AND DREAMED AND PRAYED IT WOULD BE OVER.
FOR BETTER OR FOR WORSE...

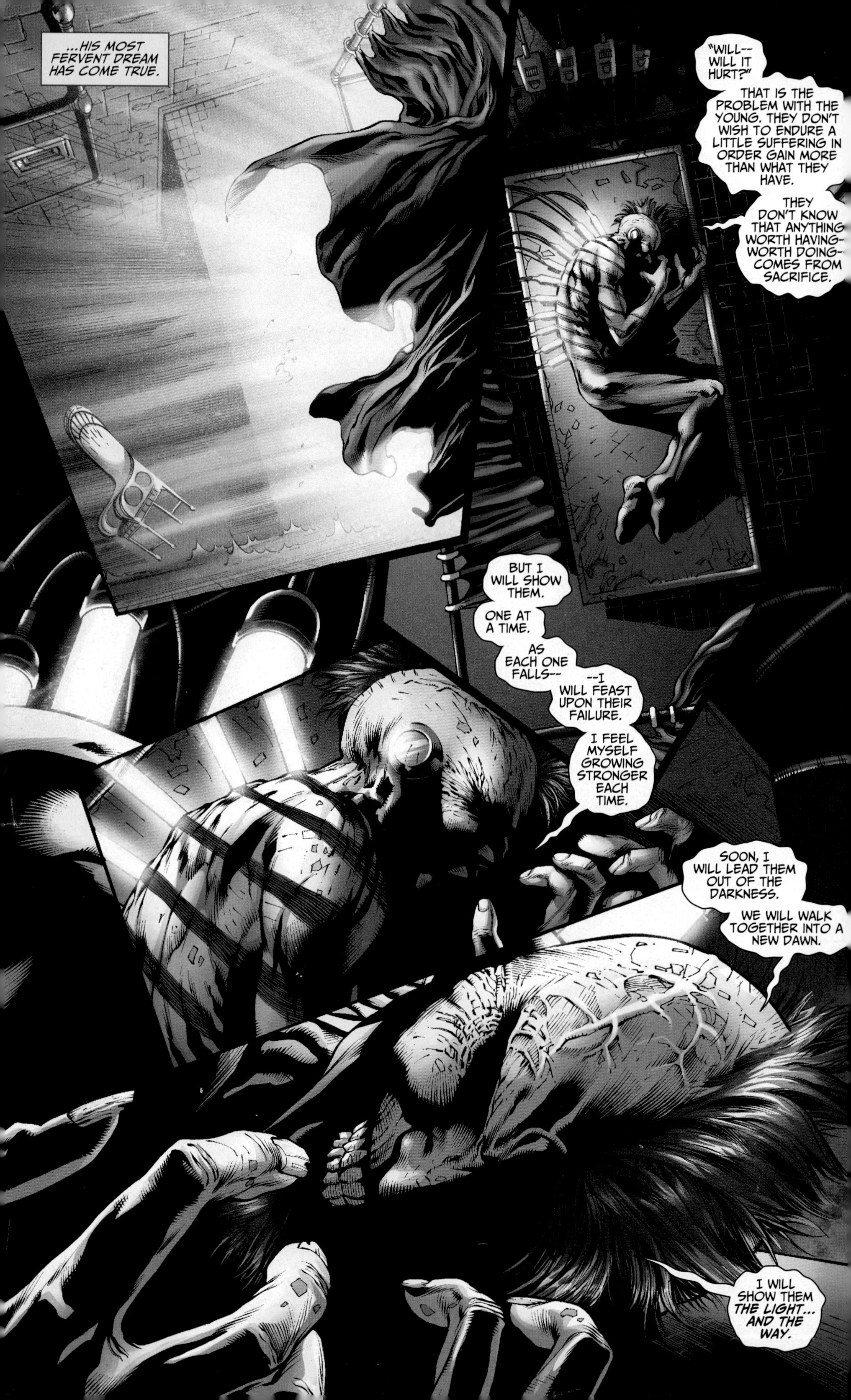
...HIS MOST FERVENT DREAM HAS COME TRUE.
"WILL-- WILL IT HURT?"
THAT IS THE PROBLEM WITH THE YOUNG. THEY DON'T WISH TO ENDURE A LITTLE SUFFERING IN ORDER GAIN MORE THAN WHAT THEY HAVE.
THEY DON'T KNOW THAT ANYTHING WORTH HAVING- WORTH DOING- COMES FROM SACRIFICE.
BUT I WILL SHOW THEM.
ONE AT A TIME.
AS EACH ONE FALLS--
--I WILL FEAST UPON THEIR FAILURE.
I FEEL MYSELF GROWING STRONGER EACH TIME.
SOON, I WILL LEAD THEM OUT OF THE DARKNESS.
WE WILL WALK TOGETHER INTO A NEW DAWN.
I WILL SHOW THEM THE LIGHT... AND THE WAY.

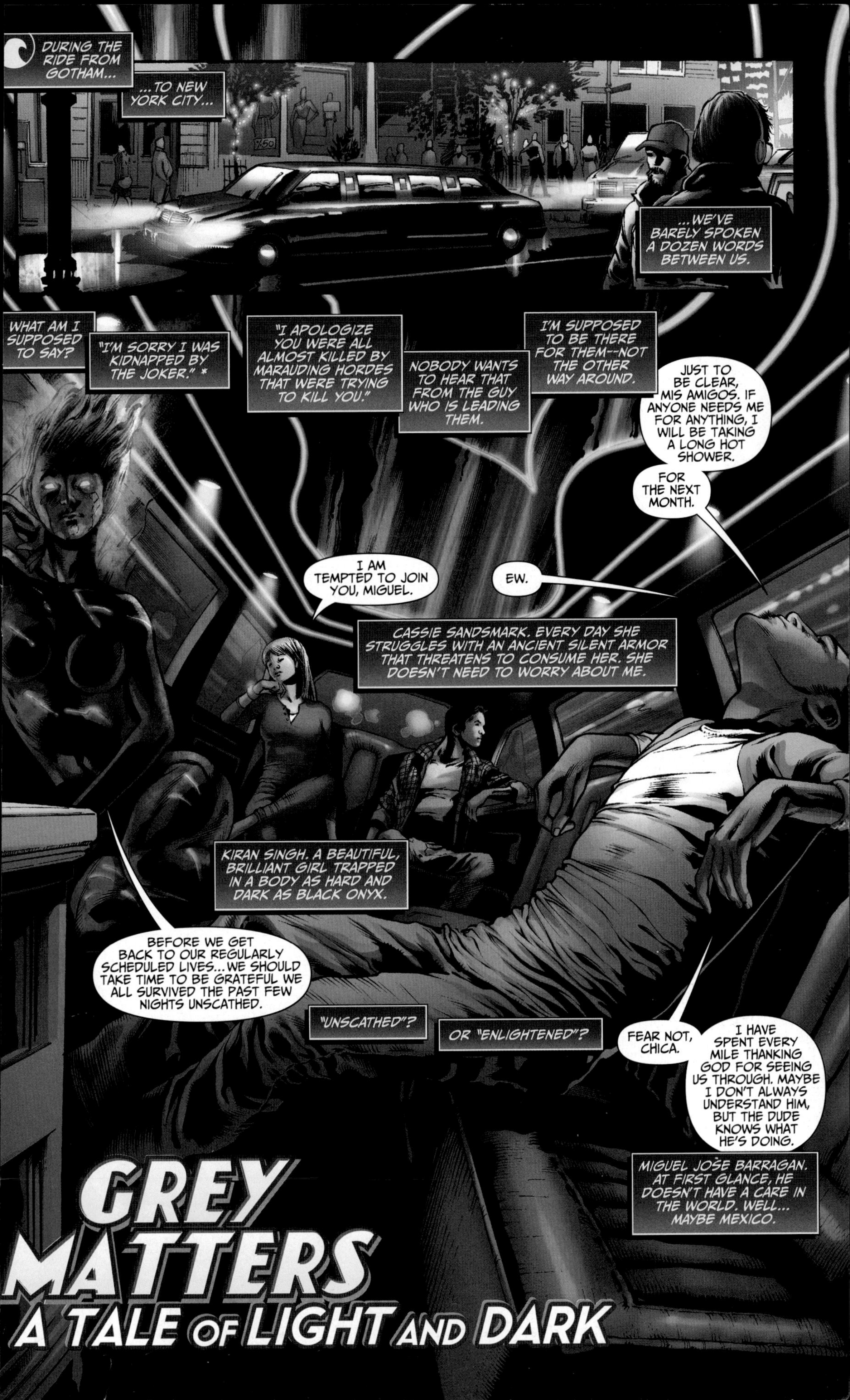
DURING THE RIDE FROM GOTHAM...
...TO NEW YORK CITY...
...WE'VE BARELY SPOKEN A DOZEN WORDS BETWEEN US.
WHAT AM I SUPPOSED TO SAY?
"I'M SORRY I WAS KIDNAPPED BY THE JOKER." *
"I APOLOGIZE YOU WERE ALL ALMOST KILLED BY MARAUDING HORDES THAT WERE TRYING TO KILL YOU."
NOBODY WANTS TO HEAR THAT FROM THE GUY WHO IS LEADING THEM.
I'M SUPPOSED TO BE THERE FOR THEM--NOT THE OTHER WAY AROUND.
JUST TO BE CLEAR, MIS AMIGOS. IF ANYONE NEEDS ME FOR ANYTHING, I WILL BE TAKING A LONG HOT SHOWER.
FOR THE NEXT MONTH.
I AM TEMPTED TO JOIN YOU, MIGUEL.
EW.
CASSIE SANDSMARK. EVERY DAY SHE STRUGGLES WITH AN ANCIENT SILENT ARMOR THAT THREATENS TO CONSUME HER. SHE DOESN'T NEED TO WORRY ABOUT ME.
KIRAN SINGH. A BEAUTIFUL, BRILLIANT GIRL TRAPPED IN A BODY AS HARD AND DARK AS BLACK ONYX.
BEFORE WE GET BACK TO OUR REGULARLY SCHEDULED LIVES...WE SHOULD TAKE TIME TO BE GRATEFUL WE ALL SURVIVED THE PAST FEW NIGHTS UNSCATHED.
"UNSCATHED"?
OR "ENLIGHTENED"?
FEAR NOT, CHICA.
I HAVE SPENT EVERY MILE THANKING GOD FOR SEEING US THROUGH. MAYBE I DON'T ALWAYS UNDERSTAND HIM, BUT THE DUDE KNOWS WHAT HE'S DOING.
MIGUEL JOSE BARRAGAN. AT FIRST GLANCE, HE DOESN'T HAVE A CARE IN THE WORLD. WELL... MAYBE MEXICO.
GREY MATTERS
A TALE OF LIGHT AND DARK

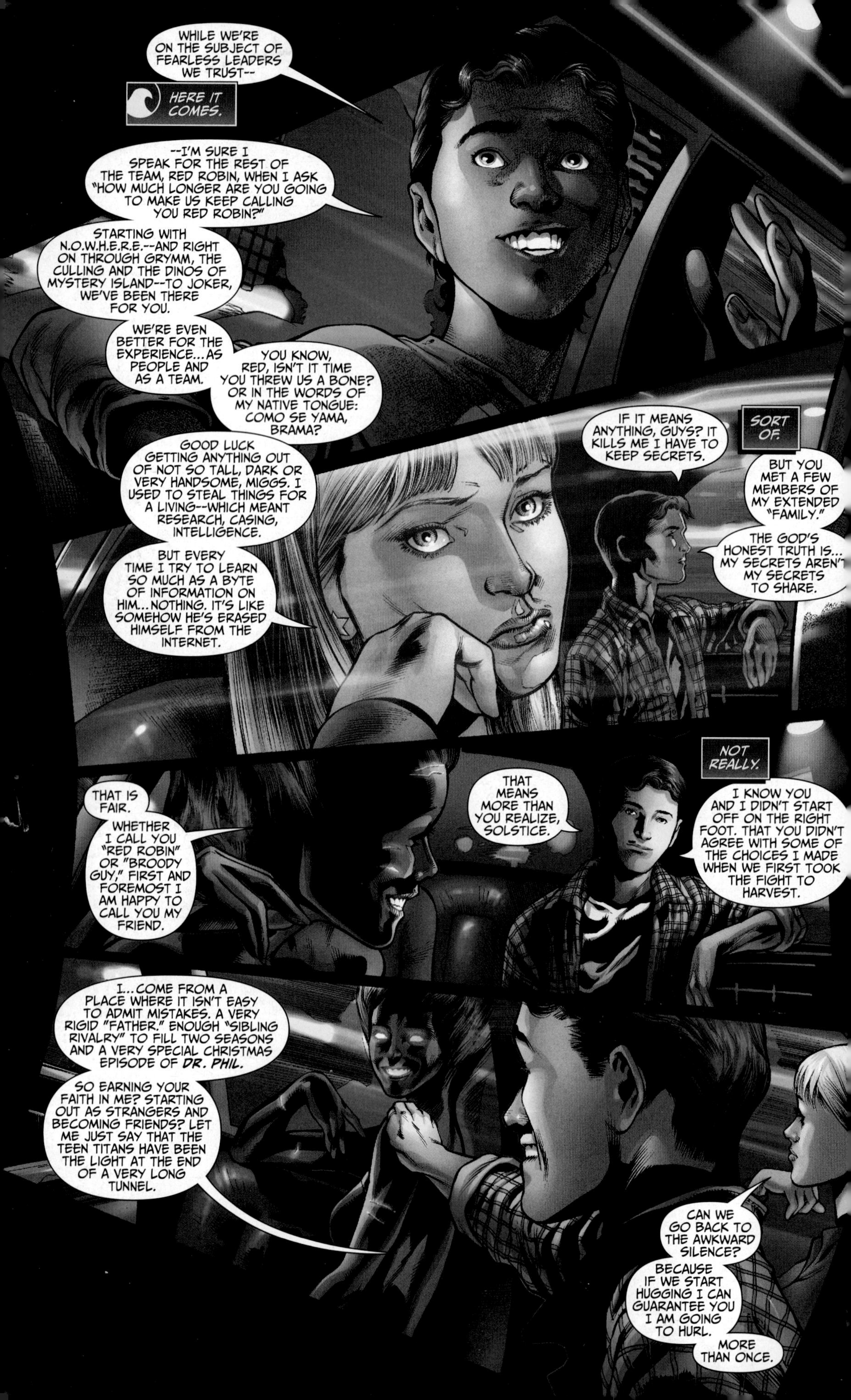
WHILE WE'RE ON THE SUBJECT OF FEARLESS LEADERS WE TRUST--
HERE IT COMES.
--I'M SURE I SPEAK FOR THE REST OF THE TEAM, RED ROBIN, WHEN I ASK "HOW MUCH LONGER ARE YOU GOING TO MAKE US KEEP CALLING YOU RED ROBIN?"
STARTING WITH N.O.W.H.E.R.E.--AND RIGHT ON THROUGH GRYMM, THE CULLING AND THE DINOS OF MYSTERY ISLAND--TO JOKER, WE'VE BEEN THERE FOR YOU.
WE'RE EVEN BETTER FOR THE EXPERIENCE...AS PEOPLE AND AS A TEAM.
YOU KNOW, RED, ISN'T IT TIME YOU THREW US A BONE? OR IN THE WORDS OF MY NATIVE TONGUE: COMO SE YAMA, BRAMA?
GOOD LUCK GETTING ANYTHING OUT OF NOT SO TALL, DARK OR VERY HANDSOME, MIGGS. I USED TO STEAL THINGS FOR A LIVING--WHICH MEANT RESEARCH, CASING, INTELLIGENCE.
BUT EVERY TIME I TRY TO LEARN SO MUCH AS A BYTE OF INFORMATION ON HIM...NOTHING. IT'S LIKE SOMEHOW HE'S ERASED HIMSELF FROM THE INTERNET.
IF IT MEANS ANYTHING, GUYS? IT KILLS ME I HAVE TO KEEP SECRETS.
SORT OF.
BUT YOU MET A FEW MEMBERS OF MY EXTENDED "FAMILY."
THE GOD'S HONEST TRUTH IS... MY SECRETS AREN'T MY SECRETS TO SHARE.
THAT IS FAIR.
WHETHER I CALL YOU "RED ROBIN" OR "BROODY GUY," FIRST AND FOREMOST I AM HAPPY TO CALL YOU MY FRIEND.
THAT MEANS MORE THAN YOU REALIZE, SOLSTICE.
NOT REALLY.
I KNOW YOU AND I DIDN'T START OFF ON THE RIGHT FOOT. THAT YOU DIDN'T AGREE WITH SOME OF THE CHOICES I MADE WHEN WE FIRST TOOK THE FIGHT TO HARVEST.
I...COME FROM A PLACE WHERE IT ISN'T EASY TO ADMIT MISTAKES. A VERY RIGID "FATHER." ENOUGH "SIBLING RIVALRY" TO FILL TWO SEASONS AND A VERY SPECIAL CHRISTMAS EPISODE OF DR. PHIL.
SO EARNING YOUR FAITH IN ME? STARTING OUT AS STRANGERS AND BECOMING FRIENDS? LET ME JUST SAY THAT THE TEEN TITANS HAVE BEEN THE LIGHT AT THE END OF A VERY LONG TUNNEL.
CAN WE GO BACK TO THE AWKWARD SILENCE?
BECAUSE IF WE START HUGGING I CAN GUARANTEE YOU I AM GOING TO HURL.
MORE THAN ONCE.

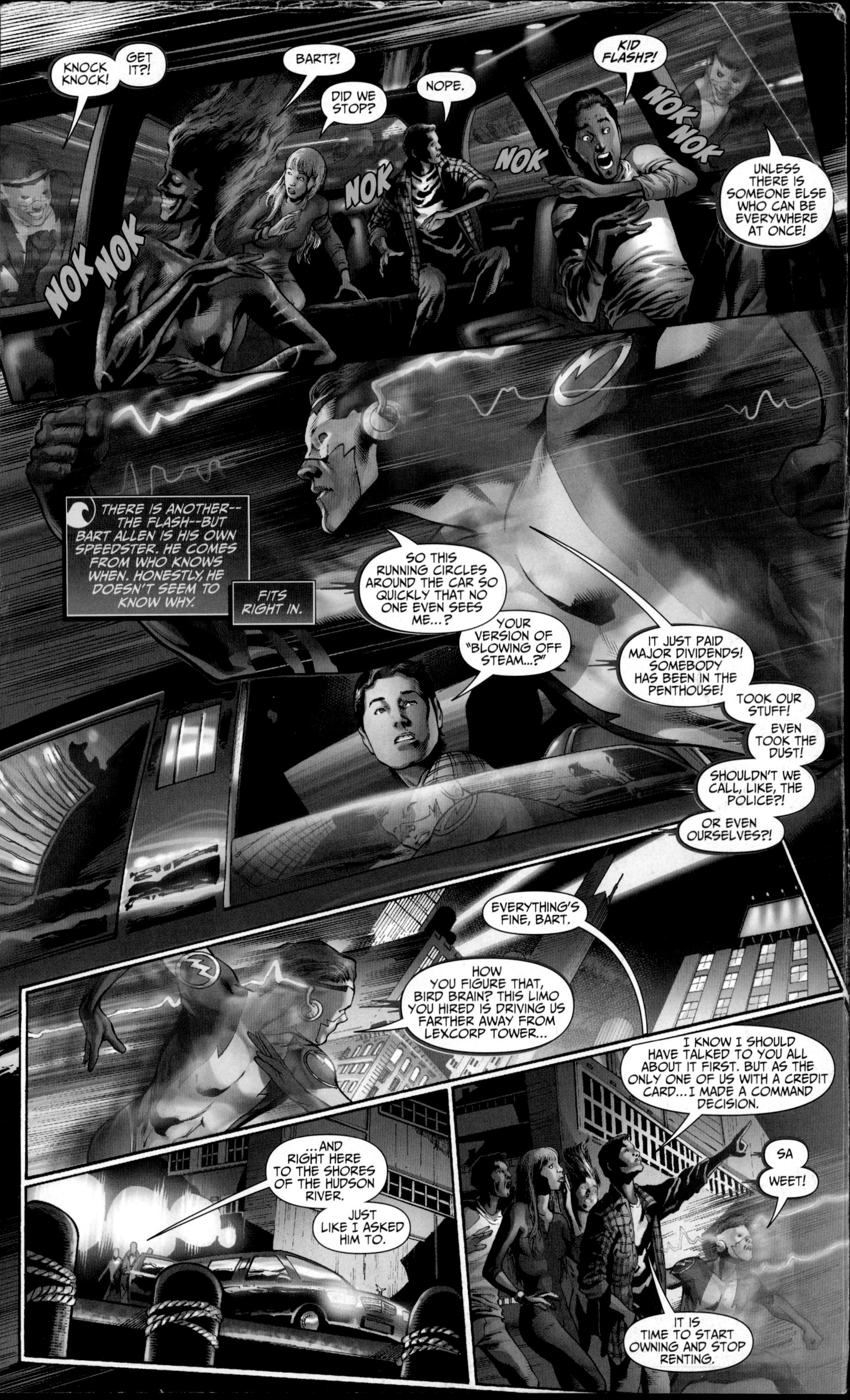
KNOCK KNOCK!
GET IT?!
BART?!
DID WE STOP?
NOPE.
KID FLASH?!
NOK NOK
NOK
NOK
NOK NOK
UNLESS THERE IS SOMEONE ELSE WHO CAN BE EVERYWHERE AT ONCE!
THERE IS ANOTHER-- THE FLASH--BUT BART ALLEN IS HIS OWN SPEEDSTER. HE COMES FROM WHO KNOWS WHEN. HONESTLY, HE DOESN'T SEEM TO KNOW WHY.
FITS RIGHT IN.
SO THIS RUNNING CIRCLES AROUND THE CAR SO QUICKLY THAT NO ONE EVEN SEES ME...?
YOUR VERSION OF "BLOWING OFF STEAM...?"
IT JUST PAID MAJOR DIVIDENDS! SOMEBODY HAS BEEN IN THE PENTHOUSE!
TOOK OUR STUFF!
EVEN TOOK THE DUST!
SHOULDN'T WE CALL, LIKE, THE POLICE?!
OR EVEN OURSELVES?!
EVERYTHING'S FINE, BART.
HOW YOU FIGURE THAT, BIRD BRAIN? THIS LIMO YOU HIRED IS DRIVING US FARTHER AWAY FROM LEXCORP TOWER...
...AND RIGHT HERE TO THE SHORES OF THE HUDSON RIVER.
JUST LIKE I ASKED HIM TO.
I KNOW I SHOULD HAVE TALKED TO YOU ALL ABOUT IT FIRST. BUT AS THE ONLY ONE OF US WITH A CREDIT CARD...I MADE A COMMAND DECISION.
SA
WEET!
IT IS TIME TO START OWNING AND STOP RENTING.

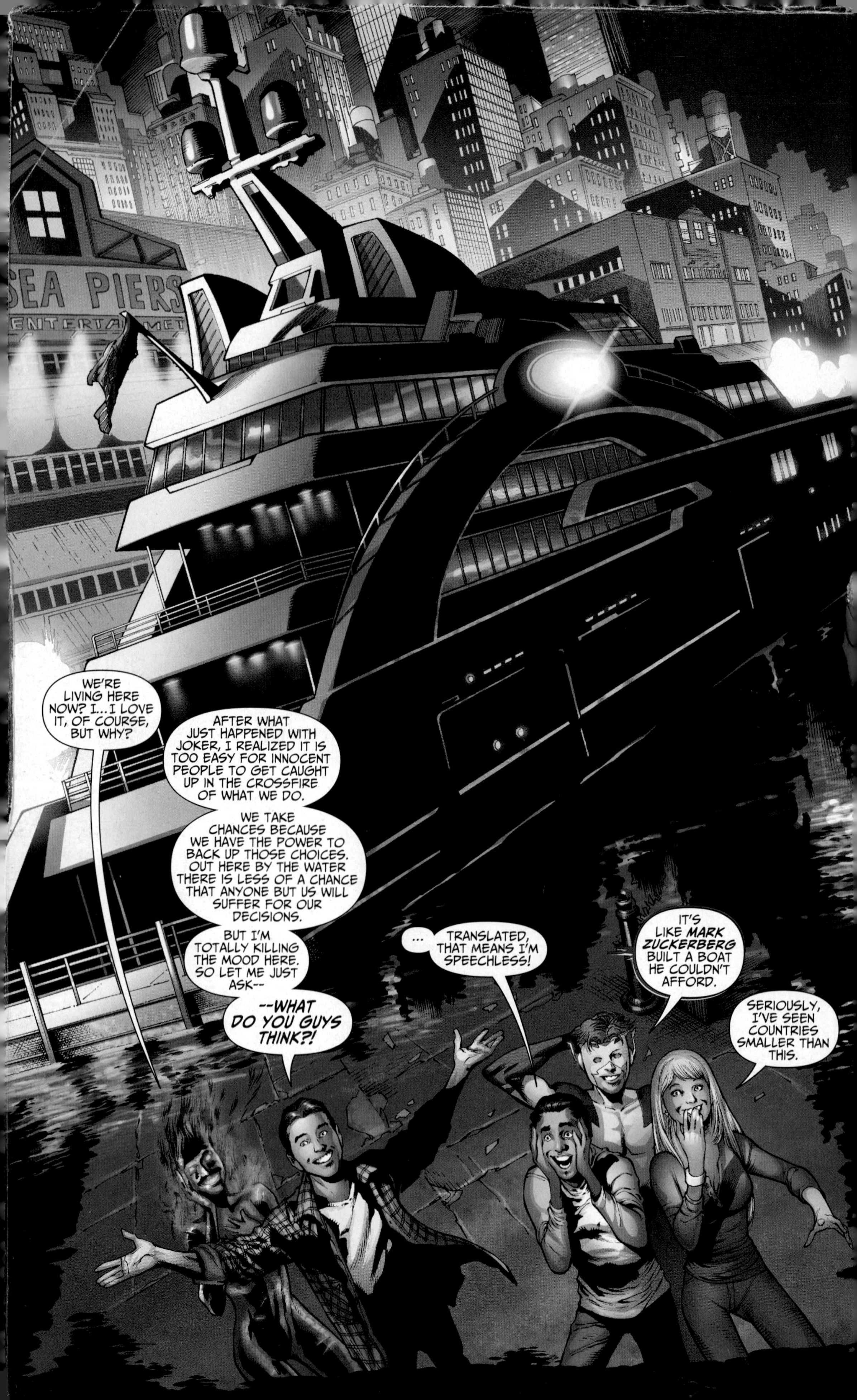
SEA PIERS
ENTERTAINMENT
WE'RE LIVING HERE NOW? I...I LOVE IT, OF COURSE, BUT WHY?
AFTER WHAT JUST HAPPENED WITH JOKER, I REALIZED IT IS TOO EASY FOR INNOCENT PEOPLE TO GET CAUGHT UP IN THE CROSSFIRE OF WHAT WE DO.
WE TAKE CHANCES BECAUSE WE HAVE THE POWER TO BACK UP THOSE CHOICES. OUT HERE BY THE WATER THERE IS LESS OF A CHANCE THAT ANYONE BUT US WILL SUFFER FOR OUR DECISIONS.
BUT I'M TOTALLY KILLING THE MOOD HERE. SO LET ME JUST ASK--
--WHAT DO YOU GUYS THINK?!
...
TRANSLATED, THAT MEANS I'M SPEECHLESS!
IT'S LIKE MARK ZUCKERBERG BUILT A BOAT HE COULDN'T AFFORD.
SERIOUSLY, I'VE SEEN COUNTRIES SMALLER THAN THIS.

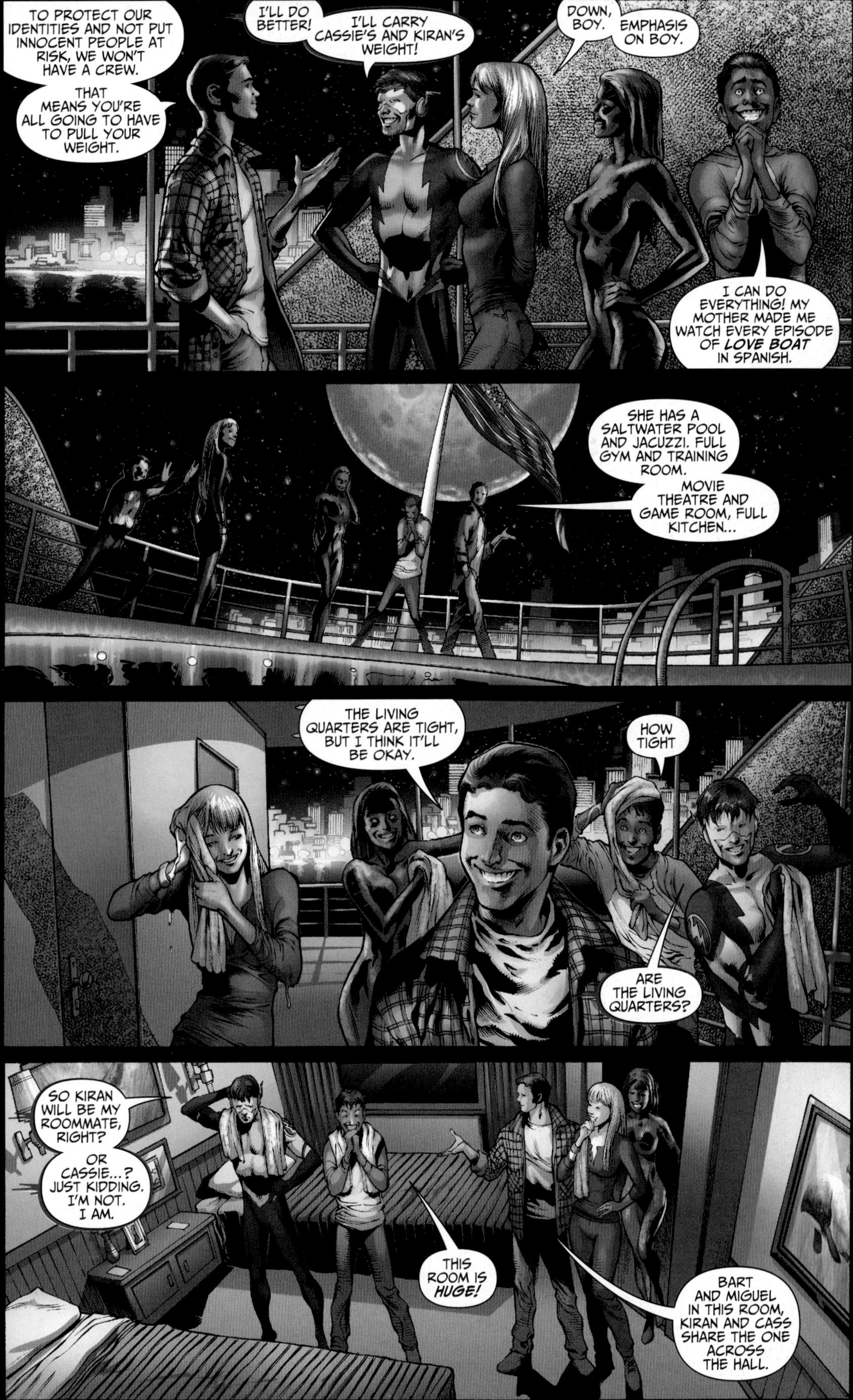
TO PROTECT OUR IDENTITIES AND NOT PUT INNOCENT PEOPLE AT RISK, WE WON'T HAVE A CREW.
THAT MEANS YOU'RE ALL GOING TO HAVE TO PULL YOUR WEIGHT.
I'LL DO BETTER!
I'LL CARRY CASSIE'S AND KIRAN'S WEIGHT!
DOWN, BOY.
EMPHASIS ON BOY.
I CAN DO EVERYTHING! MY MOTHER MADE ME WATCH EVERY EPISODE OF LOVE BOAT IN SPANISH.
SHE HAS A SALTWATER POOL AND JACUZZI. FULL GYM AND TRAINING ROOM.
MOVIE THEATRE AND GAME ROOM, FULL KITCHEN...
THE LIVING QUARTERS ARE TIGHT, BUT I THINK IT'LL BE OKAY.
HOW TIGHT
ARE THE LIVING QUARTERS?
SO KIRAN WILL BE MY ROOMMATE, RIGHT?
OR CASSIE...? JUST KIDDING. I'M NOT. I AM.
THIS ROOM IS HUGE!
BART AND MIGUEL IN THIS ROOM, KIRAN AND CASS SHARE THE ONE ACROSS THE HALL.

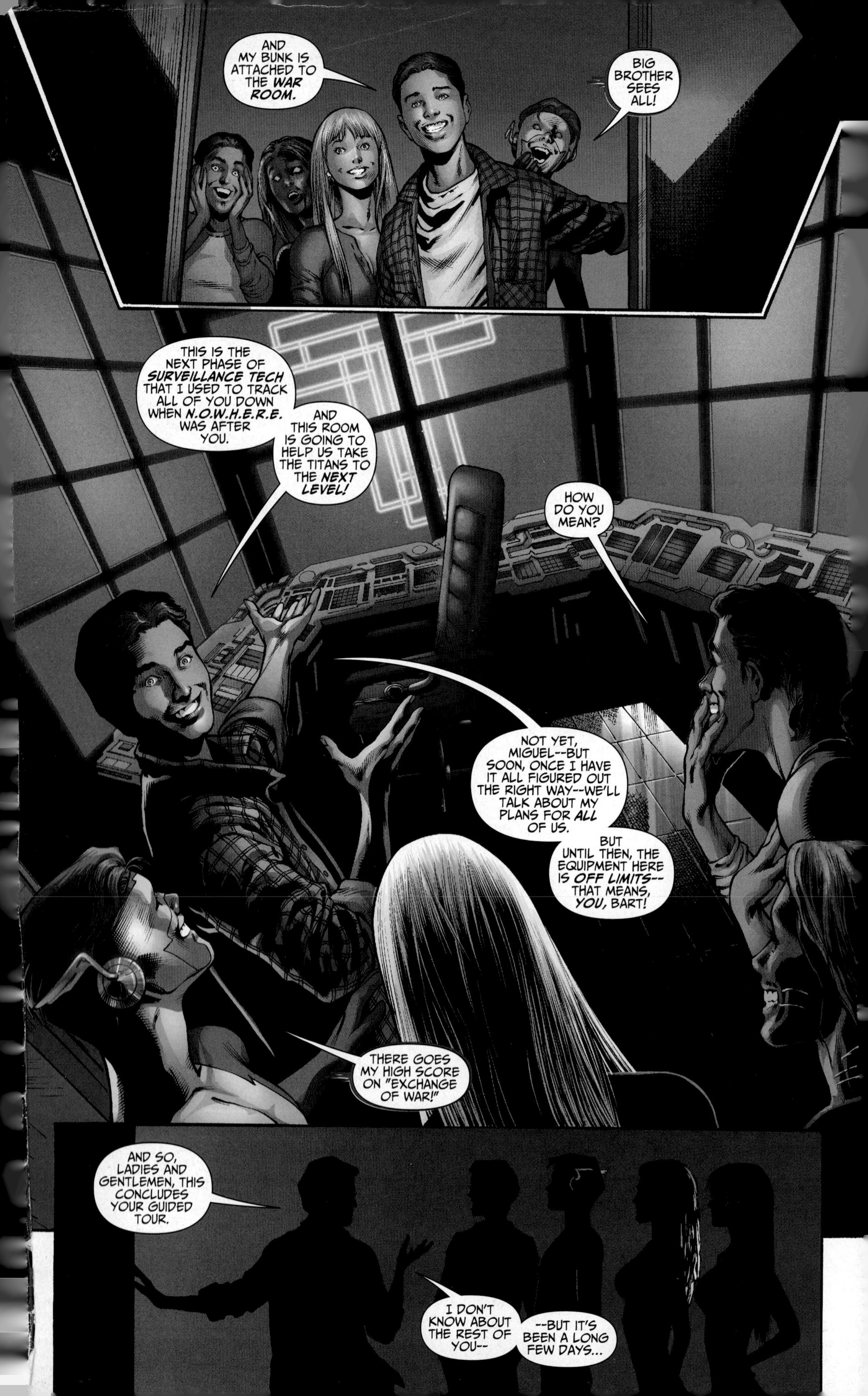
AND MY BUNK IS ATTACHED TO THE WAR ROOM.
BIG BROTHER SEES ALL!
THIS IS THE NEXT PHASE OF SURVEILLANCE TECH THAT I USED TO TRACK ALL OF YOU DOWN WHEN N.O.W.H.E.R.E. WAS AFTER YOU.
AND THIS ROOM IS GOING TO HELP US TAKE THE TITANS TO THE NEXT LEVEL!
HOW DO YOU MEAN?
NOT YET, MIGUEL--BUT SOON, ONCE I HAVE IT ALL FIGURED OUT THE RIGHT WAY--WE'LL TALK ABOUT MY PLANS FOR ALL OF US.
BUT UNTIL THEN, THE EQUIPMENT HERE IS OFF LIMITS--THAT MEANS, YOU, BART!
THERE GOES MY HIGH SCORE ON "EXCHANGE OF WAR!"
AND SO, LADIES AND GENTLEMEN, THIS CONCLUDES YOUR GUIDED TOUR.
I DON'T KNOW ABOUT THE REST OF YOU--
--BUT IT'S BEEN A LONG FEW DAYS...

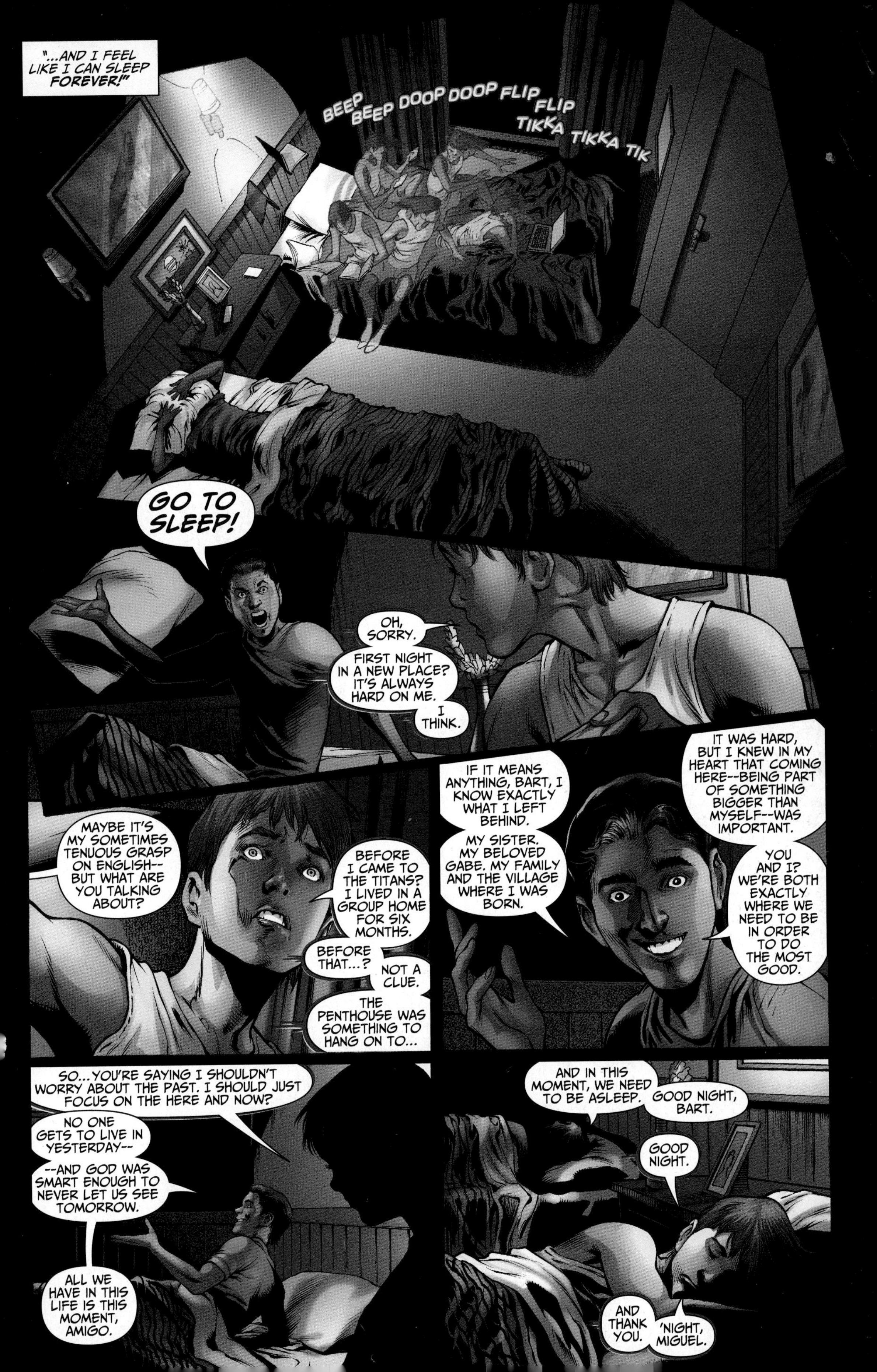
"...AND I FEEL LIKE I CAN SLEEP FOREVER!"
BEEP BEEP DOOP DOOP FLIP FLIP TIKKA TIKKA TIK
GO TO SLEEP!
OH, SORRY.
FIRST NIGHT IN A NEW PLACE? IT'S ALWAYS HARD ON ME.
I THINK.
MAYBE IT'S MY SOMETIMES TENUOUS GRASP ON ENGLISH--BUT WHAT ARE YOU TALKING ABOUT?
BEFORE I CAME TO THE TITANS? I LIVED IN A GROUP HOME FOR SIX MONTHS.
BEFORE THAT...?
NOT A CLUE.
THE PENTHOUSE WAS SOMETHING TO HANG ON TO...
IF IT MEANS ANYTHING, BART, I KNOW EXACTLY WHAT I LEFT BEHIND.
MY SISTER. MY BELOVED GABE. MY FAMILY AND THE VILLAGE WHERE I WAS BORN.
IT WAS HARD, BUT I KNEW IN MY HEART THAT COMING HERE--BEING PART OF SOMETHING BIGGER THAN MYSELF--WAS IMPORTANT.
YOU AND I? WE'RE BOTH EXACTLY WHERE WE NEED TO BE IN ORDER TO DO THE MOST GOOD.
SO...YOU'RE SAYING I SHOULDN'T WORRY ABOUT THE PAST. I SHOULD JUST FOCUS ON THE HERE AND NOW?
NO ONE GETS TO LIVE IN YESTERDAY--
--AND GOD WAS SMART ENOUGH TO NEVER LET US SEE TOMORROW.
ALL WE HAVE IN THIS LIFE IS THIS MOMENT, AMIGO.
AND IN THIS MOMENT, WE NEED TO BE ASLEEP.
GOOD NIGHT, BART.
GOOD NIGHT.
AND THANK YOU.
'NIGHT, MIGUEL.

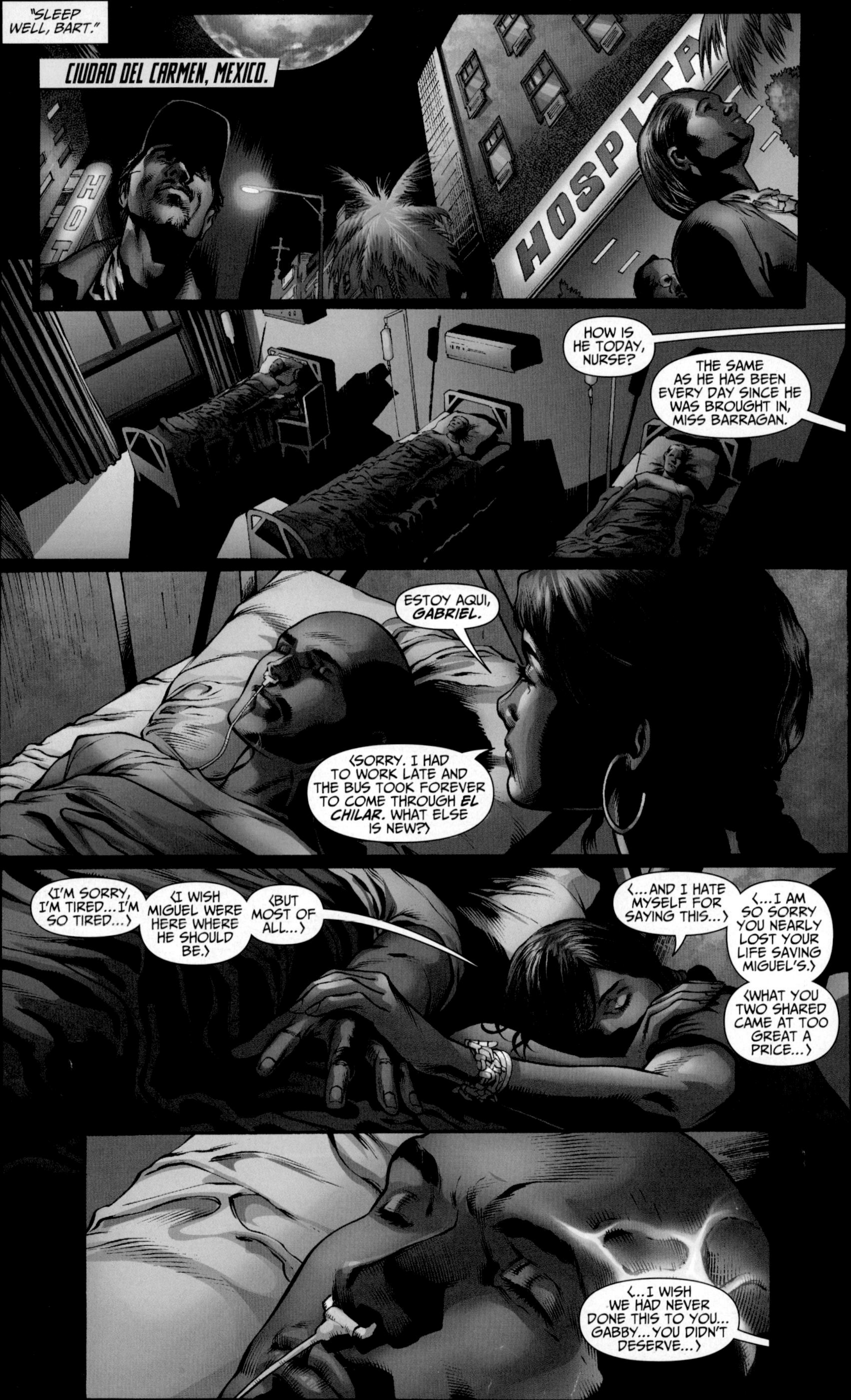
"SLEEP WELL, BART."
CIUDAD DEL CARMEN, MEXICO.
HOT
HOSPITA
HOW IS HE TODAY, NURSE?
THE SAME AS HE HAS BEEN EVERY DAY SINCE HE WAS BROUGHT IN, MISS BARRAGAN.
ESTOY AQUI, GABRIEL.
‹SORRY. I HAD TO WORK LATE AND THE BUS TOOK FOREVER TO COME THROUGH EL CHILAR. WHAT ELSE IS NEW?›
‹I'M SORRY, I'M TIRED...I'M SO TIRED...›
‹I WISH MIGUEL WERE HERE WHERE HE SHOULD BE.›
‹BUT MOST OF ALL...›
‹...AND I HATE MYSELF FOR SAYING THIS...›
‹...I AM SO SORRY YOU NEARLY LOST YOUR LIFE SAVING MIGUEL'S.›
‹WHAT YOU TWO SHARED CAME AT TOO GREAT A PRICE...›
‹...I WISH WE HAD NEVER DONE THIS TO YOU... GABBY...YOU DIDN'T DESERVE...›

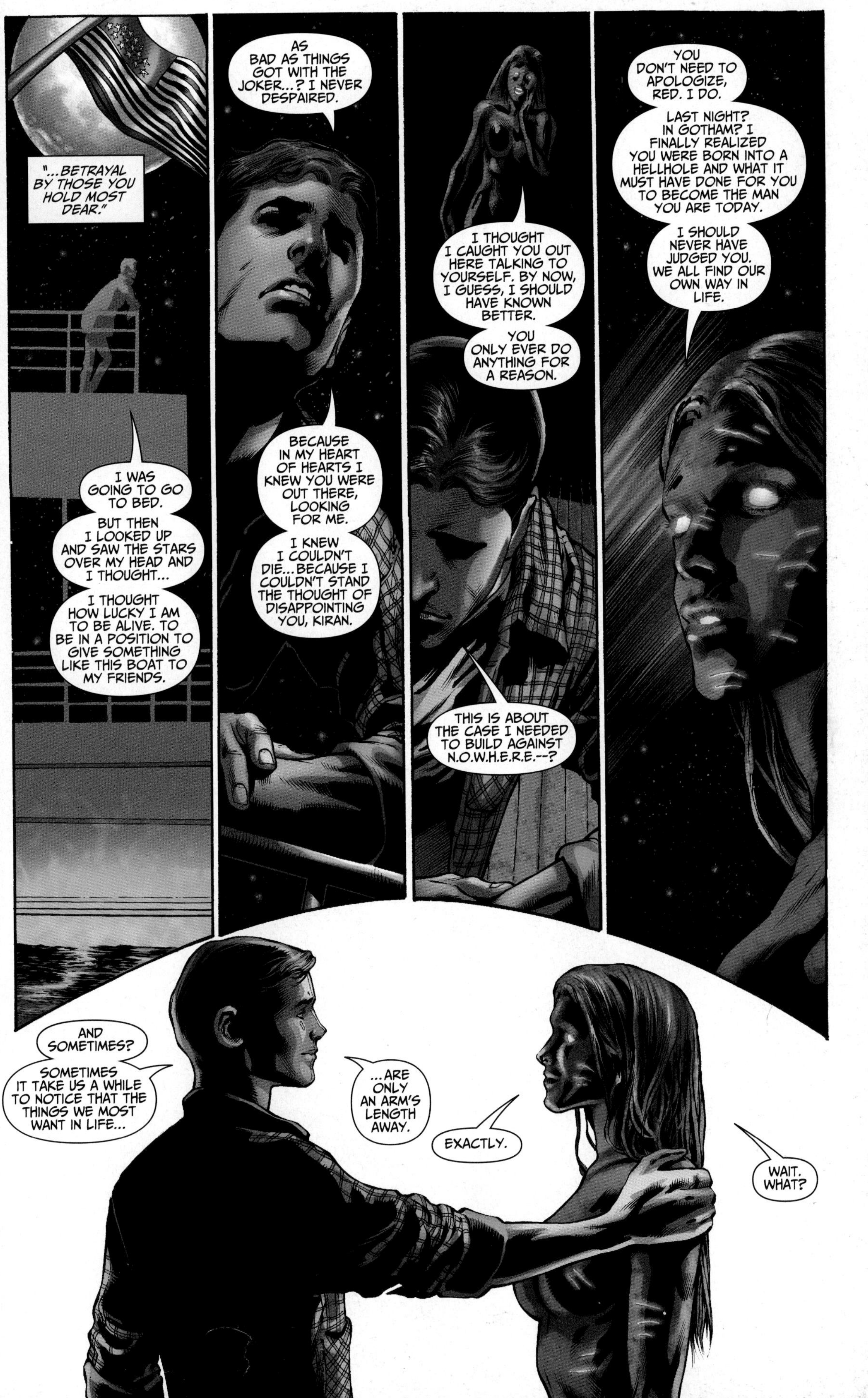
"...BETRAYAL BY THOSE YOU HOLD MOST DEAR."
I WAS GOING TO GO TO BED.
BUT THEN I LOOKED UP AND SAW THE STARS OVER MY HEAD AND I THOUGHT...
I THOUGHT HOW LUCKY I AM TO BE ALIVE. TO BE IN A POSITION TO GIVE SOMETHING LIKE THIS BOAT TO MY FRIENDS.
AS BAD AS THINGS GOT WITH THE JOKER...? I NEVER DESPAIRED.
BECAUSE IN MY HEART OF HEARTS I KNEW YOU WERE OUT THERE, LOOKING FOR ME.
I KNEW I COULDN'T DIE...BECAUSE I COULDN'T STAND THE THOUGHT OF DISAPPOINTING YOU, KIRAN.
I THOUGHT I CAUGHT YOU OUT HERE TALKING TO YOURSELF. BY NOW, I GUESS, I SHOULD HAVE KNOWN BETTER.
YOU ONLY EVER DO ANYTHING FOR A REASON.
THIS IS ABOUT THE CASE I NEEDED TO BUILD AGAINST N.O.W.H.E.R.E.--?
YOU DON'T NEED TO APOLOGIZE, RED. I DO.
LAST NIGHT? IN GOTHAM? I FINALLY REALIZED YOU WERE BORN INTO A HELLHOLE AND WHAT IT MUST HAVE DONE FOR YOU TO BECOME THE MAN YOU ARE TODAY.
I SHOULD NEVER HAVE JUDGED YOU. WE ALL FIND OUR OWN WAY IN LIFE.
AND SOMETIMES?
SOMETIMES IT TAKE US A WHILE TO NOTICE THAT THE THINGS WE MOST WANT IN LIFE...
...ARE ONLY AN ARM'S LENGTH AWAY.
EXACTLY.
WAIT. WHAT?

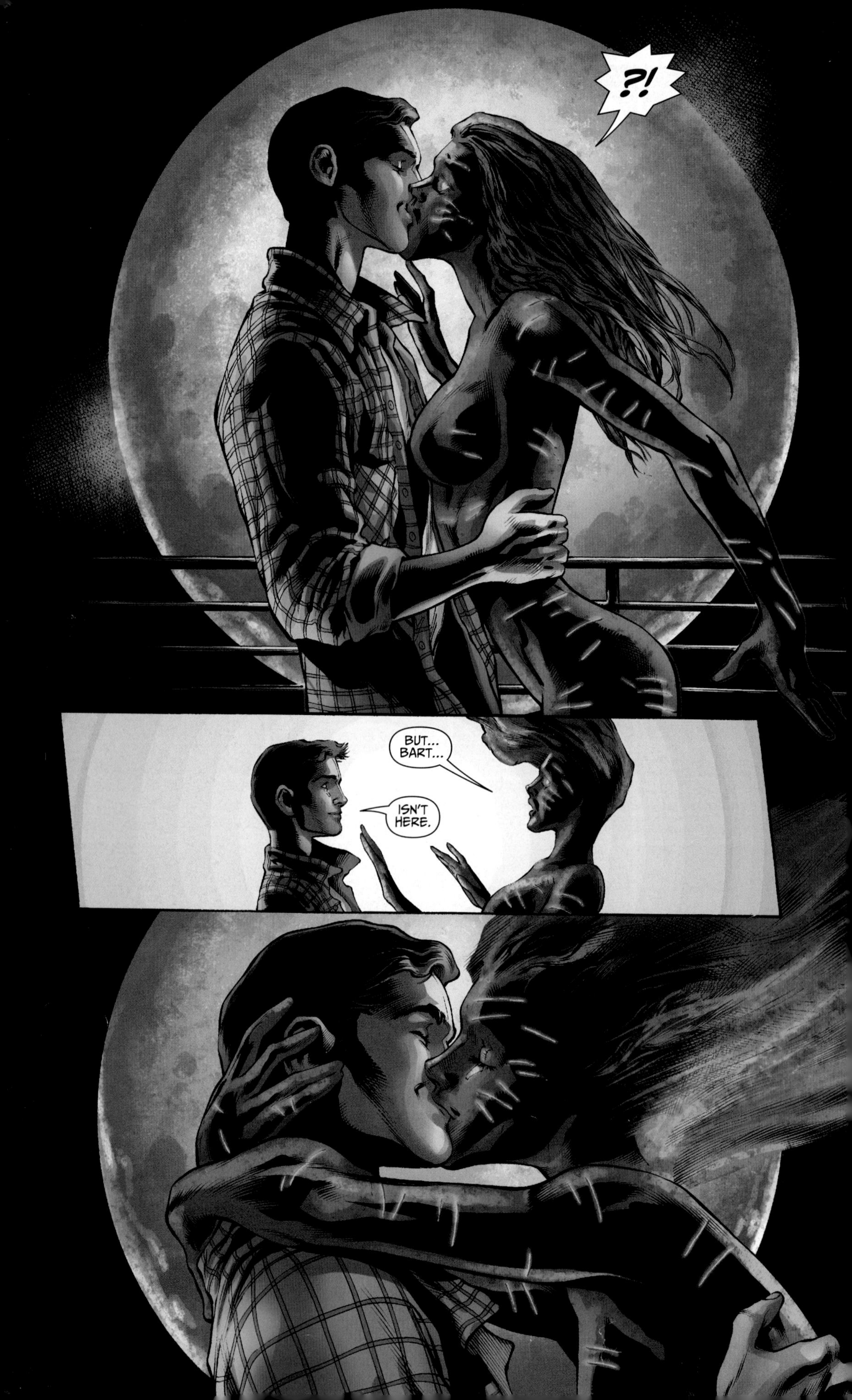
?!
BUT... BART...
ISN'T HERE.

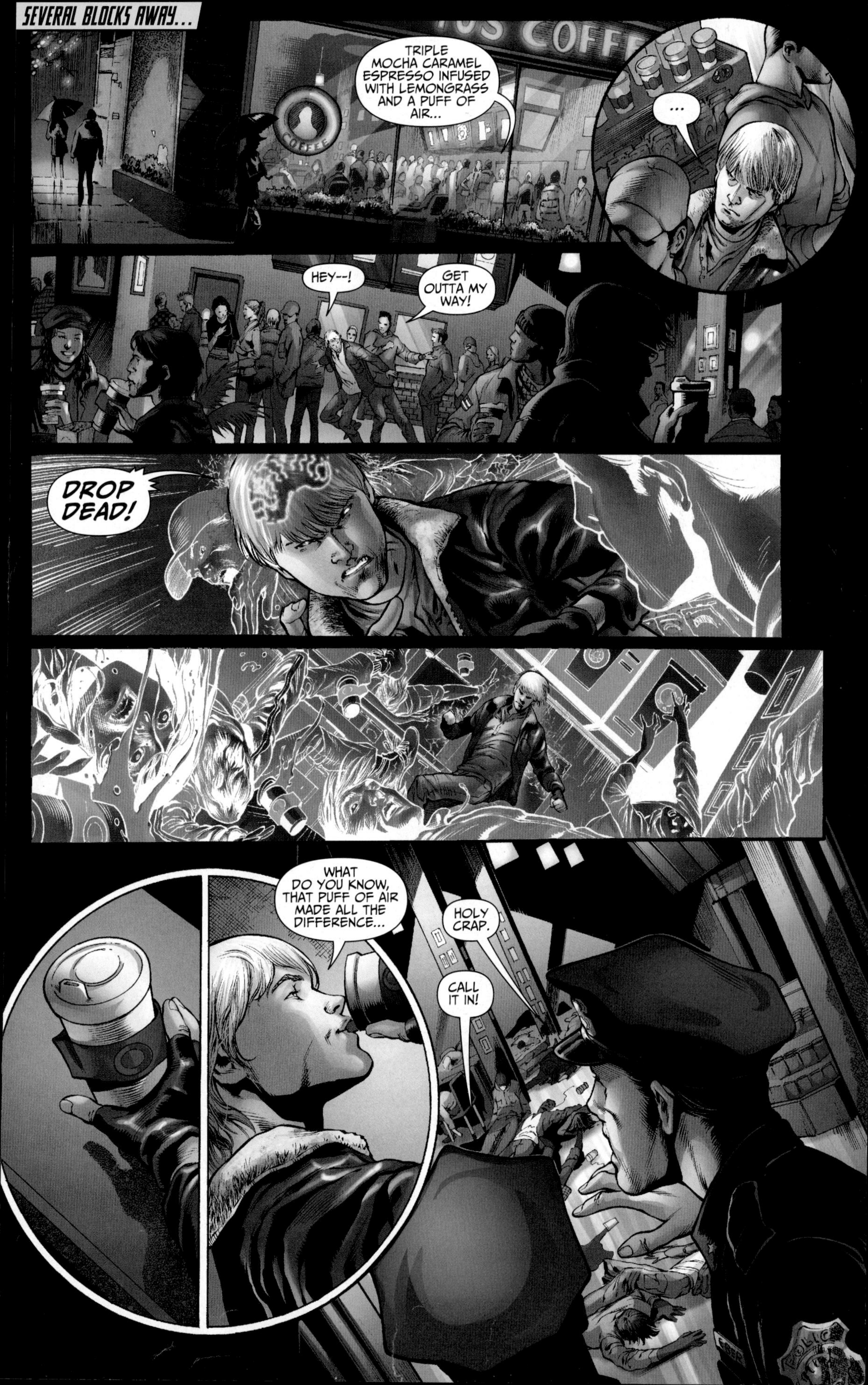
SEVERAL BLOCKS AWAY...
TRIPLE MOCHA CARAMEL ESPRESSO INFUSED WITH LEMONGRASS AND A PUFF OF AIR...
...
HEY--!
GET OUTTA MY WAY!
DROP DEAD!
WHAT DO YOU KNOW, THAT PUFF OF AIR MADE ALL THE DIFFERENCE...
HOLY CRAP.
CALL IT IN!

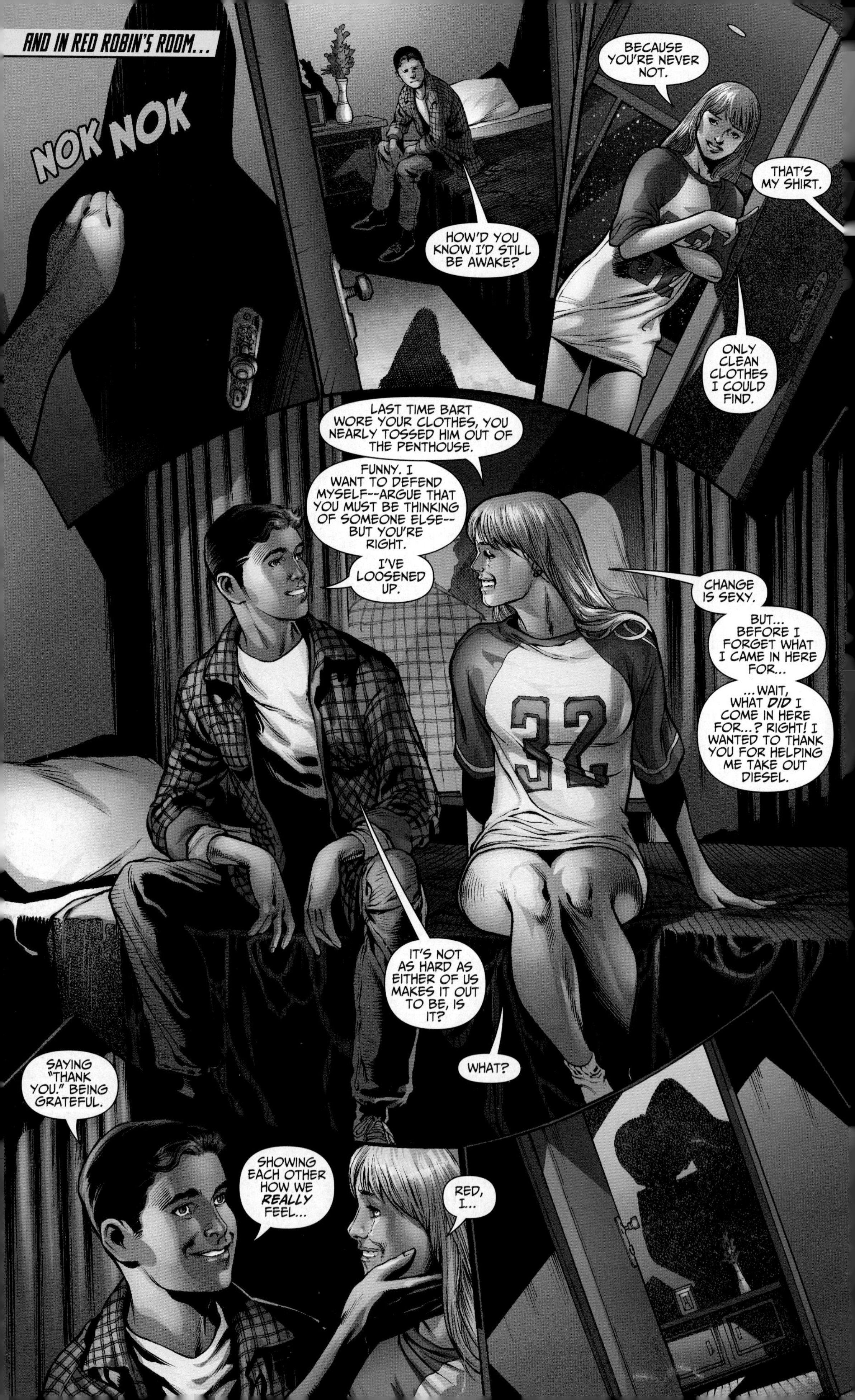
AND IN RED ROBIN'S ROOM...
NOK NOK
HOW'D YOU KNOW I'D STILL BE AWAKE?
BECAUSE YOU'RE NEVER NOT.
THAT'S MY SHIRT.
ONLY CLEAN CLOTHES I COULD FIND.
LAST TIME BART WORE YOUR CLOTHES, YOU NEARLY TOSSED HIM OUT OF THE PENTHOUSE.
FUNNY. I WANT TO DEFEND MYSELF--ARGUE THAT YOU MUST BE THINKING OF SOMEONE ELSE--BUT YOU'RE RIGHT.
I'VE LOOSENED UP.
CHANGE IS SEXY.
BUT... BEFORE I FORGET WHAT I CAME IN HERE FOR...
...WAIT, WHAT DID I COME IN HERE FOR...? RIGHT! I WANTED TO THANK YOU FOR HELPING ME TAKE OUT DIESEL.
IT'S NOT AS HARD AS EITHER OF US MAKES IT OUT TO BE, IS IT?
WHAT?
SAYING "THANK YOU." BEING GRATEFUL.
SHOWING EACH OTHER HOW WE REALLY FEEL...
RED, I...

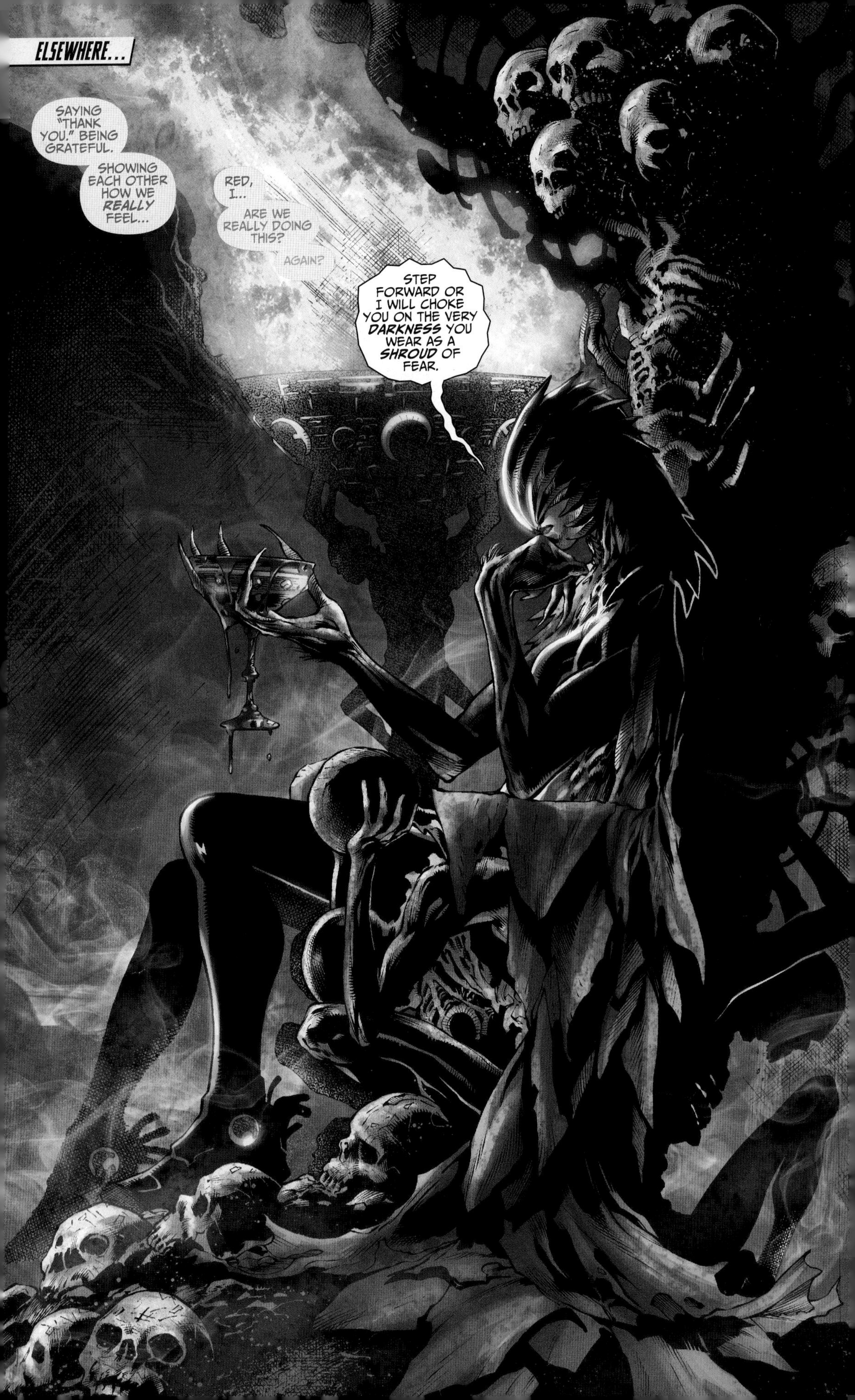
ELSEWHERE...
SAYING "THANK YOU." BEING GRATEFUL.
SHOWING EACH OTHER HOW WE REALLY FEEL...
RED, I...
ARE WE REALLY DOING THIS?
AGAIN?
STEP FORWARD OR I WILL CHOKE YOU ON THE VERY DARKNESS YOU WEAR AS A SHROUD OF FEAR.

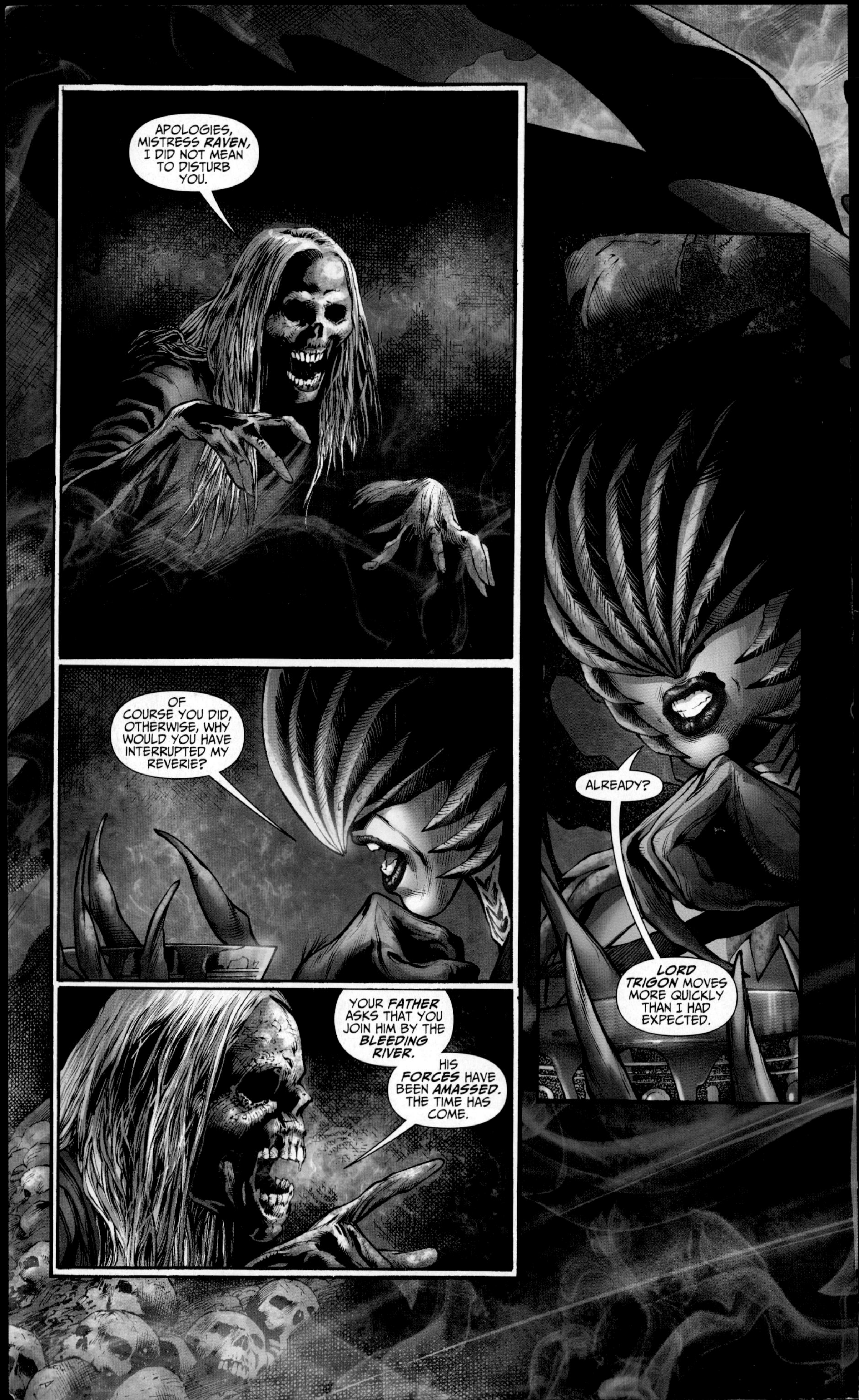
APOLOGIES, MISTRESS RAVEN, I DID NOT MEAN TO DISTURB YOU.
OF COURSE YOU DID, OTHERWISE, WHY WOULD YOU HAVE INTERRUPTED MY REVERIE?
YOUR FATHER ASKS THAT YOU JOIN HIM BY THE BLEEDING RIVER.
HIS FORCES HAVE BEEN AMASSED. THE TIME HAS COME.
ALREADY?
LORD TRIGON MOVES MORE QUICKLY THAN I HAD EXPECTED.

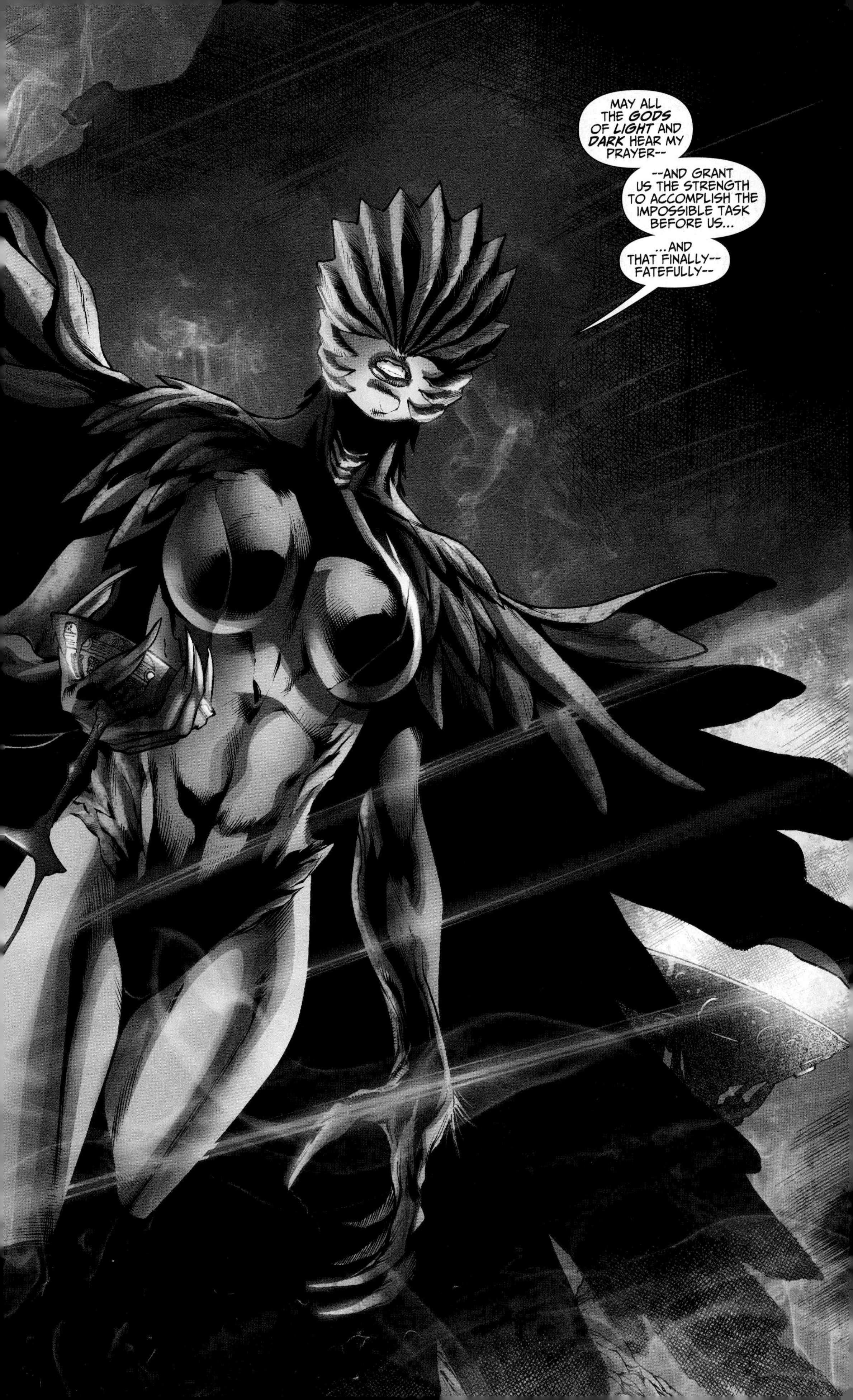
MAY ALL THE GODS OF LIGHT AND DARK HEAR MY PRAYER--
--AND GRANT US THE STRENGTH TO ACCOMPLISH THE IMPOSSIBLE TASK BEFORE US...
...AND THAT FINALLY-- FATEFULLY--

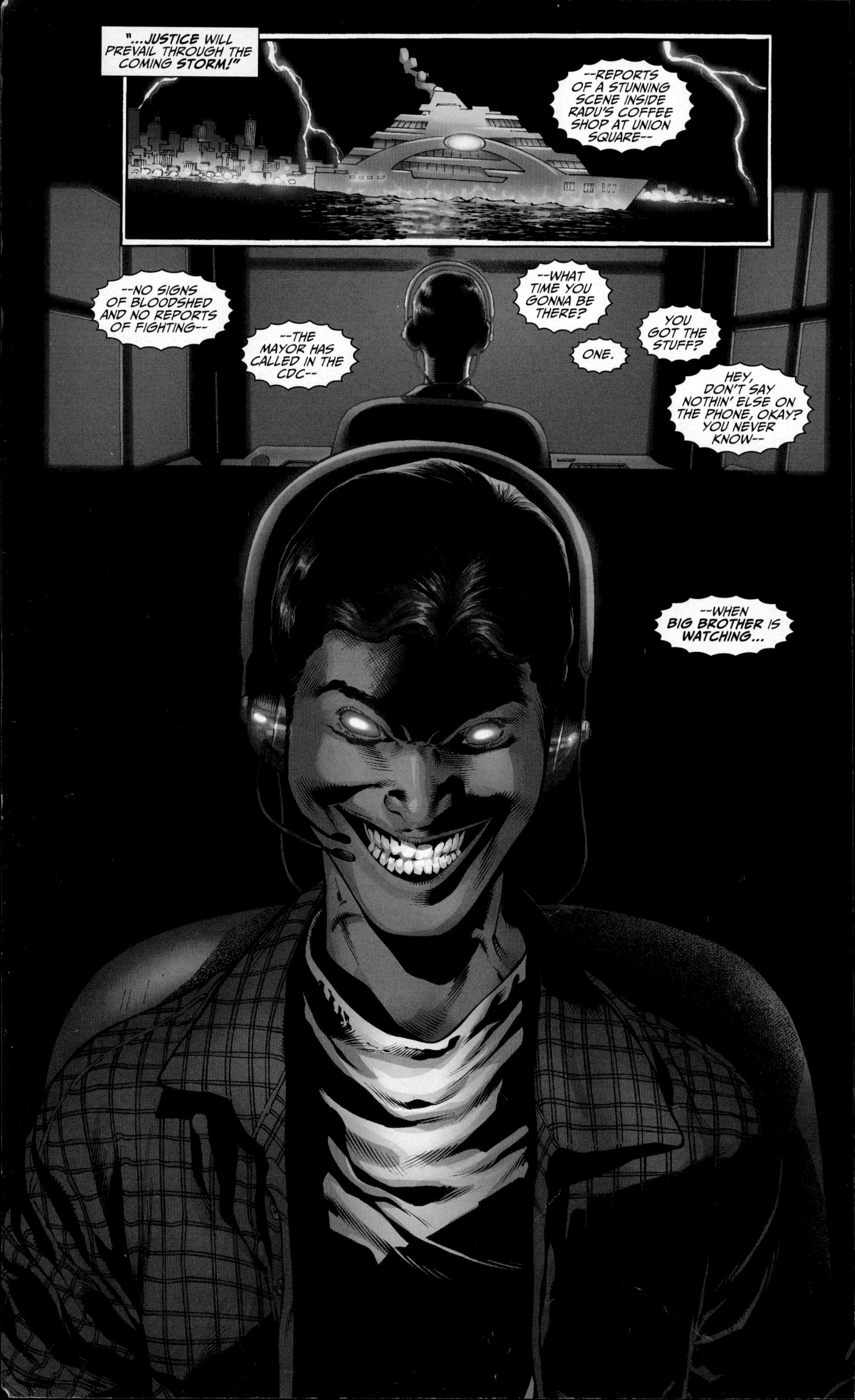
"...JUSTICE WILL PREVAIL THROUGH THE COMING STORM!"
--REPORTS OF A STUNNING SCENE INSIDE RADU'S COFFEE SHOP AT UNION SQUARE--
--NO SIGNS OF BLOODSHED AND NO REPORTS OF FIGHTING--
--THE MAYOR HAS CALLED IN THE CDC--
--WHAT TIME YOU GONNA BE THERE?
ONE.
YOU GOT THE STUFF?
HEY, DON'T SAY NOTHIN' ELSE ON THE PHONE, OKAY? YOU NEVER KNOW--
--WHEN BIG BROTHER IS WATCHING...

TEEN TITANS

TEEN TITANS ISSUE #0 PENCILS BY TYLER KIRKHAM

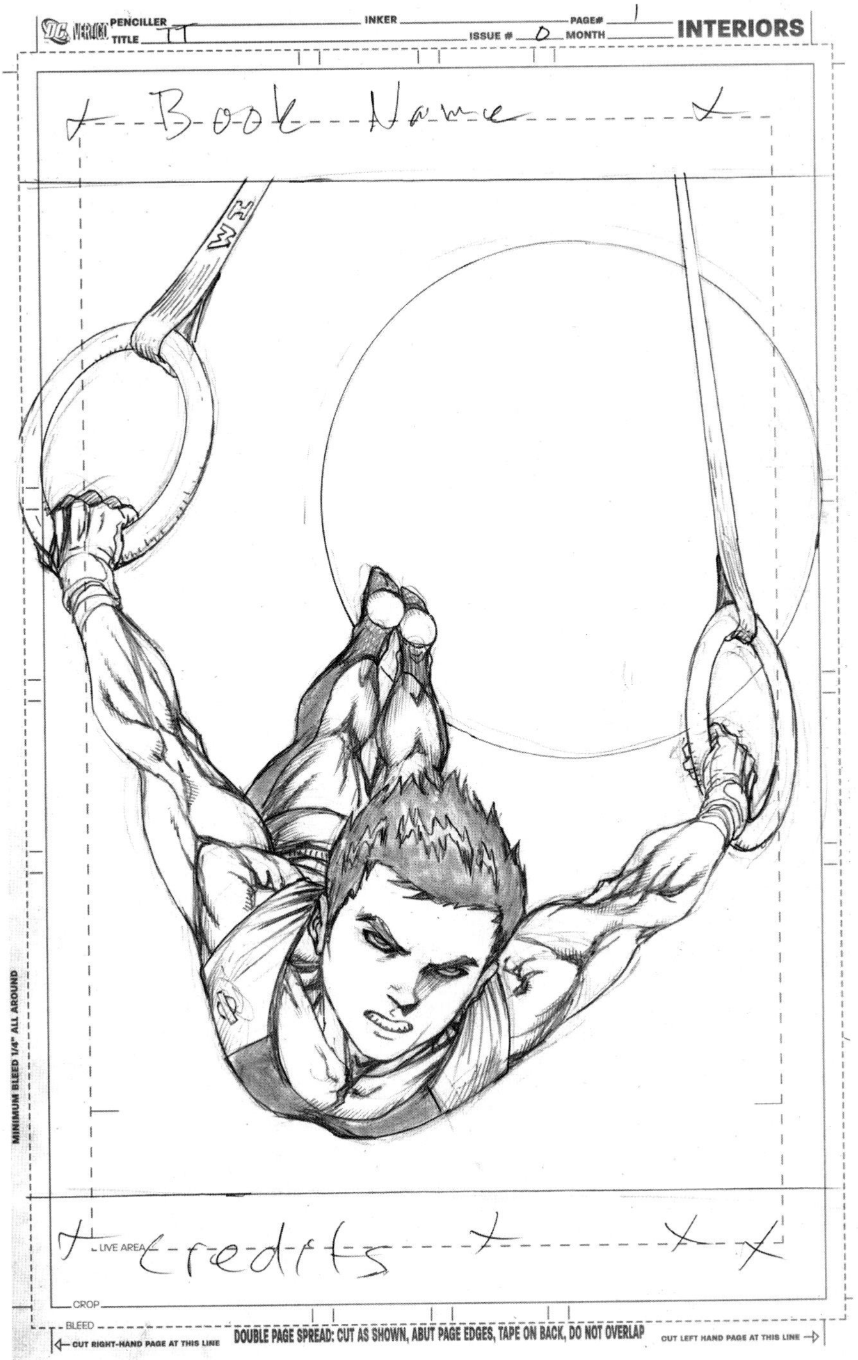
PENCILLER
TITLE TT
INKER
PAGE# 1
ISSUE # 0
MONTH
INTERIORS
Book Name
WE
credits
LIVE AREA
CROP
BLEED
MINIMUM BLEED 1/4" ALL AROUND
CUT RIGHT-HAND PAGE AT THIS LINE
DOUBLE PAGE SPREAD: CUT AS SHOWN, ABUT PAGE EDGES, TAPE ON BACK, DO NOT OVERLAP
CUT LEFT HAND PAGE AT THIS LINE

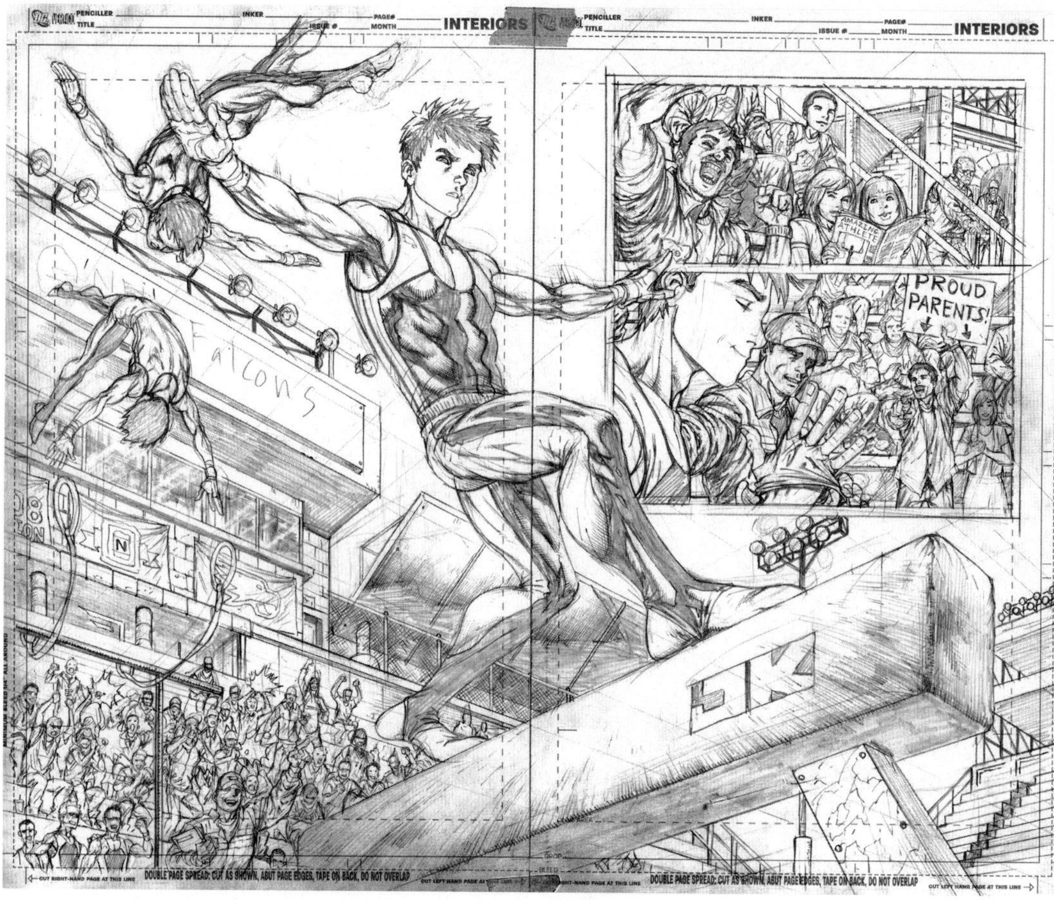
INTERIORS
PENCILLER
INKER
TITLE
PAGE#
ISSUE #
MONTH
INTERIORS
Falcons
PROUD PARENTS!
AMAZING ATHLETE
DOUBLE PAGE SPREAD: CUT AS SHOWN, ABUT PAGE EDGES, TAPE ON BACK, DO NOT OVERLAP
DOUBLE PAGE SPREAD: CUT AS SHOWN, ABUT PAGE EDGES, TAPE ON BACK, DO NOT OVERLAP

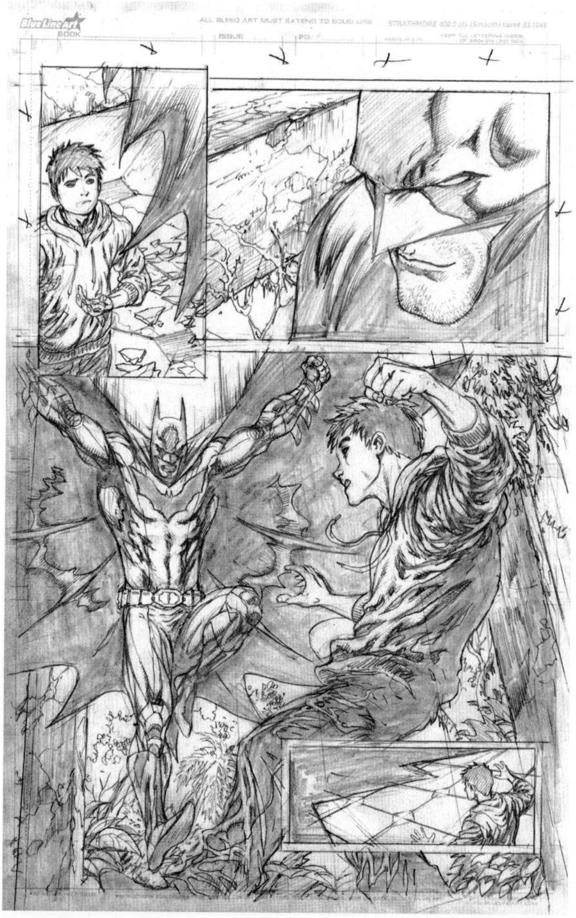
ALL BLEED ART MUST EXTEND TO SOLID LINE

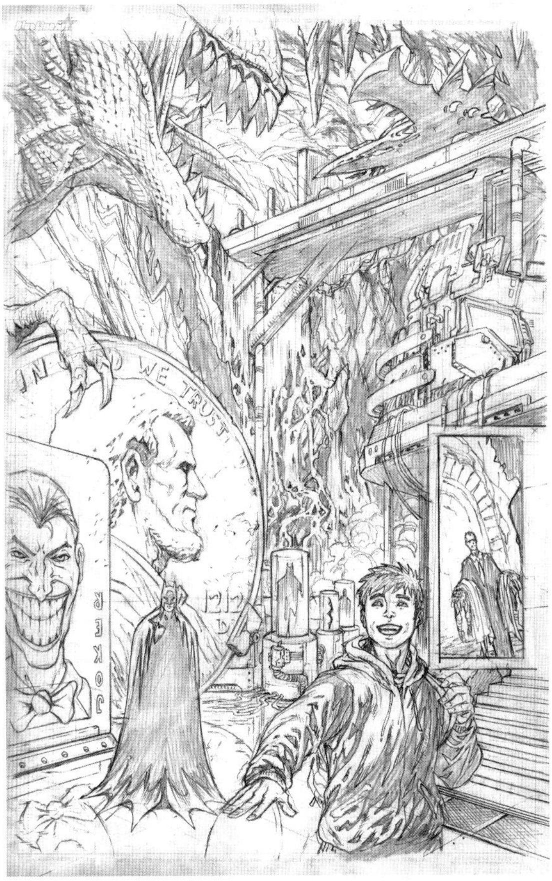

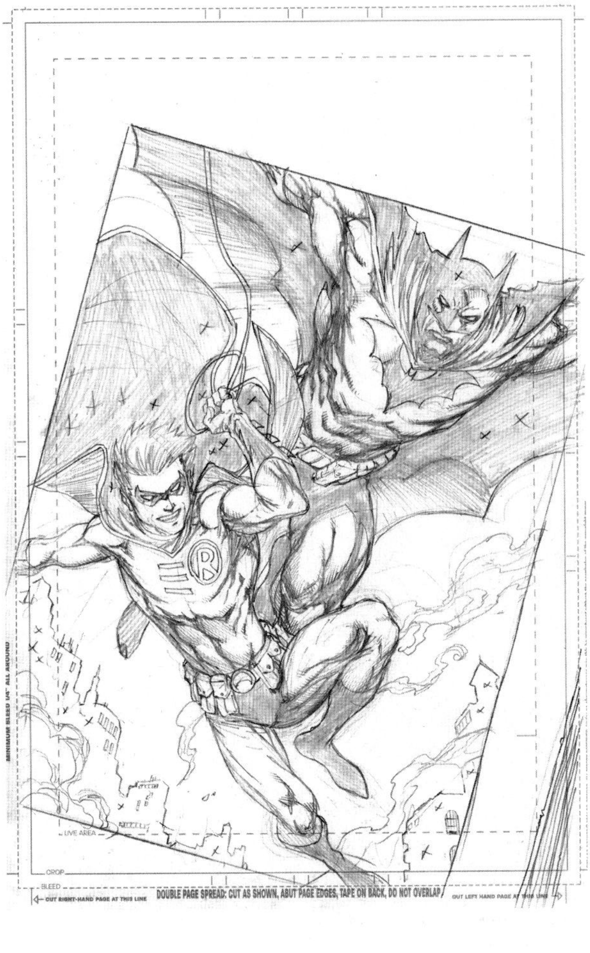
LIVE AREA
CROP
BLEED
DOUBLE PAGE SPREAD: CUT AS SHOWN, ABUT PAGE EDGES, TAPE ON BACK, DO NOT OVERLAP
CUT RIGHT-HAND PAGE AT THIS LINE
CUT LEFT HAND PAGE AT THIS LINE

TEEN TITANS

TEEN TITANS ISSUE #15 UNUSED COVER PENCILS AND FINAL ART BY BRETT BOOTH

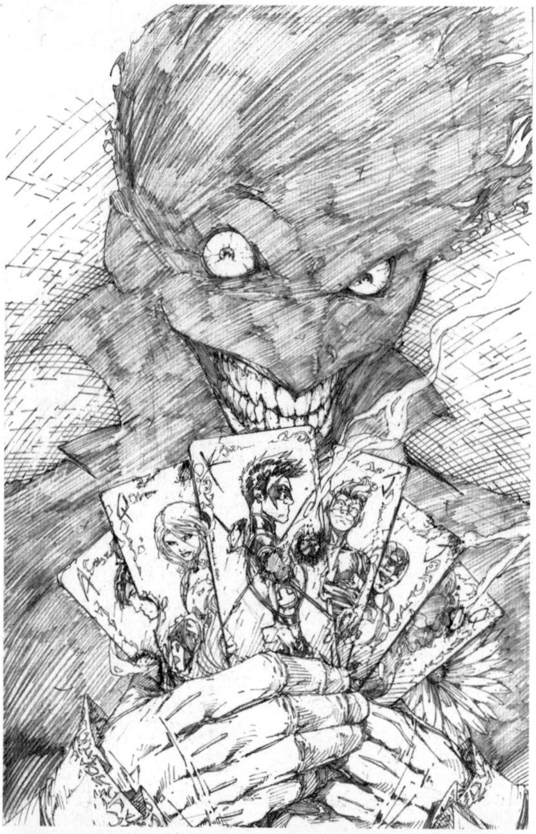

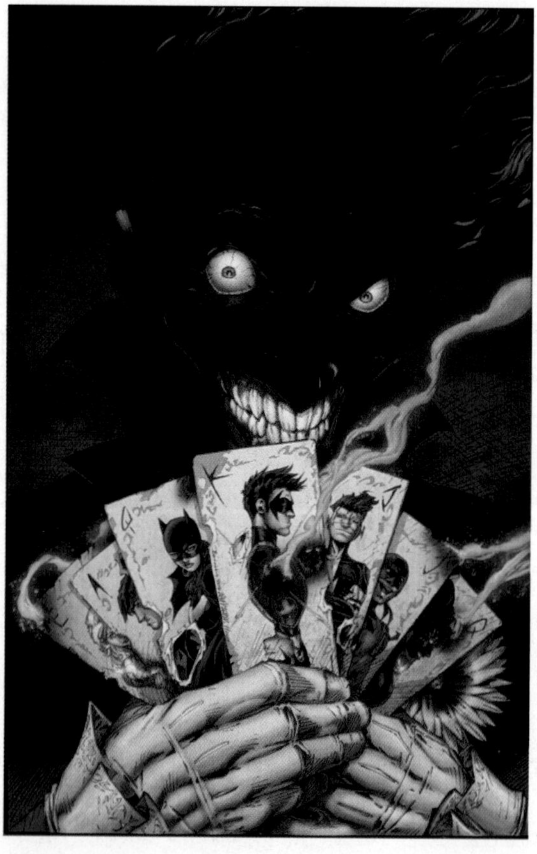

TEEN TITANS

TEEN TITANS ISSUE #16 PENCILS BY BRETT BOOTH

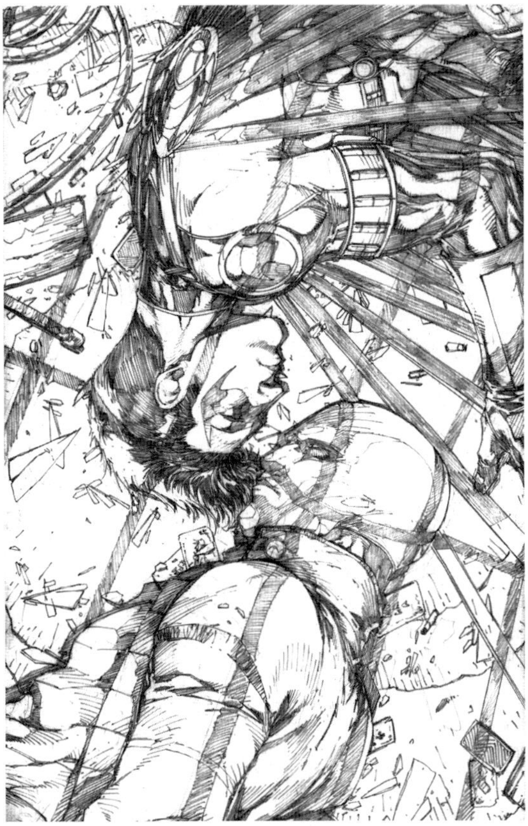

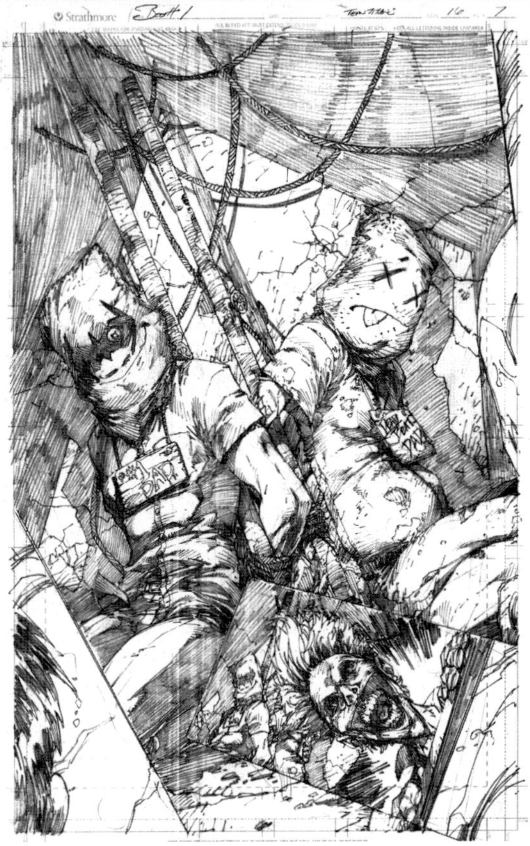

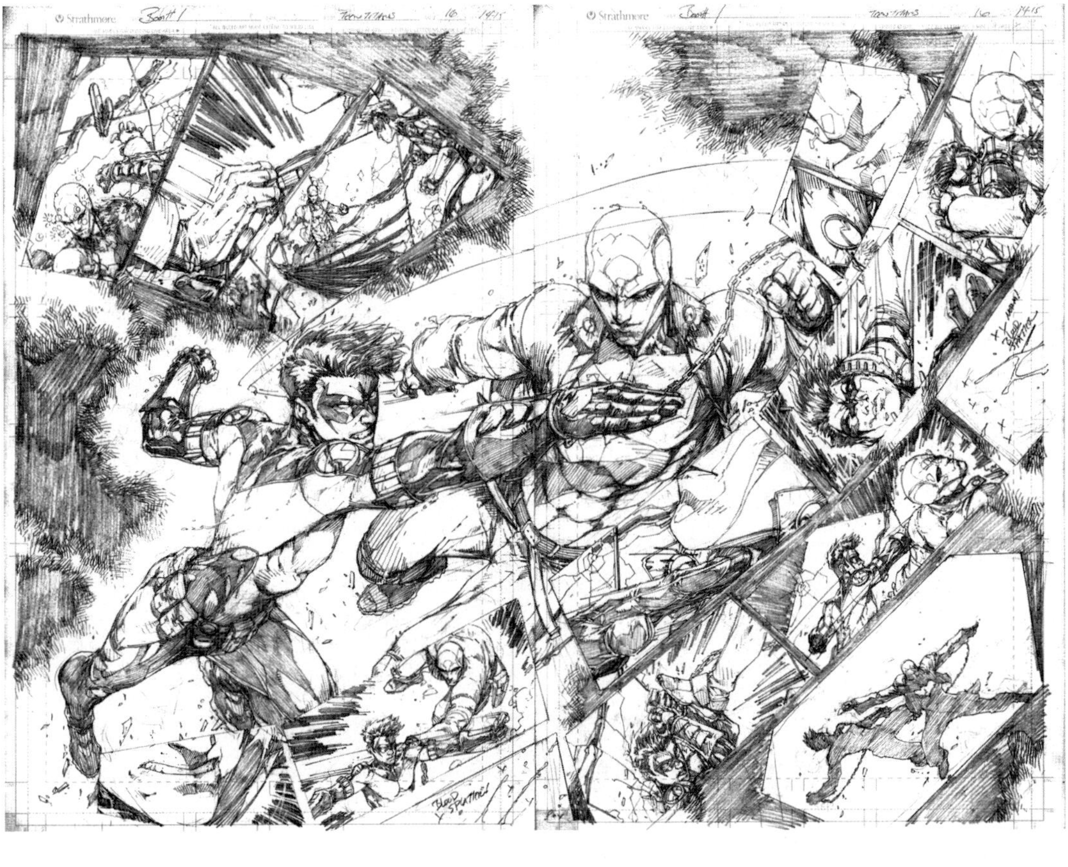

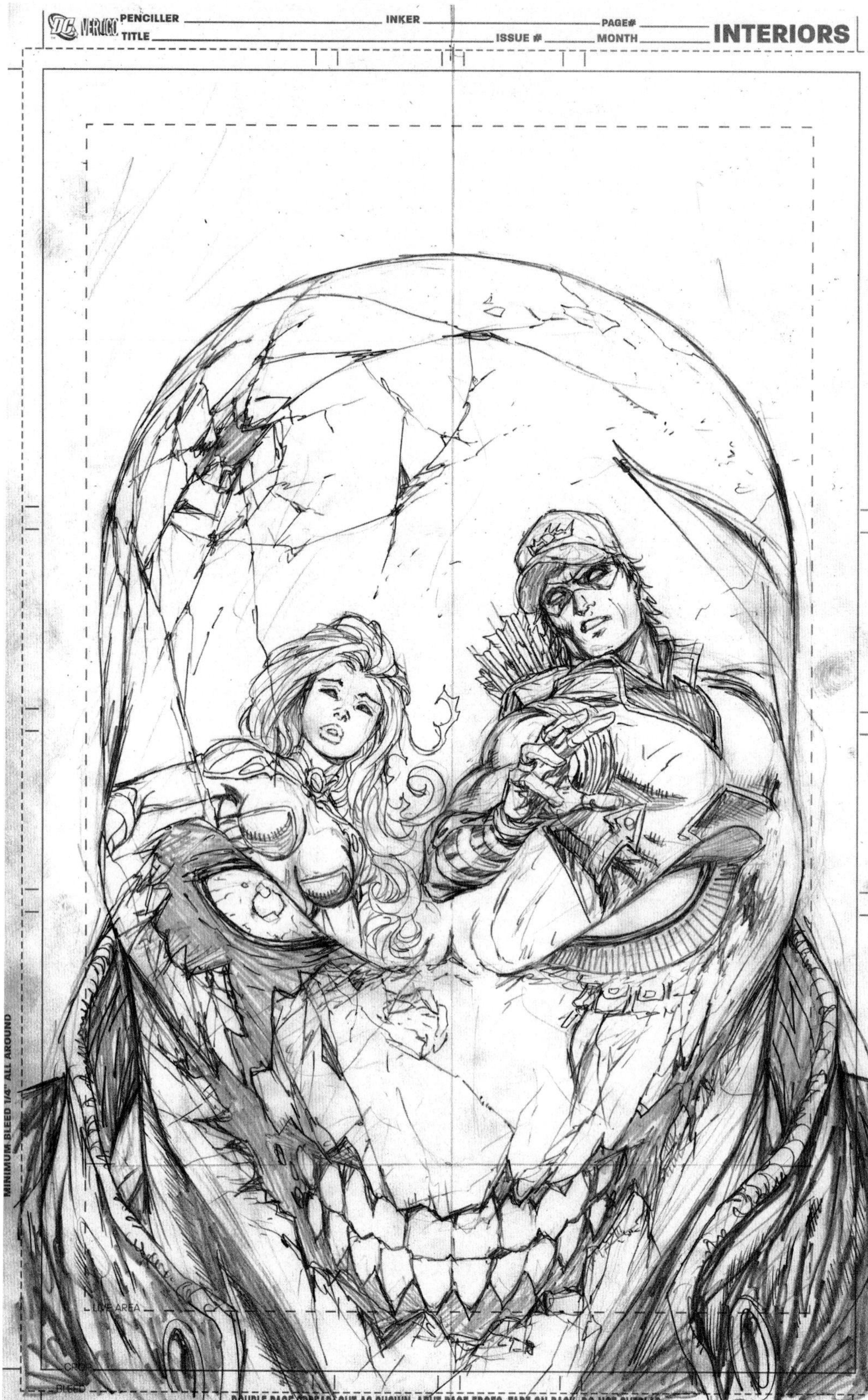
PENCILLER
INKER
PAGE#
TITLE
ISSUE #
MONTH
INTERIORS
MINIMUM BLEED 1/4" ALL AROUND
LIVE AREA
CUT RIGHT-HAND PAGE AT THIS LINE
DOUBLE PAGE SPREAD: CUT AS SHOWN, ABUT PAGE EDGES, TAPE ON BACK, DO NOT OVERLAP
CUT LEFT HAND PAGE AT THIS LINE

Cover pencils by Tyler Kirkham

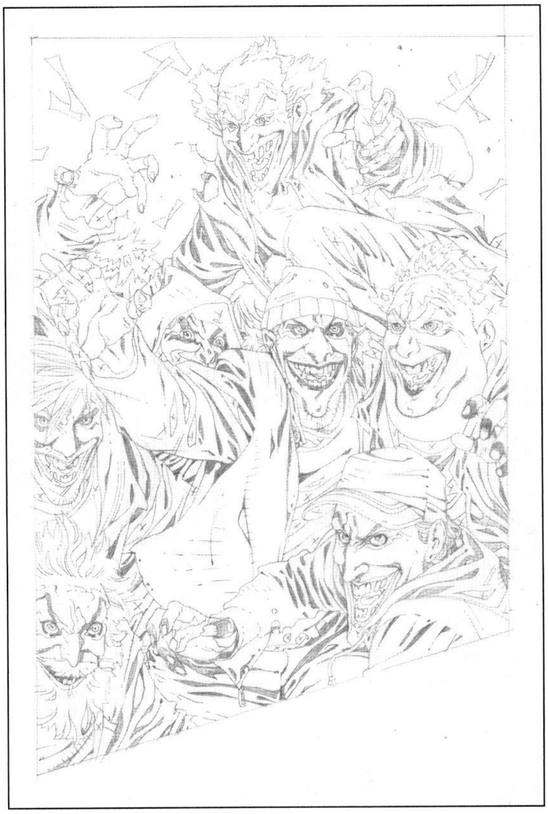

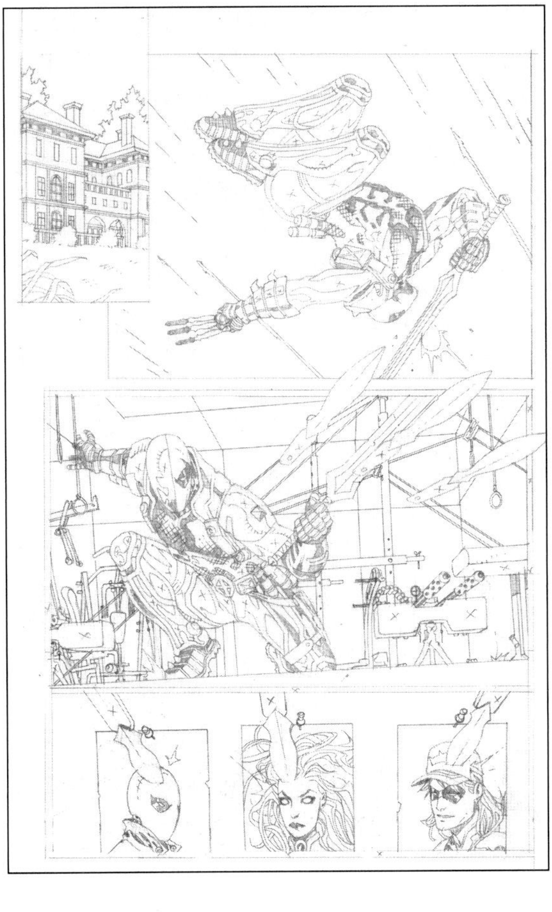

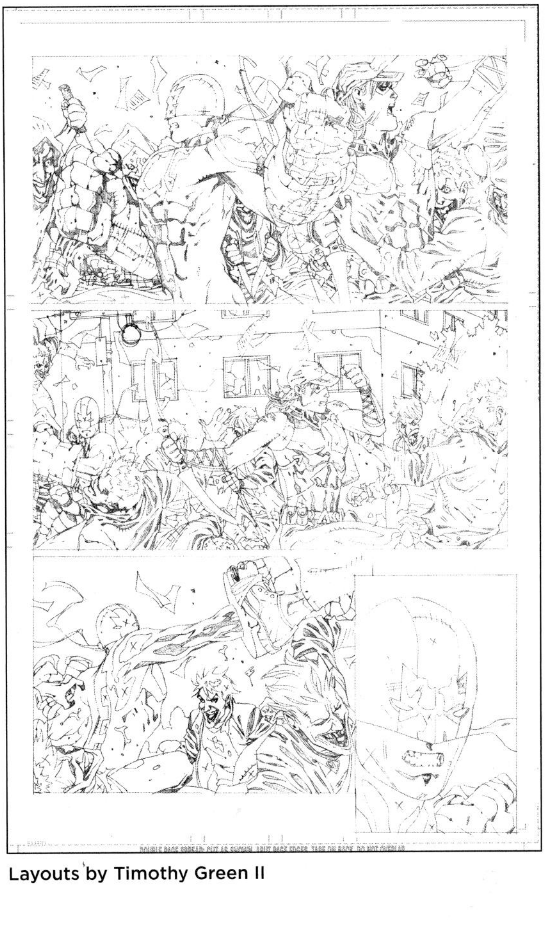

Layouts by Timothy Green II

TEEN TITANS

TEEN TITANS ISSUE #17 DESIGNS AND LAYOUTS BY EDDY BARROWS

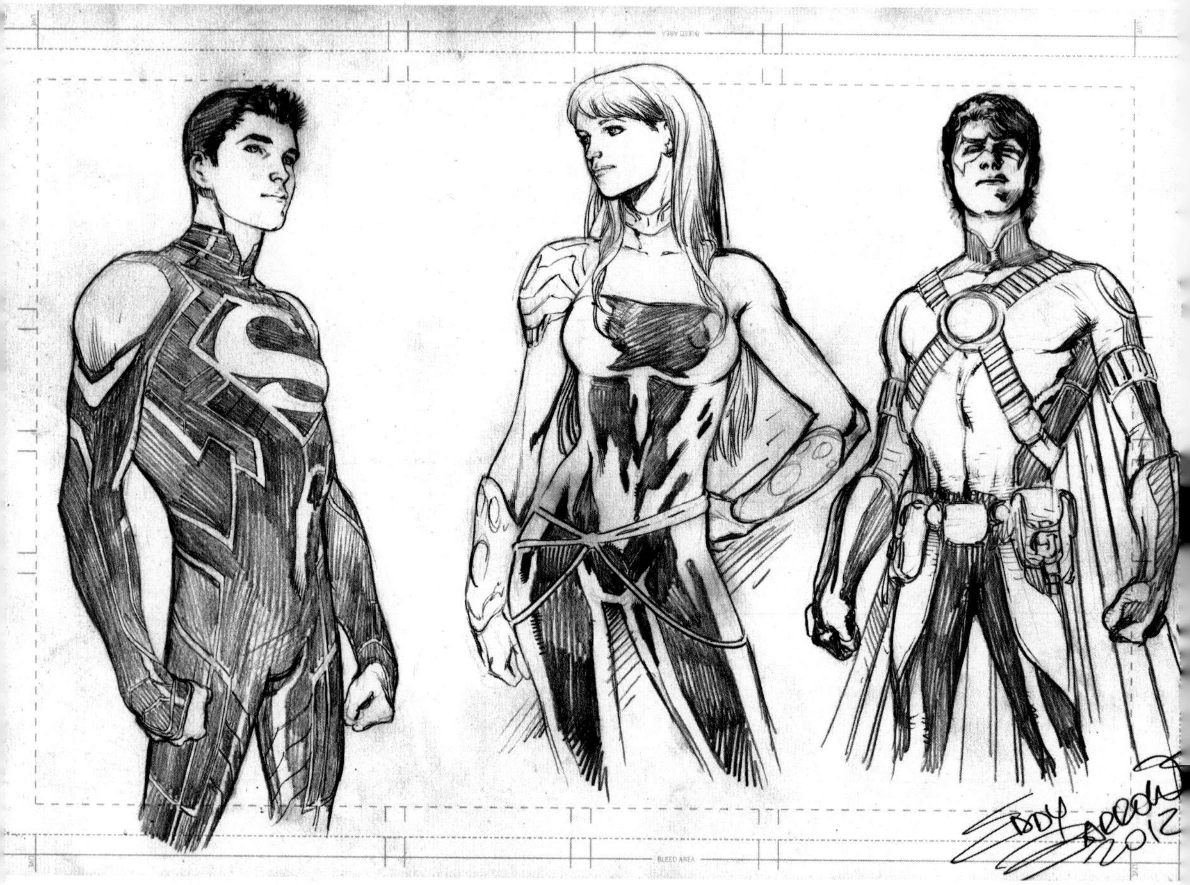

EDDY BARROWS
2012

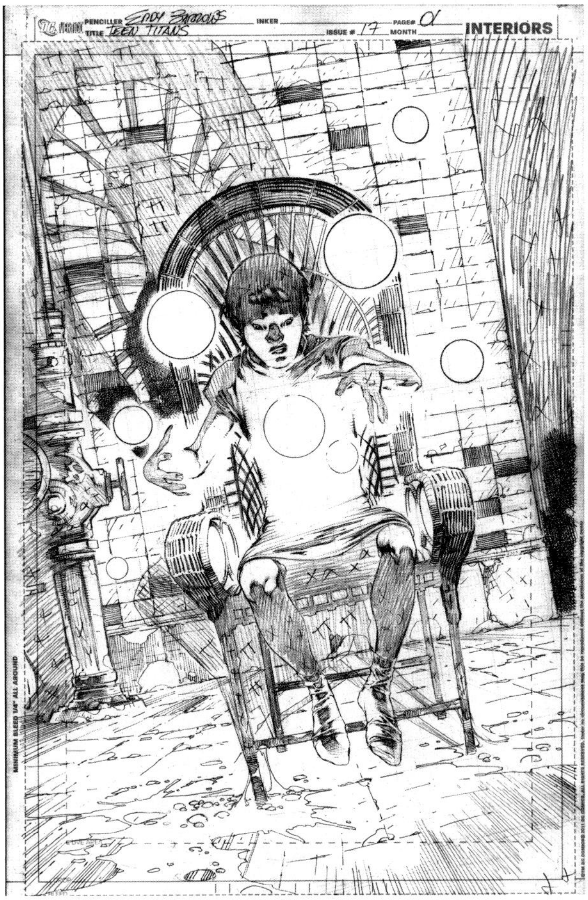
PENCILLER Eddy Barrows
INKER
PAGE# 01
INTERIORS
TITLE TEEN TITANS
ISSUE # 17
MONTH
MINIMUM BLEED 1/4" ALL AROUND

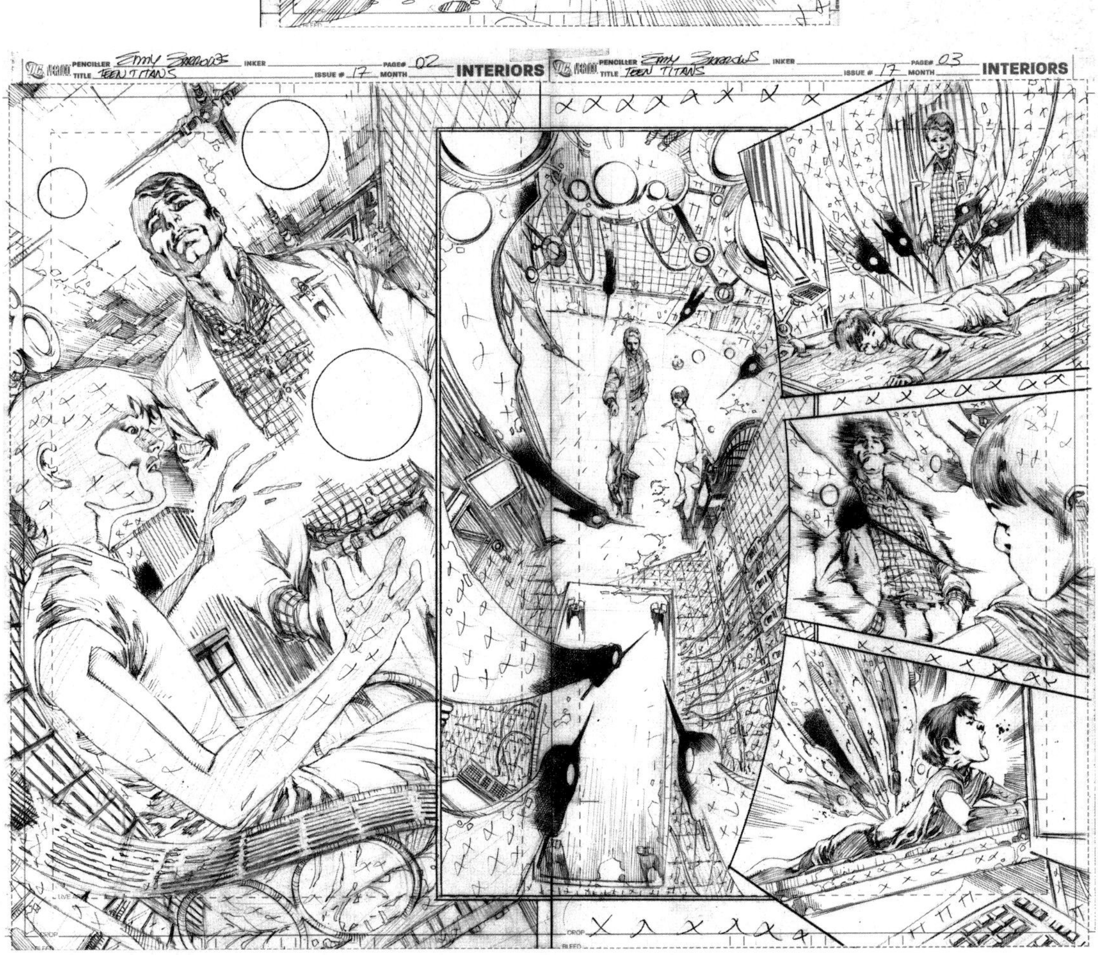
PENCILLER Eddy Barrows
INKER
PAGE# 02
INTERIORS
TITLE TEEN TITANS
ISSUE # 17
MONTH
PENCILLER Eddy Barrows
INKER
PAGE# 03
INTERIORS
TITLE TEEN TITANS
ISSUE # 17
MONTH

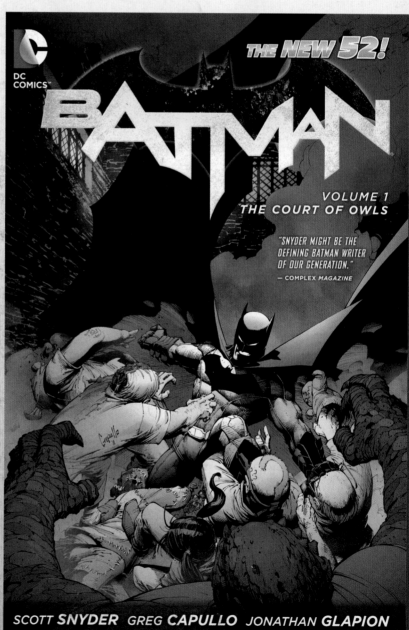

START AT THE BEGINNING!

NIGHTWING VOLUME 1: TRAPS AND TRAPEZES

CATWOMAN VOLUME 1: THE GAME

BIRDS OF PREY VOLUME 1: LOOKING FOR TROUBLE

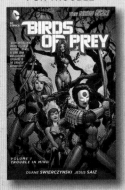

ALL-STAR WESTERN VOLUME 1: GUNS AND GOTHAM

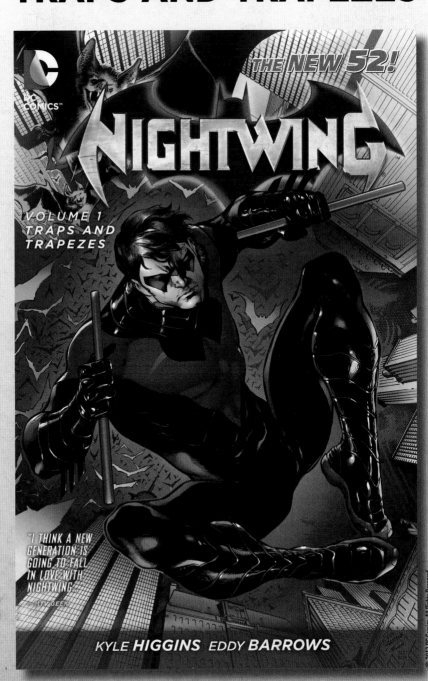

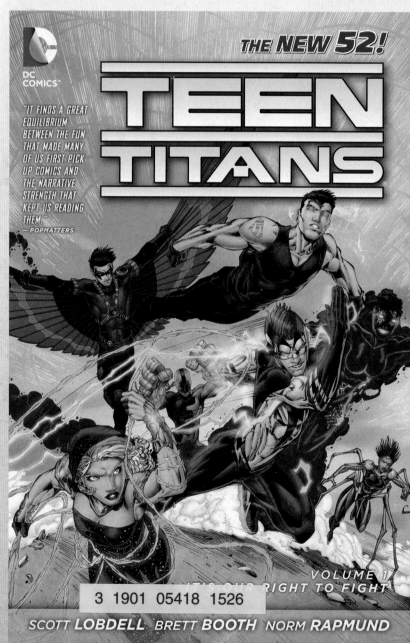